# ABOUT THE

CW00496321

Alasdair Drysdale was born in UK, rais
separate careers.

Qualifying in Edinburgh as a chartered accountant, he spent several years in two spells with a major international firm of accountants (now part of the Big 4), first in mainstream auditing and accounting, then as a national training manager and in his second spell managing receiverships, investigations and a business advisory group.

In between those spells he spent several years as an oilfield diver, logging over 500 working dives in the North Sea, Bight of Benin, Arabian Gulf, Arabian Sea and South China Sea, working mainly on offshore maintenance and structural inspection and spending three years as superintendent of a company's Arabian Gulf operations, achieving local market supremacy.

Subsequently he spent three years as group financial director on a manic and successful turnaround team rescuing a group of companies in near-terminal condition. From there he moved on to working as an interim director and has since worked on over 40 projects in 5 continents and in over 20 different industrial sectors. His clients have ranged from small owner-managed single-site businesses to worldwide groups with a multitude of operations in different countries.

This has brought him into contact with all manner of financial management methods, ranging from the unworkable to the ingenious. Having had to learn all these the hard way, he decided that they should be documented in a comprehensive practical manual before he forgets them.

For a complete list of Management Books 2000 titles
visit our web-site on http://www.mb2000.com

# THE FINANCIAL CONTROLLER

Alasdair Drysdale

2000

First published in 2010 by Management Books 2000 Ltd
Forge House, Limes Road
Kemble, Cirencester
Gloucestershire, GL7 6AD, UK
Tel: 0044 (0) 1285 771441
Fax: 0044 (0) 1285 771055
Email: info@mb2000.com
Web: www.mb2000.com

British Library Cataloguing in Publication Data is available

ISBN 9781852526399

# FOREWORD

**The mission of a business is to make money** . . . not for itself, but for the five groups of people whom it must keep happy: employees, customers (by giving them value for their money), suppliers, lenders and shareholders. If the business fails to bring a smile to the faces of any one of those groups, it will encounter difficulties. Everyone in the business is therefore involved in some way in the money generation effort, but **you** as the financial controller are or will be at the heart of this process, and largely responsible for planning, measuring and regulating it.

But there is no qualification entitled "Financial Controller". You will certainly learn by actually doing the job, or by assisting someone else in doing it, but it would be a lot easier if you had a book which sets out the principles, practices and pitfalls.

**This is that book.**

I dedicate it to those financial controllers with whom I have worked most closely and whose good ideas I have assimilated. In rough chronological order: Alison, Hugh, Liz, Peter, Julia, Liz, Gus, Roger, Angela, Dave, Richard, Terry, Mike, Gil, Wilma, Craig, Peter, Richard, Patti, Craig, Janine, Caroline, Shaun, Karen, Colin, Xenia, Jürgen, Liliane, Javier, Peter, Eddy, Manfred, Lorenzo, Bob, John, Metin, Yazdi, Hala, José Carlos, Gerard, Gail, Krishnan, Kenji, David, Raymond, Ida, Ben, Tony, Dipak, Terry, David, Neil, Helen, Chris, Louis, Andrea, Richard, Roger, Agusti, Vendula, Soňa, Zdenka, Joseph, Ute, Marita, Giovanni, Theresio, Jay, Jerome, Anna, Anna, Marta, Elzbieta, Pawel, Anja, Tom, Nick, Arndt, Finn, Jocelyne, Angelo, Agostino, Ian, Helen, Stefan, Steve, Martin, John, Jill, Mark, Mark, Rolando, Martyn, Janette, Wayne, Robbie and anyone I've missed, including an army of patiently helpful IT managers and the many financial directors with whom I've worked, this is to you with much gratitude. This book stems from your wisdom, not mine.

My thanks go especially to Liz Waugh and Helen Harper, two of the most experienced and street-wise controller/ directors in the business. They have edited my drafts, and brought me back down to earth on a number of points.

*Alasdair Drysdale*

# DEFINITIONS

At all stages in this book we assume that the financial systems are computerised. If your business is big enough to have a financial controller, it is big enough to have computerised accounting. However, the principles which we must apply to computerised controls are no different in principle from those applicable to manual accounting.

Financial terms vary from one country to another. This book uses the most suitable terms regardless of country.

| Term used | Definitions or equivalent terms |
|---|---|
| *Business* | company; division; factory; partnership; the operation for which you are responsible |
| *Manager* | head of department, regardless of seniority and whether or not he is a director |
| *Shareholders* | stockholders; investors; partners; the owners of the business |
| *Statutory accounts* | annual financial statements as required by law ("stats" in the UK) |
| *Management accounts* | internal operating financial statements as required for business management |
| *Cumulative* | from the beginning of the current financial year to the date under consideration <br> (the term "year-to-date" or YTD can mean the previous rolling twelve months) |
| *Written* | on paper, whether handwritten, typed, produced by computer or any other means |
| *Signature* | official signature whether handwritten or produced by controlled electronic means |
| *Products* | the items your business produces (goods, services, facilities or a combination thereof) |
| *R&D* | research and development; product engineering; technical design and support |
| *Inventory* | stock, including raw materials, work in progress and finished products for sale |
| *Materials* | raw materials and components included in products |

| | |
|---|---|
| *Consumables* | items consumed in production but not included in finished product (eg work gloves) |
| *Full count* | 100% physical count of all inventory |
| *Cycle count* | partial inventory count on rotational basis |
| | |
| *Receivables* | accounts receivable; debtors |
| *Receivables ledger* | accounts receivable ledger; sales ledger |
| *Sales tax* | value added tax; any tax levied on sales |
| *Despatch* | shipping, delivery of goods outward |
| *Prepayment* | calculated amount of payment made in respect of subsequent period's expenses |
| | |
| *Payables* | accounts payable; creditors |
| *Payables ledger* | accounts payable ledger; purchase ledger; bought ledger |
| *Provision* | any amount set aside for expected liability or loss of asset value |
| *Accrual* | calculated amount for liability not yet invoiced by supplier |
| *GRNI* | goods received not invoiced; uninvoiced receipts |
| | |
| *(Tangible) fixed assets* | PP&E (property, plant & equipment); software (contrary to popular practice) |
| *Intangible fixed assets* | intellectual property; long-term investments |
| *Amortisation* | any systematic writing off of fixed asset costs (the term "depreciation" is incorrect) |
| *Capex* | capital expenditure; capitalised cost of additional tangible fixed assets |
| *Expense* | any non-capital cost charged against profit (also used as a verb, meaning to charge fully against profit) |
| *Goodwill* | theoretical excess of value of assets over their book value, usually arising from buying another business at more than its stated net book value |
| | |
| *Cash* | cash balances; cheques; bank balances; any form of liquid cash |
| *Petty cash* | small funds of notes and coins kept for non-banking purposes |
| *Deposit account* | any short-term investment of surplus funds |

For simplicity I have referred to people throughout as being of the male sex. General emphasis is expressed in capital letters, and emphasis relating to a specific learning point is expressed in bold letters.

# CONTENTS

**1  THE BUSINESS**

1.1  The management team
1.2  The finance department
1.3  Other departments
1.4  External organisations

This section sets the scene — who the main players are inside and outside the business, how the financial controller should work with them and what his main responsibilities are.

**2  THE NUMBERS**

2.1  Management reports
2.2  Month-end results
2.3  Month-end processes
2.4  Month-end papers
2.5  Year-end

Everything the business does must be measured, and the results fed back to the management in such a way that they can act appropriately. It is therefore a numbers game, requiring a high degree of organisation, control and presentation. Numbers which are correctly recorded, strictly controlled and meaningfully presented are the key to successful management.

**3  THE PERFORMANCE**

3.1  Optimising profit
3.2  Optimising cash
3.3  Optimising management
3.4  Planning
3.5  Budgeting

The numbers are not an end in themselves; what matters is the team's ability to use them to identify how the many individual components of the business are performing, and to highlight what actions can and should be taken to improve the business's performance. Use of appropriate indicators will greatly assist the management in getting the best out of the business.

## 4  THE SYSTEMS

4.1  Inventory and cost of sales
4.2  Physical inventory count
4.3  Sales and receivables
4.4  Purchases and payables
4.5  Payroll
4.6  Fixed assets
4.7  Bank and cash

This highly-detailed section charts the features which should be included in your systems. You can use this section as a check-list to ensure that your systems are complete and properly controlled for the purposes of your business. You can also use it to draft the specifications for a new computer system, and to compare the features of one potential system against another. Moreover, it will provide a platform for you to implement a Sarbanes-Oxley documentation if needed.

## 5  THE CONTROLS

5.1  Losing it
5.2  Fraud
5.3  Contracts
5.4  Insurance

In addition to the regular systems are a number of controls needed to ensure the overall security of the business. These include information technology back-up and continuity planning, legally watertight documentation and adequate insurance.

## APPENDICES

A/D  General items
B    Examples – weekly reports
C    Examples – monthly reports

The appendices contain some simple examples of useful control and reporting formats, all based on examples used in a variety of businesses. There is no one-fits-all format, but these should help you design effective reports for your business.

## ALPHABETICAL INDEX

Topics indexed to subsection reference numbers

There is an occasional repetition of some minor points so that each section is largely complete within itself.

# PART 1
# THE BUSINESS

## 1.1 THE BOARD & MANAGEMENT

a   Objectives
b   Business assumptions
c   Financial controller – definition
d   Board of directors
e   Management team
f   Culture
g   Controller's master file
h   Making an impact
i   Reprise

## 1.2 THE FINANCE DEPARTMENT

a   Objectives
b   Culture
c   Staff duties
d   Staff development
e   Staff reviews & appraisals
f   Staff recruitment
g   Managing the department
h   Shared service centres

## 1.3 OTHER DEPARTMENTS

a   Objectives
b   Administration
c   Personnel
d   Company cars
e   Information technology
f   Land & buildings
g   Marketing & sales
h   Transport (distribution)
i   Credit control
j   Research & development
k   Production (goods)
l   Production (services)
m   Production (contracts)
n   Inventory control (goods)
o   Maintenance

## 1.4 EXTERNAL ORGANISATIONS

a   General
b   Customers – general
c   Customers – on contract
d   Customers of customers
e   Suppliers
f   Contractors & subcontractors
g   Bankers
h   Leasing companies
i   Public sector bodies
j   Auditors
k   Accountants – other services
l   Insurers
m   Property lessors
n   Legal advisors
o   Pension trustees
p   Shareholders
q   Group or divisional head office
r   Other group companies
s   Conclusion

## 1.1a – Objectives

This part of the book examines the typical organisational components of a business, and what is required of the various players on the business team, and of their departments. We later consider in 1.3 how the Financial Controller needs to work with these players to enable them to achieve the best results for the business.

A conventional organisation structure has been assumed in this section. Titles and lines of reporting may vary in practice, but the functions described in this section are almost universal.

**The overall objective of a business is to make money** for the following groups of people:

- **employees** – if they can make more money elsewhere, or the same amount of money in a more acceptable way, they will
- **customers** – even if they do not buy your product for commercial reasons, they will still compare it in value-for-money terms with other options
- **suppliers** – if they do not make an acceptable return from you, they will stop supplying
- **lenders** – they tend to have less power over the management, but if they are not satisfied with the performance of their borrowers, they can cease lending (in the case of overdrafts, instantly)
- **shareholders** – if the management does not give them a satisfactory return on their investment, they can appoint managers who will

Making money is measured in three ways:

- net profit after taxation
- net cash inflow
- return on capital – if the first two targets are met, the return on capital will follow

**The overall objective of the management team** is therefore to ensure that the business makes money on all three of the above measurements on

**an ongoing basis** (it is not acceptable to make short-term gains which jeopardise the future cash flows).

**The overall objective of a financial controller** is to ensure that the processes of generating profit and cash and the systems upon which the processes rely are managed to the highest possible effectiveness.

**The overall objective of this book** is to help the financial controller:
- understand and execute his duties within and beyond the business
- organise and manage the finance department effectively
- produce timely and reliable information for the management of the business
- build strong and productive working relationships with his internal and external colleagues and assist them in optimising the performance of the business
- ensure that secure and effective financial systems and controls are in place
- support the financial director and enable him to operate confidently and effectively as a board member

We begin in this section by examining the typical organisational leaders of a business, and what is required of the various players on the business team, and of their departments. We then consider in parts 1.2 to 1.5 the relationships the Financial Controller should have with these colleagues and how he should work with them to enable them to achieve the best results for the business.

## 1.1b – Business assumptions

To cater for the widest possible range of financial controllers, this book is aimed at mainstream industry and its typical requirements and problems. Although it was written in the United Kingdom, it has not assumed UK legislation or practices at any stage, but instead provides general instruction which should be relevant in most countries. In areas where the author considers that there is likely to be considerable divergence of practice from one country to another, the book draws the reader's attention to this.

The term **"products"** includes both **goods** and **services**. Throughout the book we consider a business which manufactures goods, but which also provides some services. This caters automatically for a number of other types of industrial business:
- if your business merely buys and sells, you can ignore the production and work-in-progress sections

- if your business does not sell on credit to customers, you can ignore the balance sheet aspects of accounts receivable
- if your business is a service business, you can pay less attention to the production and inventory sections, and concentrate instead on the service activities and service work-in-progress
- if your business is contracting, you should treat each contract as a business within itself
- if your business is engaged purely in production or services for a separate selling organisation within your group, you must nevertheless ensure that you have a good understanding of the requirements and problems of that selling organisation, and so most or all of this book will still be relevant

The financial, charitable and public sectors comprise specialist organisations which we do not cover here, and there are other businesses (eg mining, agriculture, property, transport, tourism) with highly specialised needs which merit specific considerations in addition to the general aspects discussed in this book.

However, in this book we cover the great majority of industrial businesses, Moreover, if you are working in the financial sector in a capacity directly involved in the financing of businesses, you should understand the contents of this book in order to gauge the management capabilities of the businesses which you are financing.

## 1.1c – Definition of a financial controller

The term 'financial controller' covers a wide range of definitions, and we shall therefore assume the most common interpretation of the role. This is best done by establishing where the financial controller functions in relation to the two other senior financial executives conventionally found in a business:

- **financial director** or chief finance officer (CFO) – strategic financial direction, corporate governance and boardroom matters
- **financial controller**, reporting to the financial director – operational management of finance function and its collaboration with all other operating departments
- **accountant** (or chief accountant), reporting to the financial controller – compilation of management accounts and statutory accounts, his responsibility being principally for production of figures rather than for management matters

The financial controller is therefore the person responsible directly to the financial director for the day-to-day operation of the finance function, which includes financial systems, controls and reporting. But note that in smaller businesses, the above functions may be combined to some extent.

It is apparent from the above that the controller's role is pivotal to the business. More than anyone else, he must be involved in every department in the business and have good working relations with all of his colleagues.

Before we consider his operational colleagues, let us begin from the top of the business and consider the board of directors, who are responsible to the shareholders for the stewardship of the business.

## 1.1d – The Board of Directors (or partners in the case of a partnership)

The board of directors is responsible for the corporate governance of the company, a wide-ranging responsibility covering all aspects of the well-being of the company and the safety of those who have any contact with it.

In larger companies and those companies with extensive external ownership and finance, the board of directors is more likely to be separate from the management team. In such a case, the board generally manages the company with regard to meeting its external strategic targets and responsibilities, in particular its relationships with the shareholders (either directly or through a stock exchange), its lenders, the financial and general public (directly or through public relations advisors), and its major trading partners, competitors and industry leaders. In the case of major personnel issues, especially those involving trade unions, it may also deal with its employees, usually as a whole body rather than individually.

The board is therefore substantially concerned with external attitudes to the business, and therefore with appearances to outsiders. That does not mean that it is not interested in the substance and dynamics of the business – far from it; good strategic decisions and external relations need accurate and reliable information which can be released to external parties in complete confidence, and in a clear and correct context. The board is therefore as concerned with understanding the true performance and circumstances of the business as any other group of people, and will come down hard on anyone presenting them with inaccurate or misleading information.

Boards can be comprised in several ways. **Executive directors**, ie those who work full-time in the business, can for example be appointed with the following responsibilities:

- as divisional directors – each division comprising a particular group of products
- as regional directors – each director representing a geographical area
- as functional directors – director of marketing, director of production, director of research etc (this functional split is particularly common in smaller businesses)
- for personal ability or speciality – ie assigned to apply a specific talent
- for temporary or historical reasons

**Non-executive directors**, ie those who do not work full-time in the business, arrive by a variety of routes. The most common are probably:

- nomination by the bank or other providers of finance (frequently as a condition of providing the finance, and with the specific remit to keep the providers informed of the financial state and prospects of the business)
- elected by external shareholders (perhaps by a pressure group therein)
- invitation by the chairman
- invitation through personal contact with an executive director

**The chairman** may be executive or non-executive, preferably the latter in order to keep his role clearly defined. He is chairman of the **board**, not of the company, and his job is to optimise the performance of the board as a collective unit. This involves:

- getting to know the individual executive directors and their particular capabilities
- coaching (this is very different from leading) the less experienced directors to enable them to be more effective board members
- understanding the business, its markets and all the external influences (for this reason, some chairmen are selected because of their contacts and reputation within the industry and associated industries)
- conducting board meetings firmly and fairly so that the issues are aired in a balanced and objective way, and no important issues are avoided or downplayed
- ensuring that rivalries, prejudices and other disruptive emotions are not allowed to develop

Managing directors have the relative luxury of dealing mainly in the quantifiable specifics of the areas in which they have worked en route to the top. The role of the chairman, however, covers less definable aspects involving politics, perceptions, public relations and boardroom relations and performance. The skills required by the chairman are therefore very different. The main difficulties faced by chairmen of smaller companies are:

- getting to know the characters and capabilities of the executive directors – this requires more than just attendance at board meetings; the chairman needs to spend some time with the individuals, and thus chairmen tend to be in demand from all quarters at once
- working with all the directors, not merely the managing director
- finding ways to help board members towards a better collective performance
- striking a balance between inputting their own considerable experience and allowing the lesser experience of the board members to develop

**The managing director**, also called the **chief executive officer** (CEO), is the director in charge of the running of the business to meet its targets and in compliance with all related legal requirements. His job is to optimise the performance of the business through leading the functional heads on the senior management team, whether or not they are board members. There are many ways in which he can operate, but he must ensure that each member of the senior management team provides:

- knowledge of and contribution to the overall strategy of the business
- knowledge of and contribution to the detailed plans to achieve that strategy
- knowledge of his individual part to play in those plans and their achievement
- completion of the day-to-day direction and management tasks required of him and of those reporting to him

In larger corporations there may be both a managing director who runs the business(es) and a chief executive officer who is largely strategic in nature, seeking development, growth, diversification etc.

The managing director may work entirely through the board members, or may also operate as the general manager through the functional managers, which is more often the case in a smaller business.

**Divisional directors** (ie directors of product groups) are common constituents of a board. The difficulty in such an arrangement is that they naturally tend to represent the interests of their product groups rather than of the business as a whole. There is also a perceived superiority of directors in charge of 'sunrise' product divisions and inferiority of directors representing 'sunset' divisions, even though managing out a sunset product group often requires considerably more skill than developing a fashionable sunrise product in current demand. Managing and financial directors must be careful to consider each divisional argument strictly on its commercial merits.

**Regional directors** can be affected by similar partisanship, but usually less so. Their concerns stem from the economic trends of their regions, currency shifts and other localised concerns, and they are often relatively uninterested in the other regions other than to identify trends that might come to affect their own regions. In a regional structure, each region usually sells all the product groups if there is a market for them, and there can be arguments as to whether the regions or the product divisions should be the dominant groupings within the business. The financial director will therefore need clear information on profit performance by product group and by region. Customer pricing and transfer pricing issues are also likely to abound as each regional director claims special circumstances for his region.

**Functional directors** tend to occur more often in companies where the board of directors is also the management team, a situation common in smaller companies. Production director and marketing director are typical titles, and of course there is the financial director.

**Hand-picked directors** function well if they are picked for defined purposes. For example, a business entering a new market may appoint a director with specific relevant experience and capability in that market.

**Non-executive directors**, who have no full-time function in the business, are a frequent source of controversy and suffer widespread criticism of their collective performance and usefulness. This is hardly surprising; non-executive directors are part-time directors expected to provide expertise in some specific useful field such as technology or markets, and often to add a degree of maturity and supervision to the board, and to help its members to develop their performance. They have to do this on a fee which reflects perhaps two or three days' work per month to cover travel and attendance at board meetings and other work such as research and external consultations. Unless in semi-retirement, they therefore have to perform other work elsewhere to make up their overall income, resulting in difficulty in obtaining sufficient time to understand the business.

As the controller, you can do yourself and the non-exec a big favour by cultivating him and voluntarily giving him a clear insight into the financial dynamics of the business. If you coach him on the inside workings, you should simultaneously glean advice and knowledge from him. But be very careful not to by-pass the financial director.

**The financial director** is your boss. His responsibility to the board is:
- co-operating with the other directors on the strategy and stewardship of the business
- providing top-end financial information and advice to the other directors
- translation of the board's strategies into viable financial plans (or intimating to the board that their plans are in his estimation not financially viable)
- leading all matters relating to funding, hedging etc
- dealing with the financial aspects of associated external bodies such as shareholders, analysts, pension funds, insurers etc
- ensuring that the financial systems and personnel of the company perform to the required standard
- ensuring that all financial aspects (and often other aspects) of the business comply with the relevant legislation, a requirement which becomes more complex as time passes

He is therefore responsible overall for the finance function, but in day-to-day practical terms most of that responsibility lies with the financial controller.

The financial director will often have to act as a counterbalance to the board when there is a strong current of feeling on any subject. For example, when the board is avoiding addressing an urgent issue affecting the financial welfare of the business (disposing of a non-performing asset, for example) he may need to insist and persist until the necessary action is taken. Similarly, when the board is enthusing about some impracticable scheme he may have to bring them gently back to earth by establishing the fundamental financial impracticality of what is being suggested.

Such necessary behaviour can result in the financial director not being regarded as a team player, but such a view would show naïveté on the part of other board members. In questioning the financial suitability of proposed action or inaction, the financial director is playing his proper rôle on the team. It is important, however, that in curbing the well-meant enthusiasm of others, the financial director is not seen as being negative. He can do this by presenting his objections in a positive way; exactly the same applies to the financial controller in working with the management team.

*Real life – a newly appointed financial director arrived at the UK group who had appointed him. The group was newly formed, having resulted from an existing business being refinanced to take over and restructure another business of similar activity and size under an ambitious business plan. There was much work to be done to ensure that the new group achieved the financial targets set for it in the plan.*

*On the financial director's second day he was notified of a serious intention by the group managing director, supported by the chairman, to purchase the group's European sales agency, who generated the group's considerable turnover in continental Europe. This purchase was not even alluded to in the business plan, and the financial and operational requirements of the expanded business left no room for such a speculative purchase. The difficulty facing the new financial director was that on his very first board meeting (due the following week) he might face the negative task of strongly opposing his chairman and managing director on what was a highly inappropriate proposal.*

*At the meeting he made no objection, merely commenting that it was an imaginative idea (the ambiguity went unnoticed). He said that he would consider the financial implications and report back to the board. He had in fact already done his research, and sent a short report the next day to the board members stating that in order to complete the purchase:*

- *there would have to be extensive due diligence to ensure that the profit stream attributed to the agent was realistically achievable and sustainable*
- *the purchase price being tentatively suggested, plus the professional costs associated with the deal, would require a second refinancing of the group (exacerbating the already-high gearing and diverting effort from the considerable tasks already in hand)*
- *as the agent's business consisted essentially of two expert telesales persons who could leave at any time to join the competition, the purchase would have to be on the basis of a lengthy earn-out agreement . . . and even short-period earn-outs are notoriously difficult to implement effectively*
- *in an industry of only a few players, amongst whom there were few secrets, the ownership of the agency would have to remain a secret from their other clients – if it was leaked (which was patently inevitable, probably within a few weeks, although he did not mention that) the other clients would take their business elsewhere and the agency's only income would be the group's own commission*

*At no time did the financial director actually object to the proposal, preposterous though it was. But by making clear the scale of the necessary actions and associated risks he gave the initiators of the proposal the opportunity to "consider it further" which in the end meant that it died a quiet death without anyone losing face.*

As the financial controller, you will have to adopt a similar approach if you disagree with the managers of the business. Do not be negative about others' views and ideas if you disagree with them; concentrate instead on giving them the facts to change their minds. It is much harder to argue with facts, particularly proven numerical ones, than it is to argue with opinions. Moreover, you can persuade others to abandon proposals which you consider unsuitable without actually denigrating their ideas. It follows that not only will you have to produce figures to substantiate your own arguments as the controller, but you will have to do the same for your financial director. The more you can help him present his case from facts, the more valuable you will be to him.

And occasionally you will find that you were wrong to doubt an idea, and you will be relieved not to have been against it from the start.

## 1.1e – The management team

Let us now move to the senior management team who actually run the business. As the financial controller, you will have to work with them, and you therefore need to understand their responsibilities, targets, concerns and individual ways of working (which may be very different from your preferred way).

There will be times when you disagree with them; on such occasions adopt a similar approach to that in the example per 1.1d above.

On the other hand, instances may occur in which it is the other departments who are in negative mode, usually where some essential action is being continually postponed (a common example is failure to resolve disputes with customers, thus causing the customers to refuse to settle old balances). The controller will therefore have to push hard to get his colleagues to resolve these matters. This means that the finance department must always be up-to-date with its work, as you will have little credibility in exhorting colleagues to deal with problems if your own house is clearly not in order. Moreover, any inefficiencies in the finance department will embarrass your boss, the financial director.

The **general manager**, whether or not he is also a director, may be the manager of the entire business, or of a specific location or sector. He will normally seek the following information from the finance department:

- monthly results – if he is a competent general manager he will focus on the capital employed as much as he focuses on the profit statement, but most managers need coaching in this aspect
- analyses of various categories of expenditure – by department, by period, by sector etc
- financial forecasts or what-ifs for various projects or hypothetical situations – new projects, new markets, closures, reorganisations; the list is endless

He will also seek the following information from the other managers, and some of this information may be derived from information systems for which the financial controller is responsible, including:

- buying and selling prices (not decided by the finance department, but recorded by them)
- payroll costs, overtime levels, absentee rates
- inventory and receivables information
- purchasing patterns (usually relating to negotiations with suppliers or potential suppliers)

The business may have a person with the title of **marketing manager** or one with the title of **sales manager**, or possibly both. Smaller businesses tend to have difficulty in distinguishing between the functions of marketing and sales and we could spend the whole book discussing them, but for this purpose let us define them thus:

- **marketing** is the science and art of examining and trying to predict the trends of the markets and deciding what products the business should offer, what specifications they should meet, how they should be packaged, priced and delivered, and how the customers could best be induced to buy them
- **sales** is the final vital process in the marketing chain; the process of getting as many customers as possible to buy the selected products at the right prices and to pay for them within the agreed timescale

As we are trying to run a perfect business, we shall assume that we have a marketing manager who has sales managers in his team. Contrary to what some innocents believe, marketing is not all about flair and intuition, although those qualities can be of great benefit in that and other fields, but mainly about hard-nosed analysis of market facts and trends, and customer preferences and behaviour. This analysis must support the development of overall marketing strategies, and detailed marketing plans to meet the strategic objectives.

The financial controller will therefore have to provide the following information for the marketing and sales managers on a regular basis:

- conventional net price and volume analysis of sales achieved
- margin analysis – the revenue from a product is the net margin after all variable costs, and this is a much more important figure than the gross or net sales price
- analysis of sales order intake, showing in particular which types of customer or region are buying which products, and at what prices and margins
- failure analysis – late deliveries, customer rejections, after-sales repairs etc
- time and cost to bring products to market – see R&D manager, below

At certain times, particularly during the planning and budgeting cycle (see 3.5), the controller may also have to provide the marketing team with financial modelling tools to enable them to forecast the sales revenue for the cycles and to perform a range of what-if and sensitivity analyses.

The **production manager** or **manufacturing manager** has equivalents in other businesses. In a contracting business he will normally be the **contracts manager**, in a service business the **operations manager**, and in a re-selling business with no production process he can have a variety of titles. Whatever his designation, we are talking here of the manager responsible for the efficient and economic flow of products through the business.

He will normally seek the following information on a regular basis:
- volumes
- costs of production
- failure rates
- overtime, absences and other direct labour statistics
- contract progress and results, if the business works to individual contracts

Many of the figures giving the above information are input into the production control system by production or contract supervisors. He will also be concerned with reliable forecast figures to enable production planning.

To establish a sound working relationship with the production manager, you must gain a sound working understanding of his business operations. It is best if you obtain this directly from him and his immediate subordinates as this will demonstrate your interest clearly to him. Concentrate on:
- the physical processes involved in making the business's products
- the materials and skills required
- storage requirements and methods

- the costs of all of the above, including the costs of failure (rejects, lost time etc)

You should also be familiar with the following disciplines, for which textbooks are recommended in Appendix D:
- general industrial processes and modern manufacturing techniques
- constraint management

An **R&D manager** (research and development manager) is normally present in a business which develops its own products. The range of responsibilities can include:
- agreeing new product concepts and specifications with the marketing manager
- designing, testing and bringing those products to production status
- technical support of products in the field (also referred to as customer support)
- continuous development of the technical aspects of the production processes
- determination of the training requirements associated with the technology to be used (the implementation of the training is usually handled by the personnel function, but it must be technically driven)

The natural tendency of the R&D function is sometimes to be a backroom boffin department, which is the exact opposite of what is required of it. This department holds the key to the business's future. The R&D manager is the person responsible for designing and bringing into successful production the products that will fulfil the marketing plan. For this reason it is essential that **the marketing, sales and R&D are located side by side** on the business premises; they must use the same stairs, elevators, photocopiers, fax machines, coffee machines, toilets, smoking rooms and be unable to escape from each other.

The reasons for this enforced juxtapositioning are:
- sales personnel will feed back customer reactions, concerns and requirements to the marketing and design staff, who will thus be kept constantly aware of what is wanted
- any concepts introduced by the design function will not be allowed to progress if they are not in line with the wants of the market, but will be actively encouraged if they are relevant
- marketing and design staff will rapidly detect ways in which the product is being mis-sold (for example, salespersons may complain that products are not working properly, but the underlying reason may be that the customer training staff are not showing them how to set up or operate the product properly)

- genuine product defects will be advised immediately to the design staff and the sales staff will maintain pressure on them to rectify the problems

The continual dialogue between the marketing and technical departments is thus essential, and can only be fully exploited when the departments are physically together.

There may also be an **engineering manager** or **technical manager**, whose functions may have a degree of overlap with the R&D manager. His responsibilities typically are:

- control of maintenance and repair, especially of production facilities
- control of capital expenditure related to production, engineering and development
- in a service business, control over the method and quality of delivery of the services
- in a re-selling business, control over the technology of storing and handling of products, and often of the testing and choice of the products themselves

The two major areas of liaison between the financial controller and the engineering department are:

- the capex budget
- the maintenance budget

and the performance of the engineering department against those budgets.

Virtually all businesses now have an **IT manager** (information technology manager), as computer systems underpin most modern activities including production, sales, purchasing, payroll, banking and accounting. The IT manager may report to the managing director or to one of the functional directors according to the priorities of the business. However, since business computer systems deal primarily with numbers, the IT manager deals extensively with the financial controller regardless of the organisation structure, and this relationship is of prime importance to the controller. We discuss it in detail in 1.3e.

Part 1.3 deals in greater depth with the specific working relationships between the financial controller and the operating departments of the business.

## 1.1f – Culture

The smaller an organisation is, the more it takes its culture from the top. This is self-evident if you consider that a one-person business has 100% the culture of the leader, but less evident as the business becomes larger. Nevertheless, a business of 50 people will reflect the culture of its leader much more noticeably than one of 500 people.

As a business becomes larger, the various departments of the business tend to assume the cultures of the department heads, who themselves tend to absorb the culture of their senior managers. That is how a business can have an overall culture at a higher level (often the culture perceived by outside parties such as customers and suppliers) and yet have pockets of individual culture across various departments or geographical areas.

Provided that none of the cultures is negative or inappropriate to its context, a mix of cultures is usually a beneficial – some would say essential – feature, since it stimulates the airing of different attitudes and approaches and thus full discussion of important issues and possible solutions. The two departments most commonly perceived by other departments as having negative cultures are the quality control and finance departments. Either or both of the following reasons could cause this:

- negative people gravitate towards those types of work (not unknown, but not common either)
- both departments often have to say "no" (this product has to be reworked; that expense is not allowable)

Both departments have the combined rôles of policing on the one hand and providing services on the other; this means that they are laying down the law to somebody one minute and at their beck and call the next. It follows that the financial controller and finance department must concentrate on providing services to other departments as prominently as they concentrate on policing the business, so they are regarded primarily as a useful resource and secondarily as a disciplinary force.

Both policing (ie systems and controls) and the provision of services are dealt with extensively in this book. However, the negative aspect of policing needs to be considered immediately before looking at the financial controller's relationship with the board of directors and the management team. As mentioned above, negative perception of the financial controller and function comes from statements beginning with "You/ we can't do that because . . . ."

Every controller will and should be making such statements from time to time. But the policing function also requires many positive exhortations, beginning with "You/ we must . . . . Examples include:

- you must get rid of that surplus inventory out of the warehouse and sell the warehouse
- you must get prices up to a gross margin level of X%
- you must cut out that expenditure
- you must ensure that all those documents are signed BEFORE the transaction

In other words, you should be stimulating necessary actions as often as you are curbing inappropriate actions. This dual necessity means that you are tend to sit metaphorically to one side of the board and management team, never allowing yourself to be caught up in the general mood, be it positive or negative. If you are doing your job correctly, you are to a large extent a counterbalance; when they are gung-ho about some wild idea you must bring them gently down to earth and when they are dragging their heels you need to kick their metaphorical backsides to get them to act.

This inevitably requires tact and maturity.

If you are always disagreeing with your colleagues you will become a pariah, especially when you are making restraining statements. Nobody likes somebody who frequently says "You can't/ mustn't . . ." so instead you have to cloak your negative views in positive statements. For example:

- "That's an interesting idea; to achieve that, we'd just need to take care of . . . [mention several major hurdles that nobody's thought of]"
- "Good thinking; so how are we [note "we", not "you"] going to handle problems X, Y and Z so that we can do that?"

You are thus seen to be going with the flow, but raising a few practical points.

Similarly, if you are always giving reminders of essential actions by other departments, you must be sure that your own department is always functioning efficiently. You will not be appreciated for pointing out lapses in other parts of the business when your own reports are produced late and are strewn with errors and omissions.

Finally, never miss an opportunity to provide other departments with a worthwhile and cost-effective service (most often in the form of information) or benefit (such as automating or achieving an economy). Don't wait for others to ask for services, but be alert to opportunities for providing them by taking a close interest in all aspects of the business.

If you perform in accordance with these principles and inculcate them upon your department you will normally find it easy to fit in with any reasonable company culture. Your attitude is what matters; if it is the right attitude, you and your department can have whatever reasonable culture you wish!

## 1.1g – The controller's master file

Given that you may be accosted by any of the aforementioned officials at any time and asked a specific question on the finances of the business, you need to have a summary of information with you most of the time. The solution to this requirement is a master file, constantly updated.

Obtain a lightweight A4 or (letter-size) folder with 40 clear pockets, giving you space for 80 sheets.

The documents in your master file should normally be:
- Contact phone numbers and email addresses
- Organisation chart(s)
- Factory plan
- Budget
- Most recent set of results
- Trend analysis
- Progress chart for major projects
- Any other information to which you may need to refer at short notice

## 1.1h – Making an impact

Each person has his own character and way of presenting himself to others. However, there are some useful general principles to observe:
- smile
- listen – much more than you talk
- don't lose your cool
- be familiar at all times with the most critical numbers
- smile
- answer in PRACTICE – not in policy nor in principle
- give reasons wherever possible
- teach, coach and train – always help people to get ahead
- smile

- concentrate always on cash and profit, not sales
- lead by example
- don't be afraid to say "I don't know" (but don't say it too often, and make sure you get the right answer immediately afterwards)
- smile

When talking, use simple, direct language. Don't say "this represents a significant window of opportunity"; say "this is a good chance". Better still, don't use the word "significant" at all; just say what the significance is.

*Real life – a weather forecaster advised that a region was going to have "significant rain". Did that mean that it would be heavy, or long-lasting, or spread over a wide front, or near-freezing, or driven by a 40-knot wind, or acidic, or a combination of those characteristics? The people in that region would probably have liked to know what was going to be significant about it.*

Remember that a very small profit is just as significant as a large profit, so be specific. Use simple words; it something is big, then say "it's big".

Avoid meaningless openers, such as:
- well/ obviously/ at the end of the day/ having said that

and similarly avoid meaningless fillers, such as:
- sort of/ if you like/ you know/ in a manner of speaking

and finally, use the proper words:
- don't call a problem a challenge; they're not the same thing (the Maginot Line was a challenge, but it certainly wasn't a problem; von Manstein simply drove round it)
- don't deliver; just do (we are awash with people "delivering solutions" and if you speak in those terms, people will soon fall asleep or start playing boardroom bingo)

Amidst all the hot air and political pronouncements, most people find it refreshing to deal with someone who speaks simply and accurately. Most importantly, speak without pretentiousness to your department. Don't begin your answer with "It's not company policy to"; instead, explain why a request cannot be granted.

If you have any criticism of members of your department, give it to them constructively and privately. How you give it depends on the attitude of the person concerned:

- if someone has done something wrong and is genuinely upset at having done it, there is little point in chastising him for it as he is already reprimanding himself
- if, however, someone is serenely ignoring a bad mistake, he should be reprimanded both for the error and for his irresponsible attitude towards it

Your success depends on your department's performance, so lead from alongside them as well as above and in front of them. When they do well or badly, make sure they know it . . . especially when they do well.

## 1.1i – Reprise

What do the following have in common: food, drink, medicine, clothing, housing, furniture, waste disposal, energy, transport, roads, electronics, communication, all other equipment, pleasure items and luxury items?

Answer: They are all manufactured.

Everything we use in life, including this book, is manufactured; even farming and mining are forms of manufacture. To regard any form of manufacture as passé or a "sunset industry" is to ignore the reality. All service industries including finance exist on the back of manufacture, no matter how indirectly. It may not seem that way if they exist on the back of manufacture in other, far-away countries, but in that case the dependence is even greater than it is on domestic manufacture. That is because the government which controls the service-based and finance-based economy does not control the manufacture upon which that economy depends and therefore has less power to influence the work flow.

No matter what your business is, be sure to understand the principles of production.

However different it may seem, your business has a production process, or even a whole set of processes.

To control your business, you must understand the processes and work with the people who operate them.

Those are principally the people described above, and they, too, are all concerned with processes.

## 1.2a – Objectives

The objectives of the finance department centre around processing, control and reporting:

- authorisations for all transactions are obtained and evidenced by the designated persons
- all financial transactions of the business are recorded promptly and correctly
- all supporting documentation is obtained, checked and filed correctly
- all financial and management reports required by the management are issued promptly and correctly
- financial assets (cash, accounts receivable, securities etc) are securely under effective control at all times
- the financial records comply fully with the relevant legal requirements
- prompt corrective action is taken to remedy any deviations from the above

The objectives of the financial controller with regard to his own department are largely managerial in nature:

- ensure that the finance department carries out its duties correctly and meets its objectives
- ensure that the department is adequately resourced at all times
- develop the capabilities of the department and of the individual members thereof
- ensure that the links between the finance department and other operating departments are fully effective
- ensure that the financial reports contain adequate provisions for liabilities and losses in asset values
- prepare medium-term forecasts (updated monthly or quarterly) and other information required by the financial director
- provide any other support required by the financial director and deputise for him when required

The financial controller's objectives in relation to the other departments are discussed in subsection 1.3.

## 1.2b – Culture

The culture of the finance department is important, because the department simultaneously performs two radically different functions:

- the department is the police force of the business's commercial activity, ensuring that all commitments and transactions are for genuine business purposes, and are properly authorised and properly processed
- the department is also a service department, providing information and occasionally systems to enable other departments to do their jobs more cost-effectively

It is also on occasion an investigative department, assisting other departments in solving problems or carrying out troubleshooting tasks, sometimes in a sensitive context.

The simultaneous role of policeman and service provider therefore requires a degree of maturity from all members of the finance department. Their attitude has to be firm, yet at the same time, cheerful and helpful. It is tempting to assume that the policing role is the dominant role, but to pursue that role at the expense of the service function would be to alienate the other departments, and in many cases to reduce the effectiveness of the business. It would also reduce the effectiveness of the finance department, since you would find it harder to obtain assistance and cooperation when required.

The smaller any organisation is, the more it takes its culture from the culture of its leader, the obvious extreme being the case of a one-person business, where the culture is 100% the culture of that person. In most businesses (with the obvious exception of the finance sector itself) the finance department is one of the smaller departments in number, and you will thus normally have a considerable influence in shaping the culture of your department.

Whatever working culture you have is entirely up to you, since there is no "correct" culture, but you must be able to lead by example in showing an appropriate mix of firmness and yet willingness. In general, departments that laugh easily together work well together, and laughter is particularly useful in a department such as finance which other departments tend traditionally to regard as somewhat straight-laced (an inevitable perception, giving the policing side of the finance role). So even if you are by nature a serious person, encourage humour within your department as far as it will go without adversely affecting their work ethic, or that of anyone else.

Moreover, people tend to visit a cheerful department more often than they do other departments, and as one of your prime functions is to keep in touch with what is happening throughout the business, you should encourage a welcoming attitude in your department (except that at month-ends this welcome will probably be extended only to those people bringing you the information you need!).

## 1.2c – Staff duties

There are an almost infinite number of ways in which finance and accounting tasks can be allocated, but the main functions listed below are standard to the majority of businesses. In smaller businesses one person may combine several of the roles, while in larger ones there may be several people performing the same role, but the allocation of tasks is approximately the same (titles may vary – controller, accountant, supervisor, operator, clerk and other titles are used in a variety of contexts, but the duties remain similar):

- accountant
- cash supervisor
- accounts receivable supervisor
- accounts payable supervisor
- payroll supervisor – this person may be in a personnel department
- costing supervisor – this person may be in a costing or production control department
- fixed assets supervisor – this person may be in a separate department such as engineering
- tax, customs duty, legal and other administration supervisor

Broadly their functions are as follows. Note, however, that much of the base data governing transactions should normally be prepared by other departments. The following examples are common, and provide a degree of internal check in that the persons establishing the standing data are not in a position to exploit that data:

- a costing department will normally enter standard or estimated costs
- a customer services department will enter customer data, including credit periods and limits
- a logistics or purchasing department will enter supplier data, including bank account details for payments
- production operators will enter details of products completed and rejected

# The Financial Controller

Note also that in addition to the routine functions listed below there will be a range of associated tasks such as resolving queries and providing analyses of certain accounts or periods.

**Accountant:**
- oversee (in a processing and accounting sense rather than a managerial sense) the clerical functions of the financial staff
- ensure that all sub-ledgers are reconciled at least monthly and all discrepancies are promptly resolved
- ensure that all periodic adjustments are correctly evidenced, calculated and entered
- prepare periodic accounts in required format and according to prescribed accounting policies
- prepare additional information for annual statutory accounts and for tax calculations (which may or may not be calculated externally)
- ensure that all periodic requirements (eg sales tax, payroll tax, government statistics) are met
- keep the financial controller advised of all major accounting issues arising or expected to arise

**Cash supervisor (see cash system per 4.7):**
- maintain day-to-day control of bank accounts, deposit accounts and petty cash floats and carry out any non-routine fund transfers in accordance with properly authorised instructions
- ensure that all cash received by post is banked promptly – direct bank payment by customers is preferable and in many parts of the world is now the norm
- reconcile with appropriate frequency (daily in a large business) all bank and deposit accounts
- prepare rolling short-term cash flow forecasts (typically every month for the following three months)
- advise the financial controller of expected foreign currency inflow and outflow and arrange hedging as and when instructed (normally by the financial director through the controller)
- reconcile all cash and petty cash sub-ledgers at least monthly with receivables, payables, payroll and general ledgers

**Accounts receivable supervisor (see receivables system per 4.3):**
- ensure that all sales invoices are correctly entered into the receivables ledger and eliminated from the finished goods records each day (normally entered by despatch or sales staff)
- ensure that the receivables ledger reconciles with the cash ledgers

- ensure that all customer debit notes and sales credit notes are correctly authorised and processed and all customer accounting queries are promptly and correctly resolved
- ensure that all other adjustments to customer accounts are correctly authorised and processed
- reconcile the receivables ledger with the general ledger at least monthly
- assist with credit control procedures and queries

Note: credit control procedures are often part of the finance department's duties, but they are so critical to the business that they are discussed in detail in 3.2e as part of the cash management.

**Accounts payable supervisor (see payables system per 4.4):**
- ensure that all purchase invoices are correctly verified, authorised and entered into the payables ledger each day
- ensure that the appropriate inventory entries have been made for inventory purchases (normally done by the goods inwards department)
- ensure that supplier credits are obtained for all disputed items and that all unresolved disputes are dealt with promptly
- flag invoices for payment approval by the financial controller and payment by the cash supervisor
- reconcile the payables ledger with the general ledger at least monthly

**Payroll supervisor (see payroll system per 4.5):**
- liaise with the personnel manager to ensure that all personnel information is up to date in the payroll system before each period's payroll is processed
- input base data from the relevant departments (eg hours worked per production or contract supervisors) to the payroll system each period
- enter all other factors affecting pay (eg holidays, maternity leave, special deductions, bonuses etc)
- run the payroll in draft and review it with the financial accountant and department heads to resolve any discrepancies
- provide the accountant with the agreed payroll posting summary
- process the payroll and initiate payment of net pay through the cash supervisor
- initiate payment of deduction and contribution accounts through the cash supervisor
- reconcile payroll accounts each month with the general ledger and agree with the accountant

- prepare related payroll statistics as required (eg annual tax deduction summaries)

**Costing supervisor (see inventory and cost of sales system per subsection 4.1):**
- maintain the material files, bills of material and other product cost data
- calculate the cost rates from the annual budget and prove the budget by running the model using the calculated rates
- provide costings to enable quotations for all customer enquiries and new products

**Fixed assets supervisor (see fixed assets system per subsection 4.6):**
- coordinate the preparation of the capex budget
- ensure that all capex is correctly authorised and accounted for
- maintain the fixed assets register and reconcile it monthly with the general ledger
- report monthly on capital expenditure incurred and committed in comparison with the budget

The specific nature of the business may require other functions – eg import/export documents and customs clearance (an integral part of the process of delivering goods to customers or getting goods from suppliers in an international environment)

All of the above members of staff have responsibility for filing the documents which they process. Some large businesses have central filing and dedicated staff, but this can be a cumbersome arrangement which does not offer rapid ad hoc retrieval of documents such as is required when dealing with queries.

## 1.2d – Staff development

Finance department staff work comprises the following general categories:
- processing transactions – coding, checking, entering in systems
- filing and related administration of transactions and documents
- reconciling ledger accounts – daily, weekly, monthly to ensure correct totals
- dealing with exceptions – queries, credits, corrections, disposals etc
- summarising and reporting – either on individual parts of the system, or the business as a whole

The work at the beginning of that list comprises mainly processing, and towards the end of the list it becomes more managerial in nature. Put a managerial person on processing duties and he will not do them well; his mind will divert to easily to related issues for which he is responsible and he is more likely to make errors. A processing person, who is used to concentrating heavily on detail, will process documents accurately but may have difficulty with more managerial tasks and may require coaching with these, especially with respect to decision-making.

The commonest example of this is in quoting figures. If the managing director asks the financial controller what the overdraft is, the controller will give a number of 3,270 (assuming units of £000), while a processor will quote £3,268,941.07 if asked the same question. You can tell a ledger operator a dozen times that you when you ask for a balance you want it to the nearest thousand pounds, but you will probably still receive it to the nearest penny because the processor is responsible for ensuring that the ledgers are correct to the penny, and quite properly thinks in those terms, leaving you to round the number to whatever level of accuracy you want.

This means that to develop processing staff who show potential for promotion, you need to:
- explain to them in all cases the wider purpose(s) of the tasks you allocate to them
- similarly, explain the purposes of all the controls which are (or will be) in place
- keep them apprised, subject to confidentiality, of the main issues occurring in the business, not just financial issues, but commercial, legal, technical and other issues – quite apart from keeping them interested and involved, this can result in some useful suggestions from your team
- always give them feedback on the effects, beneficial or otherwise, which the finance department's activities have on other areas of the business

You also need to develop them laterally, for their own personal progress and for absence cover for the department. It is not uncommon to find ledger operators who have been doing accounts receivable for years without having worked on accounts payable. This has several disadvantages:
- they do not develop their skills and hence their usefulness to the business
- they may become inflexible by nature and quite often demotivated, with a loss of care and accuracy
- the department does not have cover in times of staff absence, planned or unplanned

- there is a heightened risk of fraud, although if your systems are properly established there should be sufficient checks to ensure that this does not happen (5.2i)

Accounts receivable and payable staff usually swap fairly easily, and cash can be added to the repertoire without too much difficulty. However, the fixed assets, costing, payroll, taxes and other functions require more specific knowledge and skills, and hence more training, with the added complication of high confidentiality in payroll operation. You should therefore write into finance staff contracts when the staff are engaged that they will be expected to develop their skills by rotating within the finance department (see contracts of employment, 5.3g).

Where this becomes difficult is the point where record-keeping links into accounting. It is one thing tasking someone to reconcile the general ledger while the supervisor is on holiday, but quite another requiring the ledger supervisor to prepare the monthly management accounts. Hence in smaller businesses one sees the dangerous practice of the accountant or financial controller never taking a holiday over a month-end. That may work, but what happens when he is ill or has a domestic emergency over a month-end?

Developing staff to progress from record-keeping to preparation of financial statements can be done in several progressive stages:
- ensure that they are competent at their designated processing work
- involve them in month-end reconciliations and investigation of anomalies arising therefrom
- get them to prepare some of the month-end adjustments (accruals, prepayments, amortisation etc)
- have them transfer the figures into your accounting model (appendix C5)
- instruct them to review your draft accounts for anomalies
- task them with investigating and explaining major variances revealed in the draft accounts
- finally, let them attempt the whole process under your supervision

Most financial controllers already have an accountant preparing the monthly financial statements for them, but they will nevertheless still have to have absence cover. This could involve the controller preparing the statements, but it would normally be better to have another member of the team preparing them, so that the controller can review them; it is notably easier to spot anomalies in someone else's work than it is in your own.

## 1.2e – Staff reviews and appraisals

How often should you appraise staff?
- when they are starting a job, almost constantly – most new members need up to a week's intensive induction, followed by frequent supervision until they become self-sufficient
- in times when the business or the finance department is undergoing rapid or substantial change, appraisals should not be more than 3 months apart, because the objectives in a period of change are of a shorter-term nature than normal (on a specific project there will be frequent team reviews, perhaps even daily)
- when periods of change settle down into normality, the appraisal period can be extended to 4 months and subsequently 6 months

No more than 6 months should pass without an appraisal. If the business is in a very stable phase, it is acceptable to have full annual appraisals and lighter 6-month appraisal between them, but to let staff go for more than 6 months without a review is to risk deterioration in the performance, morale and attitude.

Split your appraisals (appendix A7) into 3 sections in which you review performance against the objectives set at an employee's previous appraisal or on induction of a new employee to the department:
- performance objectives – relations with customers, suppliers and other departments etc, accuracy, tidiness, punctuality, contribution to meetings, speed of response to queries, and any other relevant characteristics (remember that it is the behaviour you are trying to improve, not the personality)
- routine objectives – accuracy, quality of documentation, learning of new responsibilities, meeting of deadlines and any factor relating to routine work per the employee's job specification or extension thereof
- project objectives – system improvements, performance improvements, new reports, reorganisation and any other one-off projects

In all cases get the employee to give his own assessment of his progress and to state the problems he has encountered in meeting or failing to meet them.

Once a consensus has been agreed on the performance to date, agree the employee's objectives for the next assessment period. Instruct the employee before the meeting to submit his own suggestions for objectives; the better an employee he is and the better a manager you are, the more closely his objectives will match the objectives you have planned for him.

At the following appraisal, mark his objectives as fully achieved, partly achieved or not achieved; this will give you a broad measurement on which to assess his overall achievement. You may also need a "withdrawn" category, as projects are shelved from time to time and that is not the employee's fault.

There is another part to the appraisal. You also have to review how the employee has worked with the following categories of people:

- subordinates
- colleagues
- superiors
- external parties

This is because some people, although not great achievers, can build good strong relationships with other people involved in the business, and this can be a valuable contribution. Similarly, other people can achieve all of their objectives but offend many other people in doing so, thereby negating much of the benefit of their specific project achievements.

Note that this approach works for everyone from the office assistant to the chief executive. The former can be tasked with answering every telephone call within 7 seconds; the latter can be tasked with keeping the earnings per share above £X. Similarly, a sales assistant has to maintain positive relations with suppliers and a chief financial officer has to maintain them with shareholders, bankers etc.

Appendix A7 shows the simple format for conducting this type of appraisal. It is clear, easy to understand, takes a minimum of writing and can be applied to almost any business.

## 1.2f – Staff recruitment

Recruitment is one of the most daunting tasks faced by any manager in any business. Get it wrong and you can be stuck with your unsuitable choice for a long time . . . and it is not always immediately apparent whether or not you have made an unsuitable choice, as some people take time to settle in. Here are some basic rules for recruiting finance personnel, remembering the overall culture we have discussed above:

- be welcoming and put the interviewee at ease – he's not going to want to work for you otherwise

- ask technical questions – finance is a technical discipline, so you must ensure that the person you hire has the knowledge to do what is required of him
- ask open questions which require a specific explanation – for example, "what do you consider makes an effective [system, reconciliation, spreadsheet etc]?" or "how would you deal with a customer refusing to pay?" and so on, so that he must demonstrate both his knowledge and his ability to express himself
- don't recruit what you've already got, and especially don't recruit yourself, a very common failing in which you find a candidate with a similar outlook to your own, and, feeling comfortable with him in the interview you decide to hire him . . . so if you're a mover-and-shaker you now have two movers-and-shakers when what you need is one of them, plus a control-oriented person who ensures that your progressive ideas are translated into reality in a well controlled and recorded manner (and similarly, if you're a bit of an analyst you need a go-getter to deal with some of the more active aspects of your work and get things moving in your department)
- ensure that you answer all the interviewee's concerns – if he feels that he has not had fair answers he may decline your offer
- ask yourself several times during the interview: can you see this candidate gelling with the other members of the finance team? (if not, the candidate is unlikely to be suitable, whatever his other qualities; even if you are actively seeking to stimulate change in an underperforming department, the new appointee must do this in a way which makes the others want to work with him)

Let one of more of your team members help at the interview, at least for part of the time – it helps if the interviewee feels comfortable with them and it creates a more collegiate feel to the interview. But ensure beforehand that your team members will create a good impression!


## 1.2g – Managing the department

Managing a finance department is like managing any other group of people:
- they must know their team's overall responsibilities and objectives (and unless the objectives are top secret, they should always know WHY each job is required)
- they must know their own responsibilities and objectives within the team
- they must understand what their team-mates' responsibilities and capabilities are

- they must be advised of the actual and potential difficulties facing the tasks
- they must receive the necessary guidance and support from above

Firstly, ensure that you have an organisation chart for the department. In case of a very small department, a matrix of names and responsibilities will suffice, but in a larger organisation you may well need an organogram. Appendix C1, although relating only to month-end procedures, is an example of the matrix approach.

Next, ensure that you have a financial calendar for the whole business for the financial year (appendix A4) and ensure that everyone has a copy and fully understands it. The calendar will show a finance department meeting at least once per month, normally approaching the month-end to ensure that all requirements are in place for a rapid and accurate monthly accounting and reporting process. However, you may need other short meetings on a regular basis, depending on events and the speed of change in your department.

A few words about department meetings:
- don't have them if they are not needed – if your weekly meeting becomes progressively boring, it's a sign that your team has matured and fully knows the ropes, and it's time to change to a bi-monthly meeting
- keep them short and to the point – half an hour maximum unless there's a big topic on hand
- acknowledge team members' achievements of tasks from previous meetings
- keep the mood relaxed – you're a team, not a bunch of strangers, so don't forget the tea and biscuits
- finish by ensuring that each member knows exactly what is required of him
- check (lightly) in between meetings that objectives are being progressed, especially commitments made to other departments – other departments are traditionally sceptical about the value of the finance department, but if their requirements are actively being pursued and met, that will engender respect

The monthly credit control meeting is a separate issue, dealt with in 3.2e.

Finally, remember that you are only as good as the overall performance of your department.

## 1.2h – Shared service centres

*Real life – the author worked as a managing director in Singapore with the accounts processing carried out by a shared service centre in Sydney. The centre staff were cheerful, efficient, helpful and constructive and did a fine job, identifying readily with the business and understanding its needs. But if they hadn't shown those professional qualities, it would have been a difficult process to bring them up to the required standard at long range.*

So if you're going to use a shared service centre, make sure it's a very effective one in terms of both performance and cost. That may be difficult to verify without actually working with it, so before engaging a service centre, obtain references from two existing clients with similar operating circumstances to your own and discuss their experiences IN DETAIL before committing your business to using the centre. Transferring your finance operation to a service centre can be a major logistical project, and if the result is unsatisfactory you will have an even bigger project in returning it to in-house operation, because you will need to recruit and train a whole new finance department.

The author has on several occasions heard views that accounting is a non-core activity and should be outsourced if possible. Such a proposition beggars belief; given that every company's core business is MAKING MONEY, finance is the most core of core functions!

# OTHER DEPARTMENTS 1.3

## 1.3a – Objectives

As has already been stated at least twice, the objective of the business is to **make money**.

Therefore everyone in the business must be focused on that objective, although in practice this tends to be indirectly; each department will focus on its own activities, all of which should play a part in the profit and cash generation of the business

The role of the financial controller with regard to the other departments is:
- to help the managers understand how their activity and output contribute to the overall financial performance of the business
- to assist the managers in the financial planning and budgeting of their activities
- to provide them with financial information from which they can measure the financial effectiveness of their activities and their performance against budget – this may take the form of providing additional reports, or system modifications to enable them to access information directly, and usually involves close collaboration with the IT function (1.3e)
- to ensure through the relevant managers that all other departments responsible for inputting to the financial systems are doing so correctly, and that any deficiencies are promptly corrected – this may involve the provision of formal or informal instruction to the staff of other departments
- to analyse the financial reports (daily, weekly and monthly) in terms of the business's performance and instruct the appropriate actions to minimise adverse trends and maximise positive ones
- to help them with administrative and general organisation and problem-solving – this is hardly ever an official part of the controller's remit, but in practice he and the IT manager are usually the persons best placed to do it, and it creates much goodwill towards the finance and IT departments

Strictly speaking, all expenditure in a business is incurred for the purpose of making money. The controller therefore has to keep that ultimate objective very much in the minds of the other departments, so that the culture of considering the net return on all expenditure is endemic within the business. This is achieved in a number of ways:

- keeping department heads advised of the downstream effects of their work – for example, if R&D design a correction of a product fault, the controller should report back to them the value of the resultant reduction in credit notes for defective products

- keeping department heads advised of the overall financial dynamics and performance of the business – for instance, marketing may be concerned at producing more expensive components than competitors, but if the controller and R&D can demonstrate that the components can be assembled by customers much more rapidly than those of the competitors, the customers will recognise that they can generate a much higher value added per hour, and willingly buy the higher-priced components; marketing will have to adapt to marketing the products on the economics of their assembly rather than benefits such as price

Some expenditure, however, cannot be quantified easily in terms of the net revenue it generates. For example, redecorating an office does not directly generate any revenue. However, it is part of creating and maintaining an environment in which employees can work happily and effectively, and the overall morale of the employees is a considerable factor in maximising the net revenue, although it is not measurable. Even the staff turnover cost is not measurable, as you will never know how many staff would have left if the morale had been lower.

Such expenditure is therefore a matter of judgement in achieving an adequate but not excessive standard. If it remains at a modest and essentially practical level, there is probably little to worry about unless the business is experiencing difficult conditions. If, however, it becomes difficult to relate proposed expenditure instinctively to any hard monetary benefits, that is the time (ie at the proposal stage) to question strongly its suitability, and if necessary to resist it.

The concept of net revenue is discussed in 3.1c and should be kept uppermost in all managers' minds. Some successful managing directors have the habit of saying "We'd have to sell X more products to pay for that" whenever a manager suggests an item of expense. It puts the proposed expense firmly into perspective.

## 1.3b – Administration

If an administration department is separately identified as such, it is often a designated responsibility of either the financial controller or, ideally, a senior secretary reporting to him (sometimes officially to the managing director, but in practice to the controller). Functions typically included in the administration department are:

- communications (telephone, fax and postage, but not email, which is handled by IT) – monitor the various technologies, facilities, tariffs and lease options which are available, as these change with increasing frequency as communications technology develops
- stationery ordering and control – the name of the game here is physical security
- reception (including car parking and security) – collaborate with the marketing manager on this if your premises are visited by customers, as the initial impression gained by visitors to the business is an important part of establishing good relationships with them
- security – seldom as good as it should be, and can include fire and evacuation drills, first aid and first-aiders, document storage, protection of valuable materials and products, perimeter gates and fencing, alarm systems and other factors
- car parking – schemes vary from designated spaces to first-come-first-served, the optimum usually being a combination; senior personnel's time is too valuable to spend hunting for spaces, while the rest arrive at work earlier if they want a convenient space . . . but where do you differentiate between them?
- travel and accommodation booking (but not cash advances or expenses) – as it takes a considerable amount of travel to merit an in-house function, many businesses work through a travel agency, who should re-tender annually for the work; however, the ability to book travel efficiently on-line has resulted in many businesses now organising their own travel
- secretarial – as far as possible each department should handle its own secretarial functions now that electronic communication is the norm, but that sometimes results in uneven quality of communication and therefore requires a degree of central monitoring
- fleet management (company cars, distribution vehicles and others)
- filing
- archiving

**Facilities** are usually **better centralised** for practicality; they can be easily controlled as overall entities and can take advantage of economies of scale. A rigorously controlled stationery store, for example, goes some way towards preventing the business from having as many stationery stores as it has clerical staff.

**Activities** of administration, however, are generally **better decentralised**; each department should as far as practicable do its own administration. The reason is simple; if they do it badly, they will suffer immediately and will have nobody else to blame or to call to remedy matters and there is therefore a powerful incentive to keep the admin efficient. If they file documents sloppily, they will not be able to locate them and immediate action is stimulated. If a department is habitually badly administered, its management needs some attention from above.

The best barometer of the effectiveness of the administrative facilities and activities is their profile. If they are hardly visible and arouse little comment, they are probably working effectively . . . but keep an eye on them nevertheless.


## 1.3c – Personnel

The personnel function has become so specialised, and the subject of so much legislation, that in medium-sized and large companies there is almost always a qualified personnel manager in charge of the department. Even in small companies which could not afford a fully qualified manager, a designated person with training in local employment legislation is normally required – typically a senior secretarial or financial person who is already involved and experienced in handling confidential communications.

In some businesses the personnel function is part of the finance department, and in others the personnel manager reports to the financial controller or director. Even if the personnel manager reports directly to the managing director (which is preferable), the financial controller will still have considerable involvement in the personnel function, because:

- the personnel function often includes the payroll, which has widespread financial control implications, and in many businesses is the single largest item of expense
- the manpower plan normally constitutes a large part of the budgeting process (3.4h)
- the payroll may include performance pay calculations which require special attention
- the payroll also involves complex issues concerning tax, social security, pension and other financial items
- there are many contractual matters relating to personnel

- the departure of personnel, particularly if instigated by the business, can have critical financial implications

In addition, the financial director is likely to be involved in similar matters relating to the remuneration of board members.

It is clear from the above that the financial controller has to be up-to-date on payroll legislation, remuneration methods and computer systems and the various contributions and deductions involved:

- legal – the controller must ensure that all managers hiring staff are going through the proper vetting and contractual procedures, as a new employment creates an ongoing stream of expense which can be difficult to terminate (see contracts of employment, 5.3g)
- legal – in the termination of employees under conditions of redundancy or indiscipline there are many potential pitfalls, and close liaison with the business's legal advisors is likely to be needed
- financial – sickness, maternity and terminations all give rise to financial liabilities, requiring close collaboration between the controller and the personnel manager

Finally, it is essential that payroll duties are either segregated or supervised to the extent that no single person is in a position to make fraudulent remuneration payments (see payroll system, 4.5). There are still countries in which people are paid in cash, a situation which demands even greater control and supervision.

## 1.3d – Company cars

Company cars started out largely as a UK phenomenon. In the 1970s the UK government imposed a salary freeze, and to circumvent the rules businesses began to provide cars instead of pay rises for senior staff. The arrangement rapidly spiralled out of control; cars became de rigueur status symbols for executives with defective egos; all senior employees got into the act and taxation arrangements soon followed. The result is that the amount of time devoted to the company car scheme is typically out of all proportion to its importance to the company, and the disease has spread to other countries; most car manufacturers design some of their models specifically for the company executive market.

If the personnel manager is not lumbered with the company car scheme it usually falls to the financial controller, who should keep the car culture as low-key as possible. The build quality of cars is nowadays so high that there is little to choose between one make and another. Therefore you should run a simple scheme as follows:

- negotiate a fleet management arrangement with a reputable dealer, including programmed maintenance and the provision of temporary replacement cars during services and immediate replacements in the event of a breakdown anywhere in the specified territory (the main benefit of having a company car fleet is that executives are not delayed back by breakdowns, servicing or other down-time)
- offer a range of three or four cars at three levels of seniority
- stipulate estate cars for those personnel who will be carrying samples, display material or other goods
- when an employee leaves or is promoted, his car is provided for the remainder of its lease to another member of staff
- when any member of staff without a company car needs to make a journey for business purposes (eg the cashier wishes to go to the bank) he is entitled to use one of the company cars on site and the normal user must provide him with the keys
- stipulate in the contracts of employment that company staff who are dependent on driving to perform their duties are liable to dismissal if they lose their driving licences

To reduce the number of cars it may be appropriate to offer employees a cash alternative. This reduces the administration level, but incurs the slight risk that an employee may economise by having a sub-standard car which causes him to fail in his duties by missing meetings or being temporarily unable to travel.

Take advice from your tax advisors on the tax implications of your car arrangements, but avoid being drawn into any complex arrangements. Such schemes have a habit of absorbing much more management time than the savings warrant, and THE golden rule of management is to keep everything simple.

## 1.3e – Information technology ("IT")

Computer personnel are known by a variety of official labels. The two most common names are probably MIS (management information systems) and IT (information technology). The term IT is used throughout this book.

The IT department is another which often reports to the financial controller or director, although in a manufacturing or contracting or other information-intensive business the bulk of its activities may be in other areas. The association with finance is nevertheless a natural one, since IT has a strong element of control, and most of the non-financial systems have strong financial implications and usually direct linkage to finance. In some businesses the IT function is also responsible for all electronic communications.

The great majority of IT people are instinctively helpful and are natural problem-solvers, whether it is in analysing and resolving a difficulty or devising a solution to a new requirement. Most financial controllers have had many occasions to be grateful to their IT departments. In addition to his system skills the modern IT manager has a sound working knowledge of manufacturing, costing, logistics and accounting principles, and is therefore the controller's greatest ally in the day-to-day operation of the business. The quid pro quo is that the controller gives strong backing to the IT manager's reasonable requests for capital expenditure!

The main issues concerning IT tend to be security-related, and are:
- overall size and capability of IT systems – as the business prepares its strategic plans, it must also plan for commensurate computing capability
- back-up of systems and information – see 5.4c
- disaster and business continuity planning – see 5.4c
- access to enter and amend information – access to systems and entry of data must be kept constantly under review in order to balance internal control on one hand against functionality on the other

The following systems are likely to be linked:
- main finance and accounting system, including purchases, sales, cash and general ledger
- fixed asset system
- inventory control system
- manufacturing system
- production workers time recording system
- contract system (certain businesses only)
- canteen system (where meals are charged to employees by swipe-cards)
- payroll systems (weekly and monthly if applicable)

It follows that the controller and IT manager must frequently review their ongoing requirements together, liaising with departmental managers and system users. When there are system breakdowns the controller must be prepared to give priority often to the non-financial systems in order that the profit-generating processes can continue. Remedy of the accounting systems usually comes last unless there are exceptional circumstances such as a payroll run or other urgent documentation.

## 1.3f – Land and buildings

Most businesses of any size have a designated works engineer or similar official who is responsible for the premises, and usually their upkeep and security. The principal concerns of the controller in this area should be:
- health and safety
- environmental issues
- security, with regard to burglary and malicious damage
- secure storage for assets, especially perishable inventory
- general maintenance costs, and advance warning of probable major repairs
- insurance

There are many aspects of legislation in the above areas. As far as practicable these should be the responsibility of operational personnel, but the financial controller may well be involved.

Where there are cost issues, the financial controller may also have a particular interest. For example, if there is surplus building or land space, he should be seeking to have the spare resource put to profitable use.

## 1.3g – Marketing and sales

Marketing is where it all begins.

For a business to make money it has to have a market . . . and it has to design, manufacture and provide the right products for that market at the right prices. All business activities stem from there, and the finance function has to be right alongside the marketing function. The financial director is involved with the strategic aspects of the marketing plans and obtaining and managing the financial resources necessary to achieve them, while the financial controller is involved with the operational aspects of executing the plans.

The financial controller will have to work closely with marketing and sales management on many issues:
- strategic plan
- budgeting

- pricing strategy and methods
- costs of selling
- understanding net variable margins
- inventory (what is needed to support the product range?)
- receivables

To work with the marketing management on the above issues, the controller must have a sound working knowledge of the business's products and market:

- what the products do – if there is a range of similar products, the differences amongst them must be clearly understood, as there are likely to be different strategic decisions required for the different items
- how they are priced
- who buys them
- why they buy them – the answer to this is often a combination of factors, and in the case of industrial products it is seldom a simple answer
- how the products compare with those of the competition
- what the main product drivers are – price, performance, packaging, availability, appearance, trendiness, compatibility with other products, ruggedness, ease of use etc

The simplest way to gain this understanding is to list the products and their characteristics on a spreadsheet. The first column should contain the parameters applying to the business's products and the subsequent columns should detail the equivalent information for the products of the major competitors. This single sheet will give you a helicopter view of your market – put the sheet in your controller master file (see 1.1g and appendix A2).

## 1.3h – Transport (distribution)

The extent of the controller's involvement in transport will depend on whether the business uses its own transport or contracts out the work to transport companies. It is quite common for businesses to have their own transport vehicles for distribution of products outward, but less common for collection of materials inward. However, some businesses use external transport for all deliveries inward and outward, while others use their own distribution fleet to bring in materials on the return journeys, thereby negotiating lower material prices. There is also the half-way solution of having an external transport company provide you with your own fleet in your own livery, managed by your distribution manager but maintained by the transport company.

Transport is therefore one of the activities in which there may be frequent comparisons of in-house costs against contracted-out costs. Where the flow of deliveries is consistent from one day or week to the next, it tends to be cost-effective to have your own fleet, but where deliveries do not follow a regular pattern it tends to be more economical to use external carriers, to avoid having resources underutilised in one week, and overstretched the next.

If you are operating your own fleet, your distribution manager will want the products to be scheduled on the production line so that they come off the line in order of geographical area. All the south-west route products will arrive at the despatch area together, allowing swift packing and departure of the vehicle for that route, and so on. The production manager, of course, will want all products of similar specifications to go through the production process together, to minimise set-up times. Who should have priority?

In general, if the factory is not fully utilised the distribution manager should have his way, because there is spare capacity and the additional set-up time is not costing money. However, if the factory is under pressure, the production manager should have the priority to ensure that the required output is produced, and the distribution manager will have to improvise his delivery schedules.

The controller should keep in regular contact with the distribution manager on the following matters:
- overall unit cost of distribution
- recovery of distribution costs in product pricing
- capital items such as transport vehicles or the leases thereof
- evaluation of other distribution methods from time to time

See section 1.4b regarding days spent by a financial controller on a distribution truck.

## 1.3i – Credit control

Credit control is generally regarded as a finance department function, and can work quite well on that platform. However, many businesses assign credit control to one of the customer-facing functions, usually with greater success. We discuss credit control in detail in a separate subsection of the cash performance section (see 3.2e).

## 1.3j – Research and development (including technical support)

It is self-evidently stated in 1.3g above that a business has to have the right products for its markets. The rôle of the R&D department is therefore:

- understand exactly what products the market wants (this necessitates a permanently close relationship with the marketing and sales departments)
- understand what characteristics of those products are most important to the customers
- understand how well the competitors' products are meeting the customers' preferences
- design products which will outperform the competitors' offerings and **make a profit** (in addition to making them worth a good selling price, this should involve making them easy to manufacture, since the more value you can put through your factory per hour, the more profit you can make . . . and if the products contain a high proportion of standard components, that helps to keep your inventory low)
- develop these products through concept, prototype, testing, pre-production and production
- train the sales, technical support and customer service staff in the use of the products
- train the production department in the efficient manufacture of the products
- continue to develop these products to extend their profitable, cash-generative lives
- while the products are still in profitable production, identify the next generation of products

In many companies the R&D department also carries out the **technical support** for the products.

The above is a formidable list of responsibilities, and a far cry from the uneducated view which many business people have of a bunch of boffins secluded in a back room somewhere. The R&D people must be at the front end of the business alongside the marketing team, in constant touch with the sales team, au fait with the financial implications and fully conversant with the production parameters. And all that is over and above being highly skilled in the science of the business's products. They are a front-end unit, not a back-room operation.

The financial controller must therefore be very close to the R&D team:

- the cost and time required to bring new products to market will feature strongly in the strategic plans

- the department may have considerable capex, usually associated with specific projects
- the extent to which major projects are on or behind schedule can have far-reaching effects on the timing of profit and cash flow
- the examination of customer complaints will provide advance warning of future difficulties, possibly giving rise to customer credits and remedial costs, both of which will need provisions in the accounts
- the revenue costs of technical support must be separated from the capital costs of development work so that both activities can be accurately planned and the costs budgeted for

**Controller's master file** – the controller should instruct the R&D manager to present a monthly single-page summary with a column for each major project, showing:
- distinction between capital and revenue projects
- original milestones – standard font
- revised dates achieved – bold font
- previous month's forecast dates – italic font
- latest forecast dates still to be achieved – bold font
- (at foot of each column) original budget for project – standard font
- revised budget for project – bold font
- variance in monetary and percentage terms

This document will achieve the twin purpose of keeping the controller au fait with developments and keeping the pressure on the R&D department to complete their projects on schedule.

Note that the introduction of a new product involves several stages beyond the completion of the prototype:
- testing of prototype (this can be a lengthy process in simulated and actual field conditions, and may involve a series of prototypes rather than a single one)
- building of pre-production model – really an advanced prototype used for testing the production processes and other real-life aspects
- verification of the availability and performance of component supplies
- building and setting of production tooling and setting of production line
- training of the operatives and others in building, selling and maintaining the product

There is also the marketing aspect, which in addition to preceding the project by identifying the market need and profit opportunity for a new product, must also cover the following aspects:

- advertising launch campaign
- availability of demonstration models and other customer familiarity initiatives as appropriate
- general publicity
- pricing strategy
- delivery
- after-sales support of product
- discontinuation and "managing out" of product being replaced, if relevant (appendix A3)

In addition, there will be the normal accounting issues if the profitability of the product is to be reported separately.

## 1.3k – Production (goods)

Production lines vary from simple assembly to numerous linear processes with a bewildering variety of alternative routes and occasional loops, or chemical processes happening invisibly inside pressure vessels. There may also be complex processes performed off-site by contractors. Consequently, production is often the most difficult area for the financial controller to understand, and it may take months of repeated visits and persistent questioning to gain an adequate understanding of the processes involved.

A clear understanding of the production processes and their parameters is essential to the controller because he needs to understand and control:

- the costing of the product
- the systems of production control – not in production detail, but in terms of financial output
- the accounting for production, including various levels of re-work, scrap, scrap recovery, downtime and other related factors
- financial planning for future production
- cost rates for budgeting and reporting
- the need (or otherwise) for capital expenditure
- production performance – profit
- production performance – logistics and cash
- inventory control and optimum levels of raw materials, work in progress and finished goods

The disciplines underlying production normally involve:

- achieving the lowest possible unit cost

- achieving production targets
- continuous improvement of processes
- lean manufacture
- the minimising of inventory
- meeting delivery targets

all of which have a financial dimension.

## 1.3l – Production (services)

It is equally important for the financial controller to understand the production processes in a service business, or in a goods business with related services:

- the contractual nature between the business and its service clients
- the commitments within the service – not merely duties to be performed, but the extent, timing, quality and prices of those duties
- the definition and measurement of completion of the services, and the need for any troubleshooting
- the resources needed to provide those services – not merely personnel, but equipment, materials and facilities may also be involved, to very differing degrees
- the costs and revenues of all of the above, and the setting of customer charges to recover those costs with a suitable level of profit

Service businesses are as varied as manufacturing businesses. As a general rule, clients (as service customers are normally called) are not averse to paying for goods, facilities or machine time, but frequently complain about paying for personnel working on their behalf. This is because a typical personnel charge rate might be around 250-300% of a person's gross salary, in order to recover employment costs and the very considerable cost of the background organisation (staff, premises and facilities) which supports the chargeable personnel. Since clients seldom take these background factors into account, it helps to keep reminding the clients of these factors.

## 1.3m – Production (contracts)

There are basically four types of production contract:

- production of standard goods to contract terms – typically a specific quantity over a specific period
- production of bespoke goods to contract terms

- production of standard services to contract terms
- production of bespoke services to contract terms

In all cases the financial controller (and probably the financial director in the case of major contracts) must be involved from the beginning, in making and/ or checking costings, estimates, scheduling and all other planning elements before negotiations begin and any commitments are made.

In the case of standard goods sold on contract, the main practical (ie non-legal) concerns are:
- price – competitive but still profitable (do not give away profit just to gain a large contract)
- volume – within overall production capability without detriment to other products, nor excessive overtime
- service – packaging, delivery, technical back-up
- penalties – what happens if commitments are not met on either side?

In the case of bespoke goods, designed specially for a contract customer, the preceding concerns again apply, and in addition there are all the normal concerns of a new product:
- will the bespoke product perform as well as the standard product?
- are the customer's specifications realistic in terms of the cost, performance and profit of the product?
- will the bespoke elements cause financial or technical disruption of the company's normal products?

The provision of services is of a different nature to the production of goods, but nevertheless all the concerns detailed above apply equally to service contracts. Services can be more difficult to specify and quantify precisely than goods are, so additional care is needed in the contractual definitions of the services (see 5.3).

## 1.3n – Inventory control (goods)

Various terms such as **supply chain** and **logistics** are used to describe the management of inventory from the suppliers through the processes to the end customers. Some businesses use the terms only in an upstream (supplier) context, others in a downstream (customer) context and still others in a total context from supplier through to customer. Whatever they call it, inventory management is stock control.

*Real life – the author has also worked in an industry which uses the terms "upstream" and "downstream" in the opposite context, which gave rise to some strange conversations until the penny dropped. However, most people recognise that streams flow from uplands to lowlands.*

Inventory management and control is dealt with extensively in 3.2d and 4.1.

## 1.3o – Maintenance

The maintenance management may be done by an independent department, or (quite often) under the production management. The financial relationship with the maintenance department centres around:

- understanding the annual cost and budgeting for it sensibly
- understanding equally the cost of carrying out inadequate maintenance – a breakdown which causes a loss of production or any other activity can cost much more than a thorough maintenance régime
- consideration of the maintenance cost of old equipment, at a stage where the maintenance cost and any losses arising from downtime can be a major factor in assessing the financial necessity for capital expenditure

Remember that ALL equipment requires maintenance, including buildings, storage equipment, security systems, information systems and transport. Well-maintained assets generally cost less in the long run than otherwise, so ensure that you budget adequately for your needs.

## 1.4a – General

The financial controller will have to deal with a wide range of external bodies, and his ability to develop and maintain a co-operative and productive relationship with them will be fundamental to his success.

The first rule about dealing with outsiders is simple: **be the person who makes the calls**, rather than the person who receives them. People accord you much more respect if you are the person raising the issues and maintaining the momentum. If they have to keep contacting you, they come to believe that you are avoiding them, which makes them think you have something to hide, which in turn makes them doubt what you say. The other important factor about being the person who makes the calls is that if there is bad news to impart, it is less painful if the other side finds out directly from you instead of some other source

Secondly, be open and direct with them. Being direct does not mean being overbearing or aggressive; it simply means telling your story (or as much of it as you wish to tell) in simple straightforward language. Don't gloss it over with clichés or management-speak; just tell it the way it is. It may be painful at the time, but once you've told them the bad news, the pain goes quickly. If they have to drag the information out of you ("What do you mean, you've had to 'realign your payment priorities'?") it will be a much longer, more painful process.

Don't underestimate the need for simple language. Intelligent people are heartily sick of hearing about windows of opportunity, focusing on core business, thinking out of the box and leveraging one's position. Leverage is a noun, anyway, not a verb.

Thirdly, listen. You have two ears and only one mouth, and that provides a good rule for dividing your time. Listening confers great advantages, especially when accompanied by prompting:
- you learn
- you have time to decide on your response (if an external party puts you on the spot with a tough question, ask them to expand on some aspect of it and compose your response while they do so)

- with the other party doing the bulk of the talking, you need to say less than you otherwise would
- in dealing with a dispute, you save your ammunition while the other party fires his; this tends to leave you with the upper hand (ammunition fired is no longer ammunition)
- you understand your counterpart's priorities, and you only need to answer those priorities, which may limit the extent of a dispute

Understanding the other party's priorities is the fourth and most important essential. The only way to create a worthwhile relationship with any business party is for each side to give the other as much as is practicable of what he wants. Think about it. If you have concluded with your supplier a macho deal in which you've nailed him to the wall on every point, which of his customers is he going to leave in the lurch when things get tough? He will ditch the one that gives him the worst return for his effort. Both parties have to WANT to do business with each other for a relationship to work properly.

Fifthly, establish the ground rules at the beginning. Ensure that they cover all eventualities and that both parties clearly understand them, with confirmation in writing (often a quick email will suffice). If circumstances change subsequently, contact the other party and agree an appropriate amendment. If both parties are operating to a clear consensus there is much less chance of a foul-up.

Lastly, as far as time and cost allow, do your business face-to-face, at least for the first time. And try to meet at both premises, his and yours. Which you choose first is a matter of practicality, and possibly public relations.

Business is about partnerships. Yes, we sometimes get annoyed with customers, suppliers, bankers, you name it, but they get annoyed with us, too, and we all depend on each other if we are to succeed. Get used to it – and keep the relationships alive and positive.

## 1.4b – Customers – general

*Real life – following a reorganisation, a group financial controller suddenly found himself also in charge of R&D, land & buildings, purchasing and distribution. The first three were already familiar to him, but distribution, although analysed in considerable detail in financial terms, was a closed book in terms of its logistical and mechanical functions. He therefore did what any sensible person would do; he got his oldest set of overalls (to avoid being conspicuous) and set off on a trip of several days accompanying a truck driver on one of the group's long-distance distribution routes, sleeping in the truck and eating cholesterol-laden truck-stop breakfasts.*

*Throughout the trip he helped the driver and the customers' factory hands to unload the products, and afterwards redistribute the remaining load to balance the truck. On customers' premises he took a careful look round at their operations and throughout the trip he quizzed the driver on all aspects of distribution.*

*In those few days he visited dozens of customer sites, which would have taken two or three months if he had had to arrange the visits individually. He learned many things:*

- *which customers were carrying too much inventory and therefore would have difficulty in paying for it*
- *which customers had badly-organised production facilities (and therefore a host of related problems, including dissatisfied customers of their own and therefore possible claims upstream for faulty products)*
- *which customers had discontented labour*
- *which customers were genuinely busy and showed potential for expansion (and therefore also for over-reaching themselves if they expanded in an uncontrolled manner)*
- *which customers had a strong management presence in the factory area*
- *which customers had financial difficulties (there are few secrets on a factory floor)*
- *that truck drivers know and are generally welcomed by everyone – if you hire the right ones and look after them, they are the best grass-roots grapevine you can have*

*He also learned from the above a lot about the customers' management, without meeting any of them, except at one site where a hard-bitten, troublesome manager known for his dislike of accountants spotted him shouldering in a box from the truck. So nonplussed was the manager at the sight of an accountant actually doing something useful that the manager became a staunch ally thereafter – we can count that benefit as a fluke. The controller took copious notes in the cab after each visit, and used these notes to good effect in subsequent meetings with the customers (see 3.2e).*

Most of your customer visits will be arranged more conventionally, however, and should not be confined to your opposite numbers in their finance departments. Although your business will vehemently claim that every customer is equally important, the reality is that you will accord the greatest priority to those who generate or are likely to generate the **greatest net**

**variable margin** for you. You therefore need to understand in the case of each of these major customers:

- what their overall aspirations are (and if they do not have any clearly definable aspirations, that also will tell you something)
- the contribution your products make to those aspirations
- how to maximise that contribution – it is not just the product, but the way in which you supply it and support it that makes the difference
- in what ways you are failing or succeeding to maximise that contribution
- in what ways your competitors are failing or succeeding to maximise that contribution

After meeting with the majors you can meet a representative selection of some of the others, and from these two groups you will obtain a general view of the range of concerns your customers have and how they are likely to react to certain events, particularly from difficulties, whether these difficulties emanate from your business or from economic conditions in general. You should of course review a copy of each customer's latest accounts just before visiting them, so that you can put their expressed views into a financial context.

Remember that you have to sell what people WANT, not what they need. They may have a need which is obvious to you, but if you cannot persuade them that they need it, they will not want it, and you will be wasting your time trying to sell it to them. Similarly, some of their wants may appear to you to be unnecessary, but if that is what they want, you can sell it to them unless there is some financial, legal or moral reason not to do so.

Before each customer visit, ensure that you are fully briefed on:
- the products you are selling
- all major issues affecting these products and the manner of their delivery
- the contractual conditions under which you are operating
- difficulties which have occurred on either side in the relationship

After each customer visit, ensure that you ACTION the points upon which you have decided. It is too easy to return from a visit fired with enthusiasm, only to become caught up in the usual issues back at the ranch and leave all your good intentions languishing. With major customers it is often worth drafting and signing an operating agreement, stating how you will trade and how and by whom concerns will be discussed and problems solved; such a document is not a formal contract, but a statement of intent, and helps focus both parties for the common good.

In particular, ensure that there are specific individuals in your organisation who have been identified to your main (and preferably all) customers to contact in the event of queries, and that there are back-ups named for when the main contacts are absent. And ensure that the contacts and back-ups are fully aware of the financial parameters established for each customer and the implications of those parameters.

See also credit control (3.2e)

## 1.4c – Customers – on contract

Where you are a contractor to customers, the issues in 1.4b above apply just as much. But in addition you need to consider the following in respect of each major contract:

- understanding the contract and all its conditions (when you are involved in establishing a new contract, ensure that competent legal advice is obtained AND APPLIED)
- the progress of your business against the contract, in terms of time, technical and financial aspects
- problems encountered on either side, and the resolution of those problems
- potential penalties arising from those problems
- potential or actual financial issues arising from the above

Given that managers tend to devote their attention mainly to larger contracts, you may need also to satisfy yourself by test-checking some of the smaller contracts on the above issues.

Finally, ensure that all doubtful areas of performance are adequately covered by provisions which are reviewed at each month-end (see 2.4d).

## 1.4d – Customers of customers

Where your products form a key element of your customers' products, it may be advisable to visit a selection of your customers' customers on occasion to determine the role your products play for the end user. This can be critical from a financial standpoint for a number of reasons:

- it can identify opportunities for further product sales or improvements

- it can demonstrate that your own customers have strong backing from their suppliers and will thus increase the confidence of the end customers
- you can gauge the level of confidence and satisfaction the end customers have in your customers, which in turn helps to ascertain the strength and potential of your customers' businesses

However, be very careful not to offend or circumvent your direct customers. It may be politic to advise your direct customers before you speak to any of their customers, and make it clear that you are doing it to obtain a better understanding of the end-user requirements, and hence provide the best possible product/ service combination.


## 1.4e – Suppliers

If you are new to industry, customer visits can be daunting until you have acquired a reasonable knowledge of industry in general and your own industry in particular. As a newcomer, you are naturally concerned about appearing "green" and thus giving a poor impression. In that case, start by accompanying your purchasing manager on a few supplier visits; because you are the customer, the visits tend to be less daunting.

The things the supplier will be seeking from your business are:
- reassurance that you are financially secure
- an idea of the volume of ongoing business they can expect from you
- what additional plans you have which may affect what they can supply to you
- your continuing adherence to agreed payment terms
- (if they are forward-looking) a culture of partnership between their business and yours, and therefore opportunities to improve and expand the business relationship to the benefit of both parties

Establish buying parameters in consultation with your purchasing manager:
- prices (which may depend on some of the following parameters)
- batch quantities
- packaging
- frequency and locations of delivery
- methods of packaging (which can include containerisation and other shipping issues)
- back-up regarding spares, repairs and replacements
- quality control
- paperwork (invoicing, shipping and cross-border documents)

Note that if you have different streams within your overall business, they may have different requirements from the same supplier. For example, a product stream which is expanding may look to increasing its batch sizes and/ or its frequency of deliveries. However, a stream which is being run down will look to smaller deliveries, possibly at irregular intervals, so that it can balance its reducing inventory and not be left with too many of some components (appendix A3).

DO NOT treat your suppliers as bankers. If you keep your inventory and receivables levels under tight control, you should use the funds gained thereby to pay your suppliers promptly, possibly even gaining price reductions by doing so. When times get tough, as they do for all industries now and then, the suppliers will look after the prompt payers much better than the late payers. If you are a bad payer and hit a problem, are your suppliers going to move heaven and earth to help you through the problem? No.

## 1.4f – Suppliers – contractors and sub-contractors

The normal considerations in dealing with suppliers apply equally to relations with contractors and sub-contractors. However, in addition there are issues arising from the specific natures of individual contracts. These are the same as those described in 1.4c, except that in this case you are the customer, and so there are some additional factors:

- have the contract drawn up by legal advisors specialising in commercial contracts
- ensure that the contractor has the resources to complete the contract in the time and to the specification required
- ensure that their chosen subcontractors are similarly capable (you may have to nominate sub-contractors where the work concerned is critical to the overall outcome)
- ensure that they are capable of paying the penalty if they fail to complete their obligations under the contract (a performance bond lodged with a bank may be the appropriate safeguard there)
- ensure that the penalty specified is sufficient to redress the maximum default envisaged
- if you are dealing with another country, ensure that the contract is not invalidated by any overriding laws thereof (if you are in England, remember that your contract laws are in some cases fundamentally different from those of other European countries, including Ireland and Scotland)
- specify the governing law of the contract (ie the country under whose law disputes would be settled)

Your business may also be in the in-between situation where you are contracted to a customer, and you have a supplier sub-contracted to you for part of the contract work.

In all cases of any size or potential size, ensure that you have competent, robust legal advisors with a presence in both countries.

## 1.4g – Bankers

Banks earn their living from lending. Therefore they WANT to lend. If your bank is unwilling to lend, it may just be that you are dealing with a particularly cautious banker (perhaps as a result of your business's past escapades or of troubles with other businesses in your industry), but it is more likely that you have not given them sufficient confidence that your business is a good risk. The glib answer to lending reluctance is therefore to run a good business.

However, there will be times when your business is not running as well as you or they would wish, and in such times the requirement is invariably a credible remedial action plan. The remedial action invariably centres around three elements:
- liberating immediate cash by minimising working capital and any other non-performing assets
- improving the profit run-rate by a combination of increasing margins and decreasing costs (bankers are more likely to be convinced by the latter, because it is easier to pay less than to collect more)
- improving the management (beware – bankers will notice poor financial management before they notice poor operational management)

In part 3 ("the performance") we deal with these actions in considerable detail. What matters here is how we present our proposed actions to the bank.

For a routine (eg quarterly) meeting with the bank, prepare a one-page memorandum, summarising:
- the recent performance of the business (which they will probably know already from the monthly reports you send them)
- the current factors affecting your business and the expected immediate trend
- the specific actions which you are taking to deal with these factors and with the business's performance

The word "specific" above is vital. It will not satisfy them to say that you are taking steps to reduce your inventory. But if you tell them, for example, that you have identified a large number of older components which you can assemble into a quantity of lower-specification products which you can sell rapidly to some of your smaller customers as a special offer, that will carry much more weight. And be sure to mention some actions which you have already completed; the word "already" is always encouraging in such circumstances.

Whether you send the memorandum in advance of the meeting or bring it when you arrive is a matter of tactics. The latter puts you more firmly in the driving seat, but if speed is of the essence in resolving the situation an advance copy is advisable so that they have time to consider your actions and you can deal with their questions fully at the meeting. If you have prepared your memorandum appropriately, the bankers will not take any notes of the meeting; you will have done that for them and it will be your version of events in their records.

If you are not borrowing, it is very easy to forget about keeping in touch with the bank. That would be a mistake because you may suddenly meet an opportunity or a requirement which needs borrowing, leasing or other facilities and if the bank is not already familiar with your operations and your performance, it will greatly lengthen the time it takes you to persuade them to provide the finance. It may not be necessary to visit a bank quite as often if you are not borrowing, but you can, for example, send them a quarterly résumé of your activities and results, and meet them once a year. But make sure you call them, not the other way around.

If the company is in an intensive care situation, the bank will want frequent reporting.

*Real life – appendix B2 shows a format used to report weekly to a bank monitoring a business in a critical condition. The report arrived on the bank manager's desk every Monday afternoon and had a triple benefit:*

- *it gave the bank manager reassurance that the management team were controlling the situation and he continued to support the company*
- *it developed the management team's ability to forecast quickly and accurately*
- *their increased forecasting ability made them acutely aware of forthcoming difficulties (particularly dips in the flow of sales) and caused them to take action to remedy those situations before they became serious*

## 1.4h – Leasing companies

Dealing with leasing companies when you acquire assets is largely an alternative to dealing with bankers, but with some practical differences:

- instead of paying for something outright, you pay for it over an extended period (albeit at a price, which is the relatively high rate of interest built in – you don't get something for nothing)
- in the case of an operating lease for a technical asset (eg photocopier, telephone system), you often have the back-up of a technical support team which will can be called out rapidly to remedy any malfunctions
- if you need to upgrade your asset (eg a larger telephone network) you can often "roll over" your current lease into a new lease

As the above points are all in favour of leasing, many companies regard leasing as an easy financial solution and over-use it. The result of this is a fixed cost structure which becomes overloaded with lease premiums which contain relatively high interest and a degree of service costs which you may or may not use. Therefore the approach should be to use leasing companies for those essential assets which you do not have the expertise in-house to maintain, so that the operation of those assets is trouble-free. These tend for the most part to be operating leases, which are not capitalised in your balance sheet.

A curious phenomenon is that during a recession, when financial conditions generally become more stringent, it can become easier to lease. This is because leasing company sales executives have periodic targets which become increasingly difficult to meet as the recession progresses. Therefore they can become more inclined to stretch the financial parameters within which they normally operate. Businesses which take excessive advantage of this can find themselves in the high fixed cost position described above, at the very time when they should be minimising their fixed cost base.

In general, though, a leasing company will have similar priorities to a bank with regard to your business's financial position. They will want to know that you have the trading performance and the funds to meet the commitment you agree with them, and you normally have to provide some clear documentary proof of that. And remember, if you default seriously on your payments in times of difficulty, they can remove your asset at a moment's notice. However, if you speak to them when it is clear that times are becoming difficult, you may find that they will work with you through the difficulty by extending the life of the lease or making some other accommodation.

## 1.4i – Public sector (eg development authorities)

When you are dealing with the public sector, it is usually because you want something. For example:
- a low-rent industrial unit
- a grant
- free or reduced-cost consultancy or training

There are many benefits to be obtained from the various international, national and local development authorities and you should therefore maintain your awareness of what is available for your type and size of business in your location. A few phone calls, starting with your local council, are usually sufficient to put you in contact with the various bodies dispensing facilities which may be of use to you.

If you identify a benefit which you would like to claim, read carefully the conditions relating to that benefit and identify clearly what requirements will be placed on you. Remember that the authority which dispenses the benefit is looking for a demonstrable return on their assistance to you. For example:
- job creation (by far the most common motive for providing assistance to businesses)
- improved productivity through training or additional facilities
- introduction of new products, especially those for the export market

Remember that these organisations all have to justify their existence. This means that at the end of each year they must produce a glossy annual report detailing how many jobs they have helped create, what new products they have enabled businesses to develop in their area, et cetera. So they need success stories if they wish to keep their jobs, and you have to convince them beforehand that you can be one of their successes (in a perverse way this means that business which might succeed even without assistance are sometimes more likely to receive assistance than businesses which are in greater need of it).

Therefore you must present a well-constructed application for the assistance you are seeking. The points to emphasise in your application are similar to those which you would present to your bankers:
- with the exception the benefits you are seeking, you already have a well-run and properly resourced business, and you know how you want to develop it
- you have a justifiable expectation of generating satisfactory profits after you have received the training / consultancy / production space / rent holiday / grant / whatever for which you are applying – in other words, you are a good bet for the awarding authority

- all that is holding you up is the lack of the facilities for which you are applying – inevitably that also means that you are short of cash, since you would obtain the necessary benefits for yourselves if you had enough cash or borrowing facilities
- you will achieve and maintain the specific objectives demanded as part of the award of facilities – if these objectives include job creation, the awarding body may be able to claw back any cash they have awarded to you if the additional jobs created do not last for a specified number of years

Most application procedures for public sector assistance contain a set form of financial forecasts. You should therefore model these exactly on your spreadsheet package; if your model is a precise enough copy you are normally allowed to submit it instead of the format provided. By having your own integrated model you will find it much quicker and easier to produce a reliable forecast, but be careful – it is very tempting to tweak the model until it meets the exact parameters of the application (usually a cash shortfall in the early years followed by a recouping through increased profitability in the medium term).

Your forecast must be one which your management genuinely believes is attainable, allowing for a few setbacks along the way.

In general, it does no harm to keep your local authorities, grant bodies etc advised of your progress; if they are aware of what you are doing they will sometimes offer you facilities of which you were unaware. This applies particularly to areas which have suffered industrial decline in recent years and which have high unemployment.

## 1.4j – Auditors

You often hear people complaining about auditors: they don't add value; they don't understand the business; they ask stupid questions; you name it... "the auditors are a nuisance".

WRONG. When you hear a financial controller complaining about the auditors it's a sign that he probably hasn't given any thought to how to get the best out of the audit. It's very easy, but it does take a little planning.

At the beginning of the financial year, open a lever-arch file with sections corresponding to all the main audit programmes (inventory & cost of sales, receivables & sales, payables & purchases, fixed assets etc).

Immediately place in the file notes of all the outstanding or possibly contentious points from the previous year, and ensure that the outstanding ones are on your action list.

As events happen through the year, file the papers relating to any issues in which the auditors will be interested (especially problems – we shall see why in a minute). Some features will be regular items, such as all fixed asset movements and provisions against inventory and receivables). When you review your month-end working papers, ensure that all such items have been copied to the auditor file.

Keep a general section in the auditor file for system matters. When you find glitches in the systems or documentation, copy a note of them into the file.

Have a planning meeting with the audit partner early in the year to fix dates for the interim and final visits. If you leave it till late in the year, you'll be competing with all his other clients for the staff you want, and this is especially difficult if your year-end is a common one, such as 31 December, 31 March or 30 September. Auditors tend to underdo their interim visits – ensure that you receive a good long interim, which will pay dividends at the final visit (provided that you're properly ready for them, of course).

If the partner offers you the same four people that you had last year, turn him down – it means that you'll have four complete strangers the year after. Insist that you have the same two seniors but two new juniors, giving you a combination of continuity and freshness for this year, and a basis of continuity for the following year.

At the planning meeting, set the date for the audit clearance meeting. This will ensure that the audit remains targeted on a completion date, and prevents issues from straggling on for weeks after the auditors, in the manner of Elvis, have left the building. You'll know you are winning when the auditors cancel the audit clearance meeting because there are no issues to report.

At or before the start of the interim audit, give the audit team a big welcome and a thorough briefing. Include the following:
- a reasonably specific review of the financial and operational progress during the year
- your file, which will save them and you a considerable amount of time
- a written list of all of the system weaknesses of which you are aware*, with evidence (no, this is not stupid – why pay for them to spend hours of chargeable time finding problems about which you

know already, when they could be finding other issues of which you were unaware?)
- another written list of the problems you think may exist, but haven't been able to prove
- the same lists regarding any financial transactions
- all tax-relevant items (analysis of potential deductibles, interest, rents etc)

*Real life – One of the editors has pointed out that you may have no such items, but that only goes to show that the author has chosen the editors wisely. The author himself has never achieved such a state of perfection.*

There is a curious phenomenon regarding audits. If there is one error in several thousand documents, an audit junior will select that particular document to verify and come to you with a worried expression, in search of an explanation; even the auditors themselves don't know how they do that, but they do it nevertheless. So give them the gen up front and save yourself the embarrassment.

Early in the interim audit, take the audit team out with some or all of your finance team for an informal dinner and a couple of beers. You will find that the auditors are not as dumb nor as boring as they look, and with any luck they'll come to the same conclusion about you and your team. Now you've discovered that you're all human, things will go much better, and you've laid down lines for a real wing-ding at the end of the final audit.

Instruct the auditors that when they find a glitch, they report it to you at once with a written comment and documentary evidence on their observation and the implications. You will then review it immediately with the appropriate colleagues and draft your written action point (and if possible implement it). In this way, the audit 'management letter' is completed in real time by the end of the audit. But be careful; the auditors always say they'll do it because it's obviously a good idea, but somehow they don't get around to it unless you keep on your backs constantly.

If you don't do that in real time, what happens is that the audit team leaves with only hand-written notes on the weaknesses, and weeks pass without a management letter, since they've all been whisked out on other audits on return to their office. After weeks of nagging by you, one of the team returns (in the evening on overtime), picks up the file, realises he can't remember a thing from his hasty notes and arranges another visit to your site (at your expense) to compile a better set of notes and collect the evidence he'd omitted. By the time you receive the draft management letter you've also forgotten about it all and have to go back through the problems with your staff and write your responses, which will only promise remedial actions instead of advising that you've already completed them.

Real time . . . it's the only time.

The other document which causes logistical problems is the statutory accounts. Except for the narrative bits, let the auditors do them. For one thing, they're good at it; it's what they do, after all. For another thing, it's cheaper, believe it or not. If you do the accounts, the following will happen:

- you'll promise it by a certain date, but operational matters will always take precedence, and eventually you'll cobble a set together several weeks late
- a member of the audit team will be recalled from the audit and will work on your accounts in the evenings on overtime rates, at your expense
- he will then find that you haven't made some essential disclosures and weeks of correspondence will ensue because you've become out of touch with the legislation

Eventually, expensively, you will receive your accounts. But if you'd only left it to them in the first place and set an agreed finalisation date at the audit planning meeting, you'd have had your accounts ages ago without all that fuss and cost.

And of course, at the end of the final audit visit there should be another good night out, and those auditors who return the following year will do so as business friends who respect you and know how you work, and will give you value for money. And you, by managing your end of the audit effectively, will ensure that they make a high recovery rate on the audit, so that both parties are on a winner.

Always aim to be your auditors' favourite client.


## 1.4k – Accountants – other services

Unless you have particular in-house skills in corporate tax, it makes sense to instruct your auditors or another professional firm to prepare your tax computations, negotiate the liabilities with the revenue authorities and assist you in tax planning. When you prepare your annual budget, you should submit a reasonably advanced draft to your tax advisors so that you can optimise your likely tax position before you finalise your intentions. Many businesses refer to their tax advisors at or near the end of each financial year, when it is too late to take action!

There are many other services which you may require from firms of accountants. Commonly used are:

- systems selection and implementation
- shared service facilities
- acquisitions, disposals, mergers, refinancing and reorganisation
- executive recruitment

These services are like any other services; you should ask for proposals from a selection of providers and chose the providers you consider most appropriate on the bases of cost, experience, reputation, quality of presentation and your assessment of the personnel involved. Assuming your auditors are not prevented by conflict of interest regulations from providing such additional services, there is no reason why you should not use them; they have the advantage of being familiar already with your business. Alternatively you may prefer the fresh approach which another firm (not necessarily a firm of accountants) might bring.

In previous decades, smaller firms of accountants tended to concentrate on basic auditing, accounting and taxation services, leaving the less routine services to the large accountancy firms. This is no longer the case; many highly skilled advisors have set up small firms providing high quality specialist services, with the result that small and medium-sized clients should have little if any difficulty in finding advisory firms of a suitable size. In addition, they may have better local knowledge than the nearest office of a large firm and that may be of help, particularly in identifying and obtaining various kinds of assistance available locally (for example, various counties have their own local initiatives to stimulate business and employment).

Choose your service providers carefully, on the basis of value for money.

In all financial and legal advisory situations, the better the information you give to your advisors, the better the service and advice you are likely to receive from them. Your financial director will deal with the strategic matters, but it will usually fall to you as the financial controller to provide your advisors with detailed information.


## 1.4l – Insurers

Insurance is a highly specialised field, in which accountants and other financial personnel usually receive little if any training, except possibly a bare outline of the general principles of insurance. For this reason, most businesses handle their insurance affairs through a broker, the exceptions being a few very large businesses which handle their own insurance, which even then is done alongside expert external advisors.

Day-to-day contact with the broker will come through the processing of claims and informing of notifiable events, but the main business will centre around the annual review of the cover. We cover this in detail in 5.4.

Inform your insurance contact immediately of any potential claims.

*Real life – the author once dealt with a claim himself by delaying it through introducing two consecutive legal technicalities. After the second had been resolved by the pursuers, the alleged incident was more than three years past, and the claim could no longer be pursued. Pleased with himself, the author called the insurers and promptly received a roasting for not reporting the incident within 24 hours per the contract conditions.*

Lessons:
- read the small print
- don't try to be clever outside your area of expertise


## 1.4m – Property lessors

If your business is in rented property, apart from the legal conditions of the lease you should be aware of the following practical financial considerations:
- if your business is in a state of considerable change, you may wish to sub-let part of your premises if unused, or to change the use of the premises – either of these is likely to require negotiation with the property lessor
- regardless of changes, the property is likely to have specific maintenance obligations, which should be included in your budgeting
- there may be a dilapidations clause, stating that all dilapidations have to be remedied at the end of the lease, and the property returned to its original condition (this will involve undoing all the changes you have made, even if they have resulted in substantial improvements to the premises, unless you can negotiate with the landlord that some of the changes can remain) – you should have periodic estimates made of the remedial cost, and accrue for it over the life of the lease
- the lease may have break points at which there is scope for renegotiation or termination – ensure that these are considered and estimated in your strategic plans and detailed budgets

## 1.4n – Legal advisors

It will not have escaped your notice that many of the previous topics have a high legal content. As a controller you will have had some training and contact in commercial legal matters, but you will need to become familiar with at least the main aspects of:

- contracts (commercial and property in particular)
- employment matters, especially disputes
- property purchases, sales and leases
- granting of charges as security for borrowing (normally dealt with on standard legal documents issued by your bank)
- intellectual property
- acquisitions, disposals, refinancing and restructuring
- legal actions

Much of the above material is covered in section 5.3 on contracts.

In general, legislation is becoming more complex each year, and it is sometimes untidily drafted. However much you may try (and you should) to keep abreast of legal developments you should always check with your legal advisors before entering a transaction of a type in which you have not been previously involved. The charge for a fifteen-minute discussion is nothing compared with the cost of incurring a legal liability through not taking advice.

Your legal advisors should be able to provide you with a monthly or quarterly newsletter of legal developments affecting commercial activities. If your business is of a complexity where that is not sufficient to keep you apprised, consider subscribing to one of the legal manual providers. Croner's in particular provide manuals on many branches of the law, and provide updates for insertion immediately any amendments have been made (see reading material, appendix D). Which manuals you select would depend on the nature of your business, but employment law is becoming such a minefield that the employment law manual is likely to be your first priority.

Another way of keeping abreast of legislation is to pay your legal advisors a monthly retainer for them to keep you apprised of all developments. This maintains pressure upon them not to miss anything.

The main requirement for dealing with legally-sensitive activities is the same as for many other management processes: get it right at the beginning. That almost always involves consultation.

## 1.4o – Pension trustees

Fortunately for the financial controller:
- retirement benefits are largely the responsibility of the financial director and other members of the board

Unfortunately for the financial controller:
- he will have to deputise on occasion for the financial director
- pensions are at the time of writing in a state of chaos for demographic reasons that have been increasingly reported in the general press for decades but have somehow escaped the attention of those whose task it is to keep abreast of such developments

Most pension trustees can arrange for specific courses to be held for client staff, and it would be wise for the financial controller and personnel manager (and possibly a trade union representative) to attend one and thereafter keep up to date with general developments. But always take professional advice on specific queries.

## 1.4p – Shareholders

Dealing with shareholders is outside the scope of this book, and is largely a matter for the directors and secretary of the business.

However, in a smaller business it is quite common for at least some of the shareholders to play an active part in the running of the business. In theory, your relationship with these people should be defined by your respective functions within the business, but you should always be mindful of their additional status as co-owners. If anything, this should make them more acutely focused on the performance of the business, which should be a help to you as the financial controller.

A small but important rider to this is that in family-owned businesses the presence of shareholders within the management structure may have a more complex effect, since there may be sizeable intra-family (or even inter-family) agendas which do not directly concern you but which may affect the attitudes of these shareholders to various aspects of the business. Be alert.

## 1.4q – Group (or divisional) head office

There are two types of group head office:

- good ones
- bad ones

The good ones succeed largely because they have a mix of personnel who deal effectively with two very different types of activity:
- strategic direction of the group as a whole, and its relationships with the outside world
- operational management of the divisions and subsidiaries to achieve strong financial performance and a robust group balance sheet

Where a group head office consists largely of strategic personnel recruited mainly from external sources (eg the accounting professions) but lacks executives with an operational pedigree, it usually succeeds in presenting a good face to the outside world, sometimes even gaining plaudits from the financial press for its astute management. Those working in the lower echelons see a very different picture:
- instructions from the head office are impracticable, displaying ignorance of the operational circumstances and necessities
- the performance of the senior operational management deteriorates from the lack of practical leadership, control and advice from above

Eventually, the internal disarray becomes apparent the outside world, and the inflated share price falls sharply.

When the reverse happens, ie the group has a surplus of operationally experienced management at head office but a shortage of strategically experienced executives:
- operational plans proceed apace, with firm practical backing from above
- without firm and clear strategic direction, the operational objectives are not coordinated and the operating units begin progressing in conflicting directions, leading to aborted projects, internal disruption and ultimately unnecessary losses

Ultimately, the result is the same: a tumble in the share price and demands for heads to roll.

What can the financial controller of an operating unit do about this? Quite a bit, surprisingly – all summarised in two words: **constructive feedback**. Regardless of how effective or otherwise a head office appears to be, the best approach for the financial controller is:
- keep abreast of the of the group's overall progress – read the statutory accounts, press releases and the group's intranet, and if information is not available, ASK FOR IT (you will rarely be refused)
- obtain the head office organisation chart and understand who does what

- when you receive confusing or impracticable instructions, contact the originator for clarification immediately and politely – he will normally be grateful that the confusion or impracticability has been identified, and it should help towards better instructions in future
- if after carrying out instructions you have any further ideas for improving them, do the same – contact the originator and point out the additional possibilities, but without being critical
- if you have any ideas of your own for improvement of the modus operandi, put them in writing and hold them for a day or two (you are less likely to suggest something unworkable if you set it out in writing, and less still if you think further about it) – once you are satisfied that your ideas are suitable, mail them to the appropriate group personnel with a polite suggestion ("this may be useful to you" is a better approach than "you ought to be doing this")
- if for some reason you are unable to comply with an instruction, or will be late in doing so, advise the group immediately – if nineteen out of twenty companies submit figures on time and one does not, the whole group has failed to complete on time and you will not be popular, but if you warn the group of your problem, they may be able to help you deal with it
- the same goes for any other type of problem – nobody likes unpleasant surprises, especially at the last moment

There may be occasions when group instructions merit a sharp response, but such a tactic should only be used in extreme circumstances. Any major problems should be discussed with your financial director (failing that, the managing director), who may wish to take up the matter directly.

The more helpful and constructive you are to your head office and the individual people there, the better they are likely to look after you.


## 1.4r – Other group companies

If you are in a group of companies, not only will you have to form an effective working relationship with the group office, but you will have to co-exist productively with other subsidiary businesses. These may comprise:
- similar businesses with the same products as yours, but in another geographical area
- businesses selling different products (which may be complementary to yours or entirely unrelated) either in your area or in other areas
- (rarely) businesses selling the same products in the same area
- special-purpose companies, such as property-owning companies or regional warehouses

- companies either upstream (supplying some of your materials) or downstream (buying some of your products, either to process further or to sell to customers) businesses in a vertically-integrated group

Where other businesses are selling the same products in another area or other products in your area, there should be little cause for problems between you and them. You should be able to cooperate with and assist each other and share resources. However, swings in economic circumstances may result in transfers of business from one area to another, provided that the transferee area is capable of servicing the transferor's customers effectively.

Where another group business is competing directly with you, that situation is unlikely to last. The less effective business is generally likely to be subsumed sooner or later into the better one, but the exact details of the eventual solution can be affected by such factors as location, premises, production capability and accumulated tax losses. One way or another, though, change is on the cards.

Special-purpose companies should have a clearly-defined purpose, and may be an administrative nuisance, but otherwise should not cause you any difficulty.

Vertically-integrated groups are much more problematic. The chief problems are:

- establishing transfer prices from one location to the next (this is a group decision, dependent largely on economic, taxation, currency and other non-operational issues)
- comparison of buying terms from upstream group businesses with buying terms available externally (downstream subsidiaries habitually claim that they can source products more cheaply elsewhere)
- the ability of businesses to pass on problems downstream (this can only be prevented by the group laying down clear performance parameters and firmly enforcing them)

An effective group head office will maintain good relations amongst its subsidiaries, only the occasional minor dispute surfacing. But if the group office is ineffective (or is normally effective, but is seriously distracted by difficult circumstances), internecine warfare can break out at operational level. The main cause of this is that one business perceives that it has been unfairly treated by the group in relation to another business. For example:

- an unrepresentative transfer price to or from another business in the vertical chain
- the transfer of some production to another unit
- the local denial of capital expenditure which has been allowed in another location

There are also direct disputes between subsidiaries, not involving the group. These generally originate from one business perceiving that another has not performed as agreed.

Whatever the source of the disputes, they are often exacerbated by a macho stance from local managements refusing to compromise, regarding it as a sign of weakness. The disputes rumble on, credit notes are demanded and refused, and several years later there are still disputed balances on the ledgers of both parties to the dispute. These disputes are almost invariably silly, unnecessary and time-wasting. They can also on occasion be expensive. Moreover, a dispute becomes progressively more difficult to resolve as memories fade, correspondence disappears into the archives and the personnel originally involved move elsewhere.

The financial controllers can prevent much of this. Although each controller has a direct reporting responsibility to his local management, the controllers also form a network of people with a common interest across the group as a whole. When a dispute starts to intensify, the controllers should discuss the circumstances directly with each other and move as follows:

- each controller investigates the dispute thoroughly with his local heads of department (quality, logistics, transport, customer services and occasionally engineering are likely to feature)
- the controllers discuss the matters between themselves
- the controllers are prepared to make concessions (quite often, a dispute can be largely matched by another dispute in the opposite direction, and a compromise is not duly painful)
- if the compromise is not expensive, the controllers deal with it quietly and the matter is forgotten
- if the concession to be made is expensive, the controller recommends it to his financial director

Probably three quarters of intra-group disputes can be solved by the controllers behind the scenes. It is in your own interests to keep the lines of communication open and to have a give-and-take working relationship with your fellow controllers.

## 1.4s – Conclusion

Your effectiveness and therefore success as a financial controller will depend to a much higher degree than you may have imagined on establishing and maintaining good working relationships with a large number of external organisations. At the strategic level the external relationships will be with the financial director, but at your level the relationships are practical ones, sometimes involving a lot of work and some effective problem-solving.

Remember: the key to success is that you should be the one who makes the call and initiates the actions as far as possible. If the external organisations regard you as a problem-solver who acts rather than reacts, you will generally find them to be positive and helpful partners in your business.

# PART 2
# THE NUMBERS

## 2.1 MANAGEMENT REPORTS (day-to-day)

a   Objectives
b   Areas of reporting
c   Inventory & inward supply
d   Production
e   Sales
f   Receivables
g   Overheads
h   Payables
i   Product development
j   Capital expenditure
k   Cash

## 2.2 MONTH-END RESULTS

a   Objectives
b   Main reports
c   Constructing monthly reports
d   Amending monthly reports
e   Reporting priorities
f   Reporting conventions
g   Profit reports
h   Variance reports
i   Departmental or sector reports
j   Capital employed reports
k   Cash flow reports
l   Project reports
m   Closure reports
n   Foreign exchange reports
o   Narrative reports
p   Other reports
q   Consolidated reports
r   Completion & collation

## 2.3 MONTH-END PROCESSES

a   Objectives
b   Main processes
c   Accruals
d   Identifying the barriers
e   Monthly timetable

## 2.4 MONTH-END PAPERS

a   Objectives
b   Annual calendar
c   Monthly working papers – general
d   Monthly working papers – B/S
e   Monthly working papers – profit
f   Storage of accounting records
g   Conclusion

## 2.5 YEAR-END

a   Objectives
b   Processes
c   Statutory financial statements
d   Preparation (start of year)
e   Management to statutory
f   Disclosure items
g   Liquidity
h   The audit
i   Preparation for the following year

# MANAGEMENT REPORTS (day-to-day)    2.1

This part deals with the **day-to-day reporting** needed to drive the business towards its targets. As we shall see, this is a different type of reporting from the month-end reports discussed in 2.2, reporting on a cumulative basis for the whole financial year.

The use of monthly information to drive the profit and cash performance of the business is discussed in 3.1 and 3.2 respectively.

A glance at the many factors described below will show that the financial controller cannot normally follow and act upon all of the activities involved. It is therefore his responsibility to ensure that all of the monitoring activities and reports described below are carried out by appropriate personnel, and that he is KEPT AWARE of the major issues affecting the progress of the company. Although most of the remedial actions will be taken by the persons directly responsible for the actions, the controller must step in when any of the circumstances which are reported will or may result in serious financial disadvantage to the business.

## 2.1a – Objectives

The cockpit or flight deck of an aircraft is filled with instruments which give the crew a constant flow of the aircraft's performance and position, and which warn the crew of any potential threats which may prevent the craft from reaching its intended destination. The day-to-day and week-to-week management reports within a business perform much the same function for the business as the instruments do for an aircraft:

- Is the output flow, in terms of orders, production and sales, on target?
- Are the current supplies of materials, labour and services sufficient to meet requirements?
- Alternatively, are they in excess of requirements and thus wasting valuable cash?
- Are the resources being consumed at a sustainable rate?
- Is there sufficient cash (equivalent to an aircraft's fuel) to see the business to its destination?
- In all activities, what is the failure rate and what has been done to minimise it?

- What occurrences are likely to prevent the business from reaching its goal and what is being done to prevent or mitigate them?

It is apparent from the nature of the above information that the great majority of it is purely numerical. Only the EXCEPTIONS AND REMEDIAL ACTIONS REQUIRE NARRATIVE REPORTS, USUALLY OF A BRIEF NATURE.

Note that daily or weekly reporting discussed in this subsection is presented on a cumulative basis for the current month, as its objective is to drive the business towards its targets for the month. When the following month begins, the process starts all over again, thus maintaining a constant pressure on all departments to perform.

## 2.1b – Areas of reporting

Most businesses require to keep a close watch on the following groups of activity on a day-to-day basis:
- inventory (levels, usage rates, lead times, shortages, ages, condition, losses)
- production (similarly, contract progress in a contracting business or work done in a services business)
- cost of production
- sales (enquiries and orders received, despatches made, and backlogs against orders)
- receivables
- overheads
- payables
- product development
- cash

Non-recurring items such as capital spend are reported on as and when they happen. In the case of major capital projects such as building a new storage location, it may be necessary to review progress on a day-to-day business, and to receive frequent updated forecasts of the completion date and the total spend. Not only is the capital cost critical, but the date on which the project can start generating ongoing profits (or mitigating costs) is just as important.

The overall monthly report (the "management accounts" in UK terminology) should be designed to report all the essential information in a single document, compared against a budget or forecast (Appendices C6-9).

## 2.1c – Inventory and inward supply reports (generally weekly)

The following reports would be normal for a production process:

- overall stock levels against budget, and against immediate production requirements – a typical measurement of stock in addition to volume and value would be "days of production"
- stock-outs, explaining causes and remedial action to obtain the stock quickly, and also to prevent a recurrence with that stock and any other stocks (the stock-out could be caused by a supplier error or by a stock control and/ or ordering problem)
- supplier delivery performance – in addition to delays as discussed above, quality issues need to be reported, and these can include inappropriate packaging and documentary errors such as lack of quality certification, in addition to the quality of the supplies themselves
- use of express delivery inwards – excessive use of this indicates production difficulties (causing additional material needs), poor stock control, poor ordering procedures or supplier difficulties
- adjustments arising from cyclical counts (see 4.2q)
- volumes of scrap and other losses (breakages, deterioration, out-of-spec) as these are normally direct profit and cash losses, unless recycling is possible, and even that incurs additional costs
- days of raw materials held (ie expressing the stock in terms of the days of production it will cover)

The measurement of raw materials in **days of production** is an instinctively helpful measurement, as it indicates the situation clearly in relation to your activities and supply lines (are you carrying too much or not enough?). Some companies, especially US ones, use stock turn, ie the number of times stock "turns over" in a year. This is an illogical and unhelpful measurement, as it does not relate to your activity, which may vary seasonally, and is the opposite (ie upside-down) of the days-of-sales measurement used for your other current asset, the receivables (see 2.1f, below).

In a service business, reports of staff absences and shortages perform a similar function, as they indicate likely delays in completing client services on time, and may similarly result in a lower profit, particularly if a contract carries penalties for late completion or outside staff have to be used at a higher cost.

## 2.1d – Production reports (always daily)

Production of saleable output is the heart of a non-retail business, whether it sells goods or services. The finger therefore needs to be kept on the pulse of production with daily reports:

- **absolute output** – cumulative for the week or month, as you should always be working towards an overall target, and if previous days' production has been below target, you should be striving to exceed the current and subsequent daily target to get back on track
- **output per person/ per hour** – a measure of efficiency, although it may vary with the type of product, unless you are measuring against standard hours, which are calculated individually for each product and take account of its complexity
- comparison of the **output of different shifts** – this will highlight differences in personnel capabilities, supervision capabilities and differences arising from other personnel factors (for instance, weekend shifts are sometimes bedevilled by lower outputs)
- **stoppage times** ("down time") – this may result from material shortages, wrong materials, machine breakdowns, power cuts ("outages" in the USA), inexperienced operatives, poor supervision, bad scheduling and other factors; where those factors can be remedied, that must be done immediately
- **machinery difficulties** – poor maintenance, incorrect set-up, bad materials, incorrect operator actions and various other technical factors can result in machines giving trouble
- **current repair projects** – unless these are planned, they will give rise to unforecast variances
- **quality reports** – the output is as important as the processes themselves, and products which are unsaleable must be examined and the cause of the defects remedied immediately (where a process will inevitably result in a percentage of rejected output, the percentage of rejects must be reported and, if unacceptable, acted upon)
- **production scrap report** – some scrap is guaranteed (eg where discs are cut out of a rectangular sheet) and scrap must be distinguished between regular "planned" process scrap and additional scrap caused by faulty production
- **work-force absences** – a rate of absence will be inevitable and must be budgeted for, but an abnormal level of absences must be investigated and remedied
- **injuries** – the only acceptable level of injuries is zero, and the company has a duty to its employees to create the safest possible working environment; similarly, the employees have a duty to follow

the safety regulations in their entirety, and immediate investigation of accidents and elimination of their causes is paramount

Many of the above issues involve personnel, and where these issues result in variances against plan or budget, they are often the most difficult to resolve. Skill and productivity varies from person to person, and even the same person's performance can vary with personal circumstances, sometimes even trivial ones. Moreover, certain combinations of people work well together and yet the same people work less effectively when partnered with others. Leadership and supervision may also vary.

The above factors combine to make the labour aspects of production the most difficult to analyse and optimise.

## 2.1e – Sales reports (at intervals depending on sensitivity)

Production output should be geared towards ordered or expected sales; there is no point in making product merely to keep the production lines busy. It costs unrecoverable money, unnecessary wear-and-tear on the equipment, additional storage costs for unwanted products and bank interest on the cost of holding the unsold stocks. Sales volumes, values and margin levels are therefore the life-blood of the business.

The reports normally required (all compared against target or budget) are:
- **contacts by the sales force** – this report can take many forms and frequencies, depending on how the sales thrust is structured and whether the customer base is a large number of small customers, a small number of large customers or anything in between; however, a degree of targeting is normally needed to ensure that the momentum of the sales force is maintained
- **enquiry volume** (and value if measurable), and the conversion rate of enquiries into firm orders
- **order intake volume and value** (preferably expressed as total margin as well as total sales value); it is essential to be attacking the enquiry and order levels so that any drop in sales is signalled well in advance and remedial action can be taken
- **daily volume** – the sales volume is of course different from the production volume, but the production volume should be geared to the anticipated sales, so the relationship between the two needs to be monitored in addition to comparison with forecast or budget (but see also the note below on back-end loading)
- **average selling prices** are an important trend – if they are on a downward trend, you will have to increase your volume to

compensate, and sooner or later replace unprofitable products with profitable ones
- **net sales values** – net values by individual products or at least by product groups are essential
- **margins** – the same applies for margins; even more so – you must know which of your products or product groups are making you the best and worst margins
- **deductions** (credit notes, returns, rebates etc) – it is your NET sales which generate your margins, and therefore anything which detracts from the sales value must be examined and minimised . . . ensure that all such deductions are netted off directly and visibly against sales and NOT hidden in overheads; you must know what your real margins are
- **deliveries** – late, on time, express transport – as with goods inward, it is useful to see what money is wasted on express deliveries (a separate cost code may be needed) as these are normally the result of late production, which may be a planning, technical or labour efficiency problem

The appropriate frequency of review of the above figures depends upon the nature of the goods:
- a standard range of high-volume products should be reviewed daily
- products which take longer to produce, and products which are partly or fully made to customers' requirements can be reviewed less frequently, but at least weekly

*Real life – beware of a common phenomenon known as **back-end loading**. A production department is given an output target for a month, and for most of the month runs behind the target. This may be due to a lack of urgency, or simply that the manufacturing process is a long one, and the finished products scheduled for the month do not appear until late in the month. In either case there tends to be a big push in the last week of the month (often at the expense of extra overtime), and a high proportion of the month's output is despatched in the last two or three days. However, it does not reach the customer until the following month, especially in the case of export sales. What you regard as a March sale is therefore quite correctly regarded as an April purchase by your customer, who accordingly pays you a month later than you have forecast.*

*Moral – get the products out to your long-distance customers early in the month.*

It is also essential to look at the future volume of business, to establish:

- your forthcoming production requirements
- the trends of demand in your various products (you may need some new offerings)

To do this, we must examine:
- customer orders (total level) – this will highlight at an early stage any trends in demand
- customer orders (overdue percentage) – this will highlight deficiencies in your business: production difficulties or poor scheduling or shortage of supplies for various possible reasons
- enquiries (even if you are only a production unit) – this will give you an even better view of the market going forward; enquiries should be logged and analysed if practicable

For the more strategic information, such as trends in demand, a monthly analysis will usually suffice. Changes in demand can arise from:
- fashion – this occurs in every industry, even highly technical ones, and does not always follow common sense or practicality (for example, eight fingers on a keyboard are much faster than any mouse, but the mouse is used to an increasing degree)
- technical innovation – this can also lead to a fashion change, as many people and even businesses feel that they must have the latest technology; however, more often it results in a change in demand through offering an improved performance
- necessity – a change in technical, industrial, personal, economic or other circumstances

Remember always that demand for your product may be affected by circumstances well beyond your market, having a knock-on effect on your direct customers. It may also affect the way in which you do business (the most obvious example being selling over the internet instead of by catalogue or over the counter).

There are many other aspects of sales and order levels which may need constant review, probably monthly:
- other industrial sectors
- other types of customer (by activity, demographics or other defining features)
- other geographical areas

and a knowledge of the above will be essential for the budgeting process (see 3.5).

## 2.1f – Receivables reports (daily)

Cash is the lifeblood of your business. You should therefore have a cash collection target for each month and receive a report every morning stating:
- the total amount of cash collected on the previous working day
- specific amounts which have been received from identified slow-payers

You should also have prompt reports on negotiations with customers who are having difficulty in paying, or who are withholding money because of a dispute (see 3.2e).

A rolling cash forecast is an essential report, the frequency thereof dependent on the business's cash cycle and current state of liquidity – this is discussed in part 3.1f.

## 2.1g – Overheads reports (generally by exception)

It is normally adequate to consider overheads as part of the monthly review of results (see 3.1f).

However, if any category of overhead is performing unsatisfactorily it may be necessary to have a weekly or even daily review of that overhead to determine:
- where and how the overspend is occurring
- how effectively any reduction measures are being applied
- whether further measures are needed
- whether a complete new working method is required in the area of the overspend

## 2.1h – Payables reports

Since the company itself and you in particular are in control for the most part over what you pay and when you pay it, a monthly review will usually suffice. In cases where relations with a large supplier are difficult through either their fault or that of your company, you may have to monitor the position more often.

## 2.1i – Product development reports

Product development, under a variety of names (R&D, technical etc) has to be monitored on two levels:
- the cost-effective running of the department itself
- the progress towards agreed technical or development objectives

Monitoring of departmental costs are normally done in the same way as the general overheads (see 2.1g).

Progress on development projects should be monitored at least monthly (more often on a major project):
- project progress against planned milestones
- capital and revenue project costs against project budgets
- major hurdles encountered and any delays or overspends arising therefrom
- trial results and certifications
- latest estimate of time to completion
- latest estimate of remaining capital and revenue costs
- departmental difficulties arising from precedence of projects over regular work (distraction of technical staff from resolving production issues may result in lost output and late or lost cash flow)

## 2.1j – Capital expenditure reports

Capital expenditure is for the most part a strategic activity, and is planned on an annual basis. The overall plan is authorised as part of the annual budget, but each individual item must be authorised individually when the time comes to order it. Moreover, given that few businesses perform exactly to plan, there will be changes from budget: equipment will be needed earlier or later than budgeted, some unbudgeted requirements will occur and some budgeted ones may prove unnecessary.

A capex budget may also include authorised items from the previous financial year, the authorisations of which should be reconfirmed for the current year (if they are as late as that, they may well have become unnecessary).

A monthly review is therefore essential to determine whether or not:
- the budgeted expenditure which has already been specifically authorised is running close to plan
- other budgeted expenditure is still required, and on what dates

- any essential unbudgeted expenditure has been identified, and why (sometimes it results from a new set of circumstances, sometimes it is because of a change of plan, sometimes it is just wishful thinking on the part of the applicant)
- the cash flow forecast from the updated position is still within the company's capability, or whether additional finance needs to be sought

In the latter half of the year, it may be appropriate to extend the capex forecast into the first one or two quarters of the following year.

At least annually, and preferably bi-annually in a large operation, there should be a review of existing fixed assets to determine whether any are surplus to requirements and can be sold or put to another use (a common one being to provide spares for continuing items).

## 2.1k – Cash reports (daily and monthly)

The cash performance is the sum total of the activities described above. It is also a measurement of the net performance of the business, both in flow terms and as part of the balance sheet. The format and frequency of such a report varies greatly from company to company in accordance with their trading activities and circumstances (not to mention the quality of their management). It is therefore difficult to specify a catch-all cash reporting regime, but the following information on a DAILY basis would suffice for most independently-owned medium-sized companies:

- column 1 – cash receipts (trading)
- column 2 – cash payments (trading)
- column 3 – cash receipts (other – grants, loans, fixed asset sales etc)
- column 4 – cash payments (other – capex, redundancies etc)
- column 5 – closing balance
- column 6-X – closing balance by currencies
- top of page – major exchange rates at current date. The above will fit on a sheet of A4 paper, with the figures shown in thousands, and running totals of receipts and payments displayed at the bottom, preferably against budget for the month (see Appendix B1).

The monthly cash report should be in the source-and-application format (Appendix C9) and compared with budget. The statutory format of source-and-application is investor-driven and not normally suitable for running a business, so use the management format provided in this book.

## Overall performance reports

The format of overall reports for the whole business will depend on the type and circumstances of the business, but will be a distillation of the above elements. Examples are given in the appendices C6-9.

# MONTH-END RESULTS

## 2.2a – Objectives

Whereas the daily and weekly reporting described in 2.1 is designed to drive the business towards its monthly targets (ie to sustain daily pressure and optimise the trends therein), the function of the **month-end reports** is more strategic in nature. They measure the business's progress to date against its targets for the current financial year, and are used to highlight and stimulate the management actions needed to reach those targets. They are the most important document to be discussed at the monthly management meetings and/ or board meetings.

They must therefore identify and quantify the areas in which the business is ahead of or behind its targets, and by succinct narrative reports, direct the action needed to exploit the favourable trends and correct or minimise the adverse trends. They must be **rapid, reliable and relevant**.

## 2.2b – Main reports

The exact content of the month-end reports will depend on the nature of the business. Typically, a well-organised manufacturing/ service business would have the following reports, with appropriate sub-analyses:
- profit statement
- sales and margins by major product category
- variance analysis (including productivity analysis in the case of manufacture)
- costs analysis (usually a number of separate sheets supporting totals in the profit statement)
- capital employed statement (balance sheet)
- cash flow statement
- capex summary
- debt (borrowings) profile
- provisions for liabilities or diminutions of asset values
- employment statistics

Monthly figures should be presented in a budget/ actual/ variance format. It does not have to be in that order, but the budget chronologically and therefore logically precedes the actual figures; moreover, the two most important columns, the actual and the variance columns, should be viewed side-by-side. Some businesses also present a prior year figure, but that can be more of a distraction than a help, because:

- the budget process has already extrapolated the prior year's results into the current year's targets, and so the prior year has already been considered and adjusted for known or expected variations
- the prior year figures invariably reflect some circumstances and irregularities which no longer exist, and these have to be filtered out when making the comparison, and quantification of the differences is seldom readily available to enable you to do this
- the business is supposed to be going forwards, not backwards

*Real life – a financial director joined a group which habitually compared the results each month with those of the prior year. However, the largest company in the group had previously contained an activity which had been set up from the start of the current year as separate subsidiary. So when the group managing director complained in a board meeting that the performance of the largest company had deteriorated, the financial director had to point out tactfully that it had in fact improved, as the prior year's performance included the now-separated activity. As no separate accounts had been kept for that activity, nobody knew the extent of the difference in performance, and so it would have been more appropriate to compare the two activities with their budgets. The financial director conveniently failed to find any reliable figures for the previous year and the board eventually began to compare results with the budget and talk some sense.*

*Part of the reason for the comparison with the prior year was that the chairman normally worked in a publicly quoted company. Since publicly quoted companies do not make their budgets public (that would be just too helpful to competitors) the world outside has to compare their results with those of the previous year, often a highly irrelevant comparison and becoming more irrelevant as the speed of business change increases.*

The external world includes the company's bankers, who generally compare a company's results with those of the previous year; they are usually more concerned with the health of the overall business than that of the individual components thereof. However, bankers are increasingly turning their attention to the future and in many cases demand to see the annual budget as soon as it is approved by the board. Moreover, the continuing provision of finance by the bank may be dependent upon a credible and financially acceptable budget, which will include profit, cash flow and capital employed on a month-by-month basis.

And banks nowadays usually expect the company's actual results to be close to the budget!

## 2.2c – Constructing monthly reports

Most modern computer systems claim to have powerful report generators. However, these tend to be good for analysing individual sections of the financial picture (eg receivables ageing, sales by product) but are almost always too cumbersome ("clunky" in systems jargon) to produce profit, cash flow and capital employed statements in the kind of detail and quality of presentation demanded by a management or board meeting.

Most top-end financial reports are therefore produced on spreadsheet files. The most effective way of operating these is shown in appendix C5. This is an Excel spreadsheet containing columns for all 15 ledger trial balances, showing debits and credits as positives and negatives:
- opening trial balance
- 12 monthly trial balances
- pre-audit trial balance (there are normally adjustments before the audit)
- post-audit trial balance (if these are separate, it is easier to ensure that they are complete and correct)

By stating the period number and using a LOOKUP formula, the relevant figures for each period can be gathered in four columns (opening, prior cumulative, current period and current cumulative)

Then using the SUMIF formula to summarise the balances in whatever groupings you want, you can create the figures for your reports (normally to the nearest 1,000) below the trial balances. SUMIF eliminates the tiresome necessity to change the formula each time you add or remove a ledger code.

You should also create some tables in which to enter the necessary non-ledger information for your financial reports (product volumes, hours worked, personnel numbers, exchange rates etc).

You can then build reports to present the information you want in your preferred format. To report on a different period, you merely change the period number which drives the LOOKUP table.

As an essential point of control, use check-totals throughout, designed to read zero if all is square, and to show the difference if it is not.

The check-totals should confirm as a minimum that:
- the input balances are square for all periods
- the capital employed statement is square
- the prior year reserves and opening fixed asset values are the same in all periods
- the profit and cash flow statements agree with the capital employed statement in all periods

This means that when you amend the opening balances (typically in respect of external audit adjustments) you must amend the relevant rows in all periods of the data spreadsheet. Therefore, the sooner you complete your annual audit, the better!

If the disciplines described above are followed, you can maintain and develop your monthly reporting pack in a controlled and efficient manner, without an inordinate amount of time spent on maintaining the file. The secret is in making it robust and well-controlled from the outset.

## 2.2d – Amending monthly reports

**Amending the figures** in a monthly report model as described in 2.2c above involves a similar process to that which you use for entering the monthly data in the data spreadsheet (either manually or electronically, according to your preference). The check-totals will function as before.

**Amending the structure** occurs most often when additional or amended general ledger accounts are enacted. Extra rows in the data spreadsheet need to be specifically linked to the profit and/ or capital employed statement, either individually or as part of a subtotal. The cash flow statement should not normally need to be amended, as it is modelled from movements in the profit and capital employed statements.

## 2.2e – Reporting priorities

In presenting the management reports, the priorities are in this order:
- report the correct closing position, ie the correct balance sheet
- report the correct cumulative operating result
- report the correct operating result for the current month (in fact, if you report the correct closing position and correct cumulative result each month, the monthly result will automatically be correct, so the

month's operating result is very much the third accounting priority, even though it is usually management's first reporting priority)

Despite the above logic, many controllers concentrate on getting the monthly result correct. The result of this is that errors go undiscovered for long periods, sometimes accumulating until there is a disastrous discovery, often at the year-end, when everyone is expecting a different result. Think about it: if the closing position from the previous month is wrong and you get the current month's operating result correct, then the closing position for the current month must also be wrong. And if the previous month's closing position was wrong, there is an unknown problem in there, and if it is unknown it may continue to exist for some time.

## 2.2f – Reporting conventions

Balance listings from general ledgers conventionally show all debits as positive and all credits as negative.

In financial reports, however, this would be inappropriate – for example, a report on sales would be a page full of bracketed figures. Therefore the reporting convention is:

- on reports showing income and expenditure, show income figures as positive and expenditure figures as negative (which means that all your formulae are additions – ie you add negative figures rather than subtracting positive ones)
- similarly, on a report of assets and liabilities, show the assets as positive and liabilities as negative
- on reports showing a single specific stream, show figures going with the stream as positive and figures going against the stream as negative – for example, on a schedule of costs, show the costs as positive and any recoveries as negative

For negative figures in management reports, use the international convention of brackets (which are more visible than minus signs, especially in photocopies). Ensure in formatting spreadsheets that your bracketed figures are properly aligned vertically with the positive figures. If using Microsoft Excel, this means formatting a space at the right-hand end of positive figures.

## 2.2g – Profit reports

The convention is that adverse variances are shown as negative, and that variances are shown both as monetary amounts AND as a percentage of the budgeted amounts. If there is only room on your profit statement for one variance column, choose percentages, as they are more meaningful than monetary amounts. On the cash flow statement and balance sheet, however, variances will be more relevant when shown as monetary amounts.

Each business should have its own specifically-designed profit statement. The layout will depend on the structure, activity and other parameters of the business, and should include the following features:

- volume of sales (eg tonnage, number of items, number of man-hours)
- value of sales
- average unit selling price
- major categories of variable costs
- average unit variable cost
- contribution (margin) after variable costs
- contribution as a percentage of sales
- contribution per unit
- fixed costs
- operating profit (ie profit after normal fixed costs)
- non-operating items (these can be income or costs, but see below)
- profit before tax

You should have a supporting report analysing your sales, variable costs and contributions by the main sectors, be they products, outlets, markets or other main aspects. The commonest error in profit statements is to analyse the overheads in detail, but not to analyse the top end (above the contribution line) where the real business is performed. You MUST understand which of your activities are winners and losers.

Some businesses show a provision for taxation (usually as an average percentage, but some businesses present a precise monthly figure, which often requires considerable detail to calculate and may involve spurious accuracy). Where dividends are paid regularly, it would also be appropriate to provide for them, but the great majority of companies are private and do not provide for dividends until annual results are finalised.

The identification of non-operating items needs careful consideration. The purpose of showing them separately below the operating profit is to identify the real underlying profit of the business. However, almost every business incurs various unexpected costs during the year and it becomes tempting to "window-dress" the result by treating these items as non-operating costs. If they are normal business events, even if not budgeted, they should not be shown separately unless they are very large and genuinely exceptional.

A well-known and battle-hardened financial director has been known to say, "When is an exceptional item not an exceptional item? When it happens every bloody month."

## 2.2h – Variance reports

It is essential when reviewing the results of each month to investigate and understand WHY the results have differed from budget. This entails understanding the reason and the monetary amount for each major element of variance from budget. The two main reasons for sales variances are:
- the volume of products (goods or services) sold – this may include a mix variance identified separately
- the price at which they have been sold – some companies calculate their mix variance on price

The same two main streams of variance also apply to costs, but with other factors involved:
- the volume of materials should broadly vary in line with the volume of goods produced
- the volume of materials used can also vary as a result of production problems (eg wastage)
- the prices of materials and all other costs are subject to quite different factors from those causing the sales variances

Complex manufacturing operations normally have a standard costing system, which reports variances automatically to a high level of detail. Standard costing (including the systems used for that purpose) is outside the scope of this book, as it is a major discipline in its own right. Such a system typically provides a high degree of analysis, enabling the management to 'drill down' to examine variances arising from individual production categories. Typical variances highlighted by a standard costing system include:
- material usage
- material waste (sometimes in several categories)
- physical inventory count differences
- inventory write-offs (obsolescence, damage etc)
- standard revisions (standards are normally updated at least once per year)

- labour usage, sometimes with absences and overtime highlighted separately
- labour cost (overtime is often identified separately, but rate variances can be complex and difficult)
- energy or other direct production cost variances
- general spend variances on fixed overheads

Some costing systems are based on analysing costs of production, others on analysing costs of sales.

Contract costing systems are effectively a set of scaled-down business systems, one for each contract.

In the absence of a formal costing system, the financial controller should seek to provide a more empirical variance analysis as follows:
- record the volume of sales in the most appropriate units (product numbers or tonnage, hours of services charged out, days of equipment hire, or whatever is most appropriate and can be recorded reliably within or alongside the accounting system)
- use the same volume criteria in the budgeting process, allowing for targeted wastage in terms of material losses, down-time etc
- construct a statement in which the total variances are derived automatically from the profit statement in the workbook described in section 2.2c above, and in the example in appendix C7.
- examine the major transactions for the month and list and explain the major specific variances
- use a balancing figure to summarise the minor variances (remember that variances can go both ways; a $200,000 overall negative variance can consist of $300,000 of negative variances and $100,000 of positive variances)

The basic formulae for volume and price variances are:
- volume variance = (actual volume − budget volume) x budget (or standard) price
- price variance = (actual price − budget price) x actual volume

and the formula applies to material cost variances in the same way as it does to sales variances. Even if you cannot do the calculations in detail, you can still apply them, for example, to an overall actual tonnage sold against a budgeted overall tonnage.

The above process will give you a broad picture of the main undercurrents affecting your profit statement, in a much more specific way than merely quoting the overall variances between budget and actual values. They also force a more correct understanding of the variances; without splitting them between volume and price, it is often easy to assume a glib and sometimes convenient explanation of the variances instead of revealing the truth.

With some businesses you may need considerable ingenuity to devise a suitable volume unit. If your business has a large number of diverse products, for example, you may have to group them by product type or size, customer type or size, procurement or production process or some other meaningful category. Time spent on recording meaningful volume indicators will be repaid by a better understanding of the dynamics of your business.

Note that variances resulting from foreign exchange differences are normally accounted for separately from the above variances, as they are an external factor to be managed as a separate discipline.

## 2.2i – Departmental or sector reports

When a business has large divisions involving substantially different production techniques, product types, locations, markets or other factors, it is usually necessary to provide separate profit statements for these divisions so that each one is managed to its optimum capability. Often such departmental statements need only go down to contribution level, since allocation of indirect overheads is often theoretical, and sometimes even spurious.

## 2.2j – Capital employed reports

The following elements should be reported, showing budget and actual for the opening of the year, the previous month and the current month, and variances for at least the current month.

Top half (the physical substance of the business, with variables at the top and fixed items at the bottom):
- inventory
- receivables
- payables
- fixed assets

Bottom half (what is financing the business)
- all borrowings including all bank balances (credit balances shown as negative)
- tax and dividends due

- share capital and reserves

These categories are examined in more detail in part 2.4d and Appendix C8. The content of a capital employed statement varies much more from business to business than does that of the operating statement, as a result of the great differences in business structures, and especially in their funding.

## 2.2k – Cash flow reports

We show two forms of cash flow statement:
- Appendix C8 shows cash flow as variance columns to the capital employed statement – crude, but it has the great advantage of enabling the reader to see at a glance the movements to which the cash flow figures refer, without having to flip between the cash flow statement and the capital employed statement (it is also easier to explain to non-financial people who struggle with conventional cash flow statements)
- Appendix C9 shows a separate conventional cash flow statement – more detailed, and dealing more accurately with special transactions such as disposals and write-downs of fixed assets

The tortuous and fragmented statements to be found in many statutory financial reports should be avoided at all costs. Instead, show the cash flow on a single sheet in the following sequence:
- profit before taxation
- adjustments to profit to eliminate non-cash items
- working capital movements
- sub-total of cyclical (ie routine) cash flow
- fixed asset movements
- all other non-cyclical movements
- total cash flow

## 2.2l – Project reports

Most businesses have a number of projects in progress at any time. When any project is large enough or important enough to have a major effect on the business's performance (profit or cash), there should be a separate report on the progress of the project presented with the monthly management accounts.

As with all financial reports, it should be on a single page. The most effective way to do this is to use a landscape format with the project budget in month-by-month summary form on the top half of the page and the actual results in the same format immediately below it. The example in Appendix C11 shows a typical start-up situation, giving an immediate appreciation of the progress of the project against the budget.

## 2.2m – Closure reports

As with start-ups, closures must be monitored to ensure that they are rapidly and cost-effectively completed.

The example shown in appendix C12 is similar to the project report in that it gives an instant picture of the progress of the closure month-by-month (the example shows the closure of a separate business such as a subsidiary or associated company). It also highlights the main concerns of any major closure:

- establish or estimate the book value all assets and liabilities at the date of closure
- identify which assets are realisable in cash, and which cease to be assets (for example, tax recoverable may not be recovered if there are no further profits against which to recover them, and prepaid rents will no longer have a book value if the assets concerned are not in use)
- from the above considerations, estimate the realisable value of the assets; in most circumstances that will be well below the book value
- identify and forecast the costs which will be incurred as a result of the closure (for example, decommissioning, clearance and professional fees)
- prepare a closure budget and provide a timetable to the closure project leader (keep your estimate of the recoverable values of the assets confidential, so that the project leader is targeted on obtaining as high a value as possible)
- instruct the project leader to provide a month-by-month financial update (your staff will probably be needed to assist with that, and you may require separate cost and revenue codes to control the figures)

The above are merely the financial elements of controlling a closure; the operational management will also have to instruct the practical aspects, including any difficulties in dealing with discontinued suppliers and customers. Always be aware that it is much more difficult to extract money from discontinuing customers than it is from ongoing customers, and ensure that your cash collection operation is alert and in control thereof.

## 2.2n – Foreign exchange reports

If your business is trading in foreign currencies to an extent where there are considerable commitments and exposure, you should present a summary of the currency position and commitments, on a months-ahead basis. Appendix A5 shows a simple forex plan.

It may also be appropriate to show on the projection the effect of an X% rise or fall in the main currencies to illustrate the level of risk.

## 2.2o – Narrative reports ("why", not "what")

The financial statements above should be enhanced by a narrative report as follows:
- DO NOT state "sales were up 5%" – they can see that from the profit statement
- DO NOT state "the sales increase was mainly from volume" – they can see that from the variance report
- STATE "the additional sales volume was gained by . . ." (eg new outlets in Eastern Europe)

In other words, DO NOT state WHAT the numerical reports state, because it is a waste of time and effort, and often results in attendees not reading the numerical reports because they can read the news on your narrative, or vice versa. Your narrative report should state instead:
- WHY the various trends and outcomes have happened
- what the business needs to DO to maximise the good news and minimise the bad news
- what financial ISSUES should be faced now or in the future

In addition to the results themselves, there will be other financial issues to be reported, typically including:
- general economic circumstances (where not covered by the managing or marketing director)
- banking and other borrowing facilities
- major contracts, including leases
- legal matters (if not dealt with by another official)

- information systems (except where there is a chief information officer, but even if there is, systems issues tend to have strong financial and accounting repercussions)
- taxation and tax inspections
- statutory audit
- financial staff
- anything else which may materially affect the financial situation of the business (eg insurance)

Not all of the above issues will crop up at every monthly meeting, but they serve as a check-list for the contents of your narrative report each month.

AVOID using lengthy paragraphs. Your report will be much easier to write, to read and to discuss if you present each section with a short introductory sentence, followed by a series of bullet points and then a short narrative summary if needed. Your colleagues will appreciate your brevity and clarity, not to mention the lack of waffle.

Finally, avoid all current clichés:
- DO NOT SAY "we have the ability to overcome the challenge by leveraging our sunrise methodology to deliver a cutting-edge solution to the transportation scenario"
- SAY INSTEAD "we can solve the transport problem with the new system"

## 2.2p – Other reports

Do not overload your monthly meetings with information. There should be enough information for them to understand the nature and size of the issues facing the business, but the reports should be concise enough for the recipients to assimilate fully BEFORE the meeting. However, you should try to anticipate what other financial issues will arise, and in particular what questions will be asked of you at the meeting. It is sometimes a good idea to have some additional analyses which are not presented to the meeting, but which are with you in paper form to be distributed to the attendees should they question some aspects of your regular reports. As you get to know your colleagues, you will also become adept at question-spotting.

## 2.2q – Consolidated reports

If you are handling a number of business units which report separately, you may or may not have to present a consolidated financial statement. This can greatly lengthen the time taken to produce your monthly reports, especially if the units operate in different currencies. Where they are not 100% owned, the complexity is increased and so is the time taken. This is a linear problem – you cannot populate your consolidation model until the figures for the individual units are complete, although you can enter the figures for each unit as they are completed.

Ask yourself two questions:
- Do you need to consolidate at all? – in some groups, the diversity makes it hardly relevant
- If you need to consolidate, will a summarised consolidation be adequate? – more often than not, the answer will be yes, as an overall group picture needs only to present the major figures, ratios and trends, and a set of summarised statements, with estimated consolidation adjustments, will suffice.

It is useful in such situations to do a highly summarised columnar tabulation, with a column for each business unit, a column for the adjustments, and a comparison of the total with the overall group budget. That will show in one single simple page what each business unit is contributing to the group.

## 2.2r – Completion and collation of reports

How much time you have to get your reports to your colleagues attending the management meeting will depend upon the timetable.

If all your colleagues work in the same building they can operate on a very short lead time. Where members of the meeting come from other locations, more time is needed and this causes difficulties. By week 2 of any month, the previous month is receding far into history, so meetings need to be as early in the month as possible to be effective. We discuss month-end financial procedures in 2.3d, but there will be many other reports, such as sales, research and development, regional sites, systems, production etc, depending on the nature and structure of the business. These are best dealt with by having the relevant managers produce DRAFT reports on their areas by the 3$^{rd}$ last working day of the month, and editing them on the morning of day 1 of the new month for any late events or final figures.

Report packs for on-site personnel can be sent in hard copy, and off-site by email. Some companies avoid having a collection of MS Excel, MS Word and MS PowerPoint files by collating them all on an Adobe pdf. This can work well, but if there are late adjustments or insertions it can also be difficult. Whichever way you use, ensure that as much work as possible is done BEFORE the month-end.

## Sample statements

The appendices at the end of this book give examples of the kinds of reports discussed in this section.

## 2.3a – Objectives

The month-end accounting processes are essential to ensure that:
- all transactions are recorded, and recorded correctly
- all transactions are fully evidenced and the related documents are correctly filed
- all ledgers and sub-ledgers are reconciled – any unreconciled items must be reported and actioned
- all adjustments necessary to reflect the true month-end position have been correctly made
- the working papers necessary to record the trail from the ledgers to the month-end reports have been correctly and clearly prepared and filed

The above preliminary objectives are fundamental to ensuring that the main objectives are met:
- a set of prompt, accurate and relevant month-end reports is presented to the management, covering all of the main aspects of the financial performance for the month
- the management make prompt and appropriate business decisions from the management reports

If the underlying processes have been properly completed, the following situation will exist:
- every figure in the month-end reports can be analysed, evidenced and explained in full on enquiry
- every transaction can be traced from its inception to its inclusion in the month-end reports – if the transaction has not been completed by the month end, it must reside either in a balance sheet account or in an outstanding order or action report
- relevant information required by any internal or external person can be provided instantly

In practice, there are usually a small number of unresolved items at some month-ends. These must be highlighted clearly so that:
- the estimated effect of them is clearly understood
- they are resolved as soon as possible

## 2.3b – Main processes

The main processes involved in the month-end mirror the main systems in use as described in part 4:

- inventory and cost of sales
- an inventory count if the business does not have automatic perpetual inventory recording
- sales and accounts receivable
- purchases and accounts payable
- payroll
- fixed assets
- bank and cash
- accruals, prepayments, leases and other monthly journal entries

Transactions on all of the above systems except one can be controlled by the business, as the business itself initiates the transactions (although customer orders are initiated externally, they do not become transactions until work has commenced on fulfilling the order). The transactions for purchases and accounts payable, however, are frequently initiated externally, as invoices are presented by suppliers, sometimes long after the transaction date. Accurate accounting for purchases and in particular, accruals, is therefore heavily dependent upon two systems:

- the goods received system
- the accruals system

## 2.3c – Accruals

In a goods received system, the liability for all goods received is recorded automatically as "goods received not invoiced" (GRNI) or "uninvoiced receipts", where the cost of goods is entered in the systems at standard or order price, and the liability as GRNI. When the invoice is subsequently received from the supplier, the GRNI liability is then debited out and replaced by a specific supplier liability. The GRNI is therefore an automatic accrual, on which sales tax is NOT accounted for. There may be slight differences between the GRNI prices and the supplier invoice prices, but these are unlikely to be material to the month-end results.

Some companies only use the goods received system for production materials; others control the intake of ALL goods (eg stationery and canteen supplies) by directing all supplier vehicles to a specified goods inward office.

Accruals, however, are more difficult to control, as most of them involve services rather than goods. Costs which typically require accrual include:

- travelling expenses, which can be complex and are dealt with in 4.7j
- infrastructure supplies such as water, gas and electricity
- internal services such as cleaning and waste disposal
- external services and costs such as transport, customs duty and demurrage
- professional services such as marketing, advertising, recruitment and legal advice
- conferences, trade shows and other external activities
- rents or other facility usage charges paid in arrears
- repairs and maintenance, especially when performed by external parties
- other one-off items such as recruitment fees, termination costs, penalties etc
- sales credits for product defects, contract defaults, pricing errors etc

The more contact the financial controller has with the other operational heads, the more likely he is to be aware of the current activities for which accruals need to be made. However, he is unlikely to be aware of all of them, and this lack of awareness impacts in two areas:

- the current month's performance is overstated as not all costs have been accrued for
- forecasts for future months will be optimistic

Although these errors may result from activities of which the financial controller is unaware, the blame will tend to fall squarely on his shoulders. Two systems are therefore needed to minimise unrecorded liabilities.

Firstly, travelling expenses need to be strictly controlled. Regardless of what system is used, the monthly reckoning date when claims are demanded from all personnel should be set at a week before the month-end. This will give two benefits:

- any accrual needed for the remaining week will be a quarter of the normal monthly amount, so that any error in the accrual will be much smaller than otherwise
- as a result of discussing the claims, the controller will have an up-to-date view of current activities and can judge more accurately the accruals needed for conferences, exhibitions etc

For all other expense accruals, a month-end sheet (appendix C10) should be sent to all managers who approve costs, requiring that they enter estimates of all uninvoiced costs in the various categories listed above. The form should list the categories, with spaces for exact descriptions and columns for liabilities accrued by the month-end, and estimated total costs in the case of one-off exercises (eg advertising, product development). In theory every expense commitment should be the subject of a purchase order entered in the purchasing system, but this rarely works effectively for the ordering of services. For example, how many businesses send a purchase order to their solicitors to instruct them to draw up a contract?

The monthly commitments sheet can almost eliminate these surprises and covers inter alia the following:

- changes in personnel and payroll (hires, fires, secondments, one-off bonuses, permanent or temporary promotions etc)
- technical projects (eg external laboratory testing, which could be underway for several months before a large invoice is received, unexpectedly for the finance department)
- marketing projects (eg advertising campaigns, which cause the same problem)
- legal or other professional work
- repair, maintenance or other substantial non-capital projects
- negotiations (of any sort) which could lead to substantial future cost or revenue

It is clear from the above that the accruals calculation process must begin well BEFORE the month end in order to calculate an acceptably accurate result for the month. It also requires (and if performed rigorously, helps) the controller and financial staff to keep their fingers firmly on the pulse of the business.

Finally there is the problem of accruing for sales credits. If they arise from faulty documentation they are likely to be notified by customers directly to the finance department, but if they arise from faulty products, the trail is less direct. A production manager striving to achieve a monthly target is understandably reluctant to warn that some of the month's output is likely to result in a credit note in a subsequent period.

Rather than have a separate sales credit meeting (many companies already have too many meetings), ensure that a sales credit review is an specific part of the production meeting agenda, either weekly or at least in the final week of the month. The presence of the managing director will help ensure that the production manager "comes clean" on potential credits. Moreover, admitting to these problems when they are actually occurring stimulates immediate rectification of the underlying problem and prevents recurrences.

## 2.3d – Identifying the barriers

Many businesses produce their management accounts in the second or even third week of each month and they are not unknown to appear as late as the 25th of the month. Of what use is that? If the results for the previous month indicate a problem, you have already blown the current month before taking any action. Even if you produce accounts on the morning of the 3rd working day of the month, you have already lost over 10% of the working time of the current month if you are working 5-day weeks.

You therefore need your monthly results as rapidly as possible after each month-end, which requires striking a balance between speed and accuracy. The figures need to be accurate enough to be reliable and to form a basis for effective decision and action, but time should not be wasted in achieving nit-picking accuracy which would not change the interpretation of the results.

As with many problems, to achieve a positive outcome you have to identify and eliminate the negative factors. There will be many barriers to achieving rapid accounts, and you must address the barriers both individually and collectively.

*Real life: a small group suffered from producing hopelessly late accounts, usually around the 20-22nd of the month. The new finance team reduced the accounting time in one single operation by the following process. All financial personnel were given two weeks to prepare their own personal lists of barriers and if possible, solutions, in preparation for a brainstorming meeting which nobody would be allowed to leave until a solution had been found to every barrier. Two weeks later, the meeting was held in a remote room, with coffee, biscuits and toilets available, and no interruptions permitted. The barriers were divided into the following categories:*
- *computer systems*
- *internally-sourced documents (eg submission of expense claims)*
- *group-sourced documents (eg confirmation of inter-company balances)*
- *externally-sourced documents (eg supplier invoices, bank statements)*

*For each category, one or more large sheets had been mounted on the wall, each sheet with a line down the centre. As the finance team members called out the barriers they had identified, they were written up on the left side of the relevant sheets. Then there was a team review of the barriers to ensure that they had all been identified; inevitably some others were revealed and written up.*

*The team then began to devise the solutions to the barriers; firstly they presented the solutions they had thought of beforehand, and when these were agreed by the team to be feasible they were written up on the right-hand sides of the sheets, opposite the barriers. There remained a large number of unresolved barriers and there the true brainstorming began, until there were only two barriers remaining, both of them substantial ones.*

*In the brainstorming process, no idea was discounted, however impracticable it might have appeared. This gave rise to an open discussion, generally producing simple solutions, some of which were:*

- *this was before the era of electronic banking, and bank statements were not received until day 3 (Wednesday) of the following month, preventing the bank reconciliation from being prepared until after the accounts were due out (10.00hrs Wednesday) – the bank was therefore reconciled 3 days before the month-end, the month-end payments were made at 12.00hrs on the Wednesday before the month-end and no payments were allowed thereafter, and any direct transfers into the bank in the last two and a half days were adjusted for as a temporary journal immediately before the accounts were issued*
- *a sales credit review was grafted on to the final week's production meeting so that all credits due were either issued or accrued for by the month-end (see 2.3c)*
- *sales staff expense claims were demanded (and received) on the Monday of the final week; the remaining accrual was therefore for only one week and any error therein was therefore not material to the month's result*
- *unrecorded expenses were largely captured by a monthly commitments sheet (see 2.3c)*

So much for the barriers which had been resolved. There remained, however, two major hurdles:

- many suppliers were slow in sending their invoices, with the result that the business did not have an accurate record of its purchases and liabilities until more than a week after the month-end
- this problem was compounded by the lack of permanent stock records and a rudimentary costing process which was not integrated into the computer system

At the time of this problem, computerised accounting systems available for small to medium-sized businesses largely ignored the recording of goods received but not yet invoiced (a problem which still persists, although not as widely, at the time of publishing). The systems accountant therefore built an add-on facility to record liabilities as goods were received and to reverse the entries automatically when the actual invoices were processed. The liability for uninvoiced receipts was at order cost, and any differences between that and actual cost were not enough to distort the management accounts.

*The managers were enthusiastic at the prospect of receiving detailed management accounts at the beginning of the month and readily agreed to a full inventory count on the last weekend of each month (the final day of each month was always a Sunday). This and the goods received system combined to give accurate figures for inventory, cost of sales and liabilities to suppliers.*

*The agreed processes were put in place before the next month-end, and draft management accounts discussed by the management team at a meeting on the first Wednesday of the following month. As a result there was a step-change in the management of the business; problems were highlighted and actions agreed in near-real time, when the activities of the month were fresh in the memory. The financial performance of the business improved notably from that date.*

## 2.3e – Monthly timetable (see appendix C1 for example)

This subsection assumes that your business uses a month of an exact number of weeks, and thus that each month-end ends on Friday or a Sunday (appendix A4). If you use a calendar month end, you will have to refer to working days as day -2, day -1, day 1, day 2 etc instead of by their names. Even then, you will have to issue a summary each month reminding people which day is day 1 etc.

The monthly process begins a considerable time before the month-end itself, and the month-end date should appear in the middle of your chart, which will look something like the chart in appendix C1.

Instruct your team to work together to enter the month-end tasks in the necessary boxes, ensuring that they collaborate on all issues. In particular, ensure that sequential processes occur in the right order. For instance, they cannot close off the sales ledger if the cash receipts have not been posted; however, if sales credits are being accrued for as estimates, those will not delay the closing of the sales ledger. You will find that some boxes have to be expanded to accommodate several tasks, while others are not used at all; you may therefore need to apply some adjustments to the less urgent items to even out the load over the critical period.

The most appropriate person to lead the exercise is the accountant. You will need to view and question the timetable at various stages of its development to ensure that there are no practical stumbling blocks. The most common impracticalities in the building of the timetable are:
- not allowing adequate time for a task to be completed
- entering tasks out of the sequence of dependencies (see above)
- placing reliance on other departments who are not likely to meet the timetable (be careful to distinguish between "cannot do" and "will not do"!)

After a few drafts of the timetable you are likely to have a workable schedule barring two or three stumbling blocks. These normally come from other departments or external organisations and have to be worked through amicably with them. As a last resort you can go to your managing director and say "We can give you the monthly results on day 3 if you . . . ." and he will see that the departments comply!

The timetable may take a few months to settle down, as people find shorter, easier and more reliable ways of completing the tasks. Note that there are two sets of initials for each column of processes in appendix C1, so that holidays and other absences are covered.

Note also that the timetable may need to start at week minus 2 (payroll and expenses, in particular, should be out of the way well before the busy period). Similarly the timetable may be extended well forward to week plus 2, as there are many administrative tasks to be done, including:
- filing and archiving all of the month's data
- preparation of blank files, indices etc for the following month end
- copying of relevant information into the annual audit file (see 1.4j); this does not take long and saves a great amount of time and hence fees when the external auditors arrive

In addition, there are other monthly tasks that should be carried out in the first half of the next month. Principal among these is the credit control meeting (see 3.2e); customer payments are frequently received in the first few days of the new month, but by about day 9 of the month this has usually dwindled to a trickle. It will therefore be readily apparent which of the customers are overdue, and it is the most advantageous time in which to hold a review of the debts and initiate appropriate collective (in both senses of the word) action.

If you are operating the recommended 4-4-5 week accounting periods (2.4b), then every 3 months you will have a spare week between the end of week plus 2 and the beginning of week minus 2. Keep this week free of regular commitments, and through each quarter compile a list of projects for the department. Typical projects are:

- improvements to the accounting system
- reorganising the finance department
- repairs and renewals
- training
- archiving (although regular monthly archiving should be a direct part of each process)
- new services to the other departments

**After 2 or 3 months you will find that your department is doing less work in producing the financial reports promptly than they were doing when it took them 2 or 3 weeks. The effect on your working relationship with the other managers will be greatly beneficial and the business itself will benefit greatly by being constantly forward-looking instead of spending most of the time wondering where it has got to.**

## 2.4a – Objectives

Complete and correct month-end papers are central to financial control. They serve several essential purposes:
- To ensure that the correct month-end procedures are followed
- To ensure that the monthly financial statements are complete and correct, especially the closing capital employed statement
- To identify promptly any financial issues that need attention
- To instil and maintain strict discipline amongst the financial staff
- To create an accessible audit trail for internal and external purposes
- To provide evidence for subsequent enquiries

## 2.4b – Annual calendar

The annual calendar sets out the operating framework for the year. You can operate to exact calendar months, or you can operate to periods of 4 or 5 weeks (usually giving quarters of 4, 4 and 5 weeks, but not necessarily in that order). The 4/5 week system offers considerable advantages:
- it enables your weekly reporting (see 2.1) to correspond exactly with your monthly reporting, and thus avoids tiresome and time-wasting part-weeks at the beginning and end of most months
- it ensures that all your month-ends are on the same day of the week (usually Friday or Sunday) which greatly assists in having consistent month-end procedures, the only minor deviation being public holidays, which in many countries tend to be on a Monday
- it gives you a "spare" week every third month; in each 5-week month you should schedule all your normal activities into weeks 1, 2, 4 and 5 and use week 3 for special projects such as upgrading and streamlining systems, devising new reports and services, clearing out unwanted material etc

The 4-4-5 system has a few disadvantages:
- months are of more unequal length than ordinary calendar months
- in comparisons with the prior year, you may be comparing a 4-week month with a 5-week one, but this only happens once every few years

- occasionally you will have a 53-week year, and therefore a 5-4-5 week quarter somewhere
- if one has a period ending after the calendar month end, the sales on the few days of the next calendar month will be treated by your customers as their purchases in the following month, and your mathematically based cash flow forecasts may be slightly optimistic
- you may have to adjust your calculation of some accruals and cut-offs to the different month-ends
- you may need permission for statutory returns (eg VAT returns in the UK) to be adjusted to the dates

These disadvantages are relatively minor, and in most cases, a 4-4-5 period system is more efficient in terms of administration.

At least two months before the financial year starts, you must have the year mapped out in full. The two month minimum is to ensure that all directors, managers and relevant personnel have the dates of meetings, deadlines etc firmly in their diaries before the year starts, and that any possible conflicting commitments are ironed out beforehand. The items which should be included in the calendar include:

- the month-end dates
- holidays and other non-working days (if you have sites in other countries, ensure that you distinguish the countries to which the various holidays apply)
- deadlines for management reports, tax returns and other set routines
- management meetings and especially board meetings (ensure that your directors, especially external ones, are incontrovertibly aware of their commitments in this respect)
- audits, conferences, results announcements and other finance-related events

By using simple abbreviations which are explained on the calendar, you can accommodate all of the above information on a single sheet as shown in appendix A4.

## 2.4c – Monthly accounting working papers – general

The monthly accounting papers are the principal link between the accounting records and the financial statements. The complete trail is as follows:

- transactions
- transactions are evidenced by documents

- documents are recorded in accounting ledgers and filed in an appropriate sequence (see section 4)
- ledgers are summarised in monthly working papers
- working papers are summarised in monthly financial reports (management accounts)
- management accounts for the final period in the year are subject to audit adjustments
- audit-adjusted management accounts form the basis of final audited accounts for external use

It follows that the monthly papers must be complete and correct, and clearly presented and annotated. What makes sense to you at the end of the month may not make sense several busy months later at the year end.

What does that scribbled note mean? Where did that figure originate? Ensure that your notes are clear and complete so that you can trace any reported figure back to its roots and that all adjustments are fully explained.


## 2.4d – Monthly accounting working papers – balance sheet

In a typical manufacturing company, the monthly balance sheet papers should include the following schedules, with supporting evidence where they are not drawn directly from the accounting records:

**Inventory** (see 4.1, 4.2)
- summary by main relevant category (eg by product type, location, outlet, contract etc)
- summary by stage of completion (raw materials, work in progress, finished goods)
- ageing analysis
- provision movements – obsolescence
- provision movements – damage
- provision movements – non-recoverable value
- days-of-production calculation (or days-of-sales for non-manufacturing businesses)

**Accounts receivable** (see 4.3)
- receivables control account summary
- receivables ageing list by customer
- days-of-sales-outstanding calculation
- provision movements – bad debts general
- provision movements – bad debts specific
- provision movements – sales credits

- status of major contracts, including provisions for losses
- items in suspense
- list of prepayments, accrued income and miscellaneous receivables

**Accounts payable** (see 4.4)
- payables control account summary
- payables ageing list by individual supplier
- status of major contracts, including provisions for penalties
- goods received not invoiced listing
- items in suspense
- list of accruals and miscellaneous payables (maintain a 15-month spreadsheet of these, starting at 0 with the audited opening accruals and payables – as the audited figures are the most comprehensive, this ensures that you do not lose sight of any liabilities over the following months, and avoids any unpleasant shocks at the following year-end)
- schedule of deferred income (for customer maintenance contracts and other long-term commitments, maintain a spreadsheet showing the monthly deferred income over the life of every contract)

**Other liabilities** (see 4.4, 4.5)
- provisions for liabilities (warranties etc) – general and specific
- summary of payroll liabilities
- payroll control accounts
- sales tax/ value added tax control accounts
- customs duty control account
- other taxation control accounts

**Fixed assets** (see 4.6)
- financial summary (similar to that in annual financial statements)
- detail of movements in period and cumulative to date
- background to scrappings, impairments or other non-routine adjustments to value
- treatment of group adjustments relating to transferred assets
- amortisation reasonability check (does it equate to a sensible percentage overall?)
- agreement with fixed asset register (there should be no reconciling items)
- similar information for intangible assets and capital grants if relevant

**Bank, cash and loan accounts** (see 4.7)
- list of balances on all bank accounts and loose cash funds in all currencies
- bank reconciliations

- foreign exchange exposure summary and related currency hedging summary
- petty cash summary (may include approximations if foreign currency advances are provided to travelling staff for subsistence)
- bonds and other instruments

**Intra-group accounts**
- list of receivables and payables with other companies in same group, and confirmations of agreement
- note of differences where balances have not been able to be agreed

**Reserves**
- reconciliations of all movements
- provisions for dividends

**Supporting documents**
- supporting documents which are part of the normal accounting records need not be included provided that there are clear and accurate references to them; however, it is often helpful to include copies of them in complex situations, and where there are written annotations or signatures thereon to provide evidence (examples might include installation costs for a major new fixed asset, or settlement of a long-running customer or supplier dispute)
- non-system supporting documents should normally be included, at least in copy form (for example, a letter agreeing to share costs on a disputed issue)

**Accounting**
- trial balance
- trail from trial balance to financial statements (the accounting method recommended in appendix C5 provides that trail; the SUMIF codes indicate the way in which several general ledger accounts are grouped into single lines in the monthly reports)
- copies of major non-standard journal entries, with evidence of authorisation (it may be appropriate to file copies of standard journal entries also, depending on their complexity, sensitivity and degree of control, but in most cases the original copies in numerical order in the journal file will suffice)
- other confirmations
- in the case of group subsidiaries, mapping to group reporting format

The test of the above papers is that at any time after closure of the month-end results (most commonly at the end of the financial year) you can trace the origin and explanation of any figure in the financial statements. It is not difficult; it just takes care, thought and systematic presentation and filing.

## 2.4e – Monthly accounting working papers – profit statement

In terms of debits and credits, and also of the numbers themselves, the balance sheet papers detailed above do most of the checking on the numerical accuracy of the profit statement. If all the accruals, prepayments and write-downs have been included and are on a reasonable basis, then most of the movements between periods should be in order. However, it is possible for the balance sheet to be correct, but income or costs to have been charged to the wrong account in the profit statement.

The working papers for the profit statements are therefore more trend-oriented. Have the resources applied to production and sales resulted in an appropriate level of output? And looking at that from the opposite direction, are the costs in line with the output achieved? Whether you review your costs against the level of sales or the level of production or both will depend upon the nature of your business (and to some extent the way in which you operate your costing; there are standard costing systems which give the standard cost of sales and others which give the standard cost of production.)

A typical set of monthly profit working papers would include the following, WITH EXPLANATIONS where relevant:

**Sales**
- review of sales against budget and explanation of major variances
- review of sales against most recent forecast
- review of variances – volume
- review of variances – price
- review of variances – mix (you may find differing views on how this should be calculated)
- review of recent trends in actual figures
- review of low-margin sales and note of actions taken or required to prevent recurrence
- analysis of sales credit notes by reason and notes of actions taken to reduce the number thereof

**Cost of sales**
- review of material variances – cost

- review of material variances – usage
- review of material variances – scrap
- review of labour variances – rates
- review of labour variances – efficiency
- review of labour variances – personnel mix (a difficult analysis to achieve in practice)
- review of production overhead variances – cost rates
- review of production overhead variances – spend

(how the above reviews are carried out and papers are presented will vary considerably from business to business, depending on the activities involved and the costing methods used)

## Payroll (applicable to all activities including contract and professional services)
- overall numbers
- overall hours or days – normal, overtime, down-time, absences
- ratio – average costs per hour against budget or standard
- ratio – overtime hours against normal hours
- ratio – absence hours against normal hours
- ratio – down time against productive time
- ratio – bonuses against gross normal pay
- ratio – employer's oncost against total gross pay
- ratio – indirect staff numbers and costs against direct payroll numbers and costs

There may be other aspects and ratios to be considered – for example, in a professional or contracting business which charges its clients for the work of specialist personnel, the ratio of chargeable time (ie fee-earning time) to non-chargeable time is paramount.

## Direct (variable) overheads
- ratio – direct overhead costs against volume of production (this may give rise to a variety of variances resulting from the actual mix of products from the budget and/ or standard mix)

## Indirect (fixed) overheads
- spend levels against budget
- spend levels against current circumstances – programmed activities such as major repairs and exhibitions
- spend levels against current circumstances – seasonal fluctuations
- spend levels against current circumstances – unexpected events

In practice, there may be an indeterminate boundary between direct and indirect costs, many of which are semi-variable and difficult to categorise exactly. Common sense and attention to detail are required, and the monthly commitments sheet to managers (see 2.3c) is essential to the review of such costs.

Always be on the lookout for unrecorded costs – not only will they cause you to overstate your current performance, but they will probably cause you to overstate your forecasts on the same basis, leading to anguish in later periods. It will be viewed as the finance department's fault, not the fault of the people who should have reported the commitments in the first place.

## 2.4f – Storage of accounting records

Section 4 of this book details the records which are conventionally required to be maintained for each major section of the accounting systems. The combination of the month-end working papers (per this subsection) and the detailed transaction records (per section 4) must provide a complete trail of the business's activities.

Filing of the monthly accounting records is a vital process and must meet the following objectives:
- give a full explanation of all figures in the monthly financial statements (the definition of "full" is arguable, but the files should enable all reasonable and predictable queries to be answered immediately, without recourse to hunting through the accounting systems)
- from the monthly statements and final adjustments, support the annual financial statements
- provide all details necessary to support the corporate tax computations
- provide reconciliations of sales taxes, value added taxes and other external levies
- provide full reconciliations of all control accounts, and proof that all anomalies are promptly resolved
- enable the external auditors to give a full opinion on the annual statutory financial statements

Before you name a single file, establish a set of 3-letter abbreviations for all the units and departments for which you are responsible (eg NCT for Newcastle-upon-Tyne, BLF for Belfast, MFG for manufacturing, MKT for marketing). These are for use in file names to make them instantly recognisable and retrievable.

**Computer files:** establish a protocol for naming computer files; this will depend on how you wish to retrieve them; by unit, by date, by subject or whatever. For example:

- 2007-09-NCL-MFG if you wish to retrieve files by date, then by unit, then by department
- NCT-MFG-2007-09 if you wish to retrieve files by unit, then by department, then by date

Where you file by unit, establish a logical order in which to file the units and use that order for all your documentation. If the order is not alphabetical (it could be by location, date of establishment or many other criteria) consider adjusting your 3-character abbreviations so that an alpha-sort will produce the established order. For example, if you always list your units in the order Manchester, Aberdeen, Newcastle, Belfast, use the following abbreviations: 1MC, 2AB, 3NE, 4BF.

Ensure that all people submitting files use the same convention – this will make your computerised filing relatively easy to manage. Set up all the necessary computer directories (or "folders") BEFORE the start of each financial year. Also, all reports by all departments should present the units in the established order. This creates a consistency of information sequence throughout the company.

**Hard-copy working papers:** adopt a similar approach:

- before the start of each financial year, prepare a set of lever-arch files by accounting unit and by period (month, quarter or whatever will fit into the files with sufficient space for occasional additional papers)
- clear the last-but-one year's files into archive storage (see below), leave the previous year's files in place (you will still be referring to them) and set up the files for the current year (where several persons will be using the files, wall filing is the most suitable system, as the spines of the lever-arch files are visible to all)
- do not write the full names of the files on the spines – this will result in small writing which makes the files harder to locate. Use the standard 3-letter abbreviations which you have devised above and mark the file spines in large characters in heavy felt pen. For example, instead of writing "Newcastle Manufacturing Unit – September 2011-12", write as follows:

| |
|---|
| **NCT** |
| **MFG** |
| **X1-X2** |
| **SEP** |

This can be seen clearly from across a large room, and missing files are easily located.

Use dividers to divide the files into main sections and write the tabs in pencil, again using 3-letter abbreviations (eg REC for accounts receivable). At the front of each period for each unit display the index, either printed on card or held in a transparent pocket. Remember that you will use these files frequently, so they must be robust.

At the risk of appearing fussy, use paper punches with accurate alignment guides so that all working papers are punched neatly and the pages turn like a book. The reasons for this are:

- all accounting work should be carried out to a high standard of presentation
- papers are easier to locate if neatly filed
- auditors, tax inspectors and other external parties will give more credence to your papers and procedures if they are professionally filed (they shouldn't but they do)
- the appearance of the finance department will be organised and professional, an important subconscious factor in gaining and maintaining the respect of the other departments − nothing erodes confidence in a finance department as much as encountering a sea of untidy documents all over the desks and floor.

**Archive storage and date of destruction:** the length of time for which accounting records must be kept will vary according to the laws of your country, and there may be different laws for different types of records. For example, information supporting your statutory accounts, your corporate tax liabilities, your sales tax or VAT liabilities and your payroll may all have different minimum retention periods. There is at least one country which requires payroll records to be held forever, and that includes the software necessary to operate them; it is hard to believe that such a law is actually complied with. A generally held view is that accounting records should be retained for 10 years, unless the requirement is longer, in addition to the current year.

A 10-year storage period is simple to operate. You number your storage area and your boxes with the numbers 0 to 9 to denote the last digit of the year-end, and store accordingly. So when you place the 2016 records in storage, you merely remove the 2006 records from the "6" boxes or racks and replace them with the 2016 records. Before you place any records in storage, mark each file with the date of destruction − this is much easier to manage than calculating it in retrospect, and avoids indecision from questions such as "is it ten years plus the current year?" or "is it ten years from the date of the file or ten years from the year end?".

Note, however, that certain records will almost certainly need to be held for longer than 10 years. The exact requirements will vary from one country to another, but it is likely that the following documents will need to be kept for longer:

- details of long-life assets and their amortisation
- contracts which extend over long periods, or which may have legal or financial implications after their stated period (this could include tenancies, insurance, bad debts and other business arrangements)
- records regarding ownership of the business (share registers, dividend registers etc)
- records of legal meetings (members' meetings, directors' meetings etc) and of the resolutions therefrom
- all other statutory records regarding the stewardship of the company
- other records as required by the laws governing the company – take legal advice if in doubt

In addition to the ten years of routine accounting documents in the archives you will probably wish to have the prior year's files, which are frequently referred to, in your department along with the current year's files (at least until all matters relating to the prior year's audit, financial statements and tax liabilities have been finalised).

Caution: in many businesses the monthly accounting records are filed sloppily and illogically. The main mistakes are:

- failing to set up the filing space a year in advance, so that parts of the year are stored in different parts of the finance dept, according to availability of space
- failing to establish a master index and order of filing, so that different contributors file their parts of the system in different sequences
- lack of professional care: names scrawled illegibly on files, papers filed untidily or not at all

**Supporting documents** comprise:

- originating documents such as orders
- delivery documents of goods and services
- confirmations of acceptance of goods or services
- exception documents for rejections, shortfalls and other errors
- invoices and credit notes
- remittance advices and statements of account
- correspondence

There are several ways of filing the supporting documents, the main ones being:

- by serial number of document (ie the serial number allocated by *your* business)
- by date of document
- by customer, supplier or other related party
- by transaction – for example, in some companies a purchase order, delivery note, goods received note are all stapled to the purchase invoice to which they relate, providing a complete documentary trail in one place (this is a neat solution, but it can become difficult if one delivery is covered by two invoices et cetera; you must design your filing to suit your circumstances)

Which method should you use? The general rule of filing is that you should file information in the sequence in which you are most likely to want to retrieve it. However, there is the further consideration that your filing system should be able to prove that you have a complete trail of documents. The following considerations therefore apply:

- if you file sales invoices, credit notes etc in numerical order in a separate file for each customer, you should be able to answer queries from that customer rapidly, but with your documents spread over a few dozen or perhaps a few hundred files it will be difficult, perhaps nearly impossible, to ensure that you have all the documents at all times, and locating a specific document will entail checking your system to see which customer file holds that document number
- the same applies to purchase invoices and supplier files

The good business manager will instinctively gravitate towards the customer/supplier-based approach, but the reality is often that filing documents in the numerical sequence allocated by your computer system is a more effective system. When each monthly file is completed, a member of staff can check through the numerical sequence of the file to ensure that all documents are present, and mark the sequence numbers (eg 1447 – 1531) together with the unit and period data on the spine of the file. The documents can therefore be located rapidly from the filing cupboards. Only correspondence, contracts, notes and other relevant information should be kept in the customer or supplier files.

When an enquiry is received from a customer, supplier etc the operator responsible retrieves the correspondence file, and uses the computer system to bring the queried documents up on screen. That is easier than wading through a thick file containing copy invoices and credit notes mixed with correspondence, notes of phone calls etc, and so results in more effective service as well as more secure filing.

To sum up, documents should be filed numerically as follows:
- for documents generated by your systems – file in order of the numbers created by the systems
- for documents received from outside parties – file in order of the numbers which you have allocated in entering the documents into your systems (eg do not file supplier invoices by the supplier's invoice number)

It follows from the above that your formal procedure for authorising external documents must be clearly marked on the documents. The widely preferred method is by a specially-designed rubber stamp, but pre-printed stickers are used by some businesses for clarity. Writing informally on the documents is better than nothing, but in doing that you run the risk of omitting a necessary part of the authorisation process. The rubber stamp or sticker should contain the following information, the exact details depending of course on your specific approval process:
- date received
- serial number allocated
- cost code
- sales tax code
- sales tax rate
- authorisation – date
- authorisation – signature
- entered in system – date & person
- entered in system – signature

It is tempting sometimes to replicate documents which relate to more than one system. In general, try to avoid this, as one advantage of numerical filing systems is the avoidance of needless replication. However, where the documents are likely to be consulted long after their origination, it may be advisable to make an exception, and where information may be required after the document destruction date, it will be essential. For example, you may need to take photocopies of purchase invoices relating to fixed assets, and store these invoices by fixed asset number in a separate file to support the fixed assets register.

The final point about filing is that IT MUST BE DONE IMMEDIATELY. Documents lying around on desks, in drawers, in temporary folders etc are almost a guarantee of inefficiency, and in some cases loss of profits. Only documents which are awaiting verification and processing should be in any kind of pending file. As soon as the transaction or activity has taken place, the relevant document(s) must be processed, authorised, actioned and put straight into the filing system.

Numerical sequence checks should be run regularly to ensure that all documents are present (spoiled or cancelled documents should be clearly marked as such and retained on file to complete the sequence). Any missing items should be located immediately; if they cannot be found, a replacement should be requested. Ensure that your staff regularly pursue any old documents in any pending file.

## 2.4g – Conclusion

The above procedures may appear over-detailed and time-consuming, but they are emphatically not. It is much quicker to run a well-ordered documentary régime than to have documents in a state of casual disorder. The time spent in indexing and filing documents carefully is much less than the time wasted in searching for items which have not been properly indexed and have been filed in an ad-hoc location.

WORKING IN AN UNTIDY FINANCE DEPARTMENT IS A NIGHTMARE.

## 2.5a – Objectives

In addition to the normal month-end work, the following major issues arise before or upon the year-end:
- statutory accounts or financial statements **("stats")**
- external audit
- taxation – calculation of liabilities
- banks and other interested parties
- systems set-up for following year

## 2.5b – Processes

As well as the normal month-end procedures, special issues arising at the year-end are:
- additional checks on accuracy of figures (especially inventory)
- preparation of stats
- auditing of stats and underlying records
- review of covenants against stats
- approval of stats by shareholders
- lodgement of stats with companies office
- presentation of stats to other interested parties
- agreement of corporate tax liabilities
- rolling over of computer systems to new financial year
- rolling forward of fixed assets ledgers to show the new opening balances
- revaluation of inventory to the new year's standards (standard costing systems only)

## 2.5c – Statutory financial statements

Management accounts and statutory accounts or financial statements ("stats") have fundamental differences, the main ones of which are:
- management accounts are an internal document; stats are for external users, who include shareholders, banks, tax authorities and

- anyone (eg customers, suppliers, leasing companies) who is concerned about the financial strength of the business
- management accounts measure the operating performance of the business against a budget; stats measure the financial performance against the prior year (a very unsatisfactory comparison in many respects)
- management accounts can be in any format; they should be in the format that most realistically reflects the activities of the business and the format may be changed to mirror changes in the business itself; stats are to a legally prescribed format from which there is little deviation allowable
- management accounts may use any accounting principles; stats follow legally prescribed principles
- stats show many incidental disclosures not required by management accounts and vice versa
- stats are audited formally, management accounts are not audited per se, but will be reviewed by the auditors as part of the audit of the stats

It follows from the above that a set of intelligently constructed management accounts are a much more informative document to the users of the business than the stats. Businesses without prominent external shareholders therefore tend to be dismissive of the stats, particularly since in most countries they are required in an unhelpful format, under regulations which have for the most part been drafted by persons who have relatively little experience of running a business. However, the financial directors of businesses which have prominent external shareholders (especially in quoted companies) spend an inordinate amount of time worrying about how transactions and events will appear in the statutory accounts. This concern is often detrimental, since it diverts attention which should be directed to maximising the underlying performance of the business.

It is interesting to reflect that both the management accounts and the stats are specifically designed to give a true and fair view of the business, and yet can differ greatly in terms of presentation, logic and numbers. Which are the more realistic? In a well-managed business the management accounts should be the more realistic; regardless of what disclosure rules the regulators impose, the business should be dealing in hard-headed reality. Unfortunately that is not always the case – how does your company fare in that comparison?

In this book we are concerned primarily with independent companies, so we shall consider how we get from month 12 management accounts to statutory accounts in mechanical terms with a minimum of difficulty, and shall not concern ourselves with the more esoteric aspects of the stats.

## 2.5d – Preparation (start of year)

The time to prepare for the year-end is the BEGINNING of the year, not the end of it. If you do this, it will be relatively easy. When you open your filing at the beginning of the year (see 2.4f) set up a lever-arch file for the year-end. Much of the information you need for the year-end will be contained in the monthly files, so this file is for the items that will NOT be in those files. The index to your year-end file should therefore look something like this:

Prior year papers:
- audit management letter
- tax computation
- AGM minutes and dividend approvals
- final trial balance
- evidence (normally including copies of journal entries) that the final trial balance has been correctly brought forward into the current year
- any other items which will need to be re-visited in the current year

Current year papers:
- inventory counting instructions
- major fixed asset movements
- tax disallowable items
- disclosure items (directors' remuneration, political donations etc, all of which are apparent from the previous year's stats, and any new requirements announced during the current year)
- exceptional events during the year (redundancies, major repairs or projects, new business etc)
- notes of any systems problems encountered, and how they were resolved, with evidence (it is useful to break the systems section into the headings used in the auditors' programmes: sales & receivables, purchases & payables, inventory & cost of sales, fixed assets, payroll, cash etc)
- details of all provisions, showing movements from opening provisions through to final provisions
- any other items which will be of interest to the auditors (grants, insurance claims, legal disputes etc)

At the beginning of the year, review all the adjustments made at the end of the previous year, and ensure that all adjustments arising from errors, incorrect accounting practices and other inappropriate actions or omissions are corrected from the beginning of the current year, so that they do not recur at the end of this year. Then each month, when you have signed off the month-end file, instruct your staff to prepare and enter the information required for the year-end file. Alternatively, this can be done in the spare week of a five-week month, but it is better done monthly when the items are still fresh in mind. Going back through a year's repairs and renewals to analyse them for the tax computation is a thankless task; doing it monthly is easy.

You will thus arrive painlessly at the year-end with all the disclosure information ready to hand and presentable to the auditors, and all outstanding matters from the previous year dealt with. You now have to produce the final results for the year, and you will have very few adjustments to make because you have eliminated them at source following last year's review.

## 2.5e – Management to statutory

The start point is the approved management accounts for month 12. Many companies get into difficulties in monitoring the trail between month 12 and the statutory accounts, so do it properly from the start. Open up a "month 13" in your system and in your accounting pack, and merely prepare another set of management accounts, the cumulative figures of which will be your results for the year for statutory purposes. The month 13 accounts will be meaningless as accounts, but they will provide a permanent bridge between the management accounts and the stats.

If you have as recommended a narrative column in your management accounts (see appendix C6) your month 13 accounts can hold full explanations of the adjustments, and will give a full line-by-line set of accounts supporting the stats. What could be easier? If the auditors require further adjustments, you should enter them as "month 14" so that they can easily be identified, and you can ensure that they are entered in the records (appendix C5).

## 2.5f – Disclosure items

There are various areas of disclosure in the stats over and above the pure accounting issues. These are the directors' responsibility, but you may be involved in producing them, or at least providing the relevant numerical information:

- representations – the auditors cannot be expected to know every circumstance of the business and therefore protect themselves by requiring the directors to provide letters of representation certifying that there are no undisclosed circumstances which would affect the audit opinion if known by the auditors
- directors' report & review of operations – often a collection of euphemisms in the past, but legislation has put increasing pressure on the directors to report realistically on the circumstances underlying and surrounding the business
- risk assessment – in some countries, directors are required to state the company's major business risks, a disclosure which must be uncomfortable, given the information which it provides to competitors
- pensions – the status of the company's pension scheme(s) in relation to its obligations
- contingent liabilities – serious risks of a more specific nature than those in the directors' assessment
- securities – charges held by other parties (mainly lenders) against the assets of the business

The above items can be very time-consuming, so start collecting the underlying information and drafting the narratives no later than month 10 of your financial year.


## 2.5g – Liquidity

If the business is operating under tight conditions, you may have to prove to the auditors that it has sufficient funding in place to continue operating for the foreseeable future (not just beyond the year-end, but also beyond the date of signature of the audit certificate). You may therefore be required to provide:

- documentary evidence of the banks' continued support for your business for a reasonable length of time into the future
- a well-structured budget in considerable detail, consistent with current and expected market and currency conditions, demonstrating that the business has a viable path ahead – if this budget deviates

more than slightly from the current operating levels, you will need to provide detailed and credible back-up to your calculations

## 2.5h – The audit

The stats then have to be audited, and this is another area in which you can make great savings in time. Most auditors will provide you with a set of blank stats, with the previous year's final audit figures entered in the comparatives column and the current column left blank for you to compile. This acts as a useful check-list for the information you are required to provide, and should be obtained at the interim audit stage so that your preparation is complete BEFORE the final audit begins.

Section 1.4j tells you how to get the best out of the auditors; by taking a constructive attitude to your audit you can derive considerable value from it.

## 2.5i – Preparation for the following year

Your year-end isn't over yet. In addition to having the stats signed and lodged, you have to close off your ledgers and reopen them for the new year. Your computer system operating instructions will tell you how to do that, but you should also carry out a general tidying up:

- each year the accounts codes become a little untidy as random new codes are added, sometimes with unsuitable codes and/ or titles; tidy up the chart of accounts for the following year, and amend any default settings accordingly (the account codes should reflect the way in which you plan to operate the business in the following year, and should thus correspond to the budget format)
- ensure that all account headings required by your budget for the new year are in place (you should have done that when you finalised your budget; the year-end is merely a check-point)
- enter your budget into the system for the new year – you should adjust your budget to reflect the actual audited opening balance sheet, so that all comparisons of actual balances with the budget do not have to be adjusted for any opening differences
- review long-standing provisions against items in inventory and receivables and write any irrecoverable items out of the ledgers, taking appropriate tax action where required
- delete supplier and customer accounts which have had a nil balance and no transactions for a long time, with no prospect of further

transactions (this saves repetition of these accounts in every print-out, and may liberate valuable disk space)
- similarly, review and cleanse inventory part numbers in conjunction with your engineering department
- if you are operating a standard costing system, ensure that the new year's standards have been correctly entered in the costing and accounting systems, and prepare and retain a summary reconciling the movement from the old standards to the new standards for each major inventory category
- key in your period end dates and all other standing data for the year

Month-end no 1 in the new year is traditionally a nightmare for finance departments. The reason is simple; they haven't carried out the procedures described above and uncompleted year-end work prevents completion of the month-end work. But if you work methodically through the actions, preparing well ahead of time (make a detailed list to ensure that you don't miss anything), then the transition to the new financial year will happen with a minimum of disruption.

# PART 3
# THE PERFORMANCE

## 3.1 OPTIMISING PROFIT

a   Objectives
b   Elements of profit performance
c   Sales – price & volume
d   Margins & mark-ups
e   Direct (variable) costs
f   Indirect (fixed) costs
g   In-house manufacture
h   Speculative costs
i   Marketing costs
j   Borrowing costs
k   Breakeven level
l   Value added
m   Dealing with a downturn
n   Dealing with an upturn

## 3.2  OPTIMISING CASH

a   Objectives
b   Elements of cash control
c   Indicators of cash performance
d   Working capital – inventory
e   Working capital – receivables
f   Working capital – payables
g   Cash control of fixed assets
h   Research & development
i   Treasury

## 3.3  OPTIMISING MANAGEMENT

a   Objectives
b   The management cycle
c   Task allocation
d   Performance pay
e   Sales force
f   Customer service
g   Production
h   Contracts
i   Inventory control
j   Research & dev / engineering
k   Purchasing

l   Administration
m   Finance
n   Meetings
o   Sales credit notes

## 3.4  BUSINESS PLANNING

a   Objectives
b   Overall process
c   Scale & detail
d   Planning team
e   Overall considerations
f   SWOT analysis
g   Building on the SWOT
h   Planning elements
i   Calculation approaches
j   Producing the plan
k   The activity on the side
l   The controller's rôle
m   Objectives review
n   Typical strategic plan format

## 3.5  BUDGETING

a   Objectives
b   Overall process
c   Timescale
d   Documentation
e   Financial model
f   Review & approval
g   The final version
h   Making it happen
i   Interim updates

## 3.1a – Objectives

Businesses survive on cash flow. Optimising cash flow (see 3.2) involves:
- operating on a low asset base
- making a profit

We discuss the low asset base in 3.2. However, once you have offloaded all your surplus assets if you had any in the first place, there is no further cash to be generated from that source. To generate cash on a permanent basis a business has to make regular and adequate profits. Regardless of EBITDA and other fanciful measurements cooked up by bonus-chasers, the profit which matters is the profit after interest, taxation and dividends. THAT is the profit which the business gets to keep and reinvest, and which gives confidence to the bankers and backers.

## 3.1b – Elements of profit performance

In its simplest terms, ongoing profit can be maximised by improvement of some or all of the following areas:
- sales
- variable costs
- fixed costs
- borrowing costs

Each of the above categories can be divided into price and volume (ie usage in the case of costs).

Within each of these categories are many sub-categories, each of which can be attacked to improve the overall profit performance. But before considering this it is necessary to contemplate how these categories relate to each other; the relationship is by no means as obvious as the casual observer might think.

## 3.1c – Sales – price and volume

On the wall of the financial director's office of a manufacturing company in Catalunya are the following words:

> **SALES = VANITY**
> **PROFIT = SANITY**
> **CASH =REALITY**

These words should be written large on the office wall of every company director, financial or otherwise. We shall deal with the reality of cash in 3.2, but before that we must debunk forever the vanity of sales and highlight the sanity of profit.

Consider the case of two closely competing companies who are struggling at breakeven level:
- Wondrous Widgets drops its selling price by 5% and is rewarded by an immediate 20% increase in volume
- Glamorous Gizmos raises its selling price by 5% and immediately loses 20% of its sales volume

|  |  | Original |
|---|---|---|
| Sales volume | units | *1,000* |
| Unit selling price | £ | 100 |
| Unit direct cost (material + labour) | £ | 80 |
|  |  | £ |
| Sales | £ | 100,000 |
| Direct costs | £ | (80,000) |
| Gross margin | £ | 20,000 |
|  |  | *20.0%* |
| Variable overheads | £ | (10,000) |
| Fixed costs | £ | (10,000) |
| Operating result | £ | 0 |

Before turning the page, open up your spreadsheet and make a quick calculation of the result of each company after it has adjusted its selling price. No cheating!

## How do they fare?

| | | Original | W Widgets | G Gizmos |
|---|---|---|---|---|
| Sales volume | units | 1,000 | 1,200 | 800 |
| Unit selling price | £ | 100 | 95 | 105 |
| Unit direct cost (material + labour) | £ | 80 | 80 | 80 |
| | | £ | £ | £ |
| Sales | £ | 100,000 | 114,000 | 84,000 |
| Direct costs | £ | (80,000) | (96,000) | (64,000) |
| Gross margin | £ | 20,000 | 18,000 | 20,000 |
| | | 20.0% | 15.8% | 23.8% |
| Variable overheads | £ | (10,000) | (12,000) | (8,000) |
| Net variable margin | £ | 10,000 | 6,000 | 12,000 |
| | | 10.0% | 5.3% | 14.3% |
| Fixed costs | £ | (10,000) | (10,000) | (10,000) |
| Operating result | £ | 0 | (4,000) | 2,000 |

What has happened here?
- Widgets has GAINED 20% more sales for only a 5% price drop, and yet is incurring a large LOSS
- Gizmos has LOST 20% of its sales for only a 5% price rise and is somehow making a PROFIT

How can this be? Both companies reported a gross margin of 20%, but the businesses have other variable costs which are classified as overheads. Typically these could include carriage inwards (which should be classified as material costs) and outwards, export fees, sales commissions, advertising and after-sales product support costs.

The original net margin was therefore not 20% but 10%.
- Widgets therefore reduced its margin by 50% (5% is half of 10%) and therefore needed a 100% increase in sales volume just to continue breaking even, let alone make a profit
- Gizmos correspondingly increased its margin by 50% and therefore needed only 67% of its previous sales volume to break even – everything above that level would generate a profit

The lesson from this is **one of the most vital lessons in business**:
- the revenue of the business is NOT the sales figure
- the revenue of the business is NOT the gross margin

- the revenue of the business is the NET VARIABLE MARGIN, ie the margin after ALL variable costs

To prove the breakeven levels:

|  |  | Original | W Widgets | G Gizmos |
|---|---|---|---|---|
| Sales volume | units | *1,000* | *2,000* | *667* |
| Unit selling price | £ | 100 | 95 | 105 |
| Unit direct cost (material + labour) | £ | 80 | 80 | 80 |
|  |  | £ | £ | £ |
| Sales | £ | 100,000 | 190,000 | 70,000 |
| Direct costs | £ | (80,000) | (160,000) | (53,333) |
| Gross margin | £ | 20,000 | 30,000 | 16,667 |
|  |  | *20.0%* | *15.8%* | *23.8%* |
| Variable overheads | £ | (10,000) | (20,000) | (6,667) |
| Net variable margin | £ | 10,000 | 10,000 | 10,000 |
|  |  | *10.0%* | *5.3%* | *14.3%* |
| Fixed costs | £ | (10,000) | (10,000) | (10,000) |
| Operating result | £ | 0 | 0 | 0 |

The table on the following page demonstrates the danger of price reductions and should be held and fully understood by every member of your marketing and sales team:

**THE EFFECTS OF REDUCING SALES PRICES**

| Price reduction | 1.0% | 2.0% | 3.0% | 4.0% | 5.0% | 7.5% | 10.0% | 12.5% | 15.0% | 20.0% | 25.0% |
|---|---|---|---|---|---|---|---|---|---|---|---|
| Original margin | Increase in sales volume needed to achieve same monetary margin | | | | | | | | | | |
| **5.0%** | 25.0% | 66.7% | 150% | 400% | N/A | N/A | N/A | N/A | N/A | N/A | N/A |
| 6.0% | 20.0% | 50.0% | 100% | 200% | 500% | N/A | N/A | N/A | N/A | N/A | N/A |
| 7.0% | 16.7% | 40.0% | 75.0% | 133% | 250% | N/A | N/A | N/A | N/A | N/A | N/A |
| 8.0% | 14.3% | 33.3% | 60.0% | 100% | 167% | 1500% | N/A | N/A | N/A | N/A | N/A |
| 9.0% | 12.5% | 28.6% | 50.0% | 80.0% | 125% | 500% | N/A | N/A | N/A | N/A | N/A |
| **10.0%** | 11.1% | 25.0% | 42.9% | 66.7% | 100% | 300% | N/A | N/A | N/A | N/A | N/A |
| 11.0% | 10.0% | 22.2% | 37.5% | 57.1% | 83.3% | 214% | 1000% | N/A | N/A | N/A | N/A |
| 12.0% | 9.1% | 20.0% | 33.3% | 50.0% | 71.4% | 167% | 500% | N/A | N/A | N/A | N/A |
| 12.5% | 8.7% | 19.0% | 31.6% | 47.1% | 66.7% | 150% | 400% | N/A | N/A | N/A | N/A |
| 13.0% | 8.3% | 18.2% | 30.0% | 44.4% | 62.5% | 136% | 333% | 2500% | N/A | N/A | N/A |
| 14.0% | 7.7% | 16.7% | 27.3% | 40.0% | 55.6% | 115% | 250% | 833% | N/A | N/A | N/A |
| **15.0%** | 7.1% | 15.4% | 25.0% | 36.4% | 50.0% | 100% | 200% | 500% | N/A | N/A | N/A |
| 16.0% | 6.7% | 14.3% | 23.1% | 33.3% | 45.5% | 88.2% | 167% | 357% | 1500% | N/A | N/A |
| 17.0% | 6.3% | 13.3% | 21.4% | 30.8% | 41.7% | 78.9% | 143% | 278% | 750% | N/A | N/A |
| 17.5% | 6.1% | 12.9% | 20.7% | 29.6% | 40.0% | 75.0% | 133% | 250% | 600% | N/A | N/A |
| 18.0% | 5.9% | 12.5% | 20.0% | 28.6% | 38.5% | 71.4% | 125% | 227% | 500% | N/A | N/A |
| 19.0% | 5.6% | 11.8% | 18.8% | 26.7% | 35.7% | 65.2% | 111% | 192% | 375% | N/A | N/A |
| **20.0%** | 5.3% | 11.1% | 17.6% | 25.0% | 33.3% | 60.0% | 100% | 167% | 300% | N/A | N/A |
| 21.0% | 5.0% | 10.5% | 16.7% | 23.5% | 31.3% | 55.6% | 90.9% | 147% | 250% | 2000% | N/A |
| 22.0% | 4.8% | 10.0% | 15.8% | 22.2% | 29.4% | 51.7% | 83.3% | 132% | 214% | 1000% | N/A |
| 22.5% | 4.7% | 9.8% | 15.4% | 21.6% | 28.6% | 50.0% | 80.0% | 125% | 200% | 800% | N/A |
| 23.0% | 4.5% | 9.5% | 15.0% | 21.1% | 27.8% | 48.4% | 76.9% | 119% | 188% | 667% | N/A |
| 24.0% | 4.3% | 9.1% | 14.3% | 20.0% | 26.3% | 45.5% | 71.4% | 109% | 167% | 500% | N/A |
| **25.0%** | 4.2% | 8.7% | 13.6% | 19.0% | 25.0% | 42.9% | 66.7% | 100% | 150% | 400% | N/A |
| 27.5% | 3.8% | 7.8% | 12.2% | 17.0% | 22.2% | 37.5% | 57.1% | 83.3% | 120% | 267% | 1000% |
| **30.0%** | 3.4% | 7.1% | 11.1% | 15.4% | 20.0% | 33.3% | 50.0% | 71.4% | 100% | 200% | 500% |
| 32.5% | 3.2% | 6.6% | 10.2% | 14.0% | 18.2% | 30.0% | 44.4% | 62.5% | 85.7% | 160% | 333% |
| 35.0% | 2.9% | 6.1% | 9.4% | 12.9% | 16.7% | 27.3% | 40.0% | 55.6% | 75.0% | 133% | 250% |
| 37.5% | 2.7% | 5.6% | 8.7% | 11.9% | 15.4% | 25.0% | 36.4% | 50.0% | 66.7% | 114% | 200% |
| **40.0%** | 2.6% | 5.3% | 8.1% | 11.1% | 14.3% | 23.1% | 33.3% | 45.5% | 60.0% | 100% | 167% |
| 42.5% | 2.4% | 4.9% | 7.6% | 10.4% | 13.3% | 21.4% | 30.8% | 41.7% | 54.5% | 88.9% | 143% |
| 45.0% | 2.3% | 4.7% | 7.1% | 9.8% | 12.5% | 20.0% | 28.6% | 38.5% | 50.0% | 80.0% | 125% |
| 47.5% | 2.2% | 4.4% | 6.7% | 9.2% | 11.8% | 18.8% | 26.7% | 35.7% | 46.2% | 72.7% | 111% |
| **50.0%** | 2.0% | 4.2% | 6.4% | 8.7% | 11.1% | 17.6% | 25.0% | 33.3% | 42.9% | 66.7% | 100% |
| 52.5% | 1.9% | 4.0% | 6.1% | 8.2% | 10.5% | 16.7% | 23.5% | 31.3% | 40.0% | 61.5% | 90.9% |
| 55.0% | 1.9% | 3.8% | 5.8% | 7.8% | 10.0% | 15.8% | 22.2% | 29.4% | 37.5% | 57.1% | 83.3% |
| 57.5% | 1.8% | 3.6% | 5.5% | 7.5% | 9.5% | 15.0% | 21.1% | 27.8% | 35.3% | 53.3% | 76.9% |
| **60.0%** | 1.7% | 3.4% | 5.3% | 7.1% | 9.1% | 14.3% | 20.0% | 26.3% | 33.3% | 50.0% | 71.4% |

Study this table.

Note how sensitive the low margins are to small changes in price, and how robust the high margins are.

Study it again.

Now think about your business. Are you really going to give profit away just to attain the goal of higher sales? Putting it another way, are you going to sacrifice sanity (profit) for vanity (sales)?

There may be occasions when you believe it is justified. Think again, though, before you do it. And remember, the same happens as a result of any effective reduction in your selling price. Any discount is a price reduction, and so is the giving away of any sales credits, especially needless ones through poor customer service.

Always remember: **the real revenue of your business is the net margin after all variable costs**, whether they are production costs or other costs. For this reason, you should always present your profit statement with the most variable costs at the top, progressing to the most fixed costs at the bottom, regardless of what those costs happen to be (see 3.1e/f). More bad business decisions are made by including fixed costs in an appraisal of product performance than through any other accounting convention. If you are in a régime in which the absorption of fixed costs is mandatory, present an alternative layout of your operating statement each month showing the pure variable and fixed costs separately, with a margin sub-totalled between them, so that you do not lose sight of the reality.

As you can see from the foregoing example and table, a small percentage reduction in your selling price is a larger percentage reduction in your net variable margin. Therefore you must do everything possible to maintain the highest selling price you can realistically achieve, and this is especially important in difficult times when your volume is under threat – the very time when you are most tempted to reduce your price.

Another problem associated with reducing your selling price is that it is difficult to raise it again without giving some clearly identifiable benefit that you were not providing when you lowered the price. If you raise your price too high you can easily lower it, but the reverse just will not work. So if for some reason you have to go through a temporary phase of lower net prices (it would have to be a serious reason) you must make it very clear to your customers that the lowering is a special offer for a limited period. You do not have to state the length of the period as long as the message is loud and clear, and if you hold the low price for more than a short period you must issue strong reminders that it is still a special offer, so that you retain the option to raise the prices again as soon as you are able. **And do not lower your headline price – award a temporary discount instead.**

To attain and hold the highest selling price you must give your customers every possible reason to keep their business with you. As long as your selling price is not unrealistically high and you are the best supplier to deal with in terms of service, they will generally do this. The main elements of your service are:

- a helpful and knowledgeable response at the enquiry and order stage
- a polite and positive demeanour from all staff dealing with customers or potential customers
- willingness to adapt your product or service (for example, modifying your delivery schedule to suit them) provided that this does not incur losses or tie the company to unprofitable or diversionary commitments
- delivering what you have promised when you have promised it
- rapid and effective dealing with after-sales commitments and customer concerns

This clearly involves all the operational departments more strongly than it does the finance department, and you therefore have to spread and repeat this message to all concerned BEFORE you have any price pressure. It must be a permanent attitude within the business.

## 3.1d – Margins and mark-ups

The author has met a remarkably high number of people in the sales function who were not aware of the distinction between mark-up and margin:

- if your product costs £80 and you mark it up by 25%, ie £20, your selling price will be £100.
- but the margin on your sale is 20/100, which is only 20%
- the reason is simple – mark-up is calculated on cost and margin is calculated on selling price

You can imagine the chaos if your sales personnel instructed to achieve a margin of 20% are marking up the products by only 20%. The table on the following page shows the mark-ups required to achieve various margins.

| Margin required | Mark-up to use | Margin required | Mark-up to use | Margin required | Mark-up to use |
|---|---|---|---|---|---|
| 0.5% | 0.50% | 11% | 12.4% | 30% | 42.9% |
| 1.0% | 1.01% | 12% | 13.6% | 35% | 53.8% |
| 1.5% | 1.52% | 13% | 14.9% | 40% | 66.7% |
| 2.0% | 2.04% | 14% | 16.3% | 45% | 81.8% |
| 2.5% | 2.56% | 15% | 17.6% | 50% | 100.0% |
| 3.0% | 3.09% | 16% | 19.0% | 55% | 122.2% |
| 3.5% | 3.63% | 17% | 20.5% | 60% | 150.0% |
| 4.0% | 4.17% | 18% | 22.0% | 65% | 185.7% |
| 4.5% | 4.71% | 19% | 23.5% | 70% | 233.3% |
| 5.0% | 5.26% | 20% | 25.0% | 75% | 300.0% |
| 5.5% | 5.82% | 21% | 26.6% | 80% | 400% |
| 6.0% | 6.38% | 22% | 28.2% | 85% | 567% |
| 6.5% | 6.95% | 23% | 29.9% | 90% | 900% |
| 7.0% | 7.53% | 24% | 31.6% | 95% | 1900% |
| 7.5% | 8.11% | 25% | 33.3% | 97.5% | 3900% |
| 8.0% | 8.70% | 26% | 35.1% | | |
| 8.5% | 9.29% | 27% | 37.0% | | |
| 9.0% | 9.89% | 28% | 38.9% | | |
| 9.5% | 10.50% | 29% | 40.8% | 33.33% | 50% |
| 10.0% | 11.11% | 30% | 42.9% | 66.67% | 200% |

The formula to use is: Mark-up% = Margin x 100 / Cost

## 3.1e – Direct (variable) costs

We have seen above the potentially disastrous effect of lowering selling prices because of the amplified effect of the reduction on the net variable margin. It is obvious that any increase in variable cost will have the same effect on the net margin and thus the same highly-geared effect on the sales volume required to remain profitable. Many good managing directors ask the question "How many widgets do we have to sell to pay for that?" when asked to authorise some unusual item of expenditure; it puts the proposed expenditure firmly into context.

Let us consider the cost-effectiveness of the main types of variable costs:
- direct materials
- consumables
- carriage inwards
- direct labour
- other variable production overheads
- carriage outwards

- non-production variable overheads

**Direct materials** – the first area for maximising the cost of direct materials is in the buying process. Consider the potential of the following arrangements for minimising prices:
- an effective purchasing manager or department who negotiates your supplies
- provision of reliable purchasing forecasts to your suppliers so that they can match their production to your requirements
- forward purchasing contracts to stabilise prices, especially when buying in a foreign currency
- group purchasing schemes, either with other subsidiaries in a formal group, or with non-competitor associates with a shared requirement
- volume discounts, especially if you are part of a group scheme
- economic batch quantities
- storing by the supplier (if it will save you storage costs)

The other element of the material cost is the usage level, which stems from the logistics and production functions:
- proper handling and packaging – preferably re-usable packaging, but if so, it must be controlled; some businesses lose a small fortune every year in unrecovered pallets at suppliers and customers
- safe storage in small economic quantities to avoid deterioration, contamination or theft
- prompt return of unused materials to safe storage
- effective training and machine maintenance to minimise scrap
- prompt investigation and remedial action against scrap and other losses
- strict management of new and discontinued products to avoid a residue of unusable materials
- charging of consumables directly to departmental expenses when they are purchased, to discourage budget owners from holding stocks of consumables

Next, consider the methods of delivering your direct materials inward and your products outward:
- cost-effective transport inward – are your delivery vehicles bringing your materials to you when they are returning to base or are they running without a profitable load?
- express transport inward – monitor the use of express transport in a separate ledger account; frequent usage means that your buying and therefore probably production scheduling are not fully under control

- cost-effective transport outward – (*Real life – an up-market furniture company was running their own vehicle fleet at a cost of £16 per item when a commercial transport company was doing the same for competitors at £8 per item; when asked why they ran their own fleet, the furniture company said that their customers liked to see the company name on the delivery vans . . . but the transport company could have had some of their vehicles specially painted, saving half of the delivery cost*)
- express transport outward – again, monitor this; if it is the request of the despatch department it could be because your production scheduling is awry and products are completed behind schedule (it could even be a purchasing problem resulting in late material arrivals), but if it is because of urgent requests from your customers you should be charging them extra for responding so rapidly at such short notice (that should be in your conditions of sale – see 5.3d)
- overall – your purchasing manager should regularly review the comparative performance and charges of the transport organisations available

Remember that material costs include:
- carriage inwards if not included in the material price
- standard packaging, both of the materials themselves and of the finished product (but special promotional packaging, such as for a special display in a shop, is a marketing cost)
- import duty and any other charges incurred in obtaining the goods

If you do not include the above items in your material cost reporting, you may under-cost your products. You may also buy materials which appear to be cheaper, but are actually more expensive when all costs are considered. Pay attention also to exchange rates when you are sourcing goods overseas.

Finally, your accounting treatment of carriage outwards to customers will depend on whether you run specific deliveries to each customer or have a regular distribution network which is virtually a fixed cost.

**Direct labour** – management of manufacturing labour is very much the responsibility of production management, but there are a number of areas which the financial controller should monitor (some of them assume a standard costing system):
- standard hours of production output as a percentage of actual hours paid for
- standard cost of actual labour hours paid as a percentage actual cost
- down-time (if that is measurable) as a percentage of total labour hours

- absence hours as a percentage of total hours paid

A reasonably sophisticated standard costing system will normally highlight these variances automatically and the problems can be identified by discussion with the production manager. In periods of sustained high down-time, the issue of reducing the labour force must be considered.

The production process itself is an area which may be outside a financial controller's normal professional training, and he must familiarise himself with it by frequent trips around the production area (typically at least 3 times per week in a single-location business). Signs the controller should look for include:

- machinery lying idle, especially where it is in a dismantled state
- large quantities of partly-completed product stacked in front of a machine (indicating a bottleneck)
- large quantities of stock piled anywhere else where it should not normally be
- large quantities of completed components awaiting other components before being packaged in sets
- any form of untidiness

To minimise set-up time between batches, production management normally tries to schedule batches with similar set-up characteristics together. The despatch department, on the other hand, may want all the products for one geographical area together, regardless of their characteristics, so that they can schedule their transport economically. How should that conflict be resolved?

The answer requires collaboration between the despatch and production departments, with possible arbitration by sales and/or finance departments, and lies in determining:

- which is the overall financial constraint: production or delivery – if production is at full stretch and delivery is not, priority may have to be given to production, and vice versa
- whether the cost of the additional transport exceeds the cost of slowing the production – either action can cause late deliveries to customers
- whether there are any penalties for late delivery
- the sales and net margin values of the products involved if you are near the end of an accounting period and trying to reach a profit target for that period (but not at the expense of the next period's profit!)

In addition to the main production costs there are a number of other variable costs which are variously charged to production costs or variable overheads depending on the preference of each business. Whatever name you choose to give to variable overheads, they are a DIRECT cost of production, merely from the fact of being variable. Such costs include:

- electricity – for heating or air conditioning it is a fixed cost, but for production it is normally a variable cost, all though many machines are kept running throughout production hours to save start-up and shut-down delays (and perhaps costs) – note also that the heat generated by production processes may actually reduce the cost of heating the production area
- water
- gas
- cleaning materials
- loose tools and other maintenance materials

Whether you consider these to be variable or fixed costs depends on what influences the usage rates. If they rise and fall largely with production levels they should be treated as variable costs; otherwise they should be treated as fixed costs. You may even find it appropriate to take a percentage as variable and the remainder as fixed.

## 3.1f – Indirect (fixed) costs

Arguments rage over what is and is not a direct cost. The author, being unsophisticated, equates direct costs with variable costs, and indirect costs with fixed costs. The reality, of course, is that most costs have both a fixed and a variable element, and the definition will depend on which of those elements is the larger.

For example, production labour is regarded almost universally as a direct and variable cost. That is true for a company such as Boeing, who lay off large numbers of workers if demand for aircraft falls, and start hiring again when demand rises. But the great majority of businesses are not large enough to have such absolute flexibility, and their labour forces are consequently mainly fixed in nature. There will be occasional hirings and lay-offs, but the labour force remains fairly constant in size. There are small companies who account for labour quite logically and realistically as a fixed cost BELOW the gross margin line.

However, it is up to your company to decide how to classify its costs in order to manage the business, and in particular to price its products correctly. The questions you should ask in relation to minimising fixed costs are:

- do you need them (in other words, is the benefit more than the cost)? – in the case of essential costs that is easy to answer, but it can be difficult to decide in other cases
- is there a cheaper way to achieve the same result? – a different person, a different system, a different route etc
- can you meet the need more cheaply from an external source without serious loss of efficiency? – the use of external accounting centres is a common example
- can you convert them to a variable cost? – we discuss this in 3.1g

## 3.1g – In-house manufacture (variable v fixed)

When a business is expanding, there will be various points at which someone looks at a process performed outside the business and suggests that it is carried out in-house.

When you buy something from a supplier, the cost to you includes the supplier's profit margin. When the item you are buying becomes a large regular supply, you may consider making the item yourself for the following reasons:

- you will have control over the production and delivery of the items you have been buying
- subject to accurate costing, it will be cheaper to make the items yourselves, as you will not be paying for your current supplier's profit margin (you may also have spare facilities which can be used for the production at no extra cost)
- you may even have sufficient capacity to produce the items for other users (be careful; the tail is starting to wag the dog here and you may be entering a business not appropriate to your skills and resources)

However, even if the project looks profitable on paper, there are considerations:

- do you have the right skills to produce the items?
- will the operation absorb too much management time?
- If there is a downturn in the market (or the main product reaches the end of its natural life) will you be left amortising an expensive asset which no longer generates enough (or any) revenue?

In a turbulent business (nowadays it is hard to think of many that aren't) you should **keep your costs variable** as far as practicable. That way, you have the ability to re-shape your business and your supply-lines in accordance with the markets you are serving. Do not give away your flexibility lightly, and do not convert a variable cost into a fixed (make-it-yourself) cost unless the fixed cost will still be economical if a 30% fall occurs in the level of demand.

## 3.1h – Speculative costs

Some costs are neither fixed nor variable, but are discretionary. Common examples are:
- creating or improving facilities for staff
- redecorating or improving the accommodation (except where the lease demands it)
- marketing or advertising campaigns
- membership of trade or professional organisations

It is often difficult to assess the benefits from these costs in relation to the outlay thereon. What tends to happen is that the costs are assumed to be necessary until the business experiences a severe downturn, when the business decides to dispense with the costs and then finds that it does not miss the benefits therefrom.

However, if you have to downgrade the amenities provided to the staff, you should consult with them BEFORE doing so, rather than merely issuing a statement that a benefit has been discontinued. They are your business's lifeblood and they may even have alternative suggestions which would achieve the same objective at an acceptable cost.

This brings us to what is usually the biggest speculative cost of all – marketing.

## 3.1i – Marketing costs

Marketing comprises the following elements:
- study of potential and actual markets and the trends therein
- study of customers (yours and others), their products and specific preferences*, their prices and the degree to which their wants* are met by existing suppliers
- study of competitors, their products, the presentation and delivery thereof, and their qualities

- specification of appropriate products, packaging, presentation and pricing for you to offer
- contacting the potential customers and persuading them to buy your product (at this point, the marketing process crosses over into selling process – we could argue at length as to whether selling is the final stage of marketing or a different process and discipline altogether)

*Note the words "preferences" and "wants". **Marketing is about wants, not needs**. A customer may need a product (especially advice!) but if he doesn't want it, you are unlikely to sell it to him. Therefore you have to address your products to people's wants. If you consider that a potential customer has a particular need, you will have to get him to recognise the need and then to want your offering to fulfil it.

Despite the high level of systematic research and analysis involved in marketing, it remains the biggest speculative cost of most businesses.

Oddly enough, it often appears at the bottom of a profit statement (particularly in the USA) under the throwaway heading of "selling and administration". That is probably acceptable if the marketing cost is small in relation to the business's other operating costs, but if marketing spend is high in relation to sales (as in some foods and clothing) then the cost should be directly related to the margin it generates. An appropriate profit statement layout would therefore be:

| | |
|---|---|
| Sales | £1,000,000 |
| Costs of production | £(700,000) |
| Gross margin | £300,000 |
| | 30% |
| Marketing costs | £(75,000) |
| Gross margin factor | 4.0 |
| Marketing margin | £225,000 |

Note that the marketing expenditure of £75,000 has generated margin of £300,000, a ratio of 4.0 of net income to marketing spend. That is not strictly true, as marketing in one period usually generates income in future periods. However, if the ratio is falling, the marketing spend is clearly becoming less effective – whether this is a fault of the marketing team or of increasing difficulty in the marketplace needs to be considered and acted upon.

*Real life – the author was preparing for a national niche-market food company some speculative 7-year projections involving existing products and their production costs, and various not-yet-invented new products to be introduced in the later years. Upon asking the marketing director to quantify in detail the marketing spend needed for these new products, the author was told "put a million in that year and half a million each in those two."*

*Asked for some detail of the marketing spend, the marketing director replied "No idea – but we do know that a million spend will generate that level of sales." The author referred this to the managing director, who concurred, saying that the same ratios of spend to margin generated were firm and proven. The exact nature of the marketing campaigns was decided in due course once the product had been developed.*

*That may seem to be a somewhat cavalier approach, but for a business to understand so clearly the monetary effect of its marketing efforts is actually quite impressive, and their track record indicated that they got it right.*

## 3.1j – Borrowing costs

Borrowing costs are subject to four major influences:
- the financial package and interest rates which you negotiate with your banks
- running a profitable business
- your success in minimising your working capital
- operating on the minimum of fixed assets required for your activities

These factors are covered below and in 3.2.

## 3.1k – Breakeven level

The single most powerful indicator of a business's health is the **breakeven ratio**, which combines all the elements discussed above. It is a particularly robust ratio in that the numerator and the denominator are in the same units and subject largely to the same influences. There is, however, a degree of approximation in that one has to make assumptions as to which are fixed and which are variable costs, but as long as the classification is reasonable, the ratio will be reliable.

The mechanics are simple. If a business is to break even, the net variable margin generated must exactly cover the fixed costs. If one then divides the fixed costs by the margin percentage, one calculates the breakeven sales.

For example, say a business has fixed costs of £234,000 per month and a net variable margin of 22.5%, the breakeven sales value is £234,000 divided by 0.225, ie £1,080,000.

Suppose that the actual sales for the month were £1,435,000. From this we can calculate an important ratio.

| **Breakeven-to-actual ratio** | Breakeven £ | Actual £ |
|---|---|---|
| Sales | 1,080,000 | 1,435,000 |
| Variable costs | (837,000) | (1,112,125) |
| Net variable margin | 243,000 | 322,875 |
| | 22.5% | 22.5% |
| Fixed costs | (243,000) | (243,000) |
| | 0 | 79,875 |

| | |
|---|---|
| Breakeven : actual sales (1,080,000 / 1,435,000) | 75.3% |
| Breakeven : actual sales (243,000 / 322,875) | 75.3% |

The breakeven-to-actual ratio is 75.3%, or in other words, the breakeven sales of £1,080,000 are 75.3% of the actual sales of £1,435,000. However, the fixed costs are the deciding factor, being the item to be covered, so a better way to calculate the ratio is to divide the fixed costs for the period (£243,000) by the net variable margin (£322,875). The latter formula will work for every period.

What does that tell us? It says that the business is in robust health; it can lose nearly 25% per cent of its sales and still be in profit. As a rough guide, the breakeven-to-actual ratio can be interpreted thus:

- 90-100%        in danger
- 80-90%          needs improvement
- 70-80%          robust
- Under 70%      very robust

If a business is not particularly seasonal, you should review the trend of the breakeven-to-actual ratio each month. A progression of 79%, 81%, 83%, 86% indicates that action is needed – NOW. Where a business has strong seasonal fluctuations, the trend will need to be reviewed over longer intervals and periods, and should also be compared from year to year. For example, if the Christmas and post-Christmas quarters have moved from 74%-91% to 78%-96%, you must take action. That would not be apparent if you merely reviewed the two latest quarters.

Many businesses make the mistake of reviewing the fixed-costs-to-sales ratio. This can be misleading. When margin is being given away to maintain sales and fixed costs are being held static, the ratio will remain constant, creating the illusion of stability when the breakeven-to-actual ratio will show the business to be declining in real profitability.

Therefore, concentrate at all times on keeping your breakeven level as low as possible.


## 3.1I – Value added

The term "value added" means different things to different people, but for the purposes of this book it is the margin after deducting direct material costs (including carriage inwards, which is part of the cost of acquiring the material). In other words, you take a quantity of rubber, metal, plastic, adhesive and whatever, and by processing it into a finished product you increase its value from cost price to selling price. It is still the same quantity of material (minus irrecoverable scrap), but value has been added to it. The value added in respect of a single product or of all products manufactured in a period is expressed as a percentage of the sales value.

To understand the importance of this measurement, let us examine a decision that needs to be made. We have two products, A and B, and can choose to manufacture either one. Which one should we make? The costings are shown below, and for simplicity we can assume that there are no other variable costs after materials and labour.

| Which product to make? | A £ | B £ |
|---|---|---|
| Selling price | 100 | 100 |
| Direct materials | (20) | (50) |
| Value added | 80 | 50 |
| Direct labour | (40) | (20) |
| Variable margin | 40 | 30 |

Most people would answer unhesitatingly that they would make product A, which earns a net variable margin of £40 (40%) in contrast to a £30 (30%) margin for product B. But what if we asked the question differently?

Which product, A or B, would you manufacture:
- in times of weak demand for the products?
- in times of strong demand for the products?

Note that product B uses half as much labour as product A, which means that you could manufacture two of product B in the same time as one of product A. This would give you the following comparison:

| **Which product to make?** | A | B | 2B |
|---|---|---|---|
| | £ | £ | £ |
| Selling price | 100 | 100 | 200 |
| Direct materials | (20) | (50) | (100) |
| Value added | 80 | 50 | 100 |
| Direct labour | (40) | (20) | (40) |
| Variable margin | 40 | 30 | 60 |

For the same labour time (say 4 hours at £10 per hour, but the ratio is the same whatever the rate) we can make one of product A and earn £40, or two of product B and earn £60. Therefore the decision will be:
- in a lean market, manufacture product A, because you will make a higher margin and are therefore less dependent on sales volume (always maximise your margin in difficult times)
- in a strong market, manufacture product B, because you can put more profit through your factory in the same number of hours – but beware, because you will have much a higher working capital requirement (£100 of inventory against £20 and £200 (plus sales tax) of receivables against £100 (plus sales tax), and this will cause the business to absorb cash while it expands, until the money from the higher sales starts to flow in after expiry of the credit period)

Now consider that A and B are exactly the same product. A is the product made entirely in-house, buying the raw materials and doing all the processing with your own labour. B is the same product made by contracting out much of the processing to contractors, who process the material into components (hence the higher material cost) which only need to be assembled by your labour, with perhaps a secret process completed in-house to prevent pirate production of the product. The contract with the other processing business must be structured so that if the market weakens again, you can withdraw from the arrangement within a reasonable length of time and return to in-house manufacture.

So far, we have not mentioned value added in relation to this decision. And it appears to be a misleading measure, since we can earn more from product B with 50% value added than we can from product A with 80% value added. But that is only part of the necessary measure; what we need to understand and compare is value added per hour.

Product B earns £5 per hour more than product A, amounting to an excess of £20 over four hours; hence the £20 difference in gross margin between A and 2B. The lessons are therefore:
- in times of strong demand when your factory is operating at capacity, concentrate on maximising value added per hour, ie on squeezing every possible pound or dollar of added value through your factory in every working hour
- when demand slackens and you are not working at full capacity, concentrate on achieving the highest net variable margin on your products

Inevitably the decision is more complex when you are making a range of products, but the principle is the same.

## 3.1m – Dealing with a downturn

In a major downturn in the economy, the following events usually occur:
- the government insists that all is well
- the public eventually recognises that all is not well
- the government conveniently forgets its earlier statement and trumpets how much it is doing to remedy the situation, and how this will improve matters
- the public recognises that matters are not improving
- the public becomes nervous
- businesses selling to the public report a downturn in activity
- businesses selling to other businesses report a downturn in activity
- the press, whose circulation depends on headlines, highlights the downturn
- public confidence begins to fall sharply, largely as a result of the press coverage
- business confidence begins to fall sharply
- continued press exposure creates an accelerating downward spiral

- some businesses begin to panic, dropping their prices to maintain sales volumes and thus achieve even worse results than before (see section 3.1c)
- a few better-managed businesses organise themselves (see below)
- a rash of business failures occurs
- even some of the better-organised businesses fail, but most of them survive
- the government blames the previous government

The main point in the above sequence of events is that most of the better-organised businesses survive. Therefore you must do two things:
- be a better-organised business yourselves
- concentrate on getting and keeping other better-organised businesses as your customers

Both of these actions should be permanent, ie they should be in place long before any downturn occurs. This entire book is about being a better-organised, more profitable business, but what about your customers and other businesses' customers? Here is what you should do:
- identify which of your existing customers run sound, profitable, cash-generative businesses, and ensure that your position as a supplier to them is rock-solid – in practice this means understanding what their most important buying criteria are, meeting those criteria and striving constantly to improve your ability to meet their requirements (but extracting a good price for doing so)
- identify which companies in the market who are not your customers are also running highly-performing businesses and make a constant and determined attempt to obtain at least a slice of their business (in attempting that, it helps greatly if you can ascertain why they use their present suppliers, so that you know what you have to beat in terms of performance)
- if these businesses are concerned with price alone (some are) be wary of becoming beholden to them
- finally, postpone all non-necessary and non-urgent cash outflow as long as you can – remember that in a depression, cash is more important in many respects than profit
- do not invest in new products or markets unless there is a very high probability of a prompt return in cash flow terms, and that means that the income from the investment must be from a highly reliable source, such as one of the robust companies described above
- finally, be brave – do not drop your selling prices

It may sound trite, but the above actions are actions you should be taking most of the time anyway!

## 3.1n – Dealing with an upturn

An upturn may sound like good news, but be careful. The typical sequence of events is:

- the press, who helped create the downturn, exhaust their supply of bad news and start on another set of clichés, beginning with "green shoots of recovery"
- the government claims that their measures are working and use the same clichés as the press
- nothing much changes for a while
- eventually, there is a slight rise in confidence and activity (partly because people and businesses have adapted to the straitened circumstances and any small improvement is therefore more noticeable)
- the press, possibly with government assistance, produce statistics to show that the rumoured upturn is a fact
- business demand begins to improve, tentatively at first, but then gaining ground
- weaker businesses, who have somehow survived the recession by cutting back on everything possible, try to stock up and take on employees to meet the growth, but they are so cash-starved that they fail – business failures at the start of an upturn are commoner than generally realised
- the economy picks up more strongly
- people have short memories, and the recession fades into history, to be recalled later when the press are short of material
- life seems reassuringly normal and businesses start planning and investing
- the government, assuming it has survived the crisis, celebrates by calling an election (except in countries which have fixed-term governments)

It is apparent from the above that dealing with an upturn has already been largely dealt with in the process of dealing with a downturn. The business which has minimised its losses or even remained in profit as a result of the measures described in 3.1m above will be amongst the best-placed to take advantage of the upturn. Nevertheless, some precautions are required:

- review the progress and condition of your blue-chip customers to ensure that they are still as robust as they were earlier
- concentrate your efforts on expanding with them by understanding their growth plans and the supply requirements which you will need to fulfil to meet them

- if they have had difficulties in obtaining their requirements from other suppliers, ensure that your selling prices reflect your reliability to them
- review the progress of your other customers to identify those of them who are unlikely to survive the upturn, and ensure that you are not exposed to large levels of doubtful debt

Lest the above comments about the press seem somewhat cynical, one should remember that they are only doing their job, which is to generate profits by making their product interesting to consumers!

## 3.2a – Objectives

One could be simplistic and state that the objective is to maximise the business's cash, or to minimise its borrowings, which amounts to the same. Borrowings are merely negative cash, and vice versa.

In practice, most businesses go through various cycles in which the demands on the funds available vary, sometimes heavily. Cycles can be:
- regular – normally monthly, quarterly and yearly
- irregular – created by market conditions, expansion or reduction programmes and irregular external events (exchange rates, political events etc)

In practice, therefore, cash control involves not only a permanent pressure to maximise cash, but also the ability to foresee and provide for events over which the business has limited if any control. It follows that the better the business controls its regular cash flow, the more headroom it will have to cope with the irregular events, predictable or otherwise.

## 3.2b – Elements of cash control

There are four elements to cash performance:
- optimum profit performance (see 3.1)
- minimum working capital level consistent with efficient operation
- effective use of fixed assets
- well-organised treasury (banking, forex etc)

We have already dealt with profit performance in section 3.1. It is readily apparent from the cash flow statement (appendices C8 and C9) that profit is the prime generator of cash, and the only recurring one. You can improve your cash position by reducing your working capital and fixed assets, but there is a minimum level below which these elements cannot be reduced without harming the business. They therefore provide scope for one-off improvement of the cash position, but not for recurring cash flow. Your fundamental security therefore depends on an ongoing stream of adequate profit.

Nevertheless, your business will be considerably healthier if you keep your working capital and fixed assets at the minimum effective level. Moreover, if they are allowed to go out of control, particularly in times of poor profit performance, they can cause the business to become insolvent. They therefore need to be strictly managed.

Management is by operational managers – therefore the controller has to have close working relationships and, if necessary, teaching skills. Operational managers may have to be taught the fundamentals of cash flow.

Finally, there is the question of treasury, ie the management of the funds or borrowings themselves. That is a separate topic in itself, the subject of many other publications and even a separate qualification. However, we shall consider the main aspects of treasury in this section.

## 3.2c – Indicators of cash performance

Quite simply, your overall net bank balance is the indicator of your cash performance. However, you need to understand the many differing factors affecting your cash level, and this involves several specific ratios.

Your **gearing** is the ratio of your debt finance (overdrafts, loans, capital leases etc – see 3.2i) to your equity (shareholders' capital and reserves). Until the late 1980s a strict view was taken by bankers and other providers of finance. The riskier your business (eg newly-developed high technology), the lower the gearing demanded by the lenders to your business. In the case of a less risky business (eg property investment) a higher gearing would be tolerated. As a rough example, if you were operating a mainstream manufacturing business and your debt finance was 3 times your equity (ie your gearing was 300%), the bank gave you a hard time.

But in the late 1980s a strange thing happened. The word "leverage" (the US pronounce "lever" as the UK pronounces "clever", which it isn't in this case) replaced the word gearing and US banks promoted highly leveraged deals (they use nouns as verbs) as being the way forward. Within a short space of time, high gearing under the new name of leverage became a matter of pride instead of a major concern. Highly leveraged deals were considered to be at the forefront of business financing, at least until the colossal crash of the 2000s. At the date of writing it remains to be seen whether the world will regain its senses; the author is not convinced.

Whatever the foibles of the current financial markets, 3 divided by 1 is still 3, and in a mainstream manufacturing or service business you should aim to keep your gearing well below 2.0 as a general guide.

However, the gearing ratio is a result of several other ratios and we need to consider these individually, as they are subject to separate management and controls.

**Days of production** in a manufacturing business are a measure of **raw material levels**. If your overall raw material stock is equivalent to 25 days of production and your lead time from suppliers is 15 days, then you are carrying up to 10 days' worth of unnecessary stock, with an equivalent unnecessary amount of borrowing and overdraft interest.

Therefore you should seek to reduce your stock to as near to 15 days' worth as you dare, with a small surplus to avoid stock-outs in the event of a delivery delay. You may also need to make goods in advance for peak periods which exceed your production capacity, but these should be strictly controlled. Stock requirements for public customers are often more difficult to forecast than for business customers, particularly if the product is not a regular necessity.

**Days of sales** is a corresponding measure of **finished goods inventory**. If you are carrying finished goods equivalent to 60 days' sales and you can replenish your finished stocks in less than a month, then you are carrying at least twice the quantity of finished goods you should be holding. Bring your inventory level down steadily until you start suffering stock-outs and then raise the level very slightly. Of course, you may have different inventory levels for different products according to the supply and production lead times, but you should work with your finished goods supervisor to establish these and work accordingly.

An effective incentive pay for a finished goods supervisor is a monthly amount for each day of finished goods below a target level. For example you may award £50 for each day under 30 days, so that if the supervisor achieves 26 days, he has an extra £200 on his gross pay, less penalties for any stock-outs.

IMPORTANT – note that goods should be PULLED through the production process to meet actual or estimated demand, so that only goods which are expected to sell are produced. There is no point in producing unwanted goods merely to fill a production line if the goods are not required, EXCEPT when you are stock-building for a period where sales demand is expected to outstrip production capacity.

Many managers have difficulty in grasping that concept, and believe that a production line should always be running as close to 100% capacity as possible. That is ridiculous, because in that case you are expending wages, oncost, materials, power, consumables and repairs for no reward. If you pay your wages and send your staff home early, you are still saving the cost of materials, power, consumables and repairs. Better still, get your staff involved in tidying and repairing the factory. Few Western factories run at the level of cleanliness and tidiness (and therefore efficiency) of East Asian factories, and time spent in improving the workplace and engendering pride in the factory is more financially rewarding than producing products that nobody will buy.

**Days of sales** are also a measure of **accounts receivable**. If your normal credit period for customers is 30 days from date of invoice (note that that is not the same as 30 days from the end of the month) and your trade receivables (net of sales tax) are equivalent to 55 days of sales, then your cash collection process is failing and you need to work with your credit control team to bring it under control (see 3.2e).

Note that many factories tend to be **back-end loaded** in their production output. For most of each month they run behind their targeted output, and in the final few days of production the effort increases so that a high output in the final week ensures that they achieve their output target. However, the products have to be delivered to the customers, and many of the sales which they regard as April's are regarded by their customers (justifiably) as May's purchases. The customers will therefore tend to pay a month later than expected, causing a cash flow shortfall.

**Days of purchases** operates in a similar way to days of sales. Calculate your average days of supplier credit (net of sales tax) against the level of credit purchases you have made. If you are not taking the full credit allowed to you, investigate the payment patterns for the major suppliers to detect where you are paying needlessly early. Conversely, check that you are not forgoing early settlement discounts which you would rather have instead of the cash payment.

**Working capital as a percentage of annual sales** is an odd measurement, as it compares a balance at a point in time with a result or a forecast over a period of arbitrary length. The ratio on its own therefore tells you nothing. However, it can be compared with the net variable margin against sales (logically for the same year) and a non-mathematical conclusion drawn:

- if your working capital to annual sales is a high percentage in relation to your net variable margin against the sales for the same

year, your business will consume cash as it grows and liberate cash as it shrinks
- if the opposite is true, your business will generate cash as it grows, and lose it as it scales down

This can only be taken as a rough rule of thumb, as there is no basis in mathematics for choosing a 12-month period to make the comparison. However, it works! A highly reputed business turnaround specialist advises that as a rough rule-of-thumb the working capital as a percentage of annual sales should be kept below one half of the gross margin percentage.

**Bank interest actual against budget** is another useful measure, provided that you adjust your budgeted figure to the actual rate your business is paying. You may find peaks of borrowing that can be smoothed out by rescheduling some items.

All of the above measures highlight the importance of controlling your balance sheet. As has been mentioned elsewhere in this book:
- an ordinary controller keeps control of the profit performance
- a good controller also keeps control of the capital employed

## 3.2d – Working capital control – inventory

Before we discuss the cash implications of inventory, let us consider some other important aspects. The keeping of **a high level of goods in inventory can result in a wide range of problems**:
- items become more difficult to store in an orderly and accessible manner
- items are sometimes stored in the wrong place
- they therefore become harder to find, so that:
    - the wrong items are sometimes selected
    - production time is lost while the correct items are found
    - sales are lost (possibly permanently, if urgent) as a result of delays
    - items already in inventory have to be reordered because they cannot be found
- storage costs increase as a result of the additional space required
- inventory is stored in non-storage areas, such as walkways on the production floor, and causes:
    - safety hazards (by being stacked unsuitably or by exposing dangerous substances to impact)
    - a slowing of production through obstruction of movement and access

- dangerous (eg inflammable) items can become an increased hazard through being stored improperly
- inventory counting becomes more difficult, resulting in:
    - additional supervisory time spent in counting
    - inaccurate counting (especially through mis-identification of items in the wrong place)
    - further supervisory time spent in investigating and verifying inaccurate counts
    - problems in the annual audit, reducing auditor confidence in the whole business
- inventory becomes damaged or unusable because:
    - it is insecurely stacked or stored and becomes broken, faded, damp, corroded, decomposed etc
    - its shelf-life expires before it can be used or sold
    - owing to changes in regulations it becomes illegal before it can be used or sold
    - owing to changes in product design, components become unusable
- accounting problems subsequently occur:
    - unexpected write-offs have to be made when unusable surpluses are discovered
    - as a result of inaccurate estimates of material costs misleading margins can be reported or forecast (if costs are higher than forecast, profit will be below expectations, but if costs are overestimated as a result of previous write-offs etc, sales prices can be set too highly and business can be lost)
    - inappropriate decisions can be made regarding the future of products
    - the true performance of the business is not clearly understood

It can easily seen from the above that not only can overstocking result in numerous operational problems, but it can affect the recorded material costs and cause profitability problems. Inventory therefore has to be held at the lowest practicable level, the test of which is that a few stock-outs occur (if you are not getting any stock-outs, you are carrying too much inventory, and if you are getting a lot of stock-outs you are not carrying enough). The following areas need to be addressed to attain that elusive optimum inventory level:

- product design
- forecasting
- buying
- storekeeping

- process flow (and especially constraint management)
- accounting

**Product design** – the way in which your products are designed can have a major impact on your working capital. The ideal product is 99% standard off-the-shelf components and 1% design genius which makes the combination of those simple components out-perform every other product in the industry, in a way that your competitors cannot match. The more items in your product range are served by the same easily-obtainable components, the easier your inventory is to manage. If instead of using off-the-shelf parts you use custom-designed parts you will incur problems:

- your product cost will be higher (this will be acceptable only if the increase in cost is matched by a greater increase in selling price to the extent that your net variable margin increases by at least the percentage of your cost increase)
- your buying and storage activities will be more complex, risking some of the problems described above
- custom components tend to have to be bought in considerable minimum quantities; this means that in the declining period of a product's lifespan it becomes difficult to avoid being left with large numbers of surplus custom components (or else when the product's selling price has declined, you are incurring a higher cost for ordering the custom components in smaller quantities)
- if the customers for your range of products need to keep spare components, they will have to hold a wider and more expensive range; they will therefore have working capital problems of their own, and you will have more difficulty in minimising your receivables (see 3.2e).

*Real life* – be aware, however, that off-the-shelf components can also cause problems. A company designing and making sophisticated electronic equipment based their electronics on software specially designed for them. They decided to build a major new product on off-the-shelf software for the above and other reasons, and the product was brought successfully to pre-production stage. At that point the software provider (a worldwide software house whose continuing income depended on upgrades) produced the new version of their software. The old version of the software would not be supported indefinitely, but new product would not operate on the new version without substantial modification. The company therefore faced major problems:

- *it had to modify its new product, delaying the highly-publicised launch by months*

- *even with the new software platform incorporated, it could not guarantee to support its products indefinitely, since there would be further new versions and the problem would recur*

*The company therefore bought a large supply of the latest software against an estimated sales pattern, thereby increasing its inventory substantially and incurring a high unbudgeted cash outflow, causing much difficulty.*

**Forecasting** – if your company's budgeting process is reasonably accurate and your product developments are well managed, your purchasing manager will be able to give your suppliers fairly accurate forecasts of your buying levels for each year. This accuracy will confer several advantages:
- your suppliers can plan their production, stocking and despatch accurately, without panic orders, last-minute changes and other traumas which typically bedevil attempts at efficient supply
- they will be much more likely to meet your requirements on the key aspects of your buying:
   - minimum order quantities
   - delivery frequency and lead times
   - tolerances, packaging and other specifications
   - price and related terms
   - credit payment period
- because you are a well-organised customer, they will be more helpful in times of difficulty
- they will want to work with you if there are projects of potential mutual benefit

You will seldom be able to forecast your exact volume from suppliers, so err on the side of understatement. This means that you will meet your buying commitments with just a little extra (not too much), which will create the best possible reputation with your suppliers. And reputations spread.

**Buying** – how you buy your materials will depend on several factors:
- the pattern of orders to your customers (anything from very regular to entirely unpredictable)
- the lead time for delivery to your customers (the longer it is, the easier your buying will be)
- your production time (you do not want to be holding unnecessarily large inventory)
- the lead time for delivery from your suppliers (the optimum from both the cash and efficiency angles is frequent small deliveries, provided that it does not adversely affect the effective buying price, after considering the cost of stockholding)

- any safety factors built in to the above (for example, dual-sourcing essential supplies, say 70%-30%, so that you have a fall-back supplier in times of difficulty . . . but this may affect your buying price adversely)

It follows that you may have to use different buying parameters for different parts of your business. A high-volume product will typically require:
- a delivery schedule to enable you always to have just enough to meet your production needs, with only a small safety stock, thereby delaying your cash outflow as long as is practicable
- a low price to recognise the volume of business you are giving your supplier
- some businesses prefer bulk-buying to obtain substantial price advantages, but if you are a high-volume customer and a good payer, you should have enough negotiating power over your suppliers to enable a frequent low-volume supply, still at a good price

By contrast, a low-volume product (especially a highly-specialised product) would normally require flexibility on the part of a supplier to supply small quantities of materials, possibly at irregular intervals, with a consequent penalty. From a cash flow standpoint, the higher price which might arise from such a supply would normally be outweighed by the benefit of not tying up funds in long-standing stocks.

A higher-volume product approaching the end of its life can require special treatment. This is considered in the **product lifespan** analysed in appendix A3.

**Storekeeping** – there are many ways of storekeeping, and how your stores are best organised will depend upon:
- the types of materials used in your manufacture
- the processes used in your manufacture
- whether you produce a large number of small products, or a small number of large ones
- whether your products are broadly similar or not (and whether they are sold off-the-shelf or to order)

In general, however, a storekeeping system should have the following features:
- clearly designated locations for all items
- neighbouring locations for items likely to be used together
- easy access to all locations, especially those of high-volume items

- protection from all factors likely to cause deterioration of stored items
- FIFO (first-in, first out) issuing of all items from raw materials to production (not as easy as it sounds)
- real-time recording of all stock movements
- automatic provisions in the records for all out-of-date items in accordance with accounting policy
- designated areas and procedures for unsatisfactory items
- accounting facilities per section 4.1 and 4.2.

**Process flow** can either involve:
- a single material or a few materials being processed into a large number of products (eg moulding or extrusion)
- a larger number of materials being processed into a smaller number of products (eg laptop computers)

It is in the latter case where the greatest scope for problems occurs, and thus the more opportunity to take competitive advantage by minimising these problems. The modern term for this science is "lean manufacture" and any manager or supervisor involved in a production process in whatever way (finance, marketing, engineering, design etc) should be familiar with the concept.

The main elements of managing lean manufacture are:
- a detailed understanding of the upstream supply chain and a close relationship with your suppliers
- a detailed understanding of the flow and dynamics of your processes
- a process layout that specifies and allows for space for materials awaiting processing
- "pulling" rather than "pushing" materials through the production process, ie producing to demand
- immediate identification, reporting and clearance of constraints (bottlenecks)
- awareness by all production staff of these requirements

The most important point above is that of PULLING, NOT PUSHING materials through production.

*Real life – to understand this fully, carry out the following experiment next time you attend an extended family dinner of the type normally held on traditional festivals or feast days. At the end of such a dinner what normally happens is that the many participants all busy themselves stacking crockery, cutlery and glassware at the dining table, carrying it through to the kitchen, and crowding around in a confined space bumping into each other throughout the washing, drying and storing. All the available space appears to be taken up. The process takes an inordinately long time and causes considerable frustration, with people bumping into each other, putting items in the wrong places, and even dropping and breaking items.*

*To avoid this nonsense, allocate the main tasks:*
- *one person who knows where all the hardware is stored puts it away – and does nothing else*
- *one person dries the hardware and places it on a work surface for storing, but does nothing else and does not even do any drying unless there are fewer than two dry items awaiting storing*
- *one person washes the hardware and places it on the draining board, but does nothing else and does not even do any washing unless there are fewer than two items on the draining board awaiting drying*
- *one person collects hardware from the dining table, sweeps off any food remains into a receptacle and places the hardware beside the sink awaiting washing, but does nothing else and does not even bring any hardware unless there are fewer than two items awaiting washing (if the kitchen is a long way from the dining table, set up a small table half-way, and have another person operating on the same principle: no action unless there are fewer than two items waiting)*

*Everybody else must avoid the process altogether, not even passing a plate – this must be strictly enforced.*

*What happens is extraordinary. Nobody appears to do much work; they are all standing around chatting, and occasionally handling a piece of hardware. After several minutes you will be seriously worried and will check back up the production line to see what is happening. You will discover three circumstances:*
- *a remarkable amount of work has already been done*
- *those still seated around the dinner table are enjoying a warm after-dinner glow, especially your normally troublesome Auntie Histamine, who is half-way through a large cigar and what must be her fourth brandy*
- *those appointed to do the tasks are moving unhurriedly, not bumping into anyone, not dropping anything and not becoming frustrated*

That is the difference between pulling and pushing items through a production line. Pushing creates traffic jams, misroutings, breakages, missing items and frustration, while pulling means that everyone does what is required, everything that is required and only what is required.

Once you are pulling goods through a production line, you will still encounter problems because the flow through the various processes is inevitably uneven. Even if you have exactly the right capacity at each stage in the process (virtually impossible) there will be breakdowns, misprocessing, rejects and a host of other occurrences which will create imbalances in the flow. These imbalances will result in greater pressure on certain processes, and when the factory runs at full capacity your slowest process will become the **constraint** (bottleneck).

In general, a factory should not be run at full capacity; time is needed for maintenance, training, upgrading and other essential activities. Nevertheless, there may be times, especially in a seasonal or contract-driven business, when the factory has no option but to produce at full capacity. At such times, **the output of the factory is the output of the process which is the constraint**. Therefore it is crucial that you identify your constraint and take immediate action to relieve the constraint.

This is done by an approach which we shall call **QUADCOMBS**. The order in which the actions in the quadcombs approach are taken will depend on what is causing the constraint, and comprise:

- **Quality** – perform a quality check on all items waiting to enter the constraint; if you process defective items through the constraint, your entire facility is effectively doing nothing
- **Upstream** processes – give priority in the upstream processes to any products which must go through the constraint; if you delay these items to process non-constraint items, the constraint may run out of work, and again your factory will effectively be doing nothing
- **Alternatives**– if there are any available, make use of them:
  - different processes meeting the same specification as the constraint
  - contracting out the process to another business (this may cost more, but save money overall)
  - alternative materials which do not need to go through the constraint (ie pre-processed)
- **Demand** – prioritise items waiting to go through the constraint by demand; there is no point in wasting the constraint's time in processing something that is not yet needed; you are likely to hold back something which would result in an immediate sale
- **Control** – monitor the constraint closely to ensure that it performs to maximum capacity; do not leave it unattended at any time

- **Operators** – ensure that there are always trained operators available for the constraint; if it is idle because nobody is available to run it, your factory is again doing nothing
- **Maintenance** – keep a secure supply of essential spares beside the constraint, so that a minimum of time is lost in the event of a breakdown, and carry out extra levels of preventive maintenance, especially before processing critical orders
- **Batches** – if a batch being processed through the constraint does not use all of the constraint's capacity, process part of another batch to use the full capacity; never run the constraint at less than full capacity, because if your constraint is only running at 70% capacity, your whole factory is only running at 70%
- **Set-up** – arrange your batches into groups with similar set-ups on the constraint, so that there will be minimal time lost in adjusting the set-up between batches (this is called "cascading")

The above measures, applied relentlessly and intelligently, will allow the constraint to operate at its practical maximum capacity. What will happen when you have achieved this and the process is no longer creating a constraint? Quite simple – some other process will now be the constraint, and you apply the quadcombs approach all over again with the new constraint (it is also possible to have more than one constraint if there are several production lines). The logical outcome of this is that constraint management is a large and permanent part of lean production, and is a way of life for efficient production managers.

It is obvious from above that all managers are involved in lean manufacture – purchasing, inventory control, finance, engineering, production, sales, everyone. **The book "The Goal" (see appendix D) by Eli Goldratt** brilliantly explains this culture in the form of a novel about a production team who encounter every constraint difficulty imaginable in a race to prevent their factory from being shut down.


Of course, in order to eliminate your constraints, you have first to identify them:
- visual – each production process should have a area marked in front of it in which a defined maximum quantity of material for processing may be stored; if the area is empty and nothing is moving, then the constraint is upstream, but if the area is full and nothing is moving, then either this process or one downstream is the constraint
- numerical – records of quantities completed each shift by each process, together with reports of stoppages, rejects and other problems, should give a clear indication of which processes are

constraints; **the book "Continuous Improvement" by Wayne Scott Ross** gives excellent instruction on how these figures should be recorded and analysed for action – see appendix D

**Equipment set-up** – one of the main false arguments for long production runs is the avoidance of time spent on setting up production equipment for each different product. In most cases this is a false concern, because:

- the more often people perform set-ups (or any task), the more proficient and speedy they become at it (*real life: a team of divers securing 25-tonne mooring blocks for lifting on board a work vessel took 15 minutes underwater per block initially, but progressively reduced the water time to less than 1 minute*)
- production can usually be scheduled for short-term "cascading" of the products by the most critical setting – (*real life: piston-rings can be manufactured in order of diameter, and chemical mixes can be cascaded in order of the base chemicals used, starting with mixes of chemicals A-B-C in progressive percentages, then moving to A-B-D etc, thereby increasing the tolerance for minute residues from the previous mix*)

The cascading is of course within a short timescale, otherwise you will tend again to long production runs.

In cases where there is a specialist team which carries out the set-up, the performance pay of the team should be based on the good output of the shift immediately following the set-up. In the case of the chemical mixing, for example, if the team works too slowly they will be penalised by the loss of production in the following shift, and if they work too hastily they will be penalised by the detection of impurities in the output thereafter.

**Inventory accounting** – systems conventionally provide details and/ or summaries of the volumes and values of inventory held in the major categories, together with any provisions made against these values. However, the most useful information for managing inventory levels is the number of days of production or sales of each item held. This should be provided by the inventory system.

**Service industries** – in a service industry, too high a level of work in progress can also cause difficulties:

- staff become overstretched, reducing the quality of the work done
- staff of inadequate capability or insufficient familiarity with the work are assigned to cover gaps, resulting in poor quality of work
- jobs are finished in order of the customers who shout the loudest (who may well not be the customers who pay the most promptly)

- management time becomes diverted to troubleshooting, reducing the effort in obtaining ongoing work (indeed ongoing work may become undesirable, which is a dangerous state of affairs unless it is work of an unsuitable nature)

The key to minimising service work in progress is efficient project management. That is not part of the ambit of this book, but there are a number of aspects of project management in which the financial controller can play an effective part:

- set up service contracts so that **services are billed at frequent intervals** (weekly if possible):
    - this causes projects to be reviewed more frequently so that they can be billed correctly, which means that problems are resolved rapidly)
    - clients will more readily approve smaller invoices which are for work which is fresh in the mind than larger invoices for work which has become a vague memory (this also means that clients keep closer contact with projects, which helps in solving problems rapidly)
- ensure that the accounting for contracts is real-time, so that the costs expended on a service are always kept clearly in focus
- ensure that provisions for unrecorded costs are maintained up-to-date to avoid complacency and possibly under-billing of fees under the misapprehension that all costs have been incurred and charged
- when a contract begins to go off-budget or a non-contract service begins to lose profitability, report this to operational management immediately and chase them until action is taken

**Product discontinuation** – once a product is incapable of further development, it enters the "cash cow" stage, in which it should be "milked" for as much profit as it will provide, without any further investment (appendix A3). There will, however, come a time when the end of its economic life is in sight and at that stage the product must be "managed out". At this stage there is planning to be done:

- establish a precise date for discontinuation
- devise the publicity which will be needed (this may be merely a warning to the market place regarding the discontinuation, or it may concern promotion of the replacement product instead of the current product, or it could involve both streams of publicity)
- estimate the number of products and spare parts required to meet warranty commitments remaining after discontinuation (for some products you may set this level at zero on the basis that it is more economical and better publicity to provide warranty claimants with

the new product free of charge rather than to repair or replace the old product)
- harmonise your inventory and your materials purchasing (see below)
- stick to the plan, or you will be facing an uncontrollable situation

Harmonising the inventory is vital. Typically, the product being discontinued will comprise a number of materials all subject to different buying patterns, some of the materials being unique to the product and some common to other products. Some of the materials will be obtainable in small quantities, but others may only be obtainable in large quantities, negotiated by your purchasing department to obtain a low price when the product was a big seller.

Once you have calculated the material requirement for your final production phase, review your minimum order quantities and ensure that you will not be left with a collection of unusable materials after discontinuation. If you do this in good time, you may be able to negotiate part orders from your suppliers without a price penalty.

Once the product has been discontinued, ensure that the product numbers and material numbers no longer required are removed from the current list on the system (it may be appropriate to leave this until the end of the financial year, but no later).

Once all the old products are out of warranty, dispose of the related stocks as advantageously as possible. Set a date for this and ensure that it is done, otherwise the components will continue to clutter your storage area for years. Engineers (occasionally justifiably) are traditionally reluctant to dispose of old components, especially when they relate to a product which was highly successful.

*Real life – a company manufacturing diagnostic equipment had a stock of external casings complete with video screens relating to a product no longer sold. The financial director ascertained that these old exteriors could be equipped with the current internal workings, and instructed that units in the older casings be sold at a reduced price (but still profitable) offer to customers who normally found the company's products too expensive. The products were all sold in a short time and at a small profit, instead of incurring the large loss which would have resulted from scrapping the old exteriors. Note that even if the hybrid units had been sold at a small loss, there would still have been a cash flow benefit to the business. Cash and profit are sometimes in conflict!*

The process of counting inventory is discussed in 4.2.

## 3.2e – Working capital control – receivables (credit control)

*Real life: X-Co designed and distributed PVC-U window and door systems to window manufacturers throughout the UK and Ireland. Unlike aluminium windows, which can be assembled on site, the PVC-U products require welding on bulky welding machines and therefore have to be made in a factory. The industry is structured roughly as follows:*

- *window installers measure and specify windows and order them from window fabricators*
- *window fabricators manufacture from materials and components bought from window systems companies*
- *window systems companies design and test window systems, and buy the frames, cross-pieces and other linear components from extrusion companies, and other components (locks, handles etc) from specialists*
- *extrusion companies extrude the lengths, which have much more complex structures than are apparent from viewing a completed window, through dies built to the system companies' designs, using plastic granules and additives bought from plastics companies*

*Some of the larger, well-known window companies combine some or even all of the above stages, but the public only sees the installation end of the industry. The window industry in the UK has traditionally had a reputation for poor management and for sharp practices (the term "cowboy" is heard frequently), particularly at the fabricator and installer end of the chain, and bad debts are endemic therein.*

*X-Co was acquired by a larger group, who rapidly discovered that their acquisition was in much worse health than had appeared. A new managing director and then a new finance team were installed, and one of the biggest problems faced by the finance team was that of bad debts, which amounted to a horrific 4.0% of sales value. To make matters worse, X-Co's customers were typically under-funded owner-managed businesses in which the banks had effectively a greater stake than the owners. Moreover, since X-Co supplied nearly all the raw materials of the customers, X-Co had an even bigger stake than the banks.*

*As the owners of the customer businesses were untrained, few of them managed their own working capital properly and thus most of X-Co's customers had difficulty at one time or another in paying X-Co on time. Average receivables in X-Co's books stood at 78 days of sales.*

*Initially, the work involved was firefighting; there were three types of non-payer to deal with:*

- ***those who could not pay*** – where feasible, X-Co discussed the problems with the customers and agreed payment plans to help them reduce their debt while still trading with X-Co
- ***those who would not pay*** because they had a genuine grievance – X-Co resolved their grievances as rapidly as possible to get the payments flowing again (sometimes this meant helping them with their operations; for instance, were they holding more stock than they needed?)
- ***those who would not pay*** because they were being awkward – X-Co gave them one chance to pay, and if not X-Co pursued the debt by legal means, and in almost all cases did not deal with them again

While debts were being chased, X-Co started with the front end of the business. The sales force was already well trained in the technicalities of the components they sold, and in the customers' manufacturing processes. However, X-Co was developing a range of higher-performance products and further training was needed. In addition to formal practical training in selling skills, the sales force was instructed in the new product designs and the relevant manufacturing process, which could involve a wide range of differing customer machinery.

That improved the sales, but it did nothing for X-Co's appalling bad debt record.

Firstly, they moved the sales staff into the same office as the R&D/ technical department: same office, same photocopier, same coffee machine, same toilets; there was no escape. The immediate result was that every perceived problem out there in the market place was relayed promptly to R&D. The solutions could be in either direction; perhaps the customers were using the wrong settings on their production machinery or perhaps there was a genuine problem with the design of a component. Either way, the problems began to be resolved immediately on discovery; the number of customer complaints fell steadily and excuses for non-payment were reduced.

Step two was to train the sales force in basic financial dynamics. Working in groups, they attacked case studies of businesses which appeared to be doing well, but on analysis proved to be heading for a fall. From the startling figures these case studies returned, the sales force learned some of the most important lessons in business:

- ***net variable margin*** is much more important than sales value (if you have a 10% margin and reduce your selling price by 5%, you have to double your sales volume – and hence working capital – to achieve the same result before interest);

- **net variable margin per hour or day** is even more important in a busy market;
- **low working capital** is another permanent target, and in manufacturing that means low inventory as well as low receivables.

X-Co then briefed their delivery drivers to report back on disorganised storage and assembly areas at customers' premises. The sales force also began paying more attention to their customers' production processes and soon identified many customers whose processes needed streamlining, with a consequent reduction of inventory and greater ease in paying their debts. X-Co's technical people duly visited the trouble-spots and straightened their manufacture.

This caused an occasional hiatus in sales as customers consumed (and in some cases even returned) unnecessarily high stocks. The truck drivers assisted in this process by shifting some customers on to smaller, more frequent deliveries; as the fleet did a regular weekly circular route, this caused minimal extra effort. On the return journeys, the trucks picked up material from suppliers, thereby reducing buying prices and inventory levels, further enhancing X-Co's margins.

Then came the killer punch. X-Co introduced a simple performance pay scheme wherein each salesperson received an extra £50 each month for each day his area's days of debt were below 60 days. The average pay-out on the first month of the scheme was £150 and the reaction was immediate. The sales force demanded that a receivables ageing list be mailed to them every Friday afternoon for perusal over Saturday breakfast. Calls were made and sales itineraries adjusted so that delinquent payers found the sales representatives at their door the following week. The days of debt fell; the sales team's morale rose in line with their bank balances.

The credit controller began to put on weight, as he no longer had enough to worry about. So X-Co asked the sales team to identify which of their customers were having difficulty in collecting their own debts. The credit controller began visiting those customers and advising and training their sales ledger and credit control staff. He had a deep personal interest in this activity as he was also on the performance pay scheme, and X-Co's days of debt duly fell further as their customers improved their own debt collection.

R&D launched a new high-quality product range and customers immediately complained that the new items were expensive and would reduce their profit. The sales team, having been trained in the practicalities of net margin per hour (see 3.1l), demonstrated that the new products could be *manufactured much more rapidly and thus more profitably. Again, the customers responded favourably.*

*And what about the bad debts? On a static turnover of £8 million (X-Co was seeking expansion of profit, not of sales) the bad debts over 4 years were £320K, £190K, £120K and £8K. X-Co cancelled their credit insurance. The cowboys of old were nowhere to be seen, and when X-Co was sold to an acquisitive group, its annual return on capital was 106%.*

Controlling receivables is like controlling anything else; you must exert control from the very beginning of the process, or you will spend the rest of your time playing catch-up. Control of receivables therefore begins with the introduction of each new credit customer. **When a new customer applies for a credit account**, you will need to verify their creditworthiness by at least two of the following methods:

- a bank letter – this is regarded as a high-quality reference, as banks are professionally cautious about the level of credit which they recommend; however, this can work against you in that a customer can be good for a much higher level of credit than the bank is prepared to recommend, particularly if you are considering supplying a major percentage of their purchases
- a reference from a reputable credit agency is often used – this is normally a quick and effective process, but it often suffers from the lack of close contact between the agency and the customer, and can be a somewhat anodyne document
- trade references are commonly used, normally from two independent sources – the problem here is that a business which is habitually in credit difficulties usually maintains good relations with a small number of suppliers, partly because they are the most essential suppliers, and partly for the purpose of trade references (there may also be close personal relationships, of which you are unaware, with the referees)
- the latest audited accounts are often suggested – the problem is that these can legally be over a year and a half out-of-date in the UK, and longer in some other countries; moreover, while their layout gives some indication of the business's performance and position, they are far from ideally presented
- the most recent management accounts are often much more informative, and of course much more up-to-date – if they are well designed and well presented and accurately compiled they will be the best yardstick of the business's robustness, but you have no independent reassurance that they have not ignored some major adverse circumstances (however, the fact that a business can readily produce up-to-date management information is itself encouraging)

- previous knowledge of the customer or its management team – if positive, this is generally reassuring, as business is transacted amongst people, and good managers will tend to run good businesses wherever they go, although they may not always have the same level of control
- a visit to the customer's site is essential for all prospective medium-to-large customers – the instinctive impression you gain from seeing their operation and meeting and discussing business with their team is in many ways the safest information you can obtain, although you must remember that they will be putting on their best show for you

The above may make depressing reading, for it is readily apparent that there is no perfect reference available for a prospective customer. Which methods you choose will depend on your assessment on what are the most reliable in the circumstances, and sometimes simply on which methods are available.

**Calculating the credit limit** for a new customer can be difficult, but you can start with a formula:
- take their estimate of purchases in one month
- note the length of time from the first delivery to the first payment (if they purchase on day 1 and are on 30 days' credit from date of invoice, the cash should start coming in at the beginning of month 2, but in practice supplies tend to be "bundled" for payment and you may receive a single payment for the first 2 or even 4 weeks of sales)
- your assessment of the customer's creditworthiness will affect your decision: in the above circumstances you would probably award a credit limit between 40 and 60 days of the expected month's sales value PLUS sales tax or value added tax – if in doubt, set a lower limit and advise the customer that it may be raised on the basis of a good payment record
- doing increased business with a customer will often require an upward revision of the credit limit, provided that you are satisfied with the customer's payment performance to date
- if a customer wants a longer period than you would normally give, adjust the prices to cover the extra period so that you do not suffer the extra borrowing cost
- hold a general review of credit limits at least twice a year

Once you have decided to grant credit to a customer, you have to specify in writing:
- the conditions of sale under which you will be operating with them (see 5.3d)

- the credit limit (ie the total amount inclusive of sales tax)
- product specifications if appropriate
- delivery parameters (volumes, packaging, lead time, place of delivery, documentation), which are normally specified initially by the customer, but if there is any room for doubt you should specify the terms on which you are supplying your products
- any other factors which would give grounds for dispute

In the case of **export customers**, research carefully the length of the supply chain to the customer. Selling to a country on the other side of the world can result in a long time before the goods reach the customer. If you do not have nor intend to have export expertise within your business, then operate through a reputable export company and take their advice on:
- packaging
- documentation
- insurance, transfer of risk and title, and other conditions
- the extended credit period – to avoid this it is common to arrange payment through the customer's bank by one of several documentary processes

With a customer who accounts for a sizeable part of your business, it is worth signing a short operating agreement that sets out how both parties will operate together, who the main points of contact are and how any disputes or problems will be resolved. Take care to ensure that the document is merely a memorandum of understanding and cannot be construed as a deed of partnership.

Once a month, you need to hold a **credit control review**. This is best done about 8 to 10 working days after the month end, by which time it is apparent which customers are falling behind with payments. The meeting should comprise:
- the financial controller
- the credit controller
- any production, technical, despatch or sales officials whose input may be needed to understand and resolve difficult issues with any customer

The normal procedure is for the control team to work through an aged debt listing, concentrating on the old debt and nearly-old debt. The credit controller should investigate and prepare a set of brief notes beforehand. Remember that this month's 60-day debt will be next month's 90-day debt in three weeks' time. The team must initiate a series of action points:
- take whatever actions are necessary to rectify errors or omissions by the company

- contact those customers who are disputing items and resolve the disputes (sometimes this is merely a matter of providing documentary proof, or sending a copy of a missing invoice)
- agree and take action with or against those customers who are falling behind (see the can't pay/ won't pay distinction in the real life example above

The involvement of production is important. If you sell a group of components to a customer and 2% of the components have been not been delivered, the customer cannot make his product and is not going to pay for the 98% of perfect product which you delivered on time.

The credit controller is not a hatchet man. He should be a part of the sales team, attend their meetings, go for a drink with them (that can call for stamina) and visit the major customers and a few lesser ones to understand their businesses. When customers become late with payments, he should try and help them find ways out of their difficulties. Quite often, this involves a relatively minor change in the way they operate.

## 3.2f – Working capital control – payables

We have been concentrating above on minimising the amount of cash tied up in our inventory and receivables, and if you are successful at that, you will have sufficient liquidity to enable you to strike the best possible deals with your suppliers. The following aspects of supply must be considered:
- price
- special packaging and transport (eg refrigeration)
- frequency of delivery
- supplier buffer stock (ie a stock kept by the supplier to enable immediate delivery – note that this is at the supplier's premises, and should not be confused with consignment stock, which should be avoided)
- order-to-delivery lead time
- out-of-hours deliveries (for shift work, weekends and continuous processes)
- reduction in price for collection by your own sales transport returning to base
- volume discount
- credit limit
- credit period
- cash discount for early settlement
- any other advantageous terms you can negotiate

The priority you give to each of the above factors will vary with each material you purchase. For example, if you are producing a range of engineering products all from the same basic materials, you will be buying the basic materials in bulk, with easily forecast requirements and should normally be concentrating on low price. However, each of your products will have its own special components attached to the basic materials, and these components will have their own individual requirements; some may be high volume and predictable and others low volume and difficult to forecast, perhaps needing a rapid supplier response (ie short lead time).

The supplies which your purchasing manager negotiates can play a large part in the efficiency of your operation. Accordingly, the supply arrangements should be discussed by the purchasing manager beforehand with you, the production manager and the sales manager, to ensure that you have a unified approach towards the end objective of selling efficiently and profitably to your customers.

In managing your working capital, your control of inventory and receivables is aimed at cash management. In the case of suppliers, however, we have considered price (ie profitability) and efficient production (which gives profitability and good cash flow). Many business managers believe that it is clever to pay suppliers as late as possible, dragging every last day of credit out of them.

This is the worst possible thing to do to your suppliers, who are, after all, your business partners. Quite apart from being unethical, it will land you in all sorts of trouble:

- your suppliers will stop being helpful and the service on which you depend will disappear; why should they deliver according to agreed terms when you when you don't pay according to agreed terms?
- those extra little favours which your suppliers normally do will be discontinued
- you and your team and your purchasing manager will receive constant hassle by letter, fax and especially telephone, to the point where it becomes difficult to get any work done
- your suppliers will stop supplying you; remember that it only takes the absence of one material to halt manufacture of an entire product
- worse, your suppliers may send drivers round to your premises to recover materials not paid for
- if you can obtain an alternative supplier, they will eventually (sooner rather than later) also stop supplying
- the gaps in supply will lead to gaps in sales; and depending on your product, your customers may similarly lose sales of whole items

because they do not have the components you produce for them – you can be sure that they will not be paying you on time
- you will lose discounts on pricing penalties
- as supplies falter and alternatives have to be found, your production will suffer increasing delays and your unit costs will rise as your output drops
- you may lose the support of your trade referees, which will hinder you from gaining credit with other suppliers
- your customers will go elsewhere
- word will get around your industry and all of the above problems will multiply

Macho business is bad business. You should seek to be your suppliers' best customer and gain the competitive advantages which cost-effective supply lines will give you.

Above we have considered the need to stick to terms with your suppliers. But **if your business is in difficulty** for whatever reason, you may genuinely not be able to pay your suppliers promptly. This should be dealt with as follows:
- prepare a recovery plan with your management team, and if necessary, with your bankers and professional advisors
- without giving away too much detail, discuss the situation face-to-face in strict confidence with your suppliers and propose a way forward
- if you have concentrated on being a welcome and reliable customer in the past and built up a good relationship with your suppliers, they will be inclined to help you

The above statements appear trite, but many businesses simply try struggle their way through bad periods by keeping quiet and leaving their business partners in the dark. This only creates concern and mistrust, and worst of all causes rumours to echo around your business sector.

Until your recovery plan begins to bite, you may have to endure a period in which you have no alternative but to pay suppliers late, and yet you will be more dependent than ever on their support. During this fire-fighting period there are some useful tactics:
- pay the small balances first; a telephone call chasing £50 wastes as much time as a call chasing £50,000 and you can thus greatly reduce the amount of disturbance
- pay your local suppliers first; if they are unpaid, rumours will circulate in the area to your workforce and be transmitted by delivery drivers and other visitors overhearing conversations – every

industry has an effective grapevine and rumours are exaggerated as they spread, and soon your whole industry will be expecting your demise, thus worsening your already poor supply position

- contact your most important suppliers before the rumours reach them and agree a payment plan with each of them in the same way as you would with any of your customers in difficulty (see 3.2e); if you take the battle to them they will normally be much more reassured than they will if they have to initiate the dialogue
- whatever you do, do not go "underground" (avoiding contact with your suppliers); nothing creates concern and suspicion faster than avoiding speaking to people when there is a cash flow problem
- telling people that everything is under control when it patently is not is also guaranteed to create alarm and suspicion, so be straightforward about the fact that you are going through a problem period and that you have specific plans already being actioned (don't be vague, but don't be too specific either)
- once you have agreed your recovery plan and your arrangements with suppliers, WORK LIKE HELL to make everything happen, preferably ahead of schedule

It is not unknown for a business which has come through a period of difficult cash flow without going underground to find that its reputation has actually benefited from being seen to be able to deal with its problems; after all, your suppliers also have their problems from time to time and so do some of their other customers, with whom you will be compared favourably.

## 3.2g – Cash control of fixed assets

Capital expenditure has potentially the worst cash flow pattern of any outgoing. A fixed asset may have its cost charged against profit over a number of years, but the cash outflow occurs on or just after the acquisition of the asset if it is paid for outright. Even worse, in some cases a deposit must be paid before the asset is acquired, and a major capital asset such as a new factory or office will normally require large progress payments long before the asset begins to earn its keep.

Except in the most highly cash-generative businesses (and some of those, remember, are high-risk businesses) it is not practicable to fund the acquisition of major fixed assets out of normal working finance. They should therefore be funded by bank loan, hire-purchase, finance lease or a similar scheme which spreads the cash outflow over (but not beyond) the profitable life of the asset. The investment plan for the asset must therefore be realistically and comprehensively presented, and the economic risks and consequences fully understood.

Businesses which operate in highly changeable circumstances should not normally contemplate the purchase of long-term assets, but should seek to rent the assets they require for the foreseeable life of their current activities.

*Real life – the author visited the head office of a telecommunications company to discuss a potential project, and found the company's address in the heart of London's financial centre, amongst some of the highest rents on the planet. The foyer took up three storeys of inactive space, and the office, on an upper floor, was to say the least, palatial. The very nature of a telecoms company means that its HQ can be located anywhere; there was no need for an expensive address in The City. Vanity is a surprisingly common cause of bad business decisions, the two commonest examples being ostentation and a focus on sales instead of profits (itself a form of ostentation).*

Many substantial fixed assets are acquired when a business reaches a **make-or-buy decision**. When a business is young, it should keep its costs variable as far as possible, but when as it grows it reaches a stage where certain items hitherto purchased (and therefore including their suppliers' margins) can be more cheaply made in-house, after allowing for the capital cost and borrowing cost of the equipment required to make the items. When making the capital investment appraisal for such a choice, ensure that the in-house production is cheaper even if the volume of business falls 30% below the current level (or more if the business is particularly risky or volatile).

Moreover, take special care in investing in capital equipment in an industry in which technology advances rapidly. Many a business has been hamstrung by a white elephant resulting from rapid obsolescence caused by new technology. It is safer to buy the components, and although one will achieve lower profit margins, one can rapidly change one's buying patterns as technology advances.

An even bigger capital investment than buying equipment to make components is the acquisition of the business which manufactures the components. As well as being an economic move, this may be a strategic purchase to gain a foothold on the supply market. Again, the long-term future of the acquisition and its product range must be considered carefully before any commitment is made.

One curious feature occurs in almost every capex budget. The equipment requirements are reviewed most carefully with the production, technical and R&D management to ensure that all the major requirements are included in the budget (assuming there are funds available). Then, early in the new financial year, a major capex requirement surfaces, one which did not receive even a mention in the capital budgeting process. Invariably this new item is touted as the most important technical requirement facing the company, despite not even being on the horizon two or three months previously. Why this happens, the author is unable to explain, but it does. The solution is:

- either keep a contingency in the capex budget, but do not inform anyone of its existence
- or allow the purchase of the asset, but insist that another capital item is abandoned or postponed

Finally, work to the lowest level of technology that will achieve the objective. Much of the desire for new equipment comes from people's egos, and is not justified by the additional performance (if any) of the new assets they seek. Making money is much more important than having state-of-the-art technology.

*Real life – a group CFO drove to work in a top-of-the-range BMW, which did little else than occupy a substantial space in the head-office car park. However, outside office hours the car attracted numerous thefts and break-ins, to the point where the CFO, in desperation, replaced it with a Ford Fiesta. To his surprise, he found that he got to work quicker, could park it in many other places where a BMW would not fit, and that nobody was in the least bit interested in stealing or breaking into it. He kept the Fiesta.*

So when you're thinking of replacing a team of 24 workers with a large robot, remember that you can reduce the size of the team in lean times, but not the size of the robot.

## 3.2h – Research and development

As stated in 3.2e, the research and development team, aka technical department, must be **customer-facing**.

*Real life – a small company had developed the world's most capable equipment in a diagnostic application; it out-performed every other unit available. As the prototype was developed towards the production stage, trial customers expressed wishes for various additional facilities. Some of these were added, but others were omitted because the R&D director opined that the desired features were unnecessary because they did not provide any additional capability to the product. The words "they don't know what they're talking about" were heard.*

*The R&D director was right . . . but he was wrong. Despite the undoubted capability of the unit, the customers found it "clunky" (that word was also heard) because it did not have the features they had recommended. As a result, the product did not sell in the required numbers. The company stumbled on for a few years and eventually went into liquidation.*

That was a classic case of arrogance and crass disregard for customers' wants. If your customers want the product finished in Campbell tartan, that's what you give them – even if your name's MacDonald.

R&D work splits broadly into two types of activity:
- general ongoing technical advice, de-bugging and product improvements
- major (capital) projects, which need specific budgeting, cash forecasting and project control

The general ongoing work should be managed and controlled in the same way as for any other department, to an approved annual budget. There should be no need to allocate a plethora of accounting codes to the small projects; they can be simply split amongst generic headings such as maintenance, upgrading, technical advice, rectification and general development.

Major projects, however, are harder to control. Financially they should be planned, approved and controlled in the same way as any capital expenditure (see 3.2g), but there the similarity often ends. For a start, split R&D projects into two very distinct types:
- those that will proceed entirely on existing technology – that does not mean that they will be trouble-free, but they can normally be controlled as effectively as any other departments' capital projects
- those that depend on a new technology or concept – they run two additional risks: the technology may not work, and even if it does, it is much harder to harness to achieve the objective within the stated time and cost

When did you, the reader, last hear of a major capital project that finished on time and on budget? The norm in the current age is for high-profile projects to exceed budgets by a large percentage. The financial controller cannot afford even a fraction of such laxity, and in the case of new-technology projects must ensure that:

- the financial benefit from the project justifies the technological risk (ie it will confer a MUCH GREATER financial benefit than a project based on proven technology)
- there are defined points in the project when it can be wholly reviewed and cancelled in the event of insufficient progress or insufficient justification for expecting eventual success
- there are more frequent progress meetings than for less complex projects – at least twice a month in critical phases of the project

Such major projects are sometimes continued under the justification that if the company does not create the advantage expected, the consequences will be dire, including possible total failure of the business. It is an uncomfortable climate in which for a financial controller to keep a level head; fortunately the final decision is the managing director's, but he should make it as much on the financial figures as on the technical expectations.


## 3.2i – Treasury

Treasury, however simple on the surface, can be a complex science and has its own professional qualification and is normally the responsibility of the financial director, or even a company or group treasurer. Nevertheless, the financial controller is expected to understand and implement the basics.

**Overdrafts** should be used to fund working capital and minor fixed assets only. An overdraft can rise and fall as your working capital does, so it is a natural match.

**Bank loans, hire purchase and finance leases** are for capital items only. You must set the lives of the finance packages to fit the expected lives of the capital items; you don't want to be repaying instalments on a capital loan when the asset concerned has ceased generating the profits which funded the repayments. This puts pressure on you to ensure that the projection of net incremental earnings from major investments is realistic.

**Grants** can be a valuable source of free finance, so keep abreast of the grants available from all sources. Some points to remember about tactics:
- grants are available for a wide range of purposes and come from a similarly wide range of bodies: local, regional, national and international (the last are particularly prevalent in the European Union)
- every grant comes with a set of conditions which you must fulfil; these conditions can relate to your financial performance, the creation of permanent additional employment (very common),

reduction of pollution, development of new technology and various other factors, mostly relating to your region or industry

- grants must be agreed BEFORE you start the related projects (ie before making any financial commitment), otherwise you have effectively indicated that you can fund the project without the grant
- the bodies that administer the grants must produce glossy annual reports showing how much benefit the grants have created for the community, so they do need some success stories – therefore the more rock-solid your proposal is, the more likely your application is to succeed, provided that you aren't already awash with funds
- your figures must be watertight – do this by creating a spreadsheet model which exactly matches the layout of the grant application form
- present a sensitivity analysis (another reason for the spreadsheet) which shows the project has a reasonable likelihood of success even if the performance turns out to be X% above or below the forecast (X being a range appropriate to the nature and circumstances of the project)
- employment is a big feature of many grants, but technological progress often reduces employment, so grant applications for technology may have to focus on some other benefit such as bringing additional business to the region in which you operate
- finally, if your skill in presenting a written case is not as good as your financial skill, get a skilled writer to turn your notes into a well-presented case, making sure that the narrative "presses all the right buttons"

**Local debt finance**, such as invoice discounting or factoring, in which a bank or similar organisation grants you a liquid facility calculated on a high percentage of your accounts receivable total, may seem to be a good idea. It is a good idea if you have receivables which are high in value and also a high profit margin. But before you leap into an arrangement, consider the side-effects:

- you will have a considerable amount of additional administration, both internally and in your dealings with the bank
- there will be a charge on the money advanced; this may not seem high against the overall level of debt, but it often amounts to a considerable percentage of your pre-interest profit
- you will have to grant to the bank a first charge over the debtors

**Overseas debt**, inward or outward, can be complex. There are many ways of financing it, and you should take advice from your bank on the most appropriate methods. If you have a moderate to high level of international trade you should have an employee who is experienced in the voluminous documentation which is required. Instructional material is readily available on the subject, and the bank will also help with instruction if you set up arrangements for letters of credit etc.

Overseas trade also involves numerous forms of contract, in which risk and ownership pass between the seller and the buyer in different ways at different stages in the shipping process. This is another area in which you will require experience from your impex (import/ export) assistant.

**Transfer pricing** is a matter of concern if you are selling from one country to another within your organisation (normally from one subsidiary of a group to another, but sometimes from separate companies which have partly or wholly common ownership). The main concerns are:

- making your profit as far as allowable in countries with low tax rates, provided that your transfer pricing satisfies the tax authorities in the countries which are on the losing end of your transfer prices
- remitting the profits in cash to the holding company or other preferred destination
- avoiding liability to withholding taxes in the remitting countries (some countries are notoriously hard to transfer money from)
- ensuring that the overall net profits justify your investment decisions in each area

A transfer pricing investigation is often a hugely burdensome event. Consult with your bank and your financial advisors before doing any extensive trade, and before setting up foreign subsidiaries, associated companies or even agents or distributors.

**Foreign exchange** is as complex a subject as transfer pricing and needs a similar level of detailed advice. The general principles are:

- try as far as possible to buy and sell in the currency in which you publish your overall (consolidated) financial results
- this approach may need to be modified if it creates an untenable situation in some part of your organisation (eg substantial losses in a foreign subsidiary)
- consult with your bank on the range of currency hedging devices available and choose the most appropriate ones for your trading circumstances
- recognise in your calculations and forecasts that there is a price for hedging – it is a form of insurance
- prepare monthly forecasts of your movements and closing balances in each currency (appendix A5)

- decide upon the appropriate percentages to hedge (for example you might contract to sell 85% of the customer receivables for a certain month on the experience that 15% of the customers will pay late)
- apart from setting the above percentages, DO NOT SPECULATE
- if you have income and outgoings in the same currency, match them as far as possible – this may entail deliberately buying or selling an amount in that currency to minimise the net exposure
- you will need bank accounts in the currencies which you use; maintain these so that the net overall balances in each currency comprising receivables, payables and cash/ overdraft are matched by the hedging in place for each month going forward
- recognise that you will never get it completely right – you merely minimise the effects up or down

## 3.2 – Final thought

You will not have failed to notice that this is the longest section in the book

**DRAW YOUR OWN CONCLUSION**

# OPTIMISING MANAGEMENT PERFORMANCE 3.3

## 3.3a – Objectives

Most of the measures described in this book are effectively financial measures. Even measurements of volume of materials or products are considered with regard to their financial significance. In this subsection, however, we consider measurements designed to assess the performance of the management and administration.

These measurements are not merely an academic exercise. Parts 3.1 and 3.2 place great stress on close coordination with suppliers and customers to achieve and justify profitable buying and selling prices, and this coordination can only be achieved and maintained if staff performance is kept sharp. In order to ensure this, we need simple, clear indications as to how effectively the business is carrying out the support and service tasks which make the difference between being profitable and being highly profitable.

The specific measurements of management performance will vary considerably with sizes and types of business and their particular trading circumstances, but there are some general measurements which can be adapted to virtually all business and we discuss them here. Note that in any business EVERYONE is managing something.

## 3.3b – The management cycle

It has long been observed that the effective management of a routine process or set of processes entails a cycle:
- somebody carries out an **action** – either a single action such as testing a piece of technology or a routine action such as packing an item for despatch
- somebody takes a **measurement** of all relevant aspects of that action – for example, units packed, units loaded, time taken
- somebody makes an **analysis** of the measurements, which will not be fully meaningful unless they are reviewed against appropriate benchmarks such as targets, standards, previous periods, industry standards, other departments, maker's recommendations, best-ever performance etc

- somebody presents a **report** of that analysis to the management team – the report distils the analysis into summarised findings, conclusions and recommendations
- the management team issues an **instruction** for further action – if the report is satisfactory this may be to continue the action on the same basis (some praise may be appropriate); otherwise, the instruction should be directed towards improvement of the general performance and prevention of any problems which have been highlighted by the report (positive factors should be exploited and negative factors remedied)

We discuss in various other parts of this book how the financial information is used as part of this cycle. In this part we concentrate on measuring and if possible incentivising the management in all activities.

## 3.3c – Task allocation

Drysdale's First Law of Systems states: **if people can pass on pain, they will** (not always deliberately). Therefore, to achieve the maximum performance from people, all systems (the term includes all organisation structures and all contracts) should be structured so that if someone fails to do something properly, he suffers immediate pain. In other words, organise matters so that it is easier or more profitable for people to do things properly. All systems, structures and contracts should therefore be made self-policing as far as possible.

*Real life – as a short example of this, a company making aluminium components developed a simple distribution arrangement wherein the racks at the end of the production line were arranged in the areas covered by the distribution trucks: SE England, SW England, the Mid-England etc. The packers on the production team took the components, packed them in boxes in accordance with the work orders accompanying the batches, applied the address labels (included with the works orders) to the boxes and placed the boxes in the racks for their destinations.*

*It did not work. Customers in SW England complained that they were missing some items from their shipments; the driver in the Mid-England discovered that his truck contained some boxes for Scotland and so on. Not only that, but since the customers could not build their products without the full range of pieces they had ordered, they would not even pay for the items they had received. A simple system which seemed as though it should have been foolproof was causing considerable trouble.*

*An investigation found that the packers were none too careful about where they placed the boxes. If the correct rack was full, they made no attempt to clear a space on that rack or mark the boxes for attention, but merely stacked the boxes in a convenient space on another rack. As they were part of the production department, their bonus was based on output, ie on completed works orders, and therefore their motivation was to get the boxes out of the production area as fast as they could. The packers were therefore transferred to the despatch department, so that misplacing any boxes would incur the wrath of the packers' new boss, and possibly the even more fearsome prospect of an angry truck driver returning from a troublesome journey. The problem ceased.*

You can see the logic: **if people can pass on pain, they will** (not always deliberately).

*Real life – another example, this time on a bigger scale: this was a company which made large items of capital equipment for installation in various types of establishments all over the world. The company had three main types of product, each with its own production line forming a separate "business unit" with separate budgeting, accounting, targeting and responsibility. There was also a fourth business unit: a department which installed, tested and commissioned the equipment on the customer sites. The three production managers were responsible for what happened in their areas of the factory (typically 25 weeks to manufacture a capital item) while the installation manager was responsible for everything that happened on site (typically 5 weeks per installation).*

*You can imagine what happened. Products typically came off the production line 2 or 3 weeks late (which may not look too bad against a 25 week target), with some items missing, or merely taped to the product instead of being built into it. Items which were built into the product were sometimes not tested. The installation department received the equipment late on site, having booked 5 weeks' accommodation for the team, and had only 2 or 3 weeks in which to do 5 weeks' work. The team had to hire additional (untrained and sometimes not English-speaking) local technicians at exorbitant rates, work around the clock on overtime, rectify untested components and parade all of the company's incompetence in front of the customer on the his own site. They also finished late on occasion, with a knock-on effect on the next installation.*

*The management reports, of course, showed that the three production managers routinely hit their production cost targets, and only incurred a few small delays against delivery dates, while the installation manager was constantly behind time, incurred massive cost overruns and infuriated many of the company's best customers. The production managers picked up around 90% of their maximum bonuses while the installation manager was the whipping-boy of the company and in danger of being fired. The author, managing a systems development project for the company, recommended strongly to the managing director that the production managers be made profit-responsible for the entire process through to acceptance of the product by the customer and that the installation department be a central service department whose resources had to be booked by and charged to the production managers (who would therefore bear the costs and consequences of their own delays).*

Fortunately, the company was taken over by an engineering group just as the author completed his project, and the new owners recognised the need to restructure the responsibilities. The lessons from this second example are of huge importance to the financial controller:

- the controller must understand closely the structure and dynamics of the business – eg the dynamics above, wherein an 8% delay (2 weeks) in production reduced the available installation time by 40%
- the controller must especially understand the driving forces inside and outside the business
- most of these forces stem from individual people striving to achieve THEIR OWN PERSONAL OBJECTIVES rather than the objectives of the company as a whole (a natural human tendency)
- if people can pass on pain, they will – no apology for repeating this
- management reports must not merely report results – they must also report (or at least indicate) CAUSE AND EFFECT; in this case, the reports should have included statistics on late arrival of products to the installation sites, and the time and cost of finishing off incomplete products received on site, so that remedial action could have been instructed and implemented (see management cycle above)
- performance pay must be structured carefully to avoid abuse

. . . which brings us neatly to the next topic.

## 3.3d – Performance pay

The same principle applies to performance pay schemes; if people can pass on pain (in this case, something that will reduce their performance pay), they will. Therefore performance pay schemes have to be designed so that:

- they make it worthwhile for people to strive for the objectives they are given

- if the performance pay is repetitive, it is paid often enough and promptly enough to keep stimulating people to achieve their objectives and thereby the business's objectives
- the objectives they are given are entirely in line with the objectives of the business
- they do not (and cannot) gain their performance pay by causing a problem elsewhere in the business
- the net profit gained by people reaching their targets is greater than the total cost of the performance pay
- the incentives are based on factors which the people themselves can largely influence

The first two points go together in making the performance pay sufficiently worthwhile that the people concerned do valuable work in order to earn it. It is obvious that the amount of the performance pay has to be attractive, but the necessity for frequency is less apparent. It is common for businesses to pay an annual performance pay, usually based on the audited results, which in many cases are not finalised until months after the year-end. This means that someone doing good work in January 20XX may not be rewarded for it until March or April 20XY, and when a performance pay is that far away it has limited stimulating effect. Moreover, you require complex arrangements for people who join or leave the business part-way through a financial year.

The incentive effect of shortening the performance pay period to 6 months, 3 months or even 1 month is considerable, each period being substantially more attractive than the next longer one. And why should a business which pays weekly productivity performance pay to its production employees baulk at paying a monthly performance pay to others? If a person receives a bonus one month, and the next, he will get used to having it, and if he does not receive it on the third month he will generally take immediate steps to ensure that it is earned and received in respect of the fourth month, and so on; you create a degree of dependency which is a constant stimulus to good performance.

The next two points also go together. If, for example, we gave sales managers performance pay based on the monetary value of the sales they achieved, they would reduce their sales prices to increase the volume and the overall monetary amount, but as we have seen in the breakeven examples in 3.1c, we would suffer a fall in margin, and would be incentivising the sales force to make less overall profit. If instead we based the performance pay on gross (manufacturing) margin, we would not solve the problem, because they could incur excessive marketing costs to achieve the margin and we would yet again be financing a fall in profit. So we would have to base a selling performance pay on the net variable margin after all sales-related costs. This, of course, means that our sales-related costs would have to be clearly accounted for, and that they would have to be divisible on a fair basis into the territories of each sales manager.

Alternatively, you could control all prices centrally, but in many businesses this inhibits the negotiating power of the sales force (particularly when operating in widely differing markets).

Moving on to the question of objectives, it is remarkable how many businesses shoot themselves in the foot by incentivising personnel to operate against the objectives of the business as a whole.

*Real life – at the worldwide senior management conference of a manufacturing group, the chief executive officer gave the delegates two important objectives:*
- *to reduce the time-wasted on set-ups, they were to manufacture in the largest batches they could*
- *the factory managers were to achieve the highest factory utilisations they could, and this would constitute the main element of their performance pay*

*He was followed on the podium by the chief financial officer, whose main thrust was to exhort the management to improve the group's tight cash situation.*

*The CFO didn't have a hope. A business needs to manufacture the smallest practicable batch sizes in order to keep its inventory levels to a minimum. Not only that, but incentivising factory managers on utilisation would encourage them to produce even more inventory to maintain their utilisation levels, even when the output was not required. Worse still, the group used full absorption costing, further encouraging factory managers to produce for inventory in order to transfer fixed costs from the operating results into the balance sheet. Within months, the group was negotiating substantial additional funding from its backers.*

*The factory managers should have been incentivised on:*
- *low inventory levels (eg an amount per month paid on days of inventory below a set number)*
- *on-time delivery percentages to customers, less penalties for delays or returns (this incentive might be better applied further down the production management chain at shift supervisor level)*
- *the percentage net variable margin on their products*
- *the cumulative monthly amount of factory fixed costs below a set value*

That emphasises the point about incentives in one direction encouraging malpractice in another. The performance pay for any person may need to be a combination of incentives, the main ones being designed towards his main objectives and the others designed to ensure that he does not cause any collateral damage in the process (eg by holding too much inventory when pursuing a profit target). Alternatively it may be appropriate to deduct penalties from the performance pay for certain occurrences. A real-life example of this is the bad debt penalty deducted from the days of sales performance pay for sales managers (see credit control management, 3.2e)

The fifth point is that performance pay must be self-financing; in other words, someone earning performance pay must generate appreciably more cash inflow for the business than the total cost of the performance pay. Remember also that the business normally has to pay social security and pension contributions on the gross pay. Again, the subsection on credit control (3.2e) gives an example of this.

Finally, for an incentive to be fair, the performance pay must be calculated on factors for which the persons concerned are directly responsible or can influence directly. Bear in mind, however, that even the areas for which managers are directly responsible are subject to other influences. For example, a sales manager cannot meet his targets if the production manager does not make the products in time, and the production manager is similarly dependent on the logistics function having the raw materials on site in time. The principle of collective responsibility therefore plays a big part in management; if production has a problem, then sales have a problem, and the financial controller has a problem because the business is not going to meet its budget. Everyone has to work as a team, and well-designed performance pay will act as a stimulus towards this.

Since the production manager cannot control sales, he should be incentivised on having products completed on time for sales commitments, but penalised for late or faulty production. These things he can largely control, and he will have to cooperate with the purchasing or logistics manager to resolve any supply difficulties which may reduce the production bonus.

You will have noted the use of the cumbersome term **performance pay** and occasionally the word **incentive** throughout instead of **bonus(es)**. This is because performance pay should be regarded as an essential part of the earnings package, and not just a nice-to-have sum on top of it. Ideally, the remuneration package should be structured so that:

- life is somewhat unsatisfactory if no performance pay is earned
- life is satisfying if the targets are exactly met

- life is excellent if the targets are exceeded

## 3.3e – Sales force

Strange though it may seem, the one factor on which you should NOT incentivise your sales force is sales, be it by value or by volume (unless your products are sold at net prices over which they have no control). Targeting salespersons on sales value or volume creates a culture of getting the products out of the door at any price, to achieve the highest total figure. The result is that margins are sacrificed to the god of the top line, and the business becomes over-active for less profit. Even the cost structure can be affected, overtime being incurred to meet the volume sold, and reducing the net profit level even further in the process. See the example in 3.1c.

Suitable targets for a sales force will depend on the nature of the products, the way in which it is sold, and the customers' priorities. They may include:
- period targets – by net margin or net territory return (ideally, each territory should have its own profit statement, down to net profit before central costs)
- average net margins – from the sales person's gross margin should be deducted all attributable costs such as sales returns, remedial work, transport etc
- introduction of new profitable business – either new customers or new lines of sale to existing customers
- conversion rate of enquiries to new profitable customers
- absence of bad debts – reduce their performance pay by £X per bad debt, or deduct the loss from their net profit total, to discourage them from selling to or even taking on customers of dubious financial status
- days of outstanding debt each month – for every day below a specified level (eg 60 days) each month, a cash bonus will encourage them to help with cash collection, especially in helping solve customer disputes

All of the above have been used successfully in practice and are designed to create a more profitable business rather than merely more sales.

## 3.3f – Customer service (aka Sales support)

The type and purpose of customer service departments varies more than with sales forces, making it more difficult to generalise on suitable incentives. But common to all customer service functions is the objective of increasing net profit by satisfying customers. The following measurements can normally be logged and used as measurements for incentive pay:

- average telephone response time, recorded automatically by the telephone system (*real life – a sharp subsidiary managing director told his divisional director that his company's average response time to customer queries was nine, and when the divisional director commented that nine minutes was a commendable average response, the local MD told him that it was nine SECONDS*)
- problem resolution time – a log of customer queries will record and report the length of time it takes to close an enquiry

At this point one must consider the relationships between the stages of the following chain:

- production planning – for producing goods according to orders and/ or forecast demand
- production – for completing goods for sale
- finished goods store – for holding goods ready for sale and making them available for despatch
- despatch and transport – for getting the goods to the customer

and their equivalent departments in a contract or service business.

The customer service department cannot be held responsible for the performance of the entire chain, and so the measurement of its efficiency must be restricted to its own direct workings. The extent of the customer service responsibility varies greatly from company to company. A very customer-driven business may even have the finished goods store under the control of the customer service department – logical when you think upon it. In such cases, the performance measurements can focus on minimising problems in the delivery of products to the customers:

- late deliveries
- wrong deliveries
- defective products
- documentary errors
- resolution of queries

And remember that if there are 10 different components being delivered to a customer to make a product and one of them is late, then the delivery completion percentage is 0%, not 90% (see the first example in 3.3c).

## 3.3g – Production

The first rule about production targets is that everyone must be aware of them, all the time. Therefore they must be highly visible. The best financial report the author has ever seen was a blackboard which looked like this:

| OUTPUT | M | T | W | T | F | S | S |
|--------|-----|-----|-----|-----|-----|-----|-----|
| Target | 80 | 125 | 195 | 260 | 345 | 380 | 380 |
| Actual | 73 | 118 | 201 | | | | |

*Real life, real time – the upper row showed the cumulative weekly target for the product and the lower row the actual output of completed (ie quality-cleared) products. Since the controller knew both the breakeven volume and budgeted volume of production he could tell every day at a glance how well the factory was doing. There was a degree of variation in that the factory could be producing predominantly high-value or low-value products, but in general the mix was consistent, and if the actual figures appeared low, a quick conversation with the production manager would explain the situation and what, if any, remedial action was needed.*

Visibility is important in incentivising; if people are constantly aware of their targets and of their progress towards them (and hence the likelihood of receiving performance pay) they will maintain the pressure to hit the targets.

Lean production is a separate science from finance, but since the financial controller has a major vested interest in the efficiency of production, he should understand the principles of lean manufacture. The simplicity and logic of lean production will appeal to any controller, as will the mathematics. The book "Continuous Improvement" by Wayne Scott Ross (appendix D1) gives a very clear and simple picture of the logical methods used to maximise productivity.

Traditional measurements are still relevant, however, and these include:
- cumulative output against target (as above)
- output per hour and per operative and per production line, as appropriate
- percentage of rejects (by value as well as volume if products are of highly differing values)
- percentage of downtime, by individual reasons (breakdowns, spares shortage, material shortage, power failures, bottle-necks, factory holidays etc)
- percentage of overtime (planned and unplanned)

- incidence of absence, by reason
- percentage of scrap – process scrap and defect scrap
- percentage of rework, successful and unsuccessful
- late deliveries into finished goods store
- late deliveries to customers
- product rejections by customers, with reasons
- customer returns by volume, value and reason
- set-up times (times taken to adjust machinery and/ or clean vessels to produce different items)

Although the above and other measurements are the tools of production management, the financial controller needs to monitor and understand them and discuss the main trends (or lack of them) with the production, technical and supply-chain management.

## 3.3h – Contracts

Each contract with a supplier or customer is virtually a small business, the complexity of which depends on the nature of the contract. An on-running supply contract, for example, should require little extra attention provided that it is running without any penalties. A construction or engineering site contract, on the other hand, is a sizeable separate business and should be run as such. Virtually all of the management and financial controls in this book will apply to some extent to such a contract. Tailor your management to suit each individual contract.

## 3.3i – Inventory control

Computerised inventory systems enable a high degree of reporting and checking on the control of inventory. Review the following reports in respect of **raw materials**:

- raw material price variances – has the price or currency gone up, or are we ordering a different type, or is it not being bought in budgeted quantity and therefore not qualifying for volume discounts?
- raw material physical losses – in the material store(s), to be investigated
- raw material adverse variances – in the production process, possibly as a result of rejected work, or faulty processes or a different work mix from the budget

- express transport inward costs – these should be coded separately from normal transport costs, as they indicate poor order planning, unplanned wastage in production or perhaps unbudgeted products required suddenly
- book-physical differences revealed by stock counts – reasons to be found if high values are involved, and cause of discrepancies to be eliminated
- old inventory no longer usable

The reporting on **work in progress** mainly concerns efficiency of production and in practice is dependent on a high degree of labour and production recording, which may not be available to the smaller company:

- material and labour usage variances
- labour wage rate variances (often a difficult figure to extract from a system, and subject to a variety of causes which may be hard to identify separately)
- ratio of overtime to normal time
- downtime – is it caused by equipment failure, unavailability of materials, inefficiency of upstream processes, poor planning or just over-manning?
- reject volumes and re-work volumes and costs
- overall labour and materials cost as a cost of sales and/ or production, and the variances therein

The difficulty in assessing labour reports lies in the complexity of activity and the number of possible explanations for some variances, particularly.

By contrast, **finished goods** reports are relatively simple to produce and analyse:

- items unavailable for supply – bad planning, delayed production or out-of-trend demand?
- items no longer saleable – to be provided for, and probably disposed of
- items lost through damage or deterioration – causes to be eliminated
- items late for programmed despatch date – reasons to be understood and remedied
- express transport outward costs – late production, inability to locate, or some other reason?
- book-physical differences revealed by stock counts – reasons to be found if high values are involved, and cause of discrepancies to be eliminated

In a manufacturing business these will be some of the most complex issues for a financial controller to manage. They arise on the factory floor, yet they all have a financial dimension and many of the issues involve problems which if not solved may cause serious financial losses.

## 3.3j – Research & Development/ Technical/ Engineering

In 3.2 we consider the cash control of R&D projects, and the necessity to prevent them from going out of control. We also consider in 1.3j the necessity to keep R&D in close contact with the sales forces, and also with customers. Here we consider the management issues.

Frequent and close contact with the sales force is necessary on a day-to-day operating basis, but it also needs to be formalised to bring matters to the attention of general, production, purchasing and finance management. There therefore needs to be a monthly meeting to discuss and resolve issues from:

- performance of products in the field, from the viewpoint of the customers
- actions in force or needed to maximise customer impact via the product range
- solving of ongoing problems arising from the current product range
- demands for new products or amendments to existing products
- opportunities for new products, for which initial market, technical and financial appraisal are required
- current projects – measurement of progress and costs against project plans (see 3.2g)
- production issues arising from current and future product range
- purchasing and supply issues arising from current and future product range
- other external developments (market, supply, safety, technology or politics) which may affect business adversely or create a profit opportunity
- review of departmental costs against budget, and implications thereof for future cost levels

If your business does not have a formal R&D/ technical function, ask yourself who is monitoring the above issues in terms of current products and future products. Having the right products, be they goods or services, is crucial to every business and needs constant management. If, for example, you provide professional services, you need regular assessments of the effectiveness and profitability of the services, and equally regular reviews of the prospects of new services and how to provide them.

Measuring the effectiveness of R&D/ technical is not always straightforward, but there are a number of possible indicators:

- logged response time to customer and production queries
- ratio of time spent on technical issues to time spent on developments*
- actual cost against departmental budget
- project costs against project budgets
- profitability of new products against project budgets
- on-time completion performance of projects

*R&D/ technical, in common with every other department, is there to MAKE MONEY for the business.

Control of projects needs recording of not just materials and charges, but also of time spent thereon. Technical staff are not bureaucrats by nature, so give them a simple time sheet which they will complete. Quarter-days are usually sufficient for meaningful reporting, rather than accounting for every half-hour or hour. And there is normally no need to calculate different cost rates for senior and junior staff; the R&D director is just as likely to be working the equipment as the technicians are, so merely divide the total department payroll by the hours on each activity to give a reasonable estimate of the activity cost.

As the information builds up, you will come to know that a certain broad type of product takes X months and £Y,000 to bring to market – valuable, indeed essential information for taking your business forward.

Finally, the R&D department itself should monitor the maintenance and troubleshooting records of the production and other operational departments, to identify areas of problem and excess cost.


## 3.3k – Purchasing

From a regular standpoint, the effectiveness of the purchasing function is judged by three main criteria:

- price (the real net price, inclusive of all associated costs such as packaging, delivery and duty)
- timeliness of supply (not too soon, not too late – this depends on appropriate batch quantities)
- performance of goods and services bought

These are straightforward to measure, purchase price variances being the simplest of all variances.

What is more complex managerially is that the purchasing model will be different when buying materials for products in different stages of their lives (see appendix A3 for product lifespan management):

In the early stages of a new product, when the performance of the product in the field and demand for the product from customers are both uncertain, purchasing should be tailored thus:
- small batch quantities until a regular and predictable flow of sales has been built up
- short-term, low-level commitment in case materials or components are found to underperform and may need replacing or modifying
- short delivery lead time, to cope with uncertain demand and also to provide a rapid response

The above conditions may result in a price penalty.

When a product is in full swing and the volume more predictable, the purchasing department can be more demanding with the supplier:
- prices should be negotiated downward in view of the higher volume and frequency of supply, and the ability to plan the deliveries more accurately
- inventory levels are usually easier to forecast and therefore optimum batch quantities can be established
- changes in production methods to minimise production times or improve product performance may necessitate changes in supply
- further development of the product may do likewise

Finally, when a product approaches the end of its life, the purchasing requirements change again:
- volumes will decrease
- an exit strategy for the product is formulated, and this may include retaining supplies of spare parts and materials to meet estimated warranty work
- a closure date is agreed
- stocks must be balanced so that there are the appropriate quantities of all components to produce the final batches of the product, and retain the forecast quantities of warranty spares ("balanced inventory")

As with the initial build-up, the above run-down is likely to incur increased purchase prices.

There are thus different strategies for different situations. Note that maximising the use of off-the-shelf components in the design of products assists purchasing in all of the above phases.


## 3.3l – Administration

The admin department (which may be under the finance umbrella) often becomes the sink for a number of other activities, particularly when a business is reducing staff numbers. Such activities typically include:

- personnel (quaintly called "human resources" – an inappropriate piece of management-speak, given that humans are a species and resources are a commodity)
- payroll – strictly speaking, this function should be separate from both personnel and finance, but in a small or medium-sized business such a degree of separation may not be practicable
- reception
- public relations (but only in the absence of the managing director)
- electronic communications
- company secretarial work
- administrative secretarial work
- land and buildings
- company vehicles (other than distribution vehicles)
- insurance
- storage of records
- organisation structure

With the exception of insurance (5.4) and payroll (1.3c), such areas are outside the scope of this book. However, there are some general rules regarding administration:

- collect relevant information CORRECTLY at the earliest possible stage and get it CORRECTLY into the company's computer systems – if someone books a flight for Cathy McKenzie and her passport describes her as Kathy Mackenzie, she will not be allowed on the aircraft
- keep all arrangements as SIMPLE as possible – unnecessary complexity seldom helps a process
- make all arrangements as SELF-POLICING as possible – preferably by making the next stage in the process automatically refuse to accept them unless they are complete and correct

The company organisation chart is not a finance function, but given that few people have the specific skill necessary to devise such a chart, it may be worth your while to assume that responsibility (see appendix A1).

## 3.3m – Finance

See all of the rest of this book!

## 3.3n – Meetings

The actions to ensure a successful meeting culture are:
- plan your main meetings a year ahead (see appendix A4) and roll the plan forward every quarter
- adopt a daily/ weekly/ monthly/ quarterly/ yearly structure and STICK TO IT – this means publishing it well in advance, and emphasising to those involved that the timetable is a priority
- rather than re-scheduling meetings if someone will be absent, ensure that they send a capable deputy, properly briefed for the occasion (this has the occasional interesting result of the deputy outperforming his superior, and it is hence a useful pointer to future promotions)
- guillotine all meetings (except emergency meetings) or segments of meetings after a stipulated duration
- as far as possible, restrict minutes of meetings to action points with initials, completion dates and times
- review the progress on these action points at the beginning of the following meeting
- circulate minutes on the same day for morning meetings and on the next morning for afternoon or evening meetings
- don't be afraid to give constructive feedback on people's contribution to meetings – they won't get any better unless you guide them towards improvements which they can and should make
- state the objectives at the beginning and stay with them
- some meetings become stale by repetition, so don't be afraid to revise the attendance, content, frequency, timing, style, location or any other factor, or reduce the subject to part of another meeting
- use a different chairperson from time to time

How often should one hold meetings? Probably just inside the maximum interval which can pass without matters starting to drift out of control. That definition can result in any interval from a daily production meeting to an annual shareholders' meeting.

## 3.3o – Sales credit notes

This is one of the most informative areas of information.

Credit notes to customers atone for a variety of sins, including:
- sales wrongly priced (by either arithmetical error or wrong product identification)
- sales wrongly quantified
- discounts, rebates or other deductions omitted
- products containing defects
- products arriving in an incomplete or damaged state
- products arriving too late to use
- products arriving on time at the wrong location, and subsequently being too late to use
- pricing agreements (discounts, for example) being ignored
- complaints or disputes being settled by an agreed credit

The amount of a sales credit note goes straight to the bottom line; that amount of profit is lost.

Therefore the controller should demand and receive a **monthly list of sales credit notes**, analysed by the reasons listed above, and any other relevant ones. The analysis should **be by both number and value** of credit notes:
- the number indicates the frequency of errors made by staff or processes
- the value indicates the amount of money lost as a result of the problems

There are of course credit notes given for legitimate reasons such as agreed discounts, and these should be clearly identified in the report. In one single simple report, the controller will have a window on the scale of deficiencies in a range of departments.

It is the administrative equivalent of the production manager's scrap and downtime reports, and is a useful catch-all for a number of leakages – but see also 5.1c. And it must be used to stimulate REMEDIAL ACTION.

## 3.4a – Objectives

There are businesses which merely carry on doing what they have always done, selling the same products to the same customers year after year. In the early and middle 20$^{th}$ century the pace of change was steady enough that many businesses could survive comfortably in their market niches, but by the last third of the century the pace of change had become so rapid that only a small percentage of businesses can now survive without constantly realigning themselves to address their markets profitably. This increased turbulence was marked in the UK by two severe recessions, at the beginning and end of the 1980s, when business failures were prolific. These failures arose partly from poor general management, but usually from inability to keep pace with changing demands.

In the 21$^{st}$ century the pace has accelerated even further, fuelled by:
- the increasing capability and usage of technology
- changes in the demographics, interests, tastes and habits of end consumers, focusing increasingly on lifestyle (thus radically affecting housing, furnishings, clothing, food, recreation, travel, healthcare and many other factors which impacted on business in general)
- changes in the working methods of the businesses serving the consumers
- the cataclysmic upheaval of the markets caused by the less-than-sensible activities of the banking community

Therefore whether your business sells to other businesses or the public sector or the general public, it must always have:
- a reasonably accurate estimate of the direction in which your markets are heading (ie the likely changes in the interests, tastes, habits and needs of end consumers)
- a reasonably accurate quantification of the effects of these changes (increases or decreases in product consumption and design, changes in point or method of delivery etc)
- a reasonably accurate assessment of the way in which your competitors will be addressing the market

- a **strategic plan** for the way in which your business will proceed to achieve the best possible financial performance in the above circumstances

Without such a plan your business will survive for a while, but will eventually find itself seriously adrift from the trends in the market and in need of extensive surgery. The surgery may or may not be successful.

And remember always, your core business is **making money**. You may find as a result of your planning that your sidelines become your main lines, or that you move from being a manufacturer to being a distributor. Whether an activity is core business or not should be determined primarily by its money-making capability in relation to the capital and management effort involved. Do not be emotionally attached to any particular trade.


## 3.4b – Overall process

The precise details of the strategic planning process vary considerably from one business to the next, but inevitably involve the following main stages:
- analysis of the market trends to date
- research into the expected trends over the period of the plan
- research into the expected effects of technology, economic developments, exchange rates and other factors on these trends (with special note of the trend to transfer manufacturing to low-cost countries)
- research into the abilities of competitors to exploit the trends
- assessment of the business's capability (in relation to that of its competitors) to exploit the trends
- identification of the most profitable and cash-generative courses of action for the business
- quantification of the investment needed (marketing, sales channels, internal skills, production and distribution equipment, inventory and receivables) for the business to pursue those courses of action
- distillation of these factors into a numerical plan for the period under review (see 3.4n)
- expansion of the overall numerical plan into a detailed budget for the first year of the plan (see 3.5)

Although the financial plan and budget are the outcome of this process, it is not a financial exercise. It is a TOTAL MANAGEMENT EXERCISE involving all members of the management team, and each member must understand the input and parameters of all the other members.

## 3.4c – Scale and detail

Companies produce so-called strategic plans varying from a few pages to a tome the size of an epic novel. However, it is generally accepted that a true strategic plan is a large document which results from extensive research, discussion and preparation by the entire management team, while the "few sheets of paper" approach cannot claim to be anything more than an outline plan. However, a well-considered outline plan is much better than no plan at all.

The depth of detail into which a company should go to prepare a plan depends on the complexity of its business and its markets. The criterion for detail is that level which enables the management team to have a clear view of the business's prospects and how it intends to exploit those prospects to the full, so a well-thought-out simple outline plan may suffice for well-managed smaller businesses with a clear view of the future.

Similarly, the length of time which the plan should cover will depend upon the length of the business's horizons, as shaped by:

- the speed of change in the market place
- the ability of the business and its competitors to force or react to those changes
- the speed of relevant technological change
- the likelihood of opportunities or requirements for diversification or divestment

In general a more complex business will therefore plan 3 to 5 years ahead (any longer timescale becomes increasingly theoretical except in certain long-term activities such as property investment). Smaller businesses or those in an especially rapidly-changing environment tend to plan 3 years ahead. Anything less than 3 full years after the end of the current financial year is not likely to offer sufficient understanding of what lies ahead.

Whatever the period, the plan should be updated annually. This update can be either a full re-plan each year or merely a low-key adjustment of the previous year's plan, with a full re-plan after two or three years or when the circumstances have changed enough to merit a major reconsideration. A full re-writing of a major plan every year is a heavy burden on management time.

## 3.4d – Planning team

The entire senior management of the business should be involved in the plan:

- marketing and sales (and distribution if carried out directly by the business)
- research and development/ engineering
- production and quality
- buying and inventory control
- overhead control
- information systems (where constituted separately from the individual departments)
- finance

To avoid having too large a planning team, it is usually most efficient to include only the main heads, who delegate sections of the work to their managers (for example, the marketing manager delegates detailed research to the sales manager and distribution manager). Nevertheless, the second level of senior management to whom the sections are delegated must be kept fully in the picture at all times and must attend at least some of the planning meetings.

## 3.4e – Overall considerations

No matter how detailed the plan is to be, the planning process must involve the following considerations, in terms of current conditions and future trends:

- the current state of your markets and their expected directions and speed of movement
- the capability of your current competition and the likelihood of additional competition arising within your sector
- competition from other sectors; for example, if you are running a fleet of executive jets you may have competition from video-conferencing because it eliminates the need for executives to meet in the same place, and similarly a football club can have competition from video games because youngsters who would normally pay to watch the team and become lifelong supporters are now indoors repelling invasions by renegade Quargs from planet Zog
- current technology (yours and other people's) and its speed of change
- the trends in the economies in which you are or may be active

- the trends in the currencies in which you buy and sell, and also in which you invest (even economists cannot give reliable forecasts of this, so your strategy should be to minimise your exposure)
- any other major dynamics – local, national or global – which may affect your potential business activities
- from all of the above deliberations, a SWOT (strengths, weaknesses, opportunities and threats) analysis of the business, its markets and its resources; this should distil your findings and your assessment thereof on to a single sheet (see 3.4f)

## 3.4f – SWOT analysis

The SWOT (Strengths, Weaknesses, Opportunities and Threats) analysis is the most commonly used and probably the most effective method of obtaining a quick assessment of the business's position and capability in the market. The strengths and weaknesses establish where the business stands at present, and the opportunities and threats highlight the factors which the business must consider going forward.

When preparing the **SWOT analysis**, remember that:
- everything must be measured **in relation to the competition**; for example, if you have an efficient distribution network it cannot be entered as a strength if all the competitors have equally efficient networks – and if the competitors' networks are markedly more efficient than yours, your efficient network is probably a weakness; sad but true
- items should only be included in the analysis if they will, or are likely to, lead to financial gain or loss
- most entries in the analysis should have an opposite entry; for example, if one of your vital strengths is an experienced and effective group of senior sales executives, then one of your threats must be that the competition may poach them, and your plan must include making it worth their while to stay with you in the medium and longer term

Each manager should prepare the SWOT analysis for his field of operation. For example, the distribution manager may cite the following as threats, to the extent that they don't affect the competition:
- increased fuel prices
- ageing transport fleet
- new regulations limiting driver hours and thus possibly requiring more drivers

These individual threats would be summarised in the overall threat section as "X% increase in unit transport cost" to avoid the SWOT for the whole business being cluttered with detail.

The SWOT analysis is usually presented in matrix format to enable easy assimilation of the factors:

| STRENGTHS | WEAKNESSES |
|---|---|
| 1. | 1. |
| 2. | 2. |
| 3. | 3. |
| 4. | 4. |
| OPPORTUNITES | THREATS |
| 1. | 1. |
| 2. | 2. |
| 3. | 3. |
| 4. | 4. |

This presentation enables the balance between favourable and adverse factors to be gauged, especially if monetary or percentage increase and decrease estimates are shown:

- the left side of the table shows the favourable factors; the right side shows the adverse factors
- the top half shows the present situation; the bottom half shows future possibilities

If more than about 10 items are shown in any one section, the SWOT analysis is likely to lose focus. The items should be presented in order of probable financial impact on the business, thus giving a graphic one-shot picture of the business issues. However, the table is merely the summary and the full underlying detail must be studied and understood by all members of the planning team so that all members understand the complexities and the ways in which each issue affects the other issues (few if any of the issues are self-contained).


## 3.4g – Building on the SWOT

The requirements are obvious:
- strengths and opportunities must be exploited, and the strengths need to be appropriate to the opportunities, otherwise they should not be counted as such
- weaknesses must be remedied

- threats must be countered or avoided

With regard to threats, any rugby or NFL player will tell you that it is more efficient to side-step a tackle than to meet it head-on, since you are still on your feet and running. Von Manstein did not attack the Maginot Line; he simply drove round it, delivering the goods straight to the customer without cluttering his balance sheet with any unnecessary work in progress. Therefore give more consideration to avoiding threats than to neutralising them; it saves a lot of trouble and enables the business to maintain its momentum.

From the SWOT analysis or equivalent process your management team must agree:
- where you (ie the business) stand at present in relation to all that is happening around you
- where you intend to go in terms of activities and financial performance
- by what route you intend to get there (marketing tactics, distribution channels, production techniques etc – and, no matter what route you choose, a lot of hard work)
- what types of resources you will apply: people, fixed assets, technology, working capital, advertising spend etc (to be quantified by the detailed budget)

Note that some businesses state BEFORE the planning process what financial result they intend to achieve, often expressed as a growth percentage on current performance, and then go through the above process to determine how the result can and will be achieved. This approach has good and bad tendencies:
- good – it maintains pressure on the business to keep improving towards a desired target
- bad – by being dogmatic, it can tie the business to an unrealistic target, and damage it by overstretching its capabilities
- bad – it can cause a missed opportunity (for example, by demanding that sales volume is increased by 10% one can miss an opportunity to discontinue a low-margin product and replace it with a smaller volume of high-margin product, thereby achieving a higher net profit on a lower sales figure with less cash tied up in inventory and receivables)

The most effective business approach is therefore always to concentrate on **maximising profit and cash inflow**, not merely for the following year but on an ongoing basis. As a side issue, ensure that any bonus calculations do not encourage people to damage future performance by over-egging current performance.

Whatever approach you use, you must complete your plan before the end of the 3$^{rd}$ quarter of your year (ie month 9) at the latest, or you will not have time to prepare the budget properly. The dates for the planning and budgeting processes should have been fixed in the year's financial calendar (appendix A4).

## 3.4h – Planning elements

These are the main factors to be included qualitatively (in terms of performance) and quantitatively (in terms of meeting your financial targets) in the planning.

**Marketing:**
- trend in END customer demand (ie consumer preferences), taking into account overall economic factors
- trend in YOUR customer demand (if you are not selling to the end customer)
- new products which will outperform or undersell your products
- future direction of your products
- customers – who makes their buying decisions and how? (this normally originates from the end customer)
- selling – what are the product benefits most attractive to your customers' buyers?
- selling and distribution – what methods will be most effective?

**Sales:**
- persuading the customers' buyers to buy the product as defined by market research (above)
- packaging – not necessarily physical; a service can be "packaged" by the way in which it is provided
- delivery (method, frequency, speed, batch quantities, location, compatibility with customers' operation)
- installation and customer training
- after-sales support and service
- competitor performance on all above issues

**Product design (towards demonstrable benefits to customers):**
- new methods which will outperform or undercut the cost of your methods

- new materials (eg composites instead of metals) which will outperform or undercut the cost of your current materials
- ease of production of the product (including commonality of parts and use of standard components)
- ease of processing or use by customer staff
- cost and duration of design, prototyping, testing, pre-production and production
- recruitment and training of own staff
- training of customer staff (even toys and cooking ingredients carry instructions for use)

## Production methods (goods):
- quality
- set-up of existing production facilities
- cost, set-up and operator training of additional facilities
- disposal of surplus facilities where products are being discontinued
- logistics of materials and services
- contracting out of components and processes
- production control (staff, equipment, information)
- efficiency and utilisation to be achieved

## Production methods (services):
- quality
- recruitment and training of staff
- contract management
- materials and equipment
- contract management (staff, equipment, information)
- efficiency and utilisation to be achieved

## Research and development:
- all of the above, and especially quality
- capital projects (cost of development, timescale to bring product to market)
- latest developments in technology (production and products)
- probable future developments in technology

## Purchasing and logistics
- quality
- inventory levels and control and availability of supply
- delivery methods (transport, batch sizes, frequency, packaging)
- pricing – ensure that comparisons include total costs
- payment terms (payment period, special terms)

**Information systems**
- security and integrity
- future information requirements from all other departments
- economic opportunities from current and imminent technology developments
- recruitment and development of own staff
- training of other departments' staff (and in some cases, customer staff)
- capital and revenue costs

**Finance:**
- all of the above
- integrated planning model (a 3-5 year summarised equivalent of the budget model in appendix C4, with much less numerical detail and much more narrative – but see also 3.4n)
- rigorous credibility check

## 3.4i – Calculation approaches

There are three main approaches to calculating overall figures in a strategic plan and detailed figures in a budget:
- incremental
- zero-based
- targeted

**The incremental approach** begins by taking the expected result for the current year and amending it by the expected changes (eg volume, price, exchange rate, efficiency, technological innovation) for the plan years or the budget year. Each amendment can be estimated to a considerable degree of detail. For example, changes in sales volume figures can be targeted by individual product and customer, changes in capacity, higher production levels and so on. This makes it the most common method found in practice as it relies on known data and logic, and is a relatively easy thought process. The argument against it is that you do not do any serious "green field" thinking, particularly about your costs, because you accept the current figure as read.

**The zero-based approach** makes no initial assumptions; instead, each figure is based entirely on the expected circumstances for the plan or budget period. This is sometimes relatively easy for sales figures if there is reliable market information, but in practice it does not work so well for costs. For example, how would you calculate your production consumables budget starting with a blank sheet of paper? You would review the figure for the current year and amend it for expected changes in price, volume, usage and security (assuming you were incurring pilferage). In other words, you would instinctively use the incremental method. If you tried to build up an annual cost category from scratch without reference to actual cost levels you would be likely to omit costs and run immediately into an adverse variance against plan or budget.

The incremental approach is therefore a more practical one. However, you must challenge the current year's numbers and ensure that you are not carrying forward any inefficiencies or other avoidable costs.

**The targeted method** can be brutal, but is usually the best method when salvaging a seriously adverse situation. Crudely, you calculate what performance is acceptable and stipulate the minimal income and the maximum cost allowable for each category. The method is used particularly by groups in driving improved performance from their subsidiaries. However, it is not enough merely to set reduced figures for each cost category; you need to plan and commit to specific cost reductions to remain within the allowed limits. The same applies in the upward direction for income targets.

If the targeted figures are too ambitious, the following can occur in practice:
- all overheads which are not absolutely necessary are eliminated
- the business still fails to meet its ambitious targets
- the business eliminates other overheads which are not needed in the short term, but whose absence thereof will harm the business in the medium and long term
- the business may meet its targets for a limited period
- eventually, some of the core strengths of the business are lost (this is a common point at which the managing director who set the targets moves onward and upward on the strength of progress to date)
- the business loses its way in the market and begins to fall apart, with unpleasant recriminations (and possibly further retrospective kudos for the managing director who left just in time)

However, the above train of events is by no means always encountered, and in highly adverse conditions it is better to agree and follow a very tough plan with at least some chance of survival than to sit and hope for Burt Lancaster to arrive with the US Cavalry. And the managing director will be justified in his aggressive stance.

## 3.4j – Producing the plan

None of the above factors can be decided and quantified in isolation. The planning team will have to hold a series of meetings, along the following lines:
- a briefing of all departmental planning staff, giving the overall objectives and parameters
- meetings of individual departments to organise the planning process for each department
- presentation of the outline sales plan from which is derived all the other departmental plans
- quantification of each department's operational requirements (eg staff, IT, accommodation)
- quantification of each department's fixed capital and working capital requirements
- co-ordination of these factors into a single financial plan
- review and refinement of financial plan

In practice you will need several reiterations of the above cycle, the first being an outline version and review to ensure that the figures are broadly sensible. In practice the first one or two cycles reveal a number of discrepancies, in which one part of the plan does not correspond with another.

Generally, once the sales plan has been accepted as credible, it becomes the benchmark for reviewing all the other elements of the plan for consistency and realism. Typically, a number of limiting factors are revealed by the planning process. For example:
- the level of sales cannot be achieved within the production capacity
- the level of capital investment needed to achieve the production capacity exceeds the finance available
- the technology on which the plan depends will not be ready on time (it seldom is, so beware)
- other business partners (suppliers, joint venturers, component manufacturers etc) will not be able to meet the output required from them)

These problems have to be overcome by adjusting elements of the plan (eg contracting out some of the manufacturing processes or buying some of the products and selling them on for a small trading margin in your own packaging). These amendments continue until you have a plan which is regarded by the whole management team as credible.

## 3.4k – The activity on the side

If you have a side-activity which has no great relevance to your main business, but which makes money without any great input from your main business, then LEAVE IT ALONE and use it as a **cash cow**. Remember that you are here to make money, not to have high principles about what is and what isn't core business.

However, IF the sale of that business would liberate cash and/ or facilities which would enable you to achieve your medium to long term plans more profitably AND the resultant cash inflow would be demonstrably better than the projected inflow from the side-activity, then sell it. But don't sell it just because it isn't so-called core business. **Your core business is making money**.

## 3.4l – The controller's rôle

The processes described in the subsections above are normally managed by the managing director and the financial director.

The task of the financial controller is to drive the information-gathering, financial modelling and reviewing processes, and to ensure that all numbers are checked at operating department level and also in the finance department for:
- accuracy – with underlying records
- reasonability – with known circumstances
- consistency – across all departments
- consistency – with the overall plan

This concentrated mechanical input and review by the controller will enable the managing director and financial director to concentrate on the strategic realism of the plan. However, the controller should not be afraid to query their decisions; playing devil's advocate will normally provide a valuable service to the process.

## 3.4m – Objectives review

At the end of the numerical process, the planning team must do a re-run of the SWOT analysis in reverse. Reviewing the financial plan critically, the team must ask each other:

- are the figures believable and achievable given even breaks (some good, some bad)?
- do they cover all or most of the factors highlighted in the SWOT analysis?
- are the operational and financial risks involved adequately covered? (normally assessed by a sensitivity analysis showing what happens for example if sales or purchases prices and volumes change by 10%, 20% etc)

If after critical review the managing director and financial director are satisfied that the strategic plan can be published, the document then becomes "law" for the business until the next annual planning process.


## 3.4n – Typical strategic plan format

There is no specific format for a strategic plan. Indeed, changes in the format from year to year to reflect the changing parameters of the business are advisable, to prevent the process from becoming a form-filling exercise for managers who have already prepared several previous years' plans. However, the general contents of the plan should include these elements:
- summary of recent operating figures
- summary of external (market etc) statistics to date
- appraisal of the expected market, with particular references to major customers and operating areas, and the relative positions, capabilities and prospects of competitors
- appraisal of underlying economic circumstances expected during and beyond the period of the plan
- appraisal of any other circumstances (political, demographic, technological etc) likely to affect the business
- review of existing resources and opportunities within or available to the business
- estimate of additional resources (personnel, equipment, intangibles and costs thereof) required to achieve the plan
- forecast financial results of the plan

The above sequence reflects the following logic:
- this is where we are
- this is what the future economy and market look like
- this is where we intend to go
- this is why and how we mean to achieve this
- these are the resources we need
- this is what we expect and are targeting the results to be

If the planning process is entirely successful, it will finish after a few drafts with a plan which the management team considers to be ambitious but achievable. There will almost always be some reservations expressed; this is a healthy occurrence, as it combats naïveté and complacency.

**Once the strategic plan has been completed or the previous plan has been updated, it is the turn of the financial controller to co-ordinate the departments in preparing a detailed budget for the following year (see 3.5) to meet the targets in year 1 of the plan.**

The reader will have noted by now that the solution propounded for many problems is early preparation, and the budget is no different in that respect. The financial controller must have completed the preliminary organisation of the budget process (ie everything but the unknown figures) by the time the plan is finalised, so that the underlying budget to meet the plan can proceed immediately.

## 3.5a – Objectives

The strategic plan (section 3.4) establishes the financial performance which the business has to achieve over the next few years, the first of which is rapidly approaching.

But although the plan has been developed with considerable care and detail and much hard work, it is not of itself going to be achieved without a budget. For the business to meet the targets in its plan, every profit centre and cost centre in every department of the business must know what it must achieve for the business as a whole to hit its targets.

Moreover, if the business begins to fall short of its targets during the year the management must know in which areas it must take swift remedial action. To do this, the monthly reporting of actual performance against budget must highlight these points of variance. Similarly, if the business is exceeding its targets, management will seek to replicate the performance of the successful areas over other parts of the business.

The budget is therefore a bottom-up exercise designed to give each department its own share of the top-down strategic plan. The budget is also the confirmation of the feasibility of the plan (inevitably, given the different methods of preparation, there will be some final adjustment between the plan and the budget).

## 3.5b – Overall process

As with any other management process, if you give your team a sound briefing at the start, the result will be much better. The main elements you require are:
- initial briefing meeting – summarise the general objectives (with which your managers should already be familiar) and stress the differences from the previous budget (to avoid a ho-hum, "same again" attitude)

- timetable – highlight the main review dates and emphasise that if one department is late, the whole process will be delayed – stress the need to call for assistance if in difficulties
- base information – provide your team with all the information and parameters they need from the outset; most of it will emanate from the strategic plan (3.4)
- documentation – see 3.5d below

The total sales budget will normally be the starting point, as almost all areas are affected by the sales volume and the phasing (seasonality) during the year. From the sales budget will follow:

- variable costs
- fixed costs (they only remain fixed within a certain activity range; if activity rises beyond a certain level, the fixed costs are likely to take a step upward, and if activity is being reduced you will want to cut some fixed costs when a downward "step" is reached)
- inventory, receivables and payables
- capital expenditure

Therefore if possible you should have the sales budget at final or near-final stage before the budgeting of costs begins. This is normally possible since the sales function exists (or should!) in a state of perpetual forecasting, but if the sales budget is not finalised, give the departmental managers an estimated budget as a guideline by which they can start work. If this is reasonably close to the final sales budget, the departmental cost budgets should not require much, if any, alteration.

In order to achieve a uniform method and standard of calculation and presentation you should issue the department managers with a standard template for their calculations (appendix C2). This will almost invariably be on a spreadsheet (budgeting through a main computer system is seldom as effective as the system manufacturers profess it to be). The spreadsheet should have a fixed-format front sheet to give consistent collation into the total budget, and semi-free-form back-up sheets to allow each department to calculate its budget as it considers appropriate.

The overall process therefore runs as follows:

- preparation of instructions, background documents and timetable for department managers
- briefing meeting for department managers
- visits to all department managers to ensure that they are actively preparing their budgets and are fully conversant with the requirements

- collection and collation of draft department budgets and comparison with strategic plan – in 9 cases out of 10 the overall result will fall short of the plan targets, but in addition to identification of areas requiring cost reduction, be alert for omissions from cost budgets (these are harder to identify than cost over-runs and can cause serious embarrassment if not rectified at the budgeting stage)
- first review meeting – discussion of problems arising from the first draft and instructions for amending the budgets in line with the strategic plan
- further visits to department managers, concentrating on those whose first drafts were furthest adrift from the strategic plan
- second review meeting, by which time the budget should be close to the plan and any further amendments can be made by the financial controller (under discussion with the relevant managers if the amendments are substantial)
- presentation of the budget to the financial director and the board for approval
- issue of the final budget to all managers
- entry of the budget in the accounting system

Note that in a complex business it will not be practicable for the controller to monitor the work of all the department managers. In such cases he will have to work with the senior managers and ensure that they monitor the work of their subordinate managers (not as simple as it sounds).

*Real life – a company budgeted sales of complex new electronic capital equipment without including substantial customer demonstration costs in its marketing budget, nor a stock of demonstration equipment in its balance sheet. Without demonstration equipment available to customers to operate on a test basis for 1-2 weeks each, a sale was unlikely. No finance had been planned for a stock of demonstration units and the company consequently ran into a severe shortage of funds, whilst being unable to sell any equipment.*

## 3.5c – Timescale

Typically, your budget should be organised in time to begin work immediately after the results have been published for the month 9 (appendix A4) and the updated strategic plan completed:

- if you prepare the budget too early in the year you are likely to waste time adjusting it for events occurring later in the year and create the annoyance of multiple allegedly "final" versions

- you will also fail to take account of initiatives and directions in the updated strategic plan
- if you leave the budget until too late in the year you risk not having the associated practical preparation (see below) completed in time for the new year – a hasty budget is seldom a realistic one

You should aim to have the whole budget process completed by the end of month 11, leaving month 12 free for the related practical activities:

- reorganising production arrangements to accommodate the budgeted output
- reorganising supply arrangements, inventory levels etc
- creation or alteration of other facilities as assumed in the budget
- setting up the budget in your accounting system before the new year begins
- calculating and inserting the next year's detailed costings into the costing system

You should make a final adjustment to the budget to replace the budgeted opening balance sheet for the new financial year with the actual balance sheet:

- upside – you do not have to keep adjusting for the opening position when comparing actual working capital, fixed assets and cash levels against budgeted levels (although an intelligently presented cash flow statement goes a long way towards this)
- downside – if your actual opening balance sheet differs substantially from the budgeted position, you will have to tweak your balance sheet model slightly; that should not be difficult

*Real life: a group had the practice of zeroing all its subsidiary company bank accounts at each year end, so that the cash per the balance sheet always indicated the net cash flow for the year – a very good idea in theory, spoiled slightly by the fact that it could not be done until several days into the new year, resulting in a retrospective bank balance adjustment which created a difference in the opening balance between the management accounts and the statutory accounts. But then, one cannot reasonably expect Scots bankers to work on New Year's Day . . . .*

## 3.5d – Documentation

As with any other management process, if you give your team a sound briefing at the start, the result will be much better. The main elements you require are:

- either the whole strategic plan or if confidentiality prohibits that, an appropriate summary of it
- the budget timetable
- the budget template (appendix C2), one for each account category in the budget, corresponding exactly with the categories in your monthly management reports
- some guidance notes – make it as easy as practicable for the managers while still ensuring that they go through the entire thought process properly
- the master budget model (see example per appendix C4)
- (after completion) a short narrative commentary on the budget, summarising the underlying assumptions and explaining how it seeks to achieve the strategic plan targets, and any substantial deviations therefrom

As always, keep your narratives short and devoid of management clichés – and remember that your core business is making money. If you happen to make widgets at exactly the right quality and price for your customers and deliver them precisely on time, that is merely your way of making money.


## 3.5e – Financial model

A number of integrated accounting and management computer systems claim to have planning and/ or budgeting facilities, but in practice these are cumbersome and the great majority of businesses use spreadsheets for planning and budgeting. However, only a small percentage of businesses do this well.

Since every business has its own distinctive features to be incorporated in its budget, let us concentrate on the features which should be present in all budgets:
- full integration of all schedules, so that a change in one schedule automatically rolls through all the other relevant schedules (eg if you change sales, the model automatically changes the sales tax, the accounts receivable, the inventory, the bank balance, the bank interest thereon, the net profit and the tax thereon)
- a lead-in period from the most recent actual results to the start of the budget year
- an automatically self-balancing balance sheet, the cash/ overdraft being the balancing item (assuming, of course, that the balance sheet at the start of the lead-in period is correctly entered)
- an automatically self-balancing cash flow report (again, assuming a correct opening balance sheet)

- check-totals and summary check-totals (all vertical and cross-totals should be checked to zero)
- supporting schedules which set out the information in the exact format in which it will be entered in the accounting system (preferably with an account number for each category in the schedule)
- free-form schedules for underlying workings which can be linked to the input to the supporting schedules
- a profit statement and balance sheet which pick up their figures from the totals of the supporting schedules (the cash flow statement will pick up mainly from the profit statement and balance sheet, but also from the fixed assets and other supporting schedules)
- protection of the entire model except for the working schedules and the input areas in the supporting schedules

The exact contents of the model will depend on the nature of the business, but most budget models will have the following pages:

- menu – standing data (name, year, period dates, currencies etc) and check-total summary (it is also useful to have the profit and cash figure on the menu, so you can see at a glance that the result is sensible)
- assumptions (alternatively, can be included in calendar below)
- calendar – enter all expected events during the year, such as price increases, pay awards, sales exhibitions, major projects etc (if you enter events as 1 or 0, the related income and cost streams can be multiplied by the calendar rows and the income and costs rescheduled merely by amending the 1s and 0s.
- enquiries and orders (with percentages of conversion into sales)
- sales (volumes, prices and total values, less sales credits)
- direct materials including transport costs and provision for scrap and other losses
- direct labour including efficiency percentage, overtime calculations etc
- other variable costs
- marketing costs
- admin and other costs
- finance costs, taxation etc (calculated by linkage to borrowings, profits etc)
- inventory
- trade and miscellaneous receivables etc (trade balance calculated by entering days of debt)
- trade and miscellaneous payables (linked to credit items in profit and capex budgets)
- fixed assets, capex and depreciation

- borrowings, equity and reserves (including taxation and dividend balances)

In addition to the above formatted pages there should be appropriate free space for underlying calculations, which do not necessarily need to be included in the print ranges.

Note that the vertical format of the budget should be EXACTLY THE SAME as the vertical layout of your monthly management reports. It is a considerable annoyance to have a budget in one format and management accounts in another. This means that when you set up your budget model you should design next year's management accounts simultaneously. And it goes without saying that your general ledger accounts should also be in that format (usually with some additional analysis accounts which are combined in the management accounts).

## 3.5f – Review and approval

As shown in the model in appendix C2, the budget template for each department should show a rough estimate of the production or sales value and volume, and any other base figure (eg labour hours) which would influence the costs of that department. When each template is returned for the first review there is therefore an immediate correlation between the budget of that department and the overall level of activity.

The review should therefore cover:
- correlation between the budget and the agreed strategic parameters
- correct entry of all data (ie totals in the main budget model agree with sub-schedules on which budget managers have prepared their detailed figures)
- correlation between sales/ production volumes and all costs and working capital levels
- correct inclusion of fixed assets and capital expenditure
- reasonableness of all figures in main statements (profit, cash flow and capital employed)
- correlation between budgeted result and first year of strategic plan

It is easy to fall into the trap of running through the whole budget nodding one's head at the correct calculations by the departmental contributors. Concentration must therefore be directed specifically at the realism of the figures and their consistency with the overall strategic plan.

Uncertainty regarding market conditions, combined with inexperienced budgeters, will give the controller a difficult review. Conversely, an "easy" budget (same again, chaps) prepared by experienced departmental budgeters will mean that the controller has to guard against complacency in the process.

## 3.5g – The final version

When the budget has been approved by the directors the following actions are required:
- publish and distribute
- enter in system
- enter in accounting models (cum, round)
- adjust to actual opening balances when audited figures are finalised

## 3.5h – Making it happen

Once the budgeting exercise is over, those involved breathe a big sigh of exhaustion and relief. Bit by bit they pick up the threads of their normal existence, catch up on matters which have fallen behind as a result of the budgeting work and gradually get back to normal life. Within a short period of time life has returned to whatever passes for normal and the budget recedes into an accounting document used for comparison of the monthly results with the business's aspirations. This relapse is even more pronounced in groups where the budgeted targets have been to some extent forced on the local management.

YOU MUST NOT LET THIS HAPPEN.

BEFORE each month-end, the team driving the business must meet to review the prospects for the following month and the barriers in the way of achieving the cash and profit targets. At this meeting you must create the thrust towards beating the budget for the following month:
- if sales orders are not forthcoming, look to see if additional sales can be brought in from conventional and unconventional sources
- if that is not practicable, see if sales to some customers due in future months can be brought forward to the imminent month (but do not sacrifice margin in the process; if anything try and raise it)
- if production difficulties are likely to occur, take action to resolve them BEFORE the date when they will cause lost revenue, or contract out the work or supplies to other businesses

- ensure that all other issues which may impact on the achievement of the budgeted performance are mitigated as far as they can be

## 3.5i – Interim updates

Situations change so rapidly in business that a budget can (and usually does) become out of date within a few months. This does not invalidate the budgeting exercise, because the rigorous consideration, research, planning and calculation which goes into a budget causes the management to review and understand its business to a much greater depth than would otherwise be the case. The day-to-day pressures of modern management are so intense that management seldom has the time to step back and take a critical strategic look at the future. The budget forces this necessary action, and for that in itself it is valuable.

However, the almost inevitable deviation from the budget may be wide enough that a new guiding document is required. The practical way to do this is to do a re-forecast at an identifiable stage, typically at the half-year point, although some businesses have the need to do it quarterly. The re-forecast can be done empirically from scratch, but that amounts to yet another full budget, and is an excessive burden unless the business is in dire difficulties. Normally a summary forecast can be prepared and will suffice, taking into account the latest known circumstances.

Typically a business is managed for the second half-year against such a forecast. The "budget" figures in the financial statements are replaced by actual figures for the first half and the revised forecast figures for the second half, so that all variances refer to the second half only. By the time the third quarter is over, the attention is split between the current year's targets and the budget for the following year. A tough time!

# PART 4
# THE SYSTEMS

## 4.1  INVENTORY

a   Objectives
b   Physical security
c   Service & contract businesses
d   Material master file
e   Bill of materials (BOM)
f   Standard costs file (materials)
g   Standard costs file (labour & o/h)
h   Product routing file
i   Goods received records
j   Raw materials control
k   Work in progress control
l   Finished goods control
m   Despatch of finished goods
n   Inventory ledger
o   General ledger

## 4.2  INVENTORY COUNTS

a   Objectives
b   Responsibility
c   Instructions – general
d   Pre-count actions
e   Allocation of duties
f   Site plan
g   Goods inward
h   Goods outward
i   Goods in transit
j   Intra-group inventory
k   Obsolete or damaged stock
l   Counting methods
m   Recording the count
n   Issues arising from the count
o   Entry of count into system
p   Valuation
q   Cyclical counting
r   Inventory at other locations
s   Contract work in progress

## 4.3  SALES & RECEIVABLES

a   Objectives
b   New customers
c   Customer files
d   Product price files
e   Manufacture of bespoke goods
f   Sales enquiries
g   Sales contracts
h   Sales order processing
i   Despatch of goods
j   Provision of services
k   Invoice processing (goods)
l   Sales price files
m   Invoice processing (services)
n   Commission, discount, rebates
o   Sales returns
p   Customer debit notes
q   Sales credit notes (goods)
r   Sales credit notes (services)
s   Goods on consignment
t   Sales statements & reminders
u   Bad and doubtful debts
v   Sales documents filing
w   Accounts receivable ledger
x   Miscellaneous receivables
y   General ledger
z   Internal check (segregation)

## 4.4 PURCHASES & PAYABLES

a   Objectives
b   Supplier files
c   Material price files
d   Purchase contracts
e   Purchase order processing
f   Receipt of goods for inventory
g   Receipt of non-inventory goods
h   Receipt of services and facilities
i   Purchase invoices, inventory
j   Purchase invoices, other material
k   Purchase invoices, services etc
l   Goods on consignment
m   Return of goods
n   Supplier credit notes
o   Supplier statements
p   Accounts payable ledger
q   Miscellaneous payables
r   General ledger
s   Internal check

## 4.5 PAYROLL

a   Objectives
b   Personnel budget
c   Recruitment of personnel
d   Contracts of employment
e   Personnel file
f   Termination of employment
g   Payroll system
h   Calculation of remuneration
i   Verification of remuneration
j   Period payroll
k   Net pay, deductions etc
l   Casual or part-time labour
m   Payroll payments
n   General ledger
o   Monthly reviews
p   Annual information

## 4.6 FIXED ASSETS

a   Objectives
b   Capital expenditure budget
c   Definitions
d   Additions & transfers inward
e   Disposals & transfers outward
f   Revaluations & reclassifications
g   Amortisation
h   Fixed asset register
i   General ledger
j   Physical verification
k   Insurance
l   Intangible fixed assets

## 4.7 BANK AND CASH

a   Definition
b   Objectives
c   Opening & closing bank accounts
d   Cash receipts
e   Cash disbursements
f   Transfers in foreign currency
g   Bank account reconciliations
h   Deposits & investments
i   Loans, hire purchase & leases
j   Travel & other expenses
k   Petty cash funds (notes & coin)
l   General ledger

## 4.1a – Objectives

The principal objectives of the inventory and cost-of-sales system are:
- Ensure that inventory at all stages of completion is securely stored in designated locations in a manner allowing easy access and control
- Ensure that all movements of inventory into and out of all locations are promptly and correctly recorded
- Ensure that the cost of all goods sold is correctly calculated
- Ensure that the correct book value per the accounting rules is attached to all inventory at each stage
- Ensure that the financial movements of stock in the general ledger accounts are simultaneous with the relevant movements in:
  – accounts payable, materials costs, labour costs, overhead costs, accounts receivable
  – corresponding stock locations (eg transfer from finished goods stock to consignment stock)
- Ensure that intra-group stock transactions are subject to above controls and are consistent between companies
- Ensure by accounting provisions that all stocks are always valued at lower of cost and net realisable value (ie less any provisions in respect of sales value falling below cost)

Production can take many forms:
- many materials and components going into a single product
- many materials and components going into a range of products
- a single material going into many products, such as in moulding or extrusion
- many materials being physically or chemically combined into a single material or a range of materials
- part or all of the above processes being contracted to an external processor
- any of the above processes being carried out to specific contracts, each contract being effectively a separate business in terms of its control and profitability

To describe an inventory and cost-of-sales (or cost of production) system for each of the above would involve a large amount of repetition. We therefore concentrate in this section on a selection of materials and/ or components being used to produce one or more types of product in an operation of considerable size, as this is the most comprehensive situation. The reader can omit from his deliberations any sections or parts thereof which do not apply.

## 4.1b – Physical security

*Real life – a well-known department store was losing ladies' underwear from one of its branches. The losses were too regular to be attributable to shoplifting, and the management concluded that some of the staff were wearing extra sets of underwear when they left the store after closing time. But with the store busy all day, and staff coming and going on work breaks and toilet visits, it was not possible to identify any such larceny. A general warning was issued, resulting in some adverse staff reaction, but the losses continued.*

*Eventually the management reluctantly decided to involve the police, and one day when the store closed a number of policewomen appeared and carried out a strip-search of all the staff. Not only did they find no extra underwear being worn, but there was a wave of outrage from the offended staff . . . and the losses continued. The management did not dare to repeat the search, fearing that staff relations would break down completely.*

*When the auditor arrived for the pre-audit planning visit, he asked as usual if there were any exceptional circumstances being encountered, and the management told him the whole story. The auditor replied simply "You should have searched them when they arrived in the morning."*

The point of this story is that there is no limit to some people's ingenuity in misappropriating attractive stock, either for their own uses or for sale to others. There is also, unfortunately, no limit to some people's carelessness and neglect. The stock system therefore begins with physical security. Stocks must as far as practicable be stored according to the following criteria:

- in a designated location per the stock records
- in a location which gives easy access to the stock for use in production (raw or semi-processed materials) or for delivery to customers (finished goods)
- despite the above ease of access, in a location which provides security, either through supervision or lack of access, from theft
- in surroundings which will prevent or at least minimise damage from ageing or from other adverse factors such as sunlight, moisture

(including humidity) or temperature (not only heat, but cold; for example, plastics can become too brittle to work with in low temperatures)

- in a location and manner which enables ease of counting, both for stock-taking and for checking availability for production and hence re-ordering
- in accordance with any other specific requirements (especially safety) for individual items

There are certain types of inventory which have their own particular difficulties over and above the normal complexities of controlling manufacturing inventory. For example:

- commodities which are readily saleable (these can be anything from raw materials to finished products) are obviously more at risk of theft than other commodities, and need a higher level of storage security
- commodities which have a short shelf-life, being subject to some form of corrosion, disintegration, pollution or other loss of essential characteristics
- commodities which are subject to fluctuating measurement (eg grain, which can gain or lose weight according to its moisture content, which in turn is affected by ambient temperature and humidity; products which compact when stored in bulk can also be difficult to assess, the quantities near the bottom of a container being denser than those near the top)

We have already discussed in the working capital section (3.2) why inventory must be kept low for financial reasons, and the above issues reinforce that priority.

## 4.1c – Service and contracting businesses

In the case of a service business, where the inventory is mainly measured in activities rather than materials, the principles are entirely similar. Work in progress is typically measured by the hours recorded at charge-out rates by personnel engaged in individual projects, and can effectively be "stolen" by personnel charging bogus hours to a particular project). Control of inventory is therefore control of time.

In the case of contracting businesses, work in progress is often a combination of material and employee time, as charged through the records to individual contracts. Each contract or each project is effectively a separate business and should have its own set of records (typically in a contracts ledger) and controls (such as booking materials on and off a construction site). There is also the common problem of controlling and recording transfers of materials and personnel between contracts.

The principles of inventory management and control are the same, despite the differences in circumstances.

For the rest of this section we shall concentrate on the control of manufacturing inventory, which involves all of the main inventory considerations. We consider a full and detailed inventory control system, but small and simple businesses will usually have a scaled-down version of the systems described, with many of the controls being exercised by supervision and observation rather than by a stock control system. The general guideline is that the cost of operating a system should not exceed the cost of losses through not having the system.

## 4.1d – Material master file

Every single type of item, whether it is a bought-in component or a bulk chemical, which is used in the manufacture of the business's products, should be defined and identified by a material master file with the following features:

- access for entry or amendment to file restricted to authorised capable persons
- authorisation from technology/ engineering/ design department for creation of new item
- item number (a unique inventory identification number – separate numbers may be required for the same item if it is bought in different quantities, different packaging, different versions, from different suppliers or in any other way which renders one item different from another even though the basic material or component may be the same)
- item name
- unit of measure (individual items, box contents by number, weight, volume etc)
- standard unit purchase price (can be expressed also as price per kilo, price per 144 or 1,000 etc, so beware – confusion over units is a common cause of inventory variances)
- standard unit cost where item is partly manufactured internally
- currency of standard price
- agreed purchase price as authorised by purchasing department
- direct link with relevant supplier files

- direct link with contract or similar file if item is for a specific stream of activity
- printable list on demand of all item details for any defined range
- printable list on demand of all new entries and amendments in any defined period
- regular review (at least bi-annually) of files for obsolete items
- regular review (at least monthly) of all new entries and amendments
- authorised deletion and archiving of obsolete items

## 4.1e – Bill of materials (BOM)

A BOM is required for each product sold by the business (including the same product in different packaging, colours etc). It is the master document connecting the technical specification for the product with the financial control of the manufacture thereof. The BOM system should have these features:

- access for entry and amendment to file restricted to authorised capable persons
- direct links to the item master files (multiplying the costs therein by the BOM quantities to give total costs)
- item number for complete product
- item name for complete product (may have to include additional definition, such as "pack of 12")
- unit of measure
- product line
- net weight
- product structure (all components and quantities making up the product)
- definitions of semi-products (manufactured components with separate identities)
- yield and scrap percentages assumed (unless assumed in routing)
- printable list on demand of all BOMs within any defined range
- printable list on demand (reviewed at least monthly) of all new entries and amendments
- review of all BOMs (at least bi-annually) for obsolete products requiring removal or archiving

## 4.1f – Standard costs file (materials)

The annual budget (see 3.5 and appendix C4) will determine the costs to be entered within the standard costs file. The trail is normally as follows:

- the overall budget determines the volume of products to be manufactured (ie the volume sold, adjusted for any planned change in the level of inventory – typically a planned stock reduction to reduce working capital or to account for a change in business practices, such as demanded by a large customer requiring a minimum holding of finished goods)
- the volume of products determines the volume of components
- the standard cost for each component is forecast taking into account the expected volumes (see below) and entered into the standard cost file for that component
- when all the standard cost files have been prepared for the new year, the budgeted production volume is run through the standard costs system (most modern systems have the facility to do this on a trial basis) and the total cost should equal the budgeted production cost, or at least correspond closely with it

How do you set the standard cost for each item? There are various ways of doing it:

- obtain quotes from your suppliers for the following year, given the volumes you have budgeted
- take the actual costs at or near the end of the current financial year (eg end of month 11)
- take the actual costs as above and adjust them for expected variances
- predict a cost from your budget or other forecasts or calculations

If you are using the actual quantities near the end of the year, you are likely to experience material price variances during the year, and if these are large collectively, you should budget for the variances. If a fall in prices is expected, you would not normally budget for them unless they are large and very likely to happen.

Where material prices for a commodity (eg an expensive metal) are subject to unpredictable fluctuations in the commodity market, it is wise to agree a price index with your customers, so that they bear (or at least share in) the fluctuations against the price of the finished goods. The most controllable way to do this is to maintain the agreed selling price for the product as a baseline, and adjust it for an index to an agreed formula based on the commodity cost.

For example, you might sell the product for its agreed normal price, and then at intervals (typically quarterly) issue an invoice or credit note calculated against the price of the fluctuating materials per the formula agreed with the customer (eg a nickel index).

## 4.1g – Standard costs file (labour and overheads)

The standard costs for **labour and overheads** follow similar principles to those for materials.

The required **labour hours** for the year are calculated by reference to:
- the total hours (allowing for down time, etc) required to be worked to achieve the production budget
- the expected cost per hour of labour (including employer oncost) per pay negotiations or expectations thereof (it may be necessary to have separate rates for early and later months if pay rises are given during the financial year, or at least to budget for labour variances to an annual standard)
- the establishing of a standard labour cost per hour of production
- a verification by running the budgeted volume through the system as for materials

The **variable overheads** budget for production overheads will stem from the budgeted production volume, adjusted for expected price and other changes. Other variable overheads may have to be derived from other factors such as marketing and selling methods, which may move differently from production overheads. The process of establishing an hourly variable overhead rate is thereafter the same process as for the labour rate.

The inclusion of **fixed overheads** in standard costs is referred to as **full absorption costing** and is a fertile area for argument. The author considers that the inclusion of fixed overheads in the product cost is:
- one of the most misleading practices in financial management
- inconsistent with the reality of the behaviour of the costs (they would be incurred at broadly the same level regardless of the volume of products manufactured)
- the cause of some poor decision-making (see below)
- in times of expansion, an acceleration of taxes on profits (the opposite in a downturn)
- open (in fact, tempting) to abuse by management

The main problem is that inclusion of fixed costs raises the value of inventory in the balance sheet.

*Real life – managing directors working for a manufacturing group were instructed by their worldwide divisional director in month 10 of a year to "make for stock", ie produce more product than had been ordered by customers, thereby increasing the inventory. The reason was obvious: by taking fixed overhead out of the profit statements and into the balance sheets of the factories for which he was responsible, the divisional director was artificially inflating his profit to maximise his bonus based on the net result for the year. He was due to be promoted to a larger division at the start of the new year.*

*Not only was this going to give very misleading results for the current year; it was going to create a cash crisis in the first two months of the following year when the increased stocks had to be paid for. In addition, the fixed overheads being released from the balance sheet in the new year would create apparently low profits. No fools, the factory managing directors managed to achieve only a minimal increase in finished stock levels, and had sound explanations for that.*

Fixed costs are incurred regardless of activity levels and production costs should therefore include only variable costs. If an estimate of fixed costs is required for other purposes, such as quoting to achieve an acceptable net profit for finished products or costing a contract, this can readily be done on a global basis, normally by an overall percentage derived from the budget, or from recent actual results.

There is, however, an argument for inclusion of fixed costs in the work-in-progress value of long-term projects. For example, a ship-building company building vessels which take several years to complete would have several years of losses followed by an enormous profit when the vessel was sold. Such colossal fluctuations in results would be unacceptable to the sources of finance, and it would therefore be acceptable for the ship-builder to include fixed overheads in the value of the ship(s) being built. However, that type of business is very much the exception.

## 4.1h – Product routing file

Each routing file combines the materials per the relevant BOM (4.1e) with the estimated costs of the production processes to provide an overall cost estimate of the product. It therefore also provides the basis for the sales pricing, the inventory valuation and the cost of sales. Essential features are:

- access for entry and amendment restricted to authorised capable persons
- direct links to the BOM file(s), which provide all material costs
- item number for complete product
- all production operations, specifying machines used, temperatures, tooling details and other figures affecting manufacturing costs
- for each operation – set-up, labour times and machine times
- standard rates of process scrap (as opposed to material yield)

- printable list on demand of all routings within any defined range
- printable list on demand (reviewed at least monthly) of all new entries and amendments
- review of all routings (at least bi-annually) for obsolete products or processes requiring amendment, removal or archiving

In the event that there are alternative routes through the production process, the route which is likely to be used most often should be used as the standard route.


## 4.1i – Goods received records

See purchases and payables system (4.4f). A tightly controlled goods received process is essential to the overall control of materials and reporting of actual costs.


## 4.1j – Raw materials control

The exact features of the raw materials system will depend greatly on the type of materials stored. Assuming a large number of materials, you require:
- separate file for each material, showing all current year movements:
    - materials received from suppliers
    - materials returned to suppliers
    - materials issued to production
    - materials returned from production
    - materials scrapped from raw materials store
- current quantity of each material in raw material store, and total value thereof at standard cost
- location (bin) number for each material
- number of months' usage of each material in store at current consumption rates (to be averaged by system over defined period, or to be entered as forecast for defined period)
- automatic provision for products held in excess of specified period of sales
- printable reports on demand of any of the above for defined range of materials for defined period

The exact structure of the materials records will depend on the types of materials. For example:
- bought-in components can be identified and controlled individually and related in some instances to specific products

- powders and liquids may be stored in bulk containers in which individual shipments can no longer be identified
- lengths or sheets of material which will be cut to required shapes and sizes will be stored as sheets and will contain a budgeted output of shapes from each length or sheet (which may vary in practice with the product type), less a deduction for the scrap value of the off-cuts
- standard-size items such as bolts and washers may be treated merely as consumables (for which an overall value or percentage may be assumed in the standard cost), or costed specifically to individual products – whichever is more practicable

## 4.1k – Work in progress control

There are many ways of controlling goods through the production processes. They vary according many factors, including:

- the type of processes and materials involved
- the type of costing system used
- whether the products are off-the-shelf or made to order

Sales orders received from customers will be scheduled by the production control department into a grouping which gives the most efficient utilisation of the factory (see 3.2d), while ensuring that the products will be delivered when required by the customers. Production control then issues the production order (or group of orders) and the process begins.

Let us assume to begin with that a single production order will suffice to initiate a batch (or group of batches) through the whole production system:

- the production order, processed through the production system, generates an automatic materials order derived from the BOM (see 4.1e)
- materials control issues the materials specified by the order to the production line and enters the amounts involved into the system
- the system credits the materials involved out of the raw materials account and debits it into the work-in-progress account
- labour costs for each period are charged into the work in progress account
- the materials are drawn through the processes, becoming progressively more complete until a final product or batch of products emerges
- the output from the process is counted and checked for quality, and the output recorded as finished goods

- the recording of finished goods automatically deletes the materials and labour costs from raw materials and work-in-progress in the balance sheet
- any shortages in the output are debited to a scrap account
- however, if faulty completed items can be re-worked into saleable products, they are done so, normally on a separate work code which identifies the time and materials spent on remedial work

Thus the production control system will be able to report:
- the volume and value of materials and labour used
- the quantity of good product produced
- the cost of any remedial work
- the quantity and cost of scrapped product (preferably with a reason coded in)

In complex processes, there may be several intermediate stages at which production is accounted for. Each intermediate stage is treated as if the outputs were finished goods, and then the output from that stage becomes the raw materials for the next stage. The accounting is the same, but in sequential stages.

When the system is rigorously enforced it is a prompt, powerful and effective tool for quantifying the cost of the production process and for identifying areas needing remedial action. When recording is omitted or carried out incorrectly, it can give rise to major spurious variances which may require a considerable amount of time-consuming investigation.

Procedures for recording abnormal scrap levels, re-working of incorrectly made products and other non-standard events vary from one system to another but all must be subject to controls similar to those above.

## 4.1I – Finished goods control

If you are manufacturing for specific customers you should be holding relatively low finished product inventory, unless the customer lead time is considerably less than the manufacturing lead time. Off-the-shelf products require the level of finished products inventory to be based on expected demand. Assuming a medium-to-large number of products, you require on the computer system:
- a separate file for each product, showing all current year movements:
  - products received from production

- products returned to production (if this happens, you have a quality problem; nevertheless, you need to be able to record the movement)
- products despatched to customers
- products returned from customers
- products scrapped from finished products store (preferably including reasons: they could be obsolete, damaged, stolen, cannibalised for other products, used for demonstration samples, transferred to a sister-company or subject to some other fate)

- the current quantity of each product in finished products store, and value thereof at standard cost
- the location (bin) number for each product
- the number of months' sales of each product in store at current consumption rates (to be averaged by the system over defined period, or to be entered as forecast for defined period)
- automatic provision for products held in excess of specified period of sales
- printable reports on demand of any of the above for defined range of products for defined period

The finished goods inventory should be reviewed at least quarterly to identify the following problems:

- shortages of items expected to be in demand
- items increasing month-on-month, indicating either a fall in demand for the customer or a build-up for expected growth in sales (or just possibly an error in the production documentation resulting in over-production)
- the same type of goods stored in a variety of locations (indicating either haphazard storage needing reorganising, or insufficient storage space, leading to missed despatches and requiring either rationalisation or expansion)
- old items requiring a provision for unsaleability or a special initiative to sell them off)

## 4.1m – Despatch of finished goods

See sales and receivables (4.3). Despatch documentation is essential for the following purposes:

- recording and evidencing the actual despatch of the goods
- taking goods through border controls if exported
- obtaining proof of delivery to customers
- providing instructions and records for the carrier

- automatic generation of sales invoices

Despatch notes are therefore usually in four parts:
- top copy to customer
- second copy to be signed by customer for receipt of goods and returned by transporter for filing in sales or despatch department as proof of delivery
- third copy to be retained by transport company as their proof of delivery
- fourth copy to be retained by finished goods store or despatch office as proof of despatch

The above documents will prove the full trail of the finished goods. In a perfect world there would be no despatch notes; the sales invoice would perform a dual function. However, that would result in a lack of confidentiality regarding prices.

The despatch function will also have to provide the correct documentation for all exports. Since this will vary from one country to another, it is not practicable to define it here. However, most border controls require documents to be complete and correct in every respect, so the despatch department must be fully au fait with all relevant cross-border documentation and also the international shipping conventions and terminology.

Note that membership of the European Union increases export documentation rather than the expected opposite, as there are voluminous cross-border statistics required within the EU.

## 4.1n – Inventory ledger

A full computerised inventory control system, operated on the principles outlined in the foregoing sections, will give the following information in real time:
- quantity and cost of each type of material in raw materials store (some systems will link to the order system and also display the quantity of material on order from suppliers and possibly the expected date of arrival)
- quantity and cost of material, labour and direct overheads in work in progress, probably to the end of the previous day, but possibly to the end of the previous shift or even in near-real time if batches of production are logged at each stage in the processes
- the quantity and cost of finished goods in store

- the quantity and cost of scrapped materials, scrapped work in progress and scrapped finished goods
- the location of all raw materials and finished goods (locations within the production process will only be reported if completed work is booked after each process, which is relatively rare)
- adjustments to actual quantities following physical counts of raw materials or finished goods
- days of inventory held against forward orders and/ or scheduled production
- raw materials and components on order

A full production control system will produce statistics on production efficiency including labour efficiency and rate variances, down time, scrap variances (standard process scrap and abnormal write-offs) and other non-standard events arising from the production processes. The extent and detail of the information available will depend on the type and efficiency of the workshop data collection system.

Differences identified by physical counts of inventory should be shown as a separate type of variance ("book-physical adjustments").

## 4.1o – General ledger

In a fully-integrated system the inventory ledger is a sub-ledger of the general ledger. The inventory totals will automatically be reflected in the general ledger, updated at least at the end of each shift when the results of the shift have been entered. The general ledger accounts involved will normally mirror the main stages of the inventory from raw materials through the main stages of work in progress to finished goods.

It should also contain provision accounts for all of those cost accounts, and separate accounts for different locations if they are controlled separately, especially external locations if items are sent out for processing by third parties. If intra-group items are a major part of the normal process, they may need to be identified separately in the ledger for consolidation purposes, ie so that intra-group profits can be eliminated.

If the ledgers are not integrated, you will need to allocate a clerical person to the regular updating of the general ledger and reconciliation with the production records. This will need to be daily so that any discrepancies can be resolved immediately and, depending on the nature of the manufacture, may require a considerable volume of accounting. This will only be of value if it gives you prompt reporting of the level of detail indicated in 4.1n above.

# INVENTORY COUNTS                                    4.2

ALL TOPICS EXCEPT 4.2q REFER TO FULL COUNTS

## 4.2a – Objectives

Inventory can either be counted all at a single count with production stopped (a full count) or by checking certain items in rotation without stopping production (a cyclical count). Either way, the objectives are the same:

- ensure that the inventory recorded in the ledgers corresponds with the actual inventory
- identify and segregate inventory which is unusable or unsaleable
- identify and rectify any circumstances in which inventory is not being effectively managed
- make adequate provision in the ledgers for any deficiencies revealed

Although it is not a direct objective of the count, it has the additional benefit (if carried out effectively) of ensuring a thorough tidying of the manufacturing and storage areas. In this respect it is useful to accompany the work with associated housekeeping, eg repainting floor area lines and re-marking storage areas)

An annual full count is essential in almost all manufacturing businesses. Whether a count is also required on intermediate dates such as at the half-year or quarter ends depends on several factors:

- the complexity of the business, its production process and its inventory
- the effectiveness of its production and inventory records
- the effectiveness of its cyclical counting system
- the results of its cyclical counting system (frequent and/ or large differences between book and physical stocks revealed by effective cyclical counts may indicate a deep-rooted problem)

Some businesses, having no real-time inventory system, count their inventory monthly. In small businesses, which typically do not have such systems, this is often essential in order to determine their monthly gross margins.

## 4.2b – Responsibility

Whoever is responsible for the day-to-day custody of the inventory is responsible overall for the count, as that is a fundamental part of the duty of custody. Depending on how the business is organised, that responsibility could lie with the head of production or logistics, or with a number of different persons in charge of raw materials, finished goods, contract sites etc. Nevertheless, one operational person must be held responsible overall for ascertaining the **correct quantities and condition** of inventory held at the time of the count, and that person is responsible for submitting a correct record of these quantities to the financial controller, who is effectively the customer in this relationship.

The responsibility for ensuring that the inventory is recorded at the **correct values** lies with the financial controller. But since recording the wrong quantities will create the wrong values even if the correct costs are used, the controller has a deeply vested interest in the count, and must give extensive cooperation to the person responsible for the counting. The effectiveness of the count therefore depends heavily on how well the two persons and their teams work together.

Given these responsibilities, the operational management usually attends to the physical preparation of the count, ensuring that everything is in the correct location and clearly marked, and that the cut-off is well organised and all necessary movements completed beforehand. The financial management usually organises the recording paperwork and the briefing and control of the counting teams. Each side, however, must know and understand what the other side is doing, and each counting team should comprise personnel from both sides.

## 4.2c – Instructions

For the inventory count to be effective, instructions have to be issued in precise detail. They should be issued in draft to all those affected (4.2e) so that feedback can be obtained to ensure that the instructions are workable. The final instructions should be issued to the persons responsible for the following functions:
- ordering, receiving and storing raw materials
- controlling work in progress
- storing and despatching products
- liaising with customers with regard to deliveries during the count
- counting the inventory

- totalling and reconciling the counts
- entering the results in the ledgers

The points listed below should be covered in all inventory count instructions, although there are many ways of doing so. The points are listed in the order in which they would logically appear in the instructions and each point should have the initials of the responsible person noted in a column alongside. The instructions may cover the whole business, or it may be appropriate to have separate instructions for greatly different parts of the business.

With regard to the timing of the count, the instructions should state:
- dates and times of pre-count actions (see 4.2d)
- arrangements for ceasing production (or, if it is necessary to run production through the count, owing to demand or a continuous process, arrangements for counting those items separately according to an appropriate cut-off point)
- date and time of count commencement
- date and time of count completion
- date of completion of valuation
- date of submission of papers to finance department

## 4.2d – Pre-count actions

As with any management exercise, preparation is the essence of a successful count. It may take several days before the start of the count, and if the business is running short-lead-time deliveries it may necessitate the build-up of certain finished goods to cover the period when production is not running. The instructions should cover:
- tidying of all inventory areas – they should ALWAYS be tidy, but things may need to be arranged differently for ease of counting and it may be helpful to remove temporarily any items which are not to be counted, and all inventory MUST be in the correct locations and clearly identified (high-visibility tape for delineating individual areas, especially no-go areas, is recommended)
- completion of production runs – unless it is vital, there should be no production during the count
- return of surplus material to stores – the fewer locations at which materials are stored, the easier and quicker will be the count and the less chance there will be of errors and re-counts
- despatch of all products to be included in sales for the period and therefore to be excluded from finished goods inventory

- entry into raw material stores of all goods to be included as purchases for the period and therefore as raw material inventory at the end of the period
- identification of any likely difficulties and preparation of instructions to deal with them
- preparation of paperwork (count tickets, control sheets etc)

It is advisable to have instructions to cover emergencies. For example, if there is an emergency order which requires some production during the count, the movement of goods therein will have to be controlled and counted and added to or deducted from the relevant count figures.

## 4.2e – Allocation of duties

The instructions must specify every person responsible for all the count functions:

- supervision
- counting
- independent checking, and re-counting if necessary
- recording
- pricing, extending, totalling and summarising (most computerised inventory systems have a facility for doing this, requiring merely that the quantities are entered)
- resolving any anomalies revealed by the total figures
- final approval of count figures by the finance department
- entering the totals in the financial records, including the variances between recorded and actual quantities
- calculating and entering the provisions

It is also necessary to brief these persons well before the count, and to ensure that they fully understand the instructions, and what to do if any difficulties arise.

## 4.2f – Site plan

The counting team will understand their responsibilities much more clearly if they are given a site plan. This does not have to be exactly to scale but it should be reasonably accurate. The easiest way to prepare one is to use a spreadsheet and set the standard column width to the size (normally between 2 and 3) which makes every cell a square. Then by using selected borders and shading you can mark out the production areas, storage racks and all other relevant features. In a large business you may need several site plans.

If the racks and other storage areas are not permanently numbered (they should be, but in some cases it is not practicable) give them numbers on the site plan, and hang large cards prominently in each area so that the counters are very clear as to which area is which.

You should allocate and identify (eg by using high-visibility tape) quarantine areas to house goods which are subject to movements during the count. This should only happen in cases where it is unavoidable. Examples are:
- deliveries inward during the count, so that these materials are not included in the count, nor in the purchases for the period
- materials for a continuous process which cannot be stopped, and which will have materials for processing quarantined at the upstream end, and completed products quarantined at the downstream end – you will need a formula for valuing the goods in such an area
- finished goods which have been excluded and treated as sales, but which are awaiting collection and delivery to the customers (these should of course be genuine sales, despatched before the period end)


## 4.2g – Goods inward

For deliveries from suppliers:
- ensure that all deliveries up to the point of count are in the correct locations in the raw materials store and are recorded in the goods received system (ie a goods received note has been issued)
- if you have a manual goods received system, issue a goods received note of zero value marked as void to establish the cut-off point (a computerised system probably will not allow you to do this)
- print a report of goods received up to the cut-off point, to be checked by the finance department
- ensure that all goods received after the cut-off point are stored in the defined quarantine area (4.2f) and are not counted as inventory; as soon as the count has been declared satisfactorily completed they must then be promptly processed through the normal goods received system

For returns from customers, exactly the same as for suppliers above, and also:
- count goods returned and list them separately at the end of the count

- add the amounts returned to the inventory total, unless they are defective and hence of no value
- process the goods returned through the accounting system as normal, ensuring that the necessary adjustments to sales, cost of sales, finished goods inventory, scrap, provisions etc are made (see 4.1o)
- issue credit notes where required, and ensure that they are processed in the period of the count

## 4.2h – Goods outward

For deliveries to customers:
- ensure that all despatches to be recorded in the period are physically removed from inventory before the count and cannot be included in the count
- ensure that all despatches up to the point of the count have been invoiced and fully accounted for
- note the last despatch note number and sales invoice number and ensure that they are correctly reflected in the system at period end

Ensure that at the end of every period (not just those when there is a physical inventory count) the sales cut-off complies precisely with the business's definition of a sale. This is normally when the goods have been loaded on the transport, or when they have passed the gatehouse and are off the premises. However, accounting standards in some countries insist that goods must have been delivered to the customer before a despatch can be counted as a sale (a concept which can cause considerable practical difficulties). Whatever the definition, this should be a rigid and consistent discipline every month, so that it is fully understood during inventory counts.

## 4.2i – Goods in transit

Goods in transit to or from suppliers or customers at the start of or during the inventory count are dealt with as discussed in 4.2g and 4.2h above. However, procedures may also be necessary to account for when the transit is intra-business or intra-group.

Where the business has movement of inventory between its own locations (eg outlying warehouses or contract sites) the count instructions must specify how these movements are dealt with, and the instructions must be

discussed with and understood by both the sending location and the receiving location. Prepare the instructions as follows:
- complete all intra-business movements before the inventory count if possible, so that there is no inventory in transit
- if transit is unavoidable, complete the outward documentation at the sending site and add it subsequently on separate sheets to the inventory of the receiving site
- check to ensure that the inventory in transit is recorded only on the transit count sheets, and not in the main inventory of the sending site or the receiving site

If your business is part of a group, it is more difficult to avoid having inventory in transit as all sites tend to maximise their despatches in each period. Moreover, there may be considerable geographical distances between sites. In such cases ensure that you are following precisely the group instructions for items in transit. Most groups use the principle cited above in which inventory in transit is treated as belonging to the receiving location, but some countries have a legal stipulation that goods cannot be treated as sold until they have been accepted by the customer. That creates a necessity to review post-count delivery documents and include items in transit outward in the finished goods total.

Remember to isolate consignment stock:
- consignment stock INWARD MUST NOT be counted, as it belongs to your supplier until used
- consignment stock OUTWARD MUST be counted, as it remains your stock until used by the customer

(yet another couple of reasons why you should try to manage without consignment stock).


## 4.2j – Intra-group inventory

If your business is part of a group, your group office will need to eliminate intra-group profit from the inventory totals at the end of each accounting period. You should therefore have within your system a simple method of denoting inventory purchased from other group companies, and should be able to run a report of these items at any time on demand.

Similarly, when carrying out a physical count, identify group inventory separately (ideally in separate locations, but that may not be practicable) on your count sheets, so that you can total them separately and compare them with the figure held by the system and thus verify the figure you submit to your group office.

## 4.2k – Obsolete or damaged stock

In day-to-day operations, obsolete or damaged stock should be physically separated from usable stock and clearly identified as unusable. It should be disposed of on a monthly basis unless there is a clear prospect of it becoming usable at a later date. Authority for the disposal should be obtained from an appropriate department independent of production and stock control, such as purchasing (for raw materials) or sales (for finished or nearly-finished items) or design/ engineering (in general). An engineering opinion may be needed to determine whether stock is re-processable or re-usable in some other way.

In a standard costing system there may be a specific variance account for scrapped stock. Even without such a system, it is worth recording damage and obsolescence write-offs separately so that the levels and causes can be understood and future losses minimised.

## 4.2l – Counting methods

How items are counted depends on the nature of the items, the quantities and how they are packaged. The common methods are:
- count every item – this is practicable if there are small quantities
- accept unopened packages – if your experience of your suppliers is that the contents reported on their packages is accurate, this is normally an acceptable method, although some businesses prefer to break open a percentage of packages for counting
- weigh items – where there are large numbers of identical items (eg bolts) it is practicable to weigh 10 of them (to average out any slight anomalies), then weigh the total quantity and calculate the quantity against the weight of 10
- dipstick – for liquids held in large containers (it is useful if the dipstick is specifically calibrated to the dimensions of the tank, to avoid geometrical calculations, but you have to be certain you are using the correct dipstick for each tank) – always ensure that you understand the tank's geometry and dimensions
- tapping – for powders held in cylindrical silos or hoppers, tap the sides until the solid sound is replaced by a resonant sound, which happens at the level of the powder – again, to save calculation the outside of the vessel should be calibrated with the internal volume at intervals (you should also make a calculation for the meniscus, which will be convex if the last movement of powder was into the silo and

concave if the last movement was outward; a standard calculation should be available for each silo)
- internal markings in large containers – not often available in practice

You must specify the units of measure precisely in your instructions. Commonly used units include:
- units, tens, hundreds and thousands (dozens and grosses still appear occasionally)
- grammes, kilogrammes and tonnes – but beware; there are still some non-metric measurements around, and to complicate matters further a US gallon differs from a UK gallon
- millilitres (ie cubic centimetres), litres and cubic metres – again, beware of non-metric measurements, and also note that fluids are sometimes measured by weight instead of volume
- packages – see the real-life example below
- lengths or blocks – again, see the example below
- sets – several components may be provided in sets, and you must ascertain whether these components are included in your inventory and your costing system as separate items, or whether the entire set counts as a single item
- agricultural measurements – for entirely practical reasons, agricultural and fishing suppliers use methods not normally encountered elsewhere, such as the brace, meaning a pair

Confusion can arise when the quantities stated in packaging and transport documentation are quoted in different units from those used by your business. For instance, you may buy bolts in dozens for use in groups of four.

In preparing the count instructions, refer to the units per the bills of materials (see 4.1e) and use the same units throughout, except where practical considerations prevent it. Highlight such exceptions clearly. The count tickets or sheets will have a space for entering the units used for each item, but your instructions must give clear general guidelines so that counters and checkers are aware beforehand of the units which they will be using.

*Real life – a company sold 6-metre lengths of extruded plastic profile. The lengths were boxed according to the cross-section; a heavy section might have as few as two to a box, where as a small section could be packed twelve to a box. Some customers ordered the product by the metre, some by lengths and others by the box, with the result that the product had three different units of measurement in common use. To make matters worse, the extruding companies supplying the product measured and priced their output in tonnes. There was considerable scope for confusion and despite constant careful attention quite sizeable errors did occasionally occur. Such conditions require especial vigilance in preparing stock-counting instructions and in the actual counting.*

Psychologically, it is much better that the counters and checkers do not have any indication beforehand of what the quantities should be. If they are given an expected figure they will tend to work towards it, and when they reach it they will tend not to look for other quantities of the same material. This problem is especially prevalent when there are amounts of one material in several different places (generally that reflects poor organisation, but it may be unavoidable).

## 4.2m – Recording the count

There are two classic methods of recording the count:
- entering the count results on pre-printed sheets and marking the inventory as having been counted
- entering the count results on pre-printed tickets, one for each inventory item in each location, the tickets (or a tear-off portion thereof) being left at the inventory locations for the checkers to confirm

Whether sheets or tickets are used, they must be of HIGH VISIBILITY and pre-numbered sequentially. The count supervisor will record in a log which blocks of sheets or tickets are issued to each counter and will ensure that all sheets or tickets, whether used or blank, are returned to the supervisor. In this way the supervisor ensures that all items of inventory counted are progressed to the valuation stage. The instructions should state where if practicable the tickets should be placed in relation to each group of items (adhesive tickets can be useful in that context, provided that they can be removed and do not remain to confuse the next inventory count).

The sheets or tickets must show the following information – note that the counter's name and the general location (eg "electrical components rack 4") will already have been recorded when the paperwork was issued:
- exact location name or number (eg "bin A17" of rack 4 above)
- correct description of item (in accordance with bill of materials, but be careful, as items are sometimes known by a different name on the factory or warehouse floor)
- unit of measure  (see 4.2l above)
- quantity counted
- a spare column or box for noting damage or resolving discrepancies

- a spare column or box for quantity checked

Where work in progress is being counted, there is likely to be a need to define on the sheet or ticket the state of completion of the items being counted, as they will have different values according to their progress.

The ticket method, although more complex than using sheets, has several advantages:
- by leaving the ticket, or a tear-off portion thereof, on the inventory after counting, one gains a visual check that all items have been counted, and counted only once
- by checking the serial numbers of completed and unused tickets, the supervisor can confirm the exact number of locations counted, whereas a sheet of 20 rows could show anything from 0 to 20 items checked
- use of the tear-off portion means that the checker can check the location and enter his figure without knowing the original count, which makes the check more reliable
- the operational staff, in preparing the locations for the count, can place the tickets with the item details and units of measure noted beforehand on all the locations, returning the blanks to the count supervisor – this greatly reduces the time of the actual count, and also ensures visually that every location will be counted
- the count supervisor knows from the outset how many counted tickets are to be returned and can direct his resources more effectively during the count

Various designs of ticket can be obtained from commercial stationery suppliers. Failing that, they can be produced cheaply since they do not have to be of a high print quality.

When using sheets, numerical control is more difficult. The number of sheets required by each counter has to be estimated, and a greater degree of verification of the returned information is needed than it is for tickets. Moreover, each location has to be marked as counted and checked, and some items may still bear the marks from the previous inventory count, thus causing errors (colours are the obvious answer).

Whether the checkers recount every item or whether they merely check on a test basis is a management decision and will depend on:
- the incidence of error experienced on previous full counts
- the consistency and effectiveness of any cyclical counts
- the complexity of the inventory and its layout
- the values of the items involved

## 4.2n – Issues arising from the count

When the counting and checking have been completed and all tickets or sheets have been recovered, a number of actions are necessary to resolve queries which arise from the count:
- valuation/ segregation/ disposal of items identified as damaged
- resolution of discrepancies
- resolution of other queries – obsolescence, other suitability issues
- slow-moving stock, where not shown on the computer

Each must be decided on its own merits, and most of these decisions require technical and financial input. If the company is in a group making similar products, there is the added dimension that what is unusable in one part of the group may be usable in another, and consultation may be needed.

## 4.2o – Entry of count results into accounting system

If you have a system which accounts for your inventory item-by-item, it will have a function which allows you to enter the results of your physical counts for raw materials and finished products. Once you have entered and checked the total quantities, instruct the system to process the figures and it will update the quantities held, debiting or crediting the difference to a book-physical adjustment (variance) account.

How you enter the work in progress will depend on how the system accounts for work in progress, but as the work in progress volumes will flush through the system as the various products are completed, it is probably neither useful nor practicable to attempt to adjust works orders individually. Only a major adjustment should be made, and this will need an investigation of the various orders in progress to determine where the adjustments should be made.

In all cases where there are substantial adjustments, it is not enough merely to make the adjustments. You will have to determine the causes of the discrepancies to prevent or at least minimise recurrences. This involves examining the system trail to identify and examine the most likely causes for error in booking the movements of materials. Common problems are:
- scrap
- closing production orders incorrectly on completion
- returns to store not properly recorded
- double-booking

- theft (although common in the case of useful items, it is not normally a high-value issue except in the case of easily saleable materials or components – aluminium being a prime example)

In the case of contract work in progress, it is of course practicable to allocate book-physical differences to individual contracts. However, this should be an ongoing process as part of the control of each contract at each major billing stage, and each contract will have its own set of circumstances, albeit within an overall contract control system. Where a company operates a number of contract sites, simultaneous inventory counts at all sites may not be practicable, so it may be necessary to do them on different dates. Pilferage from contract sites tends to be easier than from a factory, so additional measures may be needed, including surprise counts.

## 4.2p – Valuation

Valuation of raw materials and finished goods should be at the values per your costing system, with appropriate adjustments to convert the figure to actual cost in your annual external financial statements. That adjustment is an accounting issue beyond the scope of this book; the system will value the inventory according to your costing. Provided that your accounting and tax regulations allow you to do so, set your system to value your inventory on a first-in-first-out (FIFO) basis, so that you will be carrying the minimum range of costs in your system, and your valuation will always be as close as it can to the current reality. Only in a severe case of falling purchase prices are you likely to have to make an adjustment against this basis.

Valuation of work in progress is a more contentious process, there being a variety of approaches. Common amongst them are:
- a value per the bill of materials for each state of completion for each item (rare in practice, since it would involve a degree of complexity only justifiable in items of very high value in a lengthy production process)
- value at raw material cost throughout
- value at raw material cost plus an agreed average percentage for work done (typically a half-way value between raw material cost and finished cost)

An item-by-item process-by-process valuation is only justifiable in a complex and lengthy production process in which there are substantial values involved, and where a percentage method could not guarantee reasonable accuracy. In the majority of businesses, however, the production process is short enough for the value of work in progress to be small enough in relation to the value of raw materials and finished goods for an averaging method to be accurate enough to give a true and fair view.

**Consumables** (lubricants, detergents, work clothes, stationery and other items not incorporated in the product) should not be valued as stock; they **should be expensed when they are purchased**. If they are expensed, the departments responsible immediately suffer the cost against their budgets, and they will therefore only order consumables when they really need them, instead of holding comfort stocks which absorb cash and invite pilferage. Moreover, employees are more careless with consumables when they know that there are more in inventory.

## 4.2q – Cyclical counting

Full inventory counts, as can be seen from the above points in this section, are a major undertaking in most businesses. They are time-consuming, intrusive into management and production time and distractive. As a result, they tend to be performed infrequently, typically at the year-end and half-year-end. Since a lot can go wrong in six months, good management is generally uncomfortable with such an interval and will usually wish to supplement the full counts with a degree of cyclical counting.

Some businesses consider their cyclical counting to be frequent and accurate enough to eliminate the need for full counts and others consider that they do enough full counts not to need cyclical counts, but most businesses regard the two procedures as complementary. There are no absolute rules for how to conduct cyclical counts, but the general principles are:
- rotation to cover all areas and products over a certain period (for example, every 6 months)
- greater concentration on high-value items
- greater concentration on high-quantity items
- counting at quiet times – typically in low production season or on less busy shifts
- despite the degree of predictability created above, some element of surprise counting

Evaluating the results of cyclical counts can be difficult, since they are not based on the clinical, frozen situation created by the preparations for a full count. They therefore have to be performed at times when the physical volumes counted can be agreed with opening inventory balances (for the shift, the day, the week etc) being adjusted for subsequent issues, returns, production, scrapping etc.

Despite the above difficulties, cyclical counting confers some advantages:
- it reminds personnel that they are under permanent scrutiny
- it is more likely to catch adverse situations at an early stage, avoiding escalation
- it has a degree of flexibility, and can be focused at short notice on specific areas of concern
- it smoothes out the flow of book-physical adjustments from period to period, giving a more accurate indication of real production costs
- once the routine is effectively in play, the management burden decreases, leaving more time for analysis and rectification

## 4.2r – Inventory at other locations

Even if a business is concentrated at a single factory, there may be inventory at other locations:
- contractors or subcontractors
- contract sites – quantity surveyor or site manager
- outlying warehouses
- consignment inventory inward
- consignment inventory outward

If one-time stocktaking is the procedure, the above locations should be included in the count under the normal counting procedures, although it may be necessary to appoint third party stock-counters to carry out the counting on the company's behalf.

If cyclical counting is the norm, the external locations should be included in the counting arrangements, the frequency of counting depending on the security, independence and management quality of the external locations.

## 4.2s – Contract work in progress

The principles of stock control in general in-house manufacture apply equally to contract sites, each of which should be regarded as a business within itself. Stock-counting and progress measuring at each of the contract sites should be carried out on the same principles as those described above for in-house business activity, and as far as practicable each site should have its inventory checked simultaneously.

## 4.3a – Objectives

The principal objectives of the sales and receivables system are:
- do not sell goods to a bad credit risk
- ensure that all sales are made at agreed and authorised prices and terms
- ensure that all goods and services delivered are invoiced promptly and correctly
- prevent unnecessary or unauthorised credits
- resolve all customer disputes rapidly, economically, amicably and permanently
- collect all amounts due by customers on or before the due dates
- carry a realistic provision at all times for uncollectible debts
- ensure that a full audit trail exists at all times
- maintain satisfactory relationships with customers to ensure continuing good business

Intra-group debts are governed by the same objectives, but most groups have rules for payment of intra-group debts and settlement of disputes between companies. They are therefore less of a concern.

## 4.3b – New customers

Before credit is awarded to a customer, an evaluation of their creditworthiness should be made. This is normally by one or more of these methods:
- a credit rating from a reputable credit reference agency
- recommendation from a reliable source
- credit references provided by existing suppliers of the potential customer (be careful; most businesses using suppliers as credit referees keep two or three suppliers firmly "onside" for that purpose and may not be so prompt in paying their other suppliers)
- confirmation by their bankers of funds available
- good credit experience of that customer from another company in your group

- provision of the potential customer's latest audited financial statements (but as these can be anything up to 21 months old in the UK, they should be accompanied by very recent management financials – however, some companies refuse to provide those, and others produce statements of such poor quality that you are left with a tough decision)

On engaging a new customer, arrange for them to sign your terms of sale. These should be printed on the back of ALL your sales documents: quotations, order confirmations, despatch notes, invoices and statements.
They are not a cast-iron proof of a sales commitment, but they can go a long way to help in a dispute.

## 4.3c – Customer files

The computer system should hold in respect of each customer a file with the following features:
- access for entry and amendment by authorised personnel only
- customer name, delivery address, billing address and other admin details
- price, discount and credit terms (discount terms may be applied to a standard price list, or each customer may have his own agreed prices)
- other special terms
- marketing data (eg source of enquiry, customer type, geographical area, sales person)
- date and operator of latest amendment to file
- prevention of sales transactions with any customer for which there is not an authorised and complete file
- direct links to product price files and customer transaction files
- printable report of all new entries and amendments to existing entries, monthly or on demand
- printable report on demand of customer list with required data

Credit control procedures are dealt with in detail in 3.2e. Initial credit clearance MUST be properly obtained before credit sales are made to a new customer and must be kept up to date for all ongoing credit customers (4.3b).

## 4.3d – Product price files

The computer system should hold in respect of each separately identified product a file with the following features:

- access for entry and amendment by authorised personnel only
- product name, number and other distinguishing characteristics
- product group for marketing purposes
- packaging – type and quantity (there may be several types and sizes)
- product certifications
- cost per bill of materials, price and any variations (not customer-specific)
- authorisation of price and amendments to price and margin achieved
- date of latest amendment
- direct links to product design files and product transaction files
- printable report of all new entries and amendments to existing entries, monthly or on demand
- printable reports on demand of product lists with required data

The system will draw product details from the product price file when issuing sales invoices.

## 4.3e – Manufacture of bespoke goods

The sales system processes are the same as for off-the-shelf goods, with the exception that each product is for a specific customer. This may even simplify matters as there will not be multiple prices for one product. However, a blanket pricing approach cannot be applied; the pricing will be subject to the individual trade characteristics of each customer.

## 4.3f – Sales enquiries

Recording of sales enquiries is not an essential financial control, but it is an essential business control. Not only must it ensure that business is not lost through enquiries not being processed, but analysis of the enquiries can provide valuable insight into the sources and reasons for customer calls. The system should cover:

- access for entry and amendment by authorised personnel only
- entry for each enquiry, stating source and enquiry data
- disposal of enquiry, noting sales order number where an order results

- direct links to sales order files
- monthly printable report of all new enquiries
- monthly printable report of all outstanding enquiries

## 4.3g – **Sales contracts** (normally by sales contracts dept or supervisor – see also 5.3)

Sales contracts are of two main types:
- a blanket contract to deliver standard products (this simply means that the terms of the contract are entered in the customer files and if relevant the product price files) and the contract remains a paper document which provides evidence of the terms
- a specific contract to provide specific goods and/or services for a specific and finite purpose (this type of contract requires contract costing and control (3.3h, 4.3w, 5.3)

Where specific products normally sold at a standard price are to be sold at a different price under a contract with a customer, the special prices must be distinguished by one of three methods:
- entry in a separate customer price file
- recording of the difference as a discount
- separate product numbers for the items under contract (eg 12345AC instead of 12345)

Where sales are made as part of contracts, the invoices should bear the contract numbers in addition to the information detailed above. Additional copies of documents may be necessary for storage in individual contract files, in addition to the master copies in numerical sequence (4.3v).

Each contract should be summarised monthly in a separate financial statement, showing progress and costs against the contract budget (ie the original costing of the contract). Where costs are exceeding revenue with no likelihood of being recouped, a cumulative provision should be made to cover the overall loss at the end of each month, so that the loss is charged as it occurs. If the loss is large, however, the entire loss should be provided for as soon as it can be estimated.

## 4.3h – **Sales order processing** (normally by sales dept or customer services dept)

The sales order is the beginning of the trail of each individual transaction. Full control at this point is essential to maintaining full control throughout the sales and cash collection process. The computer system should provide:
- access for entry and amendment by authorised personnel only
- credit control clearance BEFORE acceptance of order
- where goods are manufactured or services provided bespoke to an individual customer, automatic prevention of commencement of work on those products until all sums due to date by customer have been received and cleared (if this may be overridden in certain circumstances, authorisation of the override must be defined)
- dates, times, quantities and prices of all orders received from customers
- allocation of unique serial number to each order, and record of customer's own order number so that order can be accessed by either number
- automatic rejection of duplication of own serial number or customer serial number
- contract/ location/ customer distinguishing details as required
- immediate updating of inventory records with order position, to enable buying department to predict ongoing requirements
- details required by quality control procedures
- written order acknowledgement displaying standard conditions of sale and confirming any non-standard conditions (eg special carriage)
- printable list on demand of all orders or part-orders outstanding (frequency of enquiry will depend upon lead times)
- printable list on demand of all orders, cancellations and amendments for specified period
- details of potential exposure per customer (existing debt plus outstanding orders)

## 4.3i – **Despatch of goods**

Every despatch of goods must be recorded, and must generate a correct sales invoice. The system must therefore have the following features
- access for entry and amendment by authorised personnel only
- dates, items and quantities of all despatches made to customers
- sales order number for each individual despatch

- stop list, which prohibits any despatch to any customer who is "on hold" – credit hold is a mechanism which enables a credit controller to hold back despatches until a payment backlog or other dispute with the customer is resolved (the customer is referred to as being "on stop" or "on hold")
- contract/ location/ customer distinguishing details as required
- evidence that all necessary quality control checks have been completed
- subsequent proof of delivery certified by authorised customer official (normally a returned copy of despatch note, signed by customer goods inwards supervisor, filed in despatch note number order; all despatch notes must be accounted for)
- automatic simultaneous generation of sales invoice (see below)
- direct links from customer, sales orders and finished goods inventory files
- direct link to sales invoicing files
- necessary documents for exports
- printable reports on demand, normally daily, of despatches not invoiced (this should not normally be possible in a computerised system, but some systems require a separate action to invoice despatches)

## 4.3j – Provision of services

The provision of services is more complex than the delivery of goods and will normally involve some or all of the following procedures, many of which may be off the computer system

- recording and verification that services have been provided to customer as specified
- signature by customer officials to confirm satisfactory completion of services or agreed stages of a contract and correct pricing thereof
- signature by customer officials to approve outlays additional to contract price

If the service is of a very standard nature (eg office cleaning, measured only in materials and hours, plus agreed incidentals), recording is required against each customer contract of:

- all materials used on contract
- all time spent on contract at agreed hourly or daily rate
- all other agreed charges

If, however, the service is specific to each customer (eg product design, advertising, legal or financial services, software implementation), there will normally need to be a separate sales contract, however simple, to cover the service. There will also need to be specific work-in-progress accounts which may have different content from one customer to another; these accounts must provide sufficient analysis to monitor the progress of the contract against the contract budget.

If the main business is contracting, the business should have a specifically designed contract costing system, which will contain special features such as the automatic provision for a loss when the cumulative costs of the contract exceed the cumulative revenue at any stage. Purchased goods should be attributed to individual contracts at the ordering stage, so that any forthcoming losses are highlighted at the earliest possible stage.

Where an integral combination of standard goods and services is required (eg selling and fitting a new vehicle tyre or exhaust), the costed time and incidental materials should be included in the price of the goods

## 4.3k – Sales invoice processing (goods)

Invoice generation should come automatically from recording of despatches. If there are any delays (eg through overnight processing) the cut-off must be checked carefully at period ends. The system must cover:

- access for entry and amendment restricted to authorised personnel
- automatic derivation of product details from despatch records
- automatic derivation of price (4.3l)
- automatic derivation of other details from customer file
- if invoices are not posted simultaneously with despatches, but (say) overnight, a system crash will result in despatches which have not been posted – facility must be available for controlled manual entry in such cases
- date, items, quantities and prices of every despatch made
- other associated charges (eg special certification, packaging or carriage)
- allocation of unique sequential number to every sales invoice
- automatic rejection of any attempt to enter duplicate number, including same number with suffix (amendments must be dealt either by additional invoice or by credit note, or a credit reversing the entire original invoice and issue of a new correct invoice, but note that these documents also have to be reflected in finished goods records (see below)
- contract/ location/ customer distinguishing details as required
- correct general ledger codes

- correct sales tax codes (these can probably be automated, since the combination of customer and product should define the code)
- automatic simultaneous updating in customer accounts in sales ledger and relevant sales accounts in general ledger
- automatic simultaneous updating of quantities and prices in finished goods accounts in inventory ledger
- automatic simultaneous updating of relevant sales accounts and cost-of-sales accounts in general ledger
- proof that all despatches have been invoiced
- print or reprint on demand of any sales invoice (authorised users only)
- printable list monthly or on demand of all sales invoices for any defined period

Having separate recording processes for despatching and invoicing goods is normal in business, but it is wasteful. Can you issue the invoice directly on despatch, using copy invoices as priced despatch notes, thus reducing the processing and checking involved? You may have to consider the following aspects:
- confidentiality – you may not want your transporters or other parties to see your selling prices, but it is relatively simple to have some invoice copies not displaying the price
- shipping documentation – you may wish to show a different value, such as the value for insurance purposes, or the value in a different currency, but the system should be configurable to do this
- month-end cut-off – you will have to ensure that all invoiced items have actually been despatched, but you have to do that anyway

## 4.3l – Sales price files

If products are sold at established prices, there is normally a sales price file for each product.

If, however, customers have individually-negotiated pricing, the pricing information may have to be kept on the customer file.

In either case, the prices per the files should be controlled by a responsible person independent of the selling function.

## 4.3m – Sales invoice processing (services)

Invoicing of services is broadly the same as for invoicing goods above, but with considerably more attention to pricing for two reasons:

- pricing may not be standard, but may be subject to a contract or to variable terms arising from the performance of the contract or circumstances encountered during the work
- additional items such as expenses may be non-standard, and will therefore require additional procedures and controls to ensure that they are correctly calculated and that no rechargeable expenses are omitted from the invoicing – this should be achieved by specific coding of the expenses
- the contract ledger must accumulate goods, payroll charge-outs and other items (services, facilities, profit mark-up etc) from the various related sub-ledgers
- there must be independent checking by the contract sales ledger staff that the information charged to each contract for invoicing has been correctly accumulated and verified by the persons in charge of recording contract costs
- thereafter, the contract managers should in turn check and authorise the amounts to be invoiced
- it will be necessary in the case of major contracts for the financial controller to counter-authorise sales invoices after reviewing an account of each contract to date

Since contract work is particularly subject to changes in terms because of circumstances encountered during the contract, control of amendments is especially important.

## 4.3n – Sales commissions, discounts and rebates

When retrospective adjustments to sales prices are in force, the following controls are needed:

- automatic accrual of commissions when the underlying sales are invoiced
- entry of discounts on sales invoices and automatic posting thereof to relevant deduction accounts
- automatic accrual of rebates as for commissions (if rebates are triggered by attainment of an annual volume, they should be accrued pro rata unless it is patently apparent that the required volume will not be achieved)

In all of the above cases, if the necessary accrual and/ or expensing cannot be done by the system, it is an essential manual procedure in every accounting period. The finance department is not likely to be advised of such arrangements automatically, so it is advisable to check for yourself periodically whether they exist. Better still, instigate a procedure in which all such arrangements must have prior finance department approval.

## 4.3o – Sales returns

The recording of sales returns is not only for accounting purposes, but must also form the basis of analysis of the reasons for the returns, so that the errors causing them can be eliminated. The system must include:

- permission from appropriate department (normally quality control, technical services or customer services) for customer to return goods; customers should be advised from the outset that returned goods will not be accepted without prior agreement
- clearance of returns from other countries through customs
- date, customer name, quantities and serial numbers of goods returned
- original sales order, despatch and invoice numbers and dates noted on returns screen
- inspection of goods by appropriate department (see above)
- if returns are rejected and therefore not entered in system, off-system paperwork must record re-issue of goods to customers
- if returns are accepted and goods are re-saleable (with or without repair work), entry of return into system, simultaneously generating:
    - automatic credit note or credit request to customer account,
    - automatic return into finished goods inventory
    - automatic credit of original cost against cost of sales
- if returns are accepted but are not re-saleable, entry of return into system, generating automatic entries as above, followed by automatic debit of scrap cost and credit to finished goods inventory (original debit can be made directly to scrap, by-passing finished goods, but entry through finished goods is more complete and correct)
- reason for return (system must have codes to denote reasons for analysis to enable management to eliminate causes)
- printable report of returns and reasons monthly and on demand

Management should examine the returns reports monthly and seek to eliminate recurrences.

## 4.3p – Customer debit notes

Some companies enter customer debit notes in the accounts receivable, in which case they must be reversed out when the sales credit note is issued or the complaint is rejected. If customer debit notes are not entered, the relevant invoices should be flagged in the customer's account to indicate that there may be difficulty in collecting cash against the invoice.

Whichever method is used, the receipt of a debit note or any form of complaint must be notified immediately to the department responsible for resolving customer complaints (normally sales or customer services, but other departments such as technical support could be involved). If this is not done, cash inflow from the customers is likely to be delayed.

## 4.3q – Sales credit notes (goods)

The value of most sales credit notes comes straight off the profit. For this reason, the reasons must be investigated and the credits authorised at a suitably senior level before being issued. The following features are essential:
- access for entry and amendment restricted to authorised personnel
- dates, items and quantities of invoiced items subject to credit
- amounts to be credited
- reference to original invoices
- reasons for allowing amounts to be credited
- cancellation of customer debit note if debit notes are entered in system
- correct sales tax codes
- evidence of receipt of goods when returned from customer
- evidence of authorisation of credit (eg by quality control dept for defects, despatch dept for quantity adjustments, financial controller for monetary adjustments, and all items above a specified amount signed at senior level)
- simultaneous updating of customer accounts in sales ledger
- list of all expected credits not yet granted, for inclusion in sales credit notes provision (this will almost certainly be separate from the computer system)
- printable analysis monthly or on demand of all sales credit notes issued analysed by reason, for any defined period – to be reviewed by senior management and action taken to reduce causes of credits

In addition to verifying the appropriateness of any credit, there is the much bigger question of removing the problem which caused the credit. By the time you see a credit note for authorisation there may be several more instances of that problem already in play, so you must ensure that the cause has been identified and prevented from recurring.

Remember: a sales credit note may be a small amount in relation to your sales value, but it will be a much larger proportion of your profit.


## 4.3r – Sales credit notes (services)

Controlling and processing credit notes for services follows the same philosophy as for goods, but the practicalities vary according to the nature of the services provided. The main differences are:
- in most cases, there is no return of goods, and therefore no adjustment to inventory or cost of sale, and normally no scrap
- the quality inspection and approval of the granting of credit takes the form of an examination of the work carried out, both in terms of the way in which it was done and the result achieved
- any remedial work to remedy the complaint is usually merely added to the cost of sale

In all other respects, the system should function in the same way as for goods.


## 4.3s – Issue of goods on consignment to customers

Don't do it.

It causes a lot of extra work to control, and is effectively providing the customers with additional credit. Therefore if you must, just grant them the additional credit, which will have the same effect but without the need for an additional set of accounting procedures. Award the extra credit for a fixed period only (typically one quarter) and review it at the end of the period, so that the customer does not come to regard it as permanent, even if it continues for a few such periods. It will also be appropriate to reflect the additional credit in the pricing of the products.

If for some reason you have to provide consignment stock, ensure that it is covered by your insurance.

## 4.3t – Sales statements and reminders

Some companies economise by not issuing statements. This is acceptable if customers pay regularly against invoices and credit control problems are negligible, which most business do nowadays. Otherwise, the system should include:

- generation of customer statements to be in post within 2 working days of month end
- automatic generation of reminders at set intervals where payments have not been received against balances due
- escalating severity of reminders according to circumstances (exact process determined by method of customer handling)
- placing of customer accounts on credit hold when in default of payment terms (for off-the-shelf products with a regular market, credit hold should merely prevent despatch, but for bespoke or limited-market items it should prevent any work from being done on manufacturing or servicing for the customer, since those costs are not recoverable against any other customer)

## 4.3u – Bad and doubtful debts

See 3.2e for the control of accounts receivable and prevention or mitigation of bad debts. Procedures will vary from one business to another, but in general, keep the debt fully recorded in the accounts receivable until:

- there is no prospect of recovery of any of the debt, and
- sales tax has been recovered

after which, write the debt off by a journal entry in the accounts receivable, debiting the balance sheet provision and crediting the customer account.

## 4.3v – Sales documents filing

Electronic filing is now commonplace, with the result that most internally-generated documents are not printed, but accessed on screen. This is acceptable if the filing is secure, backed up and covered by a disaster/ business recovery plan (5.4c). If this is not the case, printed copies of all documents described in this subsection should be filed, but if the electronic filing is secure, the following documents should still be retained on paper:

- all documents bearing signatures of authorisation, except where the signatures are made electronically, in which case a printed report of the documents authorised may be needed

- all documents generated externally (most of these are covered above, since they must be authorised before being processed)

The recommended documents for storage for each sale are
- copy sales order acknowledgements with related customer orders attached
- copy despatch notes signed by customers for receipt of goods and returned to you by the carrier
- copy sales invoices, bearing the order and despatch note numbers
- copy goods returned notes from customers
- copies of all correspondence relating to disputed debts (including notes of telephone conversations or meetings with customers)

## 4.3w – Accounts receivable ledger

The ledger should have the following features:
- individual account for every customer to whom credit sales are made (and separate accounts for the same customer if different contracts or streams of business are being performed for the customer)
- authorisation for every opening or amendment of an account
- direct link from customer file (authorisation normally by this route)
- automatic posting of sales invoices, sales credit notes, receipts from and refunds to customers
- automatic simultaneous replication of totals of batches or daily transactions per individual customer accounts in general ledger (there should not be any reconciling items between total of accounts receivable ledger and receivables control account in general ledger)
- matching of receipts against designated invoices and credit notes
- automatic charging or crediting of exchange differences to square receipts with invoices and credit notes
- automatic separate identification of unmatched receipts
- provision for journal entries for bad debt write-offs and mispostings (all other entries should originate from invoices, credit notes and cash transactions)
- authorisation of all receivables ledger journal entries
- printable list monthly or on demand of all customer balances aged by month (this can either be aged by invoice or aged by due payment date – in the latter case, an invoice subject to 30 days' credit would appear in a different month from a simultaneous invoice on 60 days' credit)
- printable analysis on demand of any customer account
- printable list monthly or on demand of cumulative or current period sales by customer or by general ledger sales code

- printable list on demand of all customers to whom no sales have been made during the current financial year (or other defined periods) showing in each case date of last sales invoice

## 4.3x – Miscellaneous receivables

These items are normally accounted for off-system by journal entry:
- accrued income
- prepayments
- other (eg amounts due by employees, deposits for renting facilities)

Record all miscellaneous balance sheet items on a monthly tracking schedule. This is the safest way to ensure that:
- all items are included in the balance sheet
- all items which should be discontinued are removed
- provisions are made against any items not expected to recover their full book value

## 4.3y – General ledger

The general ledger should automatically record the totals of the receivables ledger transactions in the sales ledger control account (normally by batch or daily total). At the end of every day there should be no reconciling items between the receivables ledger and the control account in the general ledger, but this must be checked and confirmed monthly.

See month-end procedures (2.4d) for details of the working papers.

## 4.3z – Internal check (segregation of duties)

The exact division of duties relating to the sales and receivables processes will depend upon your company structure, but as a general rule, the persons operating the receivables ledger should be entirely independent of the persons involved in:
- control of inventory
- despatch of goods
- return of goods
- examination of quality issues and other claims by customers
- granting of credits to customers
- receipt of cash from customers

- the sales force
- non-financial relations with customers

If the above activities are mainly segregated from each other, departments will act as checks against errors by each other and any deliberate distortion of the records will be difficult to achieve without collusion.

## 4.4a – Objectives

The principal objectives of the purchases and payables system are:
- order only those goods and services which are required, and which have been authorised at agreed prices from approved suppliers
- accept liability for only those goods and services which have actually been received and meet the agreed specifications
- purchase all goods and services at the most advantageous prices and terms
- do not purchase goods and services in excess of the budgeted levels for the actual volume of activity
- pay only for verified liabilities at the correct prices and terms
- maintain satisfactory relationships with suppliers to ensure optimum service

Intra-group trading liabilities are governed by the same objectives, but most groups have rules for payment of intra-group debts and settlement of disputes between companies. They are therefore less of a concern, provided that the intra-group trade is at least as beneficial to both companies as the external trade would be.

## 4.4b – Supplier files

The computer system should hold in respect of each supplier a file with the following features:
- access for entry and amendments by authorised personnel only
- all suppliers to be vetted before inclusion, preferably with references – poor product quality or unreliable delivery performance or supplier trading difficulties could harm your business
- supplier name, ordering address and other admin details
- price, discount and credit terms (discount terms may be applied to a standard price list, or each supplier may have his own agreed prices – and note the different applications of trade, volume and cash discount)
- agreed lead times, delivery frequency and other practical arrangements

- other special terms (eg maximum acceptable moisture or impurity content)
- bank details for automatic payments to supplier bank accounts
- date and operator of latest amendment to each file
- direct links to materials (and services if feasible) price files and supplier transaction files
- printable report, monthly or on demand, of all new entries and amendments
- printable report on demand of supplier list with required data

## 4.4c – Material price files

The system should hold in respect of each separately identified item required for production a file with the following features:
- access for entry and amendment by authorised personnel only
- material name, number and other distinguishing characteristics
- product group to which material is applied (if relevant)
- packaging – type and quantity(-ies)
- material specifications and certifications required by technical and quality departments
- warranty period and point of commencement of warranty
- unit(s) of measure
- cost price per bill of materials, price and any variations (not customer-specific)
- currency of payment
- authorisation of price and amendments to price
- date of latest amendment
- direct links to product design files and bill of material files
- printable report, monthly or on demand, of all new entries and amendments
- printable report on demand of material lists with required data

It is good practice to have a secondary supplier for essential supplies, and details thereof should also be included as above.

There may also be scope for holding files of regular materials not used for production (eg maintenance, cleaning, stationery) if these items are bought regularly from established suppliers. If they are bought ad hoc, it is likely to be troublesome to include them in the price files.

## 4.4d – Purchase contracts (normally by purchasing or procurement dept)

Purchase contracts are of two main types:
- a blanket contract to supply standard products (this simply means that the terms of the contract are entered in the supplier files and if relevant the material price files) and the contract remains a paper document which provides evidence of the terms
- a specific contract to provide specific goods and/or services for a specific and finite purpose (for example, for a specific finite contract or project)

Where specific products normally bought at a standard price are to be bought at a different price under a contract with a particular supplier, the special prices must be distinguished by one of three methods:
- entry in a separate material price file, or
- recording of the difference as a discount, or
- separate part numbers for the items under contract (eg 98765KL instead of 98765)

Contract conditions are discussed in detail in 5.3.

## 4.4e – Purchase order processing

The purchase order is the start of the trail of each purchase transaction. It may be driven by and linked to a materials requirement planning system or may be initiated manually. Either way, the system should provide:
- written instructions to suppliers to accept purchase orders on official authorised order forms only
- access for order creation and amendment by authorised personnel only
- dates, times, quantities and prices of all orders issued to suppliers, less items subsequently fulfilled
- general ledger inventory or cost code for each item ordered
- allocation of unique serial number to each purchase order, and retention of evidence of cancelled orders
- automatic rejection of duplication of own serial number or supplier serial number
- contract/ location/ supplier distinguishing details as required
- immediate updating of stock records with order position
- technical and quality details and certification printed on face of order

- standard conditions of purchase printed on purchase order (normally on obverse side)
- special conditions (eg packaging, carriage) printed on front of purchase order
- printable list on demand of all orders or part-orders outstanding (frequency of enquiry will normally depend upon lead times)
- printable list on demand of all orders, cancellations and amendments entered for any defined period

Some companies operate a purchase order requisition system:
- the operating department(s) complete a numbered requisition and send it to the purchasing department
- the purchasing department checks that the items are not already available from stock and have not already been ordered from the suppliers, and amalgamates the items ordered with those requisitioned by other departments
- the purchasing department then orders the required overall quantity from the suppliers

The above system would be overkill for a small company, but in a large one it prevents a multiplicity of orders being originated from different departments, resulting in supplier confusion and possible over-ordering

The ordering department should refer to budgeted levels of spend and query major deviations therefrom before placing orders. A separate and efficient ordering department is therefore a major control against mis-spending.

## 4.4f – Receipt of goods for inventory

Stock items for production and/ or resale should be controlled thus:
- checking and entry of all received items by authorised personnel only
- access for entry and amendment restricted to authorised personnel
- links from supplier files, item master files and purchase order files
- recording of dates, items and quantities of all items received from suppliers
- matching of goods received with order for all necessary details (quantity, colour, packaging etc)
- evidence that quality control checks were completed satisfactorily and that materials were cleared by authorised inspector
- acceptance within required tolerance for quantity (eg 144 items acceptable for order of 150)
- documentation of all rejections, stating reasons

- automatic entry of material accepted in goods-received-not-invoiced (also called GRNI or uninvoiced receipts) list and general ledger account
- automatic simultaneous updating of:
    - general ledger GRNI account
    - raw material inventory records
    - general ledger raw material inventory account
    - purchase price variance (so that the material goes into inventory at standard cost, and all material variances recorded thereafter are purely quantity variances, and thus easy to track)
    - outstanding purchase orders list
- entry of assigned inventory location if relevant
- printable aged list on demand of all purchase orders outstanding (to be reviewed at least monthly)
- printable list on demand of all items accepted and rejected in defined period
- printable list on demand of all items received but rejected in defined period (these should not be entered in raw materials inventory, but should be returned to the supplier)
- printable list on demand of goods received not invoiced
- monthly review of old items received but still not invoiced

## 4.4g – Receipt of non-inventory goods

If all incoming materials, whether for inventory or not, are accepted via the goods inwards department (generally accepted as best practice, but probably impracticable in a small business), the procedure for non-inventory items will be virtually identical to that for inventory items (above) with the following exceptions:

- instead of being debited to inventory, items received will be debited to the appropriate expense code (normally by reference to the purchase order)
- acceptance of the materials may well be by a department head or other person instead of by the quality control department

If incoming materials not for inventory are received elsewhere, such as in the departments placing the orders, there is scope for misappropriation, lost documentation and other difficulties. As far as possible, route the materials through a single collection point which will record the receiving and alert the relevant departments to come and inspect and accept the materials. If the items received are not recorded on the computer system, they should be logged in a record by the gatehouse, reception or some similar suitable department.

## 4.4h – Receipt of services and granting of facilities

Control over the ordering and invoicing of services and facilities is considerably more difficult than that over materials, as there is usually no physical object which confirms that the order has been met and the invoice can be accepted. Moreover, some services such as gas, electricity and telephones are ongoing, and expected to operate continuously without being reordered. And when people call for professional services such as marketing, auditing and legal advice, conference facilities or perhaps emergency repairs, they rarely issue a purchase order for them.

It is possible, however, to maintain an ordering system for services as follows:

- allocate purchasing authority for all services as you would for materials (eg the marketing director must authorise all marketing expenditure and the production director must order electricity, gas and water)
- operate the purchase order system for services as for materials, identified separately if possible (ongoing services such as gas and electricity can be the subject of a single permanent order, with a single number)
- refer all purchase invoices for services to the authorised orderers for signed confirmation of proper completion of the services in accordance with the orders

In many businesses, practicalities prevent such a system from working well, and the emphasis therefore switches to control over invoices rather than control over ordering. This is patently less satisfactory, since the expense has already been incurred by the time the invoices are received, and if people do not inform the finance departments of expenses committed, there are likely to be under-accruals in the management accounts.

Typically, the heads of the main operating departments (production, maintenance, administration etc) look after the ordering, control and approval of services received. Not unreasonably, their priorities are operational and it may be impracticable to lock them into a formal ordering system for services.

## 4.4i – Purchase invoice processing (materials for inventory)

The essential features of system are:
- access for entry and amendment restricted to authorised personnel
- automatic matching of material details from goods received records
- automatic matching of price and trading details from supplier order file
- automatic matching of purchase order number and other details from purchase order file
- entry of invoice in system on full matching only – otherwise query must be raised and resolved (invoice for part of an order or part of a goods received entry must be allowed by system, leaving balance outstanding)
- entry of other associated charges (eg special certification, packaging or carriage)
- written evidence, eg by rubber stamp, on face of invoice of date of receipt, checks for correctness and authorisation for entry (note that authorisation for purchase occurs at ordering stage)
- allocation of unique sequential number to every purchase invoice, as well as supplier's invoice number
- automatic rejection of any attempt to enter duplicate invoice number (either internal sequential number or supplier's number), including same number with suffix (amendments must be made either by additional invoice or by credit note, or credit reversing entire original invoice and issue of new correct invoice, but note that these documents also have to be reflected in finished goods records (see below)
- contract/ location/ supplier distinguishing details as required
- correct general ledger codes (preferably derived automatically from the material file through the order)
- correct sales tax codes (this involves entry by the operator after checking the supplier invoice)
- on entry of invoice, automatic updating of supplier account in payables ledger
- automatic simultaneous elimination of invoiced items from goods received not invoiced list and general ledger account
- printable list on demand of all goods received not invoiced (to be reviewed at least monthly, and all items older than one month to be investigated)
- printable list on demand of all purchase invoices for any defined period

The following information should be entered on each purchase invoice, in a grid applied either by a rubber stamp or by a small printed control form attached to the invoice:
- date of receipt of invoice
- date and number of purchase order
- date and signature of person accepting invoice
- general ledger code(s) to which invoice is posted
- date of posting to supplier account and simultaneously to general ledger
- serial number allocated by system to invoice
- (if considered necessary) signature of person approving details above
- signature of person entering invoice in purchase ledger

Most businesses post invoices in batches of a round number, typically 20 per batch with a part-batch at the end of each accounting period. This is useful because:
- there is a frequent check that the invoices have been accepted by the system (if there is a malfunction there are only a small number of invoices to be reprocessed instead of re-running an entire month
- by marking the batches, it makes the invoices very easy to locate in storage when a query arises

*Real life – a major industrial group saved a substantial amount of time and cost by dispensing with its purchase invoicing and purchase ledger payments functions as follows:*
- *instead of entering goods received in a GRNI account (see 4.4f) they entered the liability directly into the supplier liability account at the contracted buying price*
- *they configured the system to generate a bank transfer to the supplier after the agreed credit period (a degree of supervision was still necessary to ensure that any disputed items were not paid until resolved)*
- *they negotiated with the sales tax authority to accept the delivery notes as evidence of sales tax incurred and recoverable (alternatively, being a large corporation, they could have insisted on the suppliers providing invoices with the goods)*

Consider streamlining your own system in a similar way.

## 4.4j – Purchase invoice processing (materials not for inventory)

See receipt of non-inventory goods (4.4g). In a perfect system this will be the same process as for inventory goods, except that the costs will be coded to expense codes instead of inventory codes.

If the system is separate from the inventory goods receiving system, the invoices should be checked directly with the purchase orders and with whatever informal records are maintained for receiving non-inventory goods.

In all cases the person with budgetary responsibility for the materials should be responsible overall for the control of spending on non-inventory materials.

## 4.4k – Purchase invoice processing (services and facilities)

As there is no physical receipt point, the invoices should be checked against the purchase orders.

As with materials, the persons with overall budgetary responsibility for the costs of the services and facilities should be responsible overall for the control of these costs and for the authorisation of invoices for payment. No service invoice should be paid unless the person responsible for that invoice has confirmed receipt of the service.

## 4.4l – Receipt of goods on consignment from suppliers

Consignment stock from suppliers comprises materials held on site by the business, but which remain the property of the supplier until the materials are used by the business. When the business uses the materials on consignment it notifies the supplier, who then invoices the business (often the paperwork is done monthly) for the items used. The supplier will normally check the stocks occasionally.

**Consignment stock should not be held unless absolutely necessary**, since no matter what system is used to control it, it is a potent source of mis-recording and confusion. Effectively, it achieves only two purposes:
- it makes the working capital of the business appear neater by eliminating the stock on consignment from both the inventory and the trade payables figures

- unless the usage invoices are payable on a shorter timescale, it gives the business additional credit, since the invoicing is delayed until the date of usage instead of the date of delivery to the business

The working capital effect is largely cosmetic, since it affects both current assets and current liabilities. Therefore the only real benefit is that of increased credit. The business should therefore simply negotiate this increased credit with the supplier, an arrangement which would be much easier for both parties. *Real life – subsidiary company managers have been known to arrange for consignment stock so that their figures look better when reported to head office.*

However, if you are forced to hold consignment stock, there are a variety of ways of accounting for it. Of all the methods which the author has seen, only one is simple and effective, and operates thus:
- give all materials on consignment a separately identifiable inventory code
- account for them through the normal inventory system
- show the corresponding liability in a separate (dummy) payable ledger code
- at the end of each month run a report of the consignment items still in stock
- in the monthly accounts deduct the value thereof from both inventory and payables
- reverse the journal entry at the beginning of the following month

In this way, the consignment stock is controlled on system in the same way as all other inventory, and is less likely to be subject to error. However, it can be eliminated at any time for accounting purposes.


## 4.4m – Return of goods to suppliers

The essential features of the returns system are:
- goods rejected on arrival are NOT to be recorded in the goods received records
- a report is prepared by the authorised quality or technical department stating the reason for rejection (the goods received dept may also authorise return of any excess delivery over the ordered quantity, where there is no defect involved)
- a copy of the report returned with the material to the supplier
- if an invoice is received from the supplier, there will be no goods received record against which to match it, and the invoice will therefore be rejected

- the purchase ledger department will then seek a credit from the supplier, or cancellation of the invoice

## 4.4n – Supplier credit note processing

Although not essential, it is preferable to issue debit notes to suppliers in respect of any materials or services found to be defective, or for any other amounts that should be deducted from the amounts recorded as due to suppliers. These should be cancelled when the respective credit notes from the suppliers are entered (see below).

Alternatively or additionally, the system should have a facility for locking supplier invoices which are in dispute, so that they cannot be listed for payment. The disadvantage of this is that it prevents payment of the part of the invoice which is not in dispute.

The essential features of system are:
- if debit notes are in use, entry of a debit note on instructions of the person authorised to make purchases, or persons checking goods or services received, or persons checking invoices
- if debit notes are not in use, locking (prevention of payment) of invoices on the same authority
- a written record of the request to the supplier a for credit note
- processing of the supplier credit note as for processing of a supplier invoice
- entry of the invoice number(s) to which the credit note relates
- automatic cancellation of all or part of the debit note on receipt of the supplier credit note
- automatic entry in the general ledger of any exchange differences between credit note and the related invoice(s)
- a printable report on demand of all debit notes and/ or locked invoices not yet resolved (to be reviewed at least monthly to ensure all required credits are pursued and disputes with suppliers are resolved promptly)
- a printable report on demand of all supplier credit notes processed in any defined period

## 4.4o – Reconciliation of supplier statements

For many years it was considered essential to check suppliers' monthly statements and reconcile them with the suppliers' accounts in the payables ledger. However, with the advent of integrated computer accounting systems the need for this has lessened considerably and many businesses regard the activity as superfluous, given the detailed activities and controls described in the sections above.

To a large extent the payables ledger is self-checking. If you have not paid for an item or not resolved a dispute, you will have the supplier in frequent contact with you looking for payment of the disputed item. Moreover, a modern system generates payments by marking specific invoices and credit notes (see bank and cash, 4.7e), so the scope for confusion, double-payment etc is greatly reduced.

Accordingly, many businesses either ignore supplier statements (they may retain the latest one on file for reference) or merely check them for a few suppliers who habitually have accounts which are difficult to reconcile. Whether you check none, some or all of your supplier statements will depend on the effectiveness of your payables system and the incidence of errors and disputes.

## 4.4p – Accounts payable ledger

The system must include:
- access for entry and amendment restricted to authorised personnel
- an account for every supplier from whom credit purchases are made
- authorisation for every opening or amendment of an account
- direct link from supplier file (authorisation normally by this route)
- automatic posting of purchase invoices, supplier credit notes, payments to and refunds from suppliers
- automatic simultaneous replication of totals of batches or daily transactions per individual supplier accounts in general ledger (there should not be any reconciling items between total of accounts payable ledger and payables control account in general ledger)
- matching of payments against designated invoices and credit notes
- automatic charging or crediting of exchange differences to square payments with invoices and credit notes
- automatic separate identification of unmatched payments (this should NOT happen)
- provision for journal entries for mis-postings (all other entries should originate from invoices, credit notes and cash transactions)
- authorisation of all payables ledger journal entries
- printable list monthly or on demand of all supplier balances aged by month (this can either be aged by invoice or aged by due payment date – in the latter case, an invoice subject to 30 days' credit would

appear in a different month from a simultaneous invoice on 60 days' credit)
- printable analysis on demand of any supplier account
- printable list monthly or on demand of cumulative or current purchases by supplier or by general ledger code (ie inventory or expense type)
- printable list on demand of all suppliers from whom no purchases have been made during current financial year (or other defined period) showing in each case date of last purchase invoice

## 4.4q – Miscellaneous payables

These items are normally accounted for off-system by journal entry. Examples are:
- deferred income (eg maintenance contracts for customers, paid yearly in advance)
- accrued costs
- other liabilities

In general, the more items that are accounted for through the purchase ledger and therefore the fewer that are ad hoc, the better. However, peripheral items which do not fit into a normal purchasing structure should be dealt with directly through the general ledger. As a general rule, one should not proliferate accounting by spreadsheet, but a well-controlled spreadsheet can easily look after a few dozen maintenance contracts paid yearly in advance.

## 4.4r – General ledger

The general ledger should automatically record totals of payables ledger transactions in a control account (normally by batch or daily total). At the end of every day there should be no reconciling items between the payables ledger and the control account in the general ledger, but this must be checked and confirmed monthly.

See month-end procedures (2.4) for details of the working papers.

## 4.4s – Internal check

The exact division of duties relating to the purchases and payables processes will depend upon your company structure, but as a general rule, the persons operating the payables ledger should be entirely independent of the persons involved in:

- control of inventory
- acceptance of goods and services from suppliers
- return of supplies to suppliers
- examination of quality issues and other claims against suppliers
- obtaining credits to suppliers
- payment of cash to suppliers
- non-financial relations with suppliers

With the above separation in place, departments will act as checks against errors by each other and any deliberate distortion of the records will be difficult to achieve without collusion. In addition, the more of the above functions which are performed by separate people, the better is the overall internal check.

# PAYROLL SYSTEM 4.5

NOTE THAT SPECFIC REQUIREMENTS VARY CONSIDERABLY FROM COUNTRY TO COUNTRY

## 4.5a – Objectives

The principal objectives of the payroll/ personnel system are:
- plan and budget for business personnel requirements
- avoid excess personnel costs
- authorise all personnel changes and period payrolls
- recruit only persons who are necessary and suitable for the business
- agree and record exact terms of remuneration for each person
- agree and record all amendments to those terms
- apply all current terms correctly to all pay calculations
- pay only for approved work carried out to the required standard
- pay each employee the correct entitlement
- calculate and pay correct related benefits
- accrue correctly all outstanding costs for each accounting period
- pay correct net amounts on correct dates to all parties
- comply with all local legal requirements regarding personnel and pay

## 4.5b – Personnel budget

Of all the expense commitments a business makes, those regarding personnel are the most critical:
- each recruitment creates not just a single expense, but a stream of expense which is subject to a number of associated expenses
- the stream of expenses becomes progressively more difficult and expensive to terminate
- the administration of the payroll is subject to extensive legal requirements

Accordingly, the personnel budget is crucial to the control of the process and involves many critical issues:
- determination of the manpower requirements from budgeted activity
- preparing a payroll budget to meet the manpower requirements
- estimating the optimum use of overtime

- estimating the optimum use of temporary staff to cope with fluctuating requirements
- estimating the need for an increase or reduction in permanent staff
- devising (or adapting) a management structure appropriate to the activities and objectives
- estimating and subsequently negotiating a reasonable and negotiable remuneration structure
- identifying and budgeting for training needs
- likewise for other employment benefits, facilities and needs
- in times of general recession or specific reductions in activity, redundancies
- compliance with all local laws of employment

## 4.5c – Recruitment of personnel

The precise recruitment process will depend on the organisation of the personnel function. No matter who is responsible for the recruitment, the process for every recruitment must include the following controls:

- a written request showing the economic justification for the recruitment, the recruitment cost and the ongoing total cost of employment including all associated costs
- written authorisation at senior level (normally by a director in a small to medium-sized business, but in the case of larger businesses, directors handle only senior recruitment and other recruitment is approved by a senior executive)
- comparison of the headcount in the department(s) involved with the numbers per the budget, either as a total number, or a number per unit of volume of production

For production operators recruited in numbers, the above processes may be carried out in summary, since the pay structures are generally standardised and the recruitment is tied into a known production plan (eg the operation of an additional shift, temporarily or permanently).

Economic justification may require comparison with alternative such solutions, such as:

- automating work
- computerising work
- engaging an external organisation to perform the work

In most companies, recruitment is handled by a specialist from the contractual and advertising standpoint, but operational heads will lead the specification and selection process. The finance department will be involved at senior level in considering and approving the proposed remuneration levels and structure.

## 4.5d – Contracts of employment and amendments thereto

There are numerous opportunities for an employee's conditions of employment to change, including:

- changes in work or working hours
- changes in location or other working circumstances
- temporary or permanent promotion, or simply additional responsibility
- pay increase by personal appraisal or by block negotiation
- changes to peripheral rates (overtime, travel etc)
- changes to other monetary benefits or deductions
- changes in date or method of payment (eg bank transfers instead of cheques)
- changes in legislation

These can be numerous throughout a period of employment, and to create individual amendments to all employee contracts for all of these events is not practicable. The simple way to deal with this is therefore to state in the contract that amendments will be made in writing, signed by the employer and employee, and attached to the contract, and that these amendments will form part of the amended contract. The employee may not keep all the amendments to hand, so it is essential that the personnel department does, so that the original contract and all amendments thereto can be produced at any time.

Where employment conditions are negotiated by block agreement, a copy of the general notice of amendment should be attached to each contract. If negotiations have been made by representatives on behalf of a work force, there may be no need for individual signatures.

Where the business uses contractors who work closely with the business's organisation, legal advice may have to be taken when agreeing the contract to ensure that a contractor does not technically become an employee. Each country has different rules on this subject, and you may find that someone you regard as a contractor has become technically an employee (especially if working for you for a long period) and that the business is liable to account for income tax and social security thereon, normally grossed-up on the net fees you have paid him.

In particular, if working in the UK, note the taxation rules for subcontractors, particularly in the construction and allied industries.

## 4.5e – Personnel file

A hard-copy personnel file must be maintained for each employee, permanent or temporary. This should contain:
- contract of employment and all subsequent amendments
- copies or originals (as appropriate) of personal documents per list below
- all correspondence concerning the employee
- all documentation on disciplinary matters and other matters affecting the employee's status
- all other documents which are legally required (not necessarily financial in nature)

The personal documents to be inspected and retained for each employee will vary according to the business and the law under which it and the employees operate. Copies of the following items are commonly required:
- personal identity card
- personal details completed by employee on the business's standard information form
- work permit (foreign workers) or labour office registration (local workers in some countries)
- birth certificate and marriage certificate (for claiming tax allowances)
- birth certificates of children (for claiming tax allowances)
- health insurance documents
- trade union membership card
- bank account details (for transfer of net pay)
- tax certificate and other papers from previous employment
- certificates of educational, professional and technical qualifications
- medical certificates, especially where legally required for specific types of work (eg flying, diving)
- professional confirmation of any medical conditions or restrictions
- licences to use company vehicles or specialist equipment

Even if you have a personnel manager in place, you should keep up-to-date with employment regulations and make periodic checks to ensure that they are complied with. There can be expensive financial consequences from non-compliance.

## 4.5f – Termination of employment

Legal advice should be taken in the event of any uncertainty in a termination situation, especially if large numbers are involved. In addition to obligatory legal actions, the following actions are required with regard to the financial systems and controls:

- recover all company property intact on the due dates – see below
- ensure that the tax treatment is not prejudiced by the consultation process and that the correct amount of tax is deducted in the final payroll
- document and check all pay, compensation, tax, social security, expense and other calculations
- have the termination payment authorised in writing (normally by the person authorising the employment at that level of seniority)
- file all documents relating to the termination in the personnel file
- remove the employee from the payroll system and ensure that no further payments can be made to him
- deal with accumulated pension rights in accordance with the pension scheme rules
- discontinue all access rights to all computer systems

In addition, the company must recover intact all company property held by the employee, either immediately on termination or after an agreed period or event:

- laptop computer and accessories
- company mobile phone
- medical card
- work permit and other necessary documents
- office, safe, locker, gate, vehicle and other keys
- manuals and other work-related literature
- work files
- company vehicle
- club memberships
- safety clothing
- any other company property and facilities

The length of the above list indicates the importance of keeping adequate details in the personnel files; otherwise employees will leave without returning essential company facilities.

## 4.5g – Payroll system

Use a reputable well-supported national proprietary software for payroll in each country in which you operate. Ensure that it has those of the following features that are needed by your business:

- recording of all personnel details affecting pay (including addresses for sending information, bank details for payment of net pay, family details for calculation of allowances)
- recording of all departmental allocations, and employee departments
- automatic linkage with gate and factory clocks into which employees swipe or punch time cards
- automatic linkage with piece-work completion recorded in the inventory system
- automatic linkage with any other facilities which affect employees' remuneration (eg canteen tills)
- manual entry of pay data where electronic linkage is not appropriate
- entry of absences, distinguishing between entitled absences (eg holiday, maternity, compassionate, certified illness) and non-entitlement absences (which may have to be deducted from basic pay)
- calculation of all the different elements of pay involved, plus a number of spare calculation facilities to allow for expansion, temporary pay schemes etc:
    - flat rate pay (as for salary)
    - activity-based pay from clocked-in times or from piece-work
    - special supplements (eg working in difficult conditions, overnight travel allowances)
    - regular bonus schemes as operated
    - discretionary adjustments including penalties and irregular bonuses
    - special payments (but if practicable, reimburse travel expenses through the payments system and not through the payroll)
- application of non-statutory deductions (eg canteen usage, union and social club and other subscriptions)
- calculation of all statutory contributions including income tax and social security
- automatic updating of rates of tax, social security and other calculations in accordance with statutes
- manual input of period pay details where linkage is not available to time or activity systems
- calculation of period pay by employee, by department

- printed reports of pay by department each period (available as draft for review by department heads before authorising in writing)
- automatic postings to general ledger accounts (or printed posting summary if linkage is not possible)
- automatic preparation of bank transfer list (to be printed for approval before being actioned through bank)
- printable report of payroll for each pay period and for each accounting period
- printable reports of any employee's pay history or permanent file
- printed reports of all employee and company information required for business year end
- printed reports of all employee and company information required for tax year end for legal purposes and for tax and social security control purposes

For the smaller business it may be more cost-effective to carry out some of the above procedures manually. However, the basic payroll system is still better to be a reputable proprietary one, since the onus to maintain correct tax and social security calculations remains with the provider, thus avoiding an onerous in-house task. A variation on this is to use a payroll bureau, a suitable solution where the size of the business does not merit having in-house payroll calculation.

## 4.5h – Calculation of remuneration

The following steps are required for remuneration which is dependent on activity (eg production workers' pay):
- collection of base activity data – manually or electronically
- reviewing of base data for anomalies between figures and activity levels, and correcting any errors
- ensuring that data for basic pay and data for bonus pay are separately and correctly identified
- ensuring that all employee absences are correctly reflected in base data
- checking attendance and distinguishing between entitled and non-entitled absences (it is common for workers on activity-related pay schemes to accumulate holiday pay entitlement, which is released for payment in respect of holidays taken)
- authorisation of all supporting information (eg time sheets signed by foremen)
- updating of pay and deduction rates as required
- any other calculations or adjustments required by the company

The following steps are required for remuneration dependent on the passage of time (eg salaried staff's pay):

- checking attendance
- distinguishing between entitled and non-entitled absences
- recording of additional leave

The following steps are required for all types of remuneration:

- updating of all pay and deduction rates as required for period
- updating individual employees' records for changes in circumstances (work and personal)
- checking for any other adjustments (bonuses, rises, retrospective corrections etc)

## 4.5i – Verification of remuneration

In most businesses the payroll is a large part of the operating cost. Before pay is released it is therefore necessary to perform an effective check on the payroll to ensure that:

- employees are performing to expectations
- the system and the rules are not being abused
- the staff are being deployed effectively (for example, an inordinately high level of sustained overtime may indicate that it would be cheaper to recruit additional workers, or a bonus scheme may be costing more than the net margin improvement on which it is based)
- the various categories of pay are being correctly recorded

In theory it is better to check the input documentation for anomalies before it is entered in the payroll system. In practice, however, it is often easier to produce a draft of the payroll each period and review that, because the payroll totals can readily be compared with:

- the budget
- totals of previous similar periods
- the most recent forecast for the period under review
- the level and type of activity in the period (for example, it can be illuminating to check the weekend hours per the payroll with the production achieved over the weekend)
- agreement with related systems (eg total time worked per payroll with total time worked per time system, and total deductions for meals with total charges per canteen report)
- the normal mix of costs (eg the ratio of overtime to normal time and the absentee percentage)

- records of starters and leavers (problems such as starters commencing too late to be included on the payroll may need to be adjusted for)
- any other relevant factors (for example, abuse of flexi-time)

The managers responsible for the different departments must review and sign the drafts for their departments and the financial controller must carry out a final review for overall acceptability and compatibility with the circumstances of the period.

## 4.5j – Period payroll

Following the movement in the rest of Europe, many UK companies have moved away from weekly pay for factory workers and now pay them monthly along with salaried staff. This reduces the overall workload but may create additional work in accruing overtime and other figures, especially if production is reported weekly, but calendar months are used for accounting instead of 4- or 5-week months (see 2.4b). In the USA, life is considerably more difficult, since employees are generally paid every two weeks. Calendar months which split a week or fortnight of the payroll are a nuisance you can happily live without.

The following procedures will be required:
- processing approved pay figures through system, thereby updating total figures for tax year (and in some systems, for financial year, although these totals may be achieved instead through ledger postings – note that while the UK operates on cumulative tax figures, some other countries do not)
- checking correct treatment of starters and leavers and transfers of people between departments
- posting totals to general ledger
- reviewing general ledger payroll and deduction accounts to ensure correct balances
- printing payslips and distributing to employees
- making payments (4.5k)

It is common to have a payroll system that is not part of the main accounting system, and it is therefore a natural inclination to want an electronic interface between the payroll system and the main system. Only do this if the payroll system is stable; if there are frequent modifications in the accounts code structure (common in large or changing businesses and in changing legal circumstances), use a manual journal posting, because:

- the time taken to keep amending the interface to record the changes (especially if there are several payrolls in a month) will considerably exceed the time taken to print and manually post a journal entry
- use of an established spreadsheet posting sheet gives the operator a visual check on the entries

## 4.5k – Net pay, deductions and contributions

The most common general ledger posting format is the most straightforward one:

- debit each expense account (or variance account if standard costing is used) with total payroll cost (ie gross pay plus employer's contributions)
- credit each deduction and contribution account with the total of employer's and employees' contributions
- credit the balance (ie net pay due to employees) to the net pay control account

Each deduction or contribution account will therefore show the balance due to be paid to the relevant authority. Each account will therefore be eliminated to zero when the amount is paid over, normally later in the following month. The same applies to the net pay control account, normally paid before the end of the current month.

Some businesses charge gross salaries to direct cost centres, but charge employer's contributions, overtime premiums and some other peripheral items to direct overhead or even indirect overhead. These practices are misleading; the labour cost of a product is the total cost of remuneration for the work, regardless of whether it consists of salary, social security or whatever. **Charge the total gross cost to the cost centre**, or you will be making some inappropriate business assumptions and decisions.

It is essential to review all payroll accounts to ensure that they are cleared on a monthly basis. If any balances remain on payroll accounts, investigate and resolve them immediately. The longer they remain, the more trouble they will cause, and in the case of statutory deductions and contributions they may result in an inspection from the relevant government department.

## 4.5l – Casual or part-time labour

In former years, casual labour was an easy solution to temporary peaks in production. You hired people off the street, paid them in cash and terminated them when the peak was over. Many casual labourers drifted from job to job without reporting their earnings annually to the tax authorities. Accordingly, governments were deprived of considerable amounts of tax.

Nowadays, however, legislation is much stricter in most countries and even casual labour must be employed on a strict legal basis with full documentation.

Professional workers who are genuinely self-employed, however, and have the documentation to prove it, can be hired on a fee-paying basis, and will invoice the company for their services, with the appropriate sales or value-added tax added. Even these professionals, however, have been the subject of legislation in some countries seeking to treat them as employees. If you fail to deduct tax when it is due by law, the company may be assessed for tax on the grossed-up amount of the self-employed professionals' remuneration.

## 4.5m – Payroll payments

Using the posting convention described above, the relevant general ledger accounts will display the amounts to be remitted through the payment system (see bank and cash 4.7e).

The net pay control account shows the total net pay due to employees, and this should be paid through the payments system. The payroll system should produce a standard list of the net amount due to each employee, and a signed copy of the list should be attached to the bank transfer instruction.

*Real life – with the assistance and guidance of a highly capable payroll specialist, a consultant was responsible for setting up worldwide payroll arrangements in a newly-created group, spun out from a much larger group in a private equity deal. The new group was implementing a worldwide computer system to cover the main trading activities, but the payrolls were operated separately through local bureaux in all of the operating countries, to ensure compliance with all local employment and taxation regulations.*

*The consultant was instructed to run the payroll payments through the worldwide computer system, but despite considerable pressure insisted that payroll payments were made directly via the local bureaux through the local banks in all countries. When the global accounting system went live, the payments module failed, but the 2,700 employees around the world were all paid because the payrolls had been protected separately until the main system was proven. Payroll is the most sensitive of all the systems, and your employees, who are your most precious resource, depend upon it. Do not take risks with it.*

## 4.5n – General ledger

There are various ways in which the posting trail can be set up, but they all have the same effect on the accounting:

- gross payroll cost including employer oncost is charged against profit (the oncost should be charged to the same cost centres as the pay itself)
- net pay is paid to the employees
- deductions from gross pay, together with employer oncost, are paid to the relevant authorities

In a standard costing system the entries will normally be:

Dr Standard payroll cost with standard cost of production output
    Cr Payroll variance account with same amount
Dr Payroll variance account with actual gross payroll cost
    Cr Liability accounts with amounts due to employees and deduction agencies

The payroll variance account thus shows the difference between the standard and actual payroll costs. In practice the above transaction can be split into greater detail.

## 4.5o – Monthly reviews

It is not practicable for a financial controller to review a payroll of (say) 200 employees to spot anomalies. In any case, the payroll department will have performed the detailed checks. The concern of the financial controller is with the overall cost of the payroll in relation to the production output for the period. He should therefore review the payroll for anomalies in the following:

- the overall cost in relation to the production output compared with the budget (in a standard costing system this is highlighted anyway by the variance accounts)
- the ratios among the costs of major sections of the business (for example, if transport pay is unusually high, it could be that output was late and additional hours had to be worked to get the products to the customers through extra journeys)
- the numbers of personnel in relation to activity
- the overall cost per head, taking into consideration changes in personnel mix
- the ratios of the various deductions to the gross payroll cost
- any other major deviations from the budgeted ratios and patterns

At controller level, the overview is more instructive than the detail.

## 4.5p – Annual information

Each country (and sometimes each state within a country) has its own employment and payroll reporting regulations, and these must be adhered to strictly.

The internal reporting of payroll costs is similar to that for any cost. Gross payroll costs should be allocated to those parts of the profit statement which relate to the work done by the employees, ie sales pay to selling and marketing costs, production wages to labour cost of production etc. Separate statistics of average payroll cost per person, per hour, per unit of product etc are similar to those of other costs.

# FIXED ASSETS SYSTEM                                    4.6

ALL SECTIONS EXCEPT 4.6L RELATE TO TANGIBLE ASSETS

## 4.6a – Objectives

The principal objectives of the fixed assets system are to ensure that:
- asset purchases are authorised in accordance with budget and with approved levels
- assets are capitalised or expensed in accordance with definitions
- disposals of assets are authorised and proceeds collected
- amortisation is always calculated in accordance with definitions and correct rates
- all necessary adjustments for revaluations, reclassifications etc are correctly made
- capitalised assets are always fully documented in fixed assets register
- general ledger fixed asset accounts always agree with fixed assets register
- values are not carried for assets beyond their economic lives

## 4.6b – Capital expenditure (capex) budget

The capex budget (appendix C3) is an integral part of the annual budget, and must take into account:
- activities projected in budget for current year
- activities projected in strategic plan for subsequent years
- current state of existing equipment in terms of productivity and sustainability
- other influencing factors such as legal compliance, particularly regarding health and safety
- commercial feasibility of contracting out activities rather than doing them in house
- financial issues such as lease-or-buy decisions
- availability of second-hand equipment, especially from associated businesses
- contingency amounts for unforeseen expenditure (see below)

Capex arises from three main requirements:

- the need to replace existing equipment which is failing to perform a continuing requirement
- the capital element of new projects approved by the board
- needs or alleged needs which were not foreseen at the time of the budget process

The third item needs careful consideration by the controller. In the author's experience, about three months into a new financial year the technical or production department will announce some hitherto unheard-of capex requirement upon which the entire future of the business depends, and they won't leave it alone. Why didn't they foresee this during the budgeting process? No point in asking, but the controller will have to work hard to determine whether this is a genuine requirement or just the bluebird of some enthusiastic technocrat.

But the message is clear: the controller must have a contingency in the capex budget for unexpected requirements. Equally clearly, he should not divulge the existence of this contingency – ever. If he reveals its existence one year, they'll expect it in future years. The practical way to keep the contingency secret is to publish only a small proportion of it in the capex budget, but to include the remainder in the balance sheet of the overall financial budget.

The capex budget summary (appendix C3) should contain the following sections:

- items remaining from the previous year's budget (unless they have ceased to be a requirement)
- items already authorised for the forthcoming year (ie applied for and approved in the current year but not to be purchased until the budget year)
- items planned for the forthcoming year but not authorised (some of which may spill into the year after, if part of an extensive capex project)

It may also be useful to identify and total replacement items and new (investment) items separately.

Major items in the capex budget should be supported by projections of the return on the investment. There is no point in leaving this until the item is to be purchased, and then finding out that the payback is unsatisfactory. Therefore the controller should encourage and enforce a culture of looking long-term at capex requirements and assessing the business's needs with a capex review every quarter.

An example of payback calculation is given in appendix A6.


## 4.6c – Definitions

Fixed assets are more difficult to define than expenses. Major items generally fall into straightforward categories, but smaller items which could arguably be expensed or capitalised create an endless problem, particularly in the areas of IT and office equipment. To avoid confusion and inconsistency, establish a definition along the following lines (using IT equipment as an example):

- all single items of hardware costing £X or more are capitalised
- all peripheral equipment costing £Y or more and operated as part of a system with capitalised hardware is capitalised (as part of that hardware if it is practicable to account for it as such)
- all software developed in-house is capitalised, including personnel costs, according to the project records (define what costs, such as salaries and materials, are to be capitalised)
- all software purchased for a capitalised item is capitalised as part of the item
- all consumables (eg disks, leads and peripheral equipment costing less than £Y per item) are expensed

Tooling is can also be a difficult category. If tooling lasts for (say) three or four years and comprises a mixture of low-priced and high-priced items, it can be too much to expense and not substantial enough to merit full fixed asset accounting. The answer may well be to use the pooling method: all tooling is capitalised in a pool account without being valued separately in an asset register, and an amount (say 33.3%) is amortised from the total net value each year). The disadvantage of this is that the net pool value cannot be attributed to individual tools and a degree of assessment and judgement is therefore called for to monitor the value annually. The advantage, however, is that the accounting is simple and quick to operate.

The universal term "plant and equipment" is a curiosity, since plant is obviously equipment. The terms "fixed" and "moveable" are probably more appropriate, and as fixed items tend to have a longer life than moveable items, they will often justify lower amortisation rates. Each item of equipment should include in the capital value the peripheral items which are integral to its operation, but not spares or consumables.

## 4.6d – Additions and transfers inward

Inclusion of a fixed asset in a proposed capex budget is merely a preliminary approval (in principle). When the time comes to buy the asset, a capex approval form should be submitted, with the original return-on-investment calculation (or an updated one, explaining the differences) and two or three quotations for supply and installation. This, if acceptable, should be approved by:

- the financial controller or director (for financial justification and availability of funds)
- the originating director or manager (production, marketing, research, maintenance etc)
- the managing director (probably all items, but certainly all major items)
- a group director (if such authority is required by the holding company)

When the investment has been approved, instruct the fixed asset register operator to open an asset category for the item, and provide him with full details so that he can enter the details appropriately.

If the company is part of a group, enquiries should always be made to the rest of the group when fixed assets are required, in case there is a surplus asset of suitable specification elsewhere in the group. Transfers of fixed assets from other group companies are also sometimes made on group instructions, normally when the related activity is also being transferred. Note that when an asset is acquired from another company in the group, it should normally be entered in the register as a gross value and an amortisation value, for ease of consolidation by the group, unless it has been written off by the previous owner.

Accounting for fixed assets can be done through a combination of routes:

- through the purchasing and payables system (see section 4.4)
- through a specific contract to build, install and commission a major asset
- from an intra- group transfer

The accounting is the same as for purchase or contract accounting, with the added requirement to create an entry in the fixed asset register.

## 4.6e – Disposals and transfers outward

Disposal of a fixed asset is generally simple, along the following lines:
- completion and approval of a fixed asset disposal request detailing the reasons for the disposal, through the same route as the capex request (4.6d)
- sale of the unwanted asset, either as a viable asset or as scrap, to an external organisation or to another company within the group
- invoicing of the item through a miscellaneous sales invoice
- eliminating the asset from the register and reporting a gain or loss on disposal

Many disposals are inevitably circumstantial, in that an asset ceases to be required or ceases to perform cost-effectively. However, the controller should organise an annual physical review of fixed assets throughout the business to identify assets which are no longer required and which can be sold advantageously. If this is not done, the number of such assets will increase surreptitiously, taking up useful space and sometimes even incurring storage costs; by the time they are eventually sold they are likely to fetch a lower price than they would have if sold promptly (especially in the case of highly technical assets).

Engineers will frequently present a case for retaining an asset either as a standby or for provision of spares. Listen carefully to their case and try to assess it fairly (not always easy).

Transfers outward are generally made on group instructions. The essential accounting procedures for intra-group disposals are the same as for external disposals.

## 4.6f – Revaluations and reclassifications

In addition to accounting for the normal acquisitions, amortisation and disposals, the fixed assets register should be capable of accounting for the following:
- revaluations (increases in value) – if the system cannot do this, treat it as an acquisition and account for the original asset and the additional value as one item
- impairments (decreases in value) – if the system cannot do this, treat is as a part-disposal
- push-downs; if a group has been involved in a group-wide revaluation as a result of some change in structure and/ or ownership, some of the revaluation will normally relate to the

subsidiaries and this additional value will be "pushed down" to the subsidiaries from the holding company – it should be spread across the relevant assets as a series of revaluations

Assets under construction must be accounted for separately under many régimes, and most systems can cope with this. On entry into revenue-earning service, the asset should be transferred to an operating asset category.

Where an asset is reclassified, if the system cannot cope with that, treat it as a disposal in the old category and acquisition in the new category in the same period. You will, however, need to net off these transactions in your financial statements.

### 4.6g – Amortisation

The word "depreciation" means "loss in value". When you drive a brand new car away from the showroom it loses some value immediately, and that process is **depreciation**.

What we are dealing with here is a process of writing off the cost of an asset mathematically over its economic life, and that is **amortisation**, despite the fact that the accountancy profession insists on calling it depreciation in most countries. However, they refer correctly to the amortisation of intangible assets.

Keep the policy simple: amortise each asset in the month of acquisition, but not in the month of disposal. If an asset is reclassified, amortise it at the new rate in the month in which it is transferred. Some businesses and some countries concoct unnecessary schemes which add nothing whatsoever to the truth or fairness of the accounts but which cause endless accounting problems. These largely unnecessary schemes include amortisation in the month of disposal, and half-rates in the months of acquisition and disposal.

*Real life – the pièce de résistance of nonsensical practices (mandatory in at least one large country) is that of charging a full year's amortisation for any asset installed in the first half of the financial year and half a year's amortisation for any asset installed in the second half. This means that:*
- *you must either accrue from month 1 onwards the amortisation on any asset you intend to buy later in the first half (and similarly from month 7 in the second half), or*
- *you must charge an accelerated amortisation for assets in their first year (unless bought in months 1 or 7) to make up the full year's or*

*half-year's charge, and then change to the normal rate for succeeding years*

It is small wonder that fixed asset registers can be so expensive, when they have to be able to cope with so many different forms of idiocy – and some cannot cope. It is worth reflecting that many of the people who dream up accounting policies and standards have never run a business.

If you are uncertain as to what rates to set for a new business, consult your auditors. The only criterion is that the rates must be realistic in relation to the economic (ie profit-making) life of the assets, and if that life is debatable, the rates should err on the side of a shorter life. In particular, high-technology equipment and anything which is software-intensive should be amortised conservatively, obsolescence in these areas being ever faster. The fact that one cannot accurately predict the exact economic life of most assets is another reason not to adopt complex amortisation calculations.

## 4.6h – Fixed asset register

Ideally, the fixed asset register should be part of the overall integrated computer system the business uses. Only if that register is particularly unsuitable for the purpose should a separate register be used, because this requires either an interface or journal entries between the register and the general ledger, and the additional burden of separate support, maintenance and upgrades for the separate register. It may occasionally be necessary, though; the author encountered a situation where the legal requirements for fixed asset accounting in one Eastern European country were so complex that the standard fixed asset package used internationally by the group concerned was not supported in that country, and a local solution was used instead.

A small business operating in a single country may have simple asset accounting requirements (a well-constructed spreadsheet will do many companies very effectively) but a medium-large company which is part of a foreign-owned group will need the following features in the register:
- full details of the asset, including type, manufacturer's number, location and any other essential details
- full details of cost, including installation and other associated costs (these may be built up over several accounting months before transfer out of "assets under construction")
- subsequent additions to an asset (eg a feeder bought to make a mixer run more efficiently should be added to the value of the mixer if it cannot be used independently of the mixer – this will necessitate

a composite amortisation rate to bring the feeder's net value down to zero on the same date as the mixer is fully amortised, unless the feeder can subsequently be used elsewhere)
- transfers to another category of asset (it is conceivable that a single asset may be separated into its major components and these components transferred to a number of different assets)
- disposals and reasons for disposals
- an appropriate selection of amortisation methods (including writing down the net book value, not a suitable method for large individual assets, but useful for tooling and other items which can be pooled – see 4.6c)
- facility to change end date for amortising any asset and its attachments (to allow for refurbishments and upgradings)
- facility to amortise enhancements and impairments to same end date as existing assets
- facility to enter amortisation brought in on transfers from other companies in same group
- automatic elimination of amortisation on disposals of assets
- printable report on demand of any individual asset history
- printable report on demand of total asset and amortisation movements for any defined period in current accounting year (prior year reports, if required, would have to reinstate assets subsequently disposed of, and that could be difficult)
- (for subsidiary companies operating in countries with different accounting treatment from the group policy) facility to run all above features in parallel for both local policy and group policy
- if required, facility to run all above features in accordance with local tax treatment

In general, assets held in another country are held by a subsidiary company. If, however, the company has assets in a foreign branch which is part of the same legal entity, the foreign assets are better recorded on a separate register in that country and any currency adjustments made in total through the general accounting system when consolidating the results.

## 4.6i – General ledger

In a small, simple business, cost and aggregate amortisation accounts are normally satisfactory for each fixed asset category. However, in a larger or more complex business the following categories may be needed:
- opening balance          cost    amortisation
- additions – external      cost    –

| | | |
|---|---|---|
| ▪ additions – intra-group | cost | amortisation |
| ▪ revaluations – enhancements | cost | amortisation |
| ▪ revaluations – impairments | cost | amortisation |
| ▪ reclassifications – inward | cost | amortisation |
| ▪ reclassifications – outward | cost | amortisation |
| ▪ disposals – external | cost | amortisation |
| ▪ disposals – intra-group | cost | amortisation |
| ▪ period charge | – | amortisation |

There could conceivably be exchange differences and other accounts needed. Many businesses will fall between the two extremes; for example, in an active business it is useful to maintain separate accounts for the cost and amortisation of additions and disposals, as these assist in producing cash flow and disposal gain figures. The balances on these accounts must be transferred to the overall balance at the end of each year.

## 4.6j – Physical verification

The objects of a physical check are:
- ▪ to ensure that no assets have been misappropriated
- ▪ in the case of readily saleable assets, to act as a deterrent against misappropriation and disposal (the ingenuity of thieves is not to be underestimated)
- ▪ to confirm that the locations and condition of the assets is as stated in the register (assets are often moved without informing the asset register holder, and are sometimes cannibalised to repair other assets of the same type)
- ▪ to review the condition of the assets with a view to replacement (although this is an engineering responsibility, it has an obvious financial dimension)
- ▪ to note whether assets are actually in use, or should be considered for disposal

How often should a check be performed? At least once per annum. In some companies it is a very large exercise and can only practicably be done in several stages. In that case, count all assets of a certain type in a single stage, otherwise assets of the same type can be moved between stages to cover missing items.

In which direction should one check the assets?

- Checking from the register to the assets will ascertain that all the assets in the balance sheet do actually exist (this is generally the priority and will also be the main concern of the external auditors)
- Checking from the assets to the register will reveal any unrecorded assets (in a large group where assets are transferred from one site to another, especially in the case of company closures, this is a surprisingly common occurrence, and this check may reveal surplus assets that can be sold for cash)

How the check is performed will therefore depend on your main concern. It may be appropriate to alternate between the two, particularly if there is the prospect of finding surplus assets.

In the case of old assets which have been cannibalised, you may find that asset serial numbers differ from the register as the parts of the assets bearing the numbers are used elsewhere.

## 4.6k – Insurance

Your monetary level for capitalisation of assets is for accounting purposes. However, many of the assets you have expensed are essential to the running of the business and must nevertheless be insured. This can be dealt with in several ways, all of them with disadvantages:

- maintain in your fixed asset register a memorandum category in which you record the cost of all your small assets which have been expensed (you will have to review them, probably bi-annually, to ensure that defunct or disposed assets are removed from the list, and you will have to assume an overall percentage uplift to calculate the replacement value)
- monitor your annual expenditure on non-capitalised equipment and assume a number of years' worth of expense (typically 7 to 12) to give you an appropriate replacement value
- take an inventory of uncapitalised assets at appropriate intervals (perhaps two years) and value them
- make a round-sum estimate and take the risk that your estimate is sufficient

## 4.6l – Intangible fixed assets

Intangible assets, by their very name, are assets that one cannot touch. They include:

- external investments (one can touch the share certificates, but not the ownership)
- trade investments, ie subsidiary companies
- intellectual property such as patents and trade marks
- other rights which have a life longer than one year
- goodwill (although accounting treatments vary from time to time and place to place, and the concept has been the subject of considerable argument)

These are amortised in the same way as tangible fixed assets, ie over the expected period in which they are expected to confer economic benefits to the business. In some cases, such as a licence, the period is specified in the document creating the asset.

The treatment of **goodwill** has been argued over for decades, and whatever your views are on the subject you probably have to comply with the accounting rules in whatever jurisdiction you operate.

At the next level of credibility is the capitalisation of **development costs**. Yes, money has been expended on these, but it is seldom possible to foresee accurately the likely return on a development. Moreover, even ultra-large companies with great experience in developing highly technical products suffer their share of failures in the market place. Development costs are therefore in most cases better written off when incurred.

**Computer hardware** (other than minor accessories) is correctly classified as a tangible fixed asset, but strangely, **computer software** is regarded by the accounting intelligentsia as an intangible asset. This is by any logic inappropriate, because:

- software is an integral and essential part of hardware – without it, the hardware is useless
- software can be located in one place and moved to another
- software performs a physical (ie electronic) function
- software reacts to the actions of the users
- software can break down (who ever heard of an intangible fixed asset breaking down?)
- software in cars and other equipment is not classified separately
- software can be modified into new and improved models in the same way as (say) motor vehicles

Boffins have also argued that one often does not own software, but merely the licence thereto. But since the same boffins have adopted the dogma of substance over form, they are contradicting themselves.

Software does what the mechanical insides of adding machines used to do, only much more effectively. For the better understanding of your business and its assets, you should classify software as a tangible asset, included with your computer hardware. If you have to treat it separately for your published financial statements, so be it, but do put up a fight before you surrender.

Note, however, that in the case of a **software company**, the software which it has developed for licensing to users IS an intangible asset, ie the rights which it is licensing to other companies to obtain its income. In that case, the intellectual arguments hold good.

From time to time, people who should know better come up with harebrained schemes for recording intangible assets to decorate their balance sheets. Two examples are:

- **valuing a brand** owned by the business – but the value of the brand will already be in the balance sheet, as the business will have been performing accordingly if it is well managed (and although there is an ongoing value in some brands, the work has yet to be done in realising that value)
- **valuing the work-force** of the business – again, the value will already be reflected in the balance sheet, and there is the additional dichotomy that management spends a considerable part of its effort in minimising its work force, an approach which hardly merits including it in the balance sheet (especially since the most valuable personnel are the most likely to be poached by competitors)

One catch-all way of considering intangible assets is to ask: would the business be materially undervalued if the intangibles were not included the balance sheet? If the answer is yes, than they should probably be capitalised. But the whole subject is still a minefield.

## 4.7a – Definition

We use the term "**cash**" to cover **all liquid funds**, be they cheques, bank transfers, bills of exchange or whatever.

Where we refer to **notes and coin** specifically, we use the term "**petty cash**".

This part of the systems section differs from the others in that there is little to discuss in the way of computerised systems, as the cash functions are largely contained in the other systems discussed, especially receivables (4.3), payables (4.4) and payroll (4.5). If any software is provided by a company's bank, they will provide their own instructions. We therefore concentrate here on authorisation and security, since funds are the most attractive and transferable asset of any business, with the possible exception of bullion or gems.

Appendices C4, C8 and C9 deal with cash flow budgeting and part 3.2 with regular cash management.

## 4.7b – Objectives

The principal objectives of the bank and cash systems are to ensure that all cash and cash equivalents are:
- kept in secure custody accessible only to authorised persons
- accounted for promptly and accurately so that the funds position is known on a daily basis
- not disbursed unless necessary, properly evidenced and properly authorised
- held and transacted in the currencies most appropriate to the needs of the company
- held and transacted in accordance with treasury requirements
- hedged against currency fluctuations where applicable

Ensure that no speculation occurs with cash or cash equivalents.
Ensure that transactions in notes and coin are kept to a minimum.

## 4.7c – Opening and closing bank accounts

Try to operate with as few bank accounts as practicable. Even then, you may find yourself operating a plethora of accounts, each with a specific practical purpose:

- main trading account
- invoice discounting account
- short-term deposit account
- payroll account
- US dollar account
- Euro account
- dividend account

There are many more possibilities. As banking is one of the "pure" finance functions which can be handled without the involvement of any other department, any new bank account or facility should be authorised in writing by the managing director as well as the financial director.

It is now almost essential to have electronic banking; it enables you to operate your cash accounting almost in real time instead of having to wait several days to verify transactions and balances, and to complete reconciliations. Similarly it is preferable to deal electronically with your customers and suppliers, although you may occasionally meet some resistance, particularly from customers. If you do not bank electronically, you may find it difficult to keep pace with your business, particularly if you deal internationally.

Negotiate the following facilities when opening a bank account:

- borrowing limits
- foreign currency facilities and their interaction with borrowing limits
- interest rates
- charges – transactions, safe deposits, currency conversions, internal transfers, meetings, arrangement fees (large fees rendered for arranging a facility and renewing it annually); be careful, because bank fees can be more onerous than they appear at first glance
- speed of lodgements, withdrawals and transfers (domestic, international and special) – ensure that the bank can meet its commitments, so that you do not advise suppliers that they will receive funds in X working days only to find that a transfer takes X+2 working days
- security for electronic banking (eg a card-operated system in your office)
- full account details provided daily by bank (preferably on-screen) downloadable into your spreadsheet

- signatures required for withdrawals
- discounting of inward letters of credit, bills of exchange etc (if required)
- provision of letters of credit to overseas suppliers (if required)
- any other arrangements you require

In part 1.4g we discuss the relationship aspects of dealing with the bank.


## 4.7d – Cash receipts

Payments directly into bank accounts have become the norm in most of Europe, but there are still many countries and also small businesses who pay mainly by cheque. The USA is more cheque-intensive, having a less-developed banking system (and they spell cheque as "check", sometimes causing confusion).

For receipts of cash in the mail, handling procedures should include:
- receiving incoming mail in a safe area
- opening of mail by a responsible authorised person who is independent of the accounts receivable ledger and of all credits and journal entries (eg bad debts) related thereto
- listing of cheques received
- entry of cheques in accounts receivable ledger (or accounts payable ledger for supplier refunds or general ledger for miscellaneous receipts)
- reconciliation of accounts receivable ledger movement with cheque listing
- preparation of bank lodgement
- agreement of bank lodgement total with cheque listing and accounts receivable ledger (or others)
- clearance of any customer orders awaiting receipt of cheque (assuming that you are satisfied that cheque will not be rejected)
- lodgement of cheques in bank on same day (or if not practicable, storage in safe)
- filing in date sequence of all bank receipts and lodgements

For receipts paid directly into your bank account, procedures should include:
- downloading and printing daily bank statement
- listing of transfers received
- posting of transfers received to ledgers and reconciliation thereof as for cheques (see above)
- clearance of any customer orders awaiting receipt of transfer
- filing in date sequence of all bank statements and transfer lists

For letters of credit and bills of exchange received (this should be by prior arrangement only), discount with your bank per the procedures you have agreed with them.

## 4.7e – Cash disbursements

Whatever the method of payment, there should be signatories agreed with the bank for each bank account. The same signatures should be applied whatever method of payment is used. Management time is best concentrated by grading the authority required for payments. For example:

- payments at or above level A – the managing director and one other signatory
- payments below level A and at or above level B, and all payments for payroll or expenses – one director and one other signatory
- payments below level B except for payroll or expense reimbursement cheques – any two signatories

Levels A and B are set so that the bulk of small routine payments (ie those on which there is a minimum of decision-making) can be authorised by reasonably competent and independent persons. The restriction of involvement of directors (or senior management, depending on the business structure) to large or sensitive payments only means that they will give these payments their full attention, something difficult to do if the larger items are in amongst a long list of small payments.

The number of signatories authorised depends on practical circumstances. If there are too many signatories, there is a dissipation of control. If there are too few signatories, there will be frequent difficulties in having payments made on time because the signatories are not on site, and this in turn can lead to unacceptable practices such as a signatory signing a number of blank cheques or transfer authorities before going on holiday. Another circumvention is the splitting of a large payment into several small ones to take them down to a lower authority level; this should be expressly forbidden. Whatever number of signatories you appoint, they must communicate their forthcoming absence dates to those responsible for making payments, so that the payments can be authorised slightly in advance if necessary, and activated on the due dates.

For bank transfers to suppliers per the accounts payable ledger, procedures should include:

- strict security over password and keycard access to the electronic banking system (you will also need to cover staff absences in a controlled way)

- flagging of individual invoices for payment per accounts payable ledger
- printing of list for authorisation by approved signatories (normally two copies, one for the bank and one for filing)
- testing by signatories of an agreed proportion of items on each list, by reference to supporting documentation, before signing the list (the uppermost level of payments should be checked 100%), and the supporting documents should also be signed by the signatories
- transmission of one copy of the signed payment list to the bank
- entry of the payments in the accounts payable ledger (normally done automatically by confirming the items flagged for payment) and other ledgers if relevant
- filing of the other copy of the signed list in date sequence
- checking the list against the subsequent bank statement

For cheque payments, procedures should include:
- keeping of the blank cheques in a safe, accessible only to authorised persons who are independent of the accounts payable ledger, other purchasing functions and the payroll functions
- all procedures as for bank transfers above, except that individual cheques will have to be signed instead of a single signature being applied to a total listing

For payroll payments, whichever method is used:
- the payroll system should produce a payment listing from the period payroll and the personnel files, and this should be processed in the same way as an accounts payable listing (see above)
- deduction and contribution account balances should be paid in the same way as any other miscellaneous payments, the ledger account and payroll summary being presented as supporting evidence for signature

Miscellaneous payments should be authorised by presenting the appropriate documents together with the cheque or miscellaneous payment list to the signatories.

Standing orders and direct debits must be subject to the same authorisation requirements as any other payments. The authorisation level must be set at the total commitment where there is a defined payment period. Where an arrangement is open-ended (not generally advisable) the commitment should be assumed to be at least 5 years' worth of payments (ie 60 monthly payments) when being authorised.

Note also that many direct debits are in respect of operating leases that are for items which are essentially capital in nature. These items must go through the same authorisation process (4.6d) as other capital expenditure.

## 4.7f – Transactions in foreign currency

Foreign exchange ("forex") is complex enough to occupy a whole book in itself. Nevertheless, only the larger businesses normally have in-house treasury functions, and the controller of a small or medium-sized business often has to wrestle with a number of forex issues, which we shall deal with in simple terms here:

- sales in foreign currency (or whether to price them in the home currency)
- purchases in foreign currency
- assets and liabilities in foreign currency
- hidden currency influences
- interest rates in different currencies
- total facility available from bank

In a perfect world you will buy and sell in the same currency. If your total purchases in a foreign currency equal the sales in that currency, you will normally only have a few minor exchange gains and losses caused by timing differences in the receipts and payments. Consequently, if you maintain a bank account in that currency with an adequate balance you may be able to operate with little or no hedging.

If, however, you have an excess of purchases or sales in a foreign currency, you will have to buy or sell forward in that currency (transactional hedging) if you wish to hedge against (ie minimise) any strong adverse movement in that currency. It is here that the difficulties arise:

- if you buy currency forward at the purchase date so that you are covered at the right exchange rate when you come to pay for the purchases, your overall available bank facility will be reduced by this amount – if you are operating with very little headroom, you therefore may not be able to hedge
- if you sell currency forward to cover sales in that currency, you are dependent on receiving the cash from your customer on the due date, so if the customer does not pay you may have a commitment that you cannot meet
- if you hedge effectively, you will not incur any substantial exchange losses, but neither will you make any large gains (many a business's operating results have been improved by a large, fortunate exchange gain)

It is seldom possible to forecast sales and purchases precisely, and even less so the cash flows resulting from those transactions. You therefore risk encountering a situation in which you have committed to buy or sell currency, but the underlying cash flow has not occurred to plan. To avoid this, many businesses hedge short of the forecast cash flows – for example, 80% or 90% of the expected exposure. The percentage which you hedge will depend on the predictability of your cash flows, and given that you pay your suppliers out of cash received from customers, your sales cash flow tends to dominate your calculations. See appendix A5.

How far forward should you hedge? The rolling period of a transaction hedge will depend on the length of credit you allow or are allowed, and how closely that period is adhered to, especially by your customers. For example, if your customers typically pay about three months after despatch of goods or completion of services, you should seek to sell forward in January for April net currency receipts. Once your hedge is up and running, you will normally become acquainted with the pattern and your hedge will become more accurate with increased familiarity (interrupted by an occasional minor crisis to keep you alert).

A more difficult situation occurs in the balance sheet – structural hedging as opposed to transactional hedging. If you are investing in another currency (eg opening a branch or a subsidiary in another country), not only will you have income and expenditure in the currency of that currency, but you will also have to consider the consolidation of the balance sheet items of that enterprise. A movement in the exchange rate can dramatically affect your balance sheet. Consult with the forex specialists of your financial advisors before setting up a foreign enterprise under your company's ownership, to ensure that you have the safest structure.

Remember always that you are a financial controller, not a currency expert, so resist any temptation to play the currency markets – you may get away with it once or twice, but they will hit you in the end.

As a warning, take note of the sorry tale in "short term deposits and investments" in 4.7h below.

## 4.7g – Bank account reconciliations

If you do not know how to reconcile a bank account, you will not have bought this book. However, there are some practical concerns, particularly when your banking is complex or high-volume or both.

Some general ledger systems have a useful facility for you to mark off receipts and payments which have gone through the bank statements, printing out an automatic reconciliation therefrom.

A complex bank reconciliation may slow down the month-end procedures, because the ledgers cannot be closed off if the bank transactions are not correctly entered. There are two possible solutions to this problem:

- carry out interim (perhaps weekly) reconciliations during the month to even out the work flow and minimise the work load at the month-end
- ensure that all payments for the month are made by the third last working day of the month, so that the traffic for the last three days is greatly reduced

Always work to the TRUE BALANCE, as follows:

| Bank reconciliation [date] | £ |
|---|---|
| Balance per statement | (551,309.44) |
| Outstanding lodgements | 12,638.09 |
| Outstanding withdrawals | (104,562.80) |
| True balance | (643,234.15) |
| | |
| Balance per ledger | (644,254.13) |
| Lodgements not entered | 1,500.00 A |
| Withdrawals not entered | (234.10) B |
| Unreconciled items | (245.92) C |
| True balance | (643,234.15) |

Items A, B and C should not exist in practice, unless there is some difficulty which cannot be resolved in time to finalise the period-end results. At all month-ends, the ledger balance should be the TRUE BALANCE. If items A, B or C appear, the controller may decide to exclude them if they are not material, or enter a temporary (reversible) adjustment if they are material.

All anomalies such as unreconciled items must be pursued relentlessly until they are resolved, and not allowed to remain longer than one month. The longer they remain, the harder they will become to resolve.

## 4.7h – Short-term deposits and investments

If you are in one of the minority of businesses with spare cash (either regularly or temporarily as a result of an event such as the disposal of a major asset), you will seek to make that cash generate the best possible return until it is used. Therefore as soon as you become aware that you will have free cash, you should consult with your bankers and other advisors and set up your facilities in advance. The authorities for these facilities should be at least as rigorous as those for setting up a new bank account (see above), and when the time comes to move money in and out of investment accounts, the transfers should similarly follow your banking rules.

*Real life – a UK group which had just sold a major division had £60 million on the money market, awaiting an acquisition in the final stages of negotiation. The cash was placed on the money market and moved each Monday by authorised members of the finance team to obtain the best interest rates. By an unexpected combination of circumstances it was discovered one Friday that all members of the group's finance team would be away the following week – except one. He had not initiated any money transactions before, so was given a piece of paper with some names and telephone numbers, and duly called the names on the Monday, selected the investments and authorised them, all over the telephone with a faxed confirmation to follow.*

*None of the persons placing the money had ever heard of him, nor seen a copy of his signature, but the £60 million was promptly moved as instructed. For continuity, he did some of the following Monday's movements when handing the reins back to the usual players. He then had to wait a further two weeks until there was someone in the building who could approve his (unrelated and fully documented) travel expense claim for under £100.*

*No authorisation needed to uplift and re-invest £60 million, but a signature needed for £100!*

*To make matters worse, the forthcoming acquisition was in a different currency, which moved strongly against the UK£ in the intervening period, resulting in an exchange loss much greater than the interest received from the money market. As the overwhelming likelihood had been that the acquisition would take place (it was between a willing seller and a willing buyer, with most of the conditions agreed), the money should have been invested in the currency of the acquisition to hedge against any intervening movement. Members of the finance team pointed this out to the group directors at the time, but were ignored. Fortunately, the exchange loss did not affect the finance team's bonus for that year!*

This incident highlights the psychological danger of having spare funds. Working against an overdraft limit keeps one aware of the constraints and constantly focused on cash control. Having funds to spare tends to cause a relaxation of attitude. For an unaccredited person to be able to shift £60 million on the strength of a telephone call (when the norm was for all expense claims to be authorised at a senior level) was extreme slackness, as was the absence of a hedge against the forthcoming purchase.

Be very careful, however healthy the state of your funds; they can disappear remarkably easily.


## 4.7i – Loans, hire purchase and leases

There are seldom any separate systems for loans, hire purchase and leases, which are largely a matter of accounting.

In the case of operating leases, which in most countries are purely an expense item, the lease costs can normally be dealt with through the direct debit procedure (see cash disbursements, above). It is customary for the first payment to include a sizeable deposit, so try to obtain an additional cash flow advantage by including the total sales tax in the first payment, so that it can all be recovered at the start.

Loans and finance leases are easily dealt with by MS Excel spreadsheets:
- set out your loan / lease details at the top, including the monthly payment amount
- allocate a notional interest rate (eg 10.0000%) in one cell
- deduct the deposit and any other opening adjustments (eg sales tax)
- allocate a row to each repayment, and enter the month of repayment on each row
- deduct the interest from the outstanding capital, linking it to the interest cell, and allocate the rest of the payment to reducing the capital (round the interest to the nearest penny)
- carry the balance of capital down to the next row and repeat for all payment periods
- place your cell pointer on the closing capital balance after the last payment
- select Tools/ Goal Seek and instruct that the closing balance cell should be made to equal zero by setting the interest rate cell to the required percentage
- the spreadsheet will now eliminate the capital correctly, and will show you what the real interest rate is, which may come as a shock

to you (it is useful to have the draft spreadsheet to hand for this purpose when negotiating with the leasing company)

If you have a number of loans or finance leases, create a top spreadsheet summarising them, and note the date in a separate cell top of the summary. Use a lookup table to select the closing balances for the month you have entered on the summary, and the summary will display the closing balances for that month. Prepare the journal entry for the month's payments, so that the correct capital balance is displayed in the balance sheet and the remainder of the payments total is expensed. Whenever you add a new loan or lease, check that the summary is picking up the correct capital balance, and check the total payments per the summary with your bank records. Always, always, always do your accounting towards **the correct capital balance** at the end of the month, then check to ensure that your period charge is reasonable.

With all kinds of loans and leases you normally have some choice regarding the phasing of the payments. There is usually a choice of paying monthly, quarterly or sometimes even annually. In all such cases, opt for the monthly period, for two reasons of control:

- you do not have to operate a cycle of controls; the monthly requirements will be constant (but check whether you are running one month in arrears, one month prepaid, or paid-up at each month-end)
- the business accommodates and accepts the regular outflow; if cash flow is tight, the larger quarterly payments can be more traumatic because the intervening months have been easier, whereas monthly payments keep the business sharp

Ensure when entering any major loan or lease commitments that the business is authorised to do so by its articles of association or equivalent constitutional document and that all necessary board resolutions have been obtained.

## 4.7j – Travel and other expenses

Travel expenses can tie up a considerable amount of time. To operate an effective expenses system:

- establish and issue a written set of rules
- create a practical claim form, preferably on a password-protected spreadsheet allowing the claimant to complete it either manually or electronically

- ensure that the print command prints the instructions on the back of every sheet
- divide the form into defined expense categories as required
- ensure that the treatment of sales tax or value added tax is clear and easy (some companies prefer that this is done by the finance department, as claimants frequently enter the tax incorrectly – in that case, it may be easier for the claimants to enter the gross amounts on the form and for finance staff to deduct the tax from the totals to show net expense totals and tax total for posting to the ledger)
- brief every new member of staff on the process before he travels for the first time

From the point of view of the business the simplest solution for travelling expenses is to let the employees incur the expense on their own credit cards and have their expenses reimbursed directly to their bank accounts. This will actually offer them two advantages:

- provided they submit their expense claims promptly (and the business pays them promptly) they will receive the cash before they receive the credit card statement and will therefore not be out of pocket
- the fact that they have a high level of purchases on their cards and pay them off promptly will tend to increase the level of credit given to them by the credit card company

Unfortunately, this often does not work in practice:

- some employees have longer-term debt on their credit cards, and do not pay their cards in full each month; the reimbursement from the business can therefore encourage even more credit for personal use, which they cannot afford
- employees on long trips over long distances may not be able to submit their expense claims regularly (especially when incurred in several currencies) and it is not fair to expect them to shoulder this burden

**Company credit cards** may therefore be required. When issuing company credit cards, the exact arrangements will depend on the credit card company. The procedures should include:

- request to finance department from head of department of employee requiring credit card, stating reasons for request and amount of credit required
- signed approval of request by financial controller (and financial director in smaller business)
- formal request to credit card company

- tax invoices and analysis– use same form as for expense claims, but prepare separate claim to match each credit card statement
- credit card settlement by direct debit, and matching of each bank debit with card statement, expense form and supporting invoices etc
- signature of employee and department head on expense claim
- journal entry posting claim to general ledger
- permanent list of all company credit card holders and their limits

If credit card statements are received before the expenses are claimed, a useful method is to open an account in the receivables ledger for the employee(s):

- when the credit card statement is paid, debit the employee's receivable ledger account and credit the bank account with the gross amount of the claim
- when the employee provides the expense claim and supporting invoices, credit his receivable ledger account and debit the expense and VAT accounts

A considerable amount of work can be involved, and where foreign currencies are involved, you may have to wait until receiving the card statement before recording the transaction. This means that you are likely to have to accrue for such expenses at each month-end. The credit card company may be able to assist by making the statement date around the 23$^{rd}$ of each month, so that there is time to process the expenses before the month-end, and only one week of expenses to accrue, with less scope for over/ understatement.


## 4.7k – Petty cash funds (notes and coin)

Does your business really need to handle notes and coin? Even some quite small businesses manage without it these days. This should be possible in most European businesses, but in other continents it can be necessary to make quite large payments in notes and coin, because many of the people needing to paid insist on notes and coin. Draw your own conclusions.

If you have to operate a petty cash system, use it for as few transactions as practicable. The system should include the following features:

- a lockable cash box with compartments for all currencies
- a safe in which the box can be stored
- cash amounts which are sufficient to enable the system to operate without frequent drawing of cash from the bank, but not large enough to cause a security risk

- a simple debit-and-credit account (normally a book) recording the expenses and imprest reimbursements
- expenses only – all income should be banked direct and intact, and no expenses should be paid from cash received
- an imprest system – if the cash float is £500 and the expenditure for the period is £367.19, leaving a balance of £132.81, a cheque for £367.19 should be drawn to restore the float to its normal level of £500 (in that way, the cheque through the bank account will always match the expenditure, leaving a much clearer audit trail)
- replenishment to the full float at each month-end, and certainly at the year-end
- a separate file of receipts for expenses paid from petty cash
- monthly review by the financial controller, who should sign the closing balance on each currency at each month-end, test-counting the cash
- posting of the expenses to the general ledger, debiting expense accounts and crediting cash floats, where the credits will cancel the debits of the replenishments from the bank

If you have frequent **overseas travel** by staff members, you are likely to have to hold petty cash in several currencies. Even if your employees buy their foreign currency from a cash machine at the airport of arrival, they will return with unused notes and coin which they are entitled to convert into your home currency. You are therefore likely to have balances in several different currencies, and the balances will seldom square with the petty cash book (which will need an account for each currency). The balances will be advanced and recovered at different exchange rates, and you will have to enter a forex adjustment to square to the balance at each month-end. Provided that the difference is small, do not waste time on this; you have much bigger things to worry about. However, do not display this relaxed attitude to your staff. Cash is a matter of fidelity and they should always seek to be precise.

Exhort the travelling staff to give as much advance notice of their foreign cash requirements as practicable, to help your cashier decide on what is an appropriate level of currency to hold.

## 4.7l – General ledger

In modern computer systems, the bank transactions are automatically integrated with the relevant general ledger, and the processing of receipts and payments will be automatically recorded.

Petty cash will normally be recorded manually. Exceptions may occur where there is a large volume of cash, such as in a factory canteen using employee cards swiped directly through to the payroll.

# PART 5
# THE CONTROLS

## 5.1 LOSING IT

a    Objectives
b    Inventory & production
c    Sales & receivables
d    Purchases & payables
e    Payroll & expenses
f    Fixed assets
g    Cash

## 5.2 FRAUD & THEFT

a    Definition & scope
b    Objectives
c    Limitations
d    Employee fraud – engagement
e    Employee theft – facilities
f    Employee fraud – pay
g    Employee fraud – goods
h    Collusion
i    Segregation of duties
j    Third party theft & fraud
k    Fraud at high level
l    Blowing the whistle

## 5.3 CONTRACTS

a    Objectives
b    Contract structure
c    Other rules affecting contracts
d    Conditions of sale
e    Distributor or agent contracts
f    Importing & exporting
g    Employment contracts
h    Employment termination
i    Contracts dictated by others
j    Drafting contracts

## 5.4 INSURANCE

a    Objectives
b    Types of cover
c    Business continuity & disasters
d    Personnel

# LOSING IT

## 5.1a – Objectives

This section considers some easy ways to lose money. Some of these may seem blindingly obvious, but you'd be surprised at how easily some businesses give away their hard-earned profits. There are many other errors and misdeeds than those listed here; these are errors in processes where the financial controller could be expected to be active.

## 5.1b – How to lose money via inventory and production

Allow diversion of goods
- on intake
- between locations
- between processes
- from premises (*real life – a company stored lengths of aluminium profile with a cross-section of 70mm in a yard protected by a fence with a mesh of 100mm – the local wide-boys had a field-night*)
- on despatch

Hold excess stock
- diverts cash from other uses
- incurs borrowing costs
- causes crowding, and therefore:
  - difficulty in storing items properly, causing damage
  - selection of wrong items
  - additional storage costs
  - delay in findings items, causing lost production and therefore lost business
  - accidents
  - crowded and therefore inefficient production area
  - difficulty in counting items
  - incorrect re-ordering of items
  - concealment of slow-moving items
  - deterioration of hidden items

Hold insufficient stock
- causes production delays, and thus lost output
- causes delivery delays and possibly additional (perhaps even express) transport costs
- loses business
- results in claims from customers for failing to meet commitments

Value stock incorrectly (by wrong product definition or wrong calculation)
- gives misleading product margin figures
- causes wrong pricing decisions
- results in selection of wrong products
- causes errors in future periods' figures
- conceals actual performance of business

Fail to apply price changes correctly – causes same problems as value errors above
Misallocate costs between products – causes same problems as above

Fail to operate on suitable batch quantities and lead times
Fail to order correct stock on correct dates
Fail to control production processes
Fail to operate stock control systems properly

Run production for a long time at full capacity – there is therefore no time for:
- equipment maintenance
- staff training and customer demonstrations
- trialling new products and processes
- implementing improvements (better controls, more efficient layouts etc)

and a variety of problems occur

*Real life – a company set minimum production volumes for each of its products. The worldwide sales team were not receiving a high enough level of enquiries to justify production of many of the products. They therefore overstated the forecasts in the sales system to establish quantities above the minimum production level. The products were duly made but only a small proportion of them could be sold, and the finished goods inventory began to rise by around USD 1 million per month, the increase consisting largely of products that nobody wanted. The situation was exacerbated by a culture of 100% factory utilisation (see above).*

*The sales force met their targets, but not for long – the company went into administration.*

## 5.1c – How to lose money via sales and receivables

Fail to establish conditions of sale
Establish conditions of sale but fail to agree with customers
Fail to set customer credit limit
Set credit limit too high for customer's financial capability
Set credit limit at appropriate level but allow customer to exceed it
Set credit limit too low and cause good customer to buy elsewhere
Despatch goods to customers on credit-hold (ie on the "stop list")
Produce goods (especially bespoke products) for customers on credit-hold

In accepting sales orders, fail to agree exact requirements:
- items (especially part numbers)
- specifications
- quantities and tolerances
- prices, discounts and currency
- packaging and delivery details

Fail to obtain written proof of customer's acceptance of delivery (ie a signed despatch note)

Fail to generate sales invoice from despatch of product (should be an automatic process on system)
Invoice sales late, delaying receipt of cash and incurring interest

Invoice sales incorrectly:
- wrong items
- wrong quantities
- wrong prices, discounts and currency
- omission of special terms
- wrong address or other customer details

Mismanage sales credits:
- fail to resolve disputes rapidly, so that cash collection is delayed
- continue to fail to resolve disputes, to the extent that they become insoluble, with the result that the cash due is never received
- issue credits or discounts to which the customer is not entitled
- fail to act to reduce a high reported incidence of credits (see 3.3o)

Fail to pursue collection of cash (due, overdue and in legal hands)
Fail to follow procedures specified by credit insurers, resulting in rejection of claims against defaults

Fail to prevent fraud and theft:

- diversion of receipts
- misposting of cash
- issue of unauthorised credits
- making unauthorised contras
- making unauthorised write-offs
- making unauthorised adjustments

Fail to operate management reports:
- fail to produce control reports
- produce control reports but fail to review them
- review reports but fail to take management action

Fail to operate control systems as specified

## 5.1d – How to lose money via purchases and payables

Fail to establish conditions of purchase
Establish conditions of purchase but fail to agree with suppliers

In placing purchase orders, fail to agree exact requirements:
- items
- build, performance or other specifications
- certification
- quantities
- prices and discounts
- packaging
- delivery

Allow unauthorised purchase orders to be made (this can be particularly difficult in a smaller business)
Allow orders to exceed budgeted levels of expense without special authorisation
Account for consumables as stock, allowing unnecessary stocks to build up – always write off consumables!

Fail to control goods inward:
- accept goods or services which were not ordered
- fail to record receipt of goods or services (and therefore order those items again)
- fail to inspect goods and services on receipt
- inspect items received but fail to record results of inspection
- fail to act on unsatisfactory inspection results
- fail to enter direct materials into inventory records

Fail to control purchase invoices:
- record and process invoice more than once, resulting in double payment
- fail to check satisfactory receipt of invoiced items (normally automatic in modern systems)
- fail to check prices and all other terms on invoice
- fail to code purchase to correct cost code or stock category
- fail to record purchase invoice in payables ledger, incurring late payment charge or loss of discount
- issue invoice to management for approval and fail to recover – again a late payment results

In the event of a dispute with a supplier:
- fail to record and contest the dispute
- fail to issue a debit note to the supplier
- fail to record a credit note sent by the supplier

Note 1: always process and record invoices in a register or in the payables ledger BEFORE physically passing them out for approval, otherwise you may never see them again. Once the invoices have been approved by the relevant managers you can mark them in the payables ledger as cleared for payment. Managers regard approving purchase invoices as the least and last of their tasks, especially when they are operating against a tight budget.

Note 2: invoices for services are much harder to control than invoices for goods. How do you verify that an invoice for a repair or a regular maintenance visit is correct, and that the service was carried out properly? There is no physical movement of measurable goods to evidence the provision of the service. Gate controls help, and in some companies a service register is maintained, but it is still difficult.

## 5.1e – Losing money via payroll and expenses

Allow fictitious persons to be entered on payroll
Allow leavers to remain on payroll
Treat employee(s) illegally and incur financial penalties

Terms of employment:
- fail to establish terms of employment
- establish terms, but fail to record them, or record them incorrectly
- allow unauthorised increases to remuneration and/ or benefits
- define terms of employment but fail to communicate them to supervisors or managers

Work done:
- fail to control recording of piece-work – measurement
- fail to control recording of piece-work – authorisation
- fail to control recording of hours worked – measurement
- fail to control recording of hours worked – authorisation
- fail to control recording of type of work – measurement
- fail to control recording of type of  work – authorisation
- fail to control absences – measurement
- fail to control absence – authorisation

Pay processing:
- fail to check pay rates
- fail to check pay calculations
- fail to submit correct deduction money to authorities and so incur penalty

Fail to deduct tax, social security etc and thus be liable for it, because:
- employee documents (eg P45 in UK) have not been obtained
- benefits have not been taxed
- the above items have been dealt with, but the wrong rates have been applied

(the company will be liable for any amounts due but not deducted from employees)

Expenses are fertile ground for losing money:
- fail to define eligibility rules for expense claims
- define eligibility but fail to communicate definition to managers authorising claims
- fail to check validity of claims
    - journeys and distances travelled
    - amounts spent (by examination of receipts etc)
    - reasons for spending (by examination of receipts and details of work)
    - calculations
- fail to authorise claims in writing (normally by signature) after checking

## 5.1f – Losing money via fixed assets

Fail to prepare asset purchase justification (preferably a return-on-investment calculation – see appendix A6)
Receive asset purchase justification but fail to check calculations and underlying reality

Buy asset when market projection does not support it

Fail to obtain competitive quotes for asset
Buy the asset in another currency and do not hedge the transaction

Buy asset for occasional use when one can be spot-hired
Buy new asset when second-hand one would have sufficed
Replace asset when existing asset could have been refurbished
Buy asset for process which can more cheaply and just as efficiently be contracted out
Buy asset of unproven technology*
Buy asset when one of a lower specification would have sufficed*

*Real life – conceit can find its way into business transactions. Some business leaders feel the urge to have the latest technology or a prestige asset in the same way that others simply must have an expensive car. You are not in business to parade the latest technology; you are there to make money. Remember that a hot water bottle does the same job as an electric blanket.*

Fail to keep moveable assets where they are not accessible to theft
(especially where you are operating on remote sites such as in a contracting business)

Fail to maintain adequate insurance cover over all practical risks arising from assets
Fail to enforce rigorous and effective maintenance régime

Buy asset for which there is no effective after-sales support (especially a newly-developed foreign asset)
Buy asset which causes pollution or which breaches pollution or safety regulations

Fail to give adequate training to operators of asset(s)
Buy asset that needs specially-trained and therefore expensive operators (as opposed to standard ones)

You will not have failed to note that most of these issues relating to the fixed assets are the responsibility of operational management rather than financial management. However, as a matter of financial prudence, you should ensure that these matters are carefully considered by your technical colleagues when buying and operating fixed assets. You can do this to a large extent by ensuring that these considerations are mentioned in writing in the justification for asset purposes

## 5.1g – Losing money via cash management

Unlike fixed assets, cash falls fairly and squarely into the domain of the financial controller! Moreover, most cash mistakes are uncomfortably obvious at board level. Most of the real cash management comes from the stewardship of the business as a whole as discussed throughout this book and especially from avoiding the errors highlighted in the foregoing topics of this section, but you can still lose sizeable amounts of money by the following actions or inactions:

- Negotiate inappropriate borrowing terms by not matching the types of finance to the assets and activities being financed (see 3.2i)

- Fail to negotiate the lowest borrowing costs (unless the financing you have chosen offers genuine alternative benefits, such as greater flexibility or less stringent security terms)

- Fail to hedge transactions in foreign currencies – there is no perfect hedging system, and you may spend more money hedging than you would have if you had not hedged, but you cannot afford to take the risk of leaving a material currency exposure unhedged

- Fail to implement and maintain the detailed controls in 4.7

## 5.2a – Definition and scope

Theft is the unlawful or unpermitted abstraction of another party's goods or services.

Fraud is the obtaining of another party's money under false pretences. Fraud is therefore a form of theft.

From the company standpoint, anyone can commit theft. Fraud, however, is more specific; there are three main types of fraud perpetrator, with potentially differing intentions:
- employee
- director
- third party

All three categories of person may have the intention of defrauding the business of cash, or of goods or services (which effectively defraud the business of cash), for personal use. Directors may have additional intentions with regard to the manipulation of the business's apparent financial results, but these intentions still tend towards personal gain in some form.

## 5.2b – Objectives

The principal objectives of this section are:
- to identify the main circumstances in which fraud is likely to occur
- to identify the preventive actions which are needed
- to consider the legal implications

## 5.2c – Limitations

The financial controller, as a steward of the business's assets, is directly concerned with the prevention, or in less successful circumstances the detection, of theft or fraud. Considerable attention is therefore required of the controller towards the controls and internal checks within the business and its systems.

However, a sense of proportion is necessary. There are so many opportunities for theft and fraud that to prevent or detect them all is probably impossible. Besides, the cost of prevention or detection is likely to outweigh the loss in the great majority of cases.

In particular, people in general have an emotional fixation about cash.

*Real life – an entire board of directors of a private company were up in arms over the removal of UK£50 from a cash box, while they were quite unconcerned about the loss of thousands of pounds of raw materials through inadequate storage. Moreover, the small theft was the first in several decades of operation, while the inventory losses continued year after year. What upset the directors most was the betrayal of trust, and yet they themselves were betraying the shareholders' trust on a grand scale . . . accidentally through negligence, but nevertheless culpably.*

Concentrate therefore on the issues that really matter, with measures which save more than they cost.


## 5.2d – Employee fraud – engagement

As fraud is the obtaining of money by false pretences, an employee who obtains a position and commensurate salary by overstating the achievements in his CV is perpetrating a fraud. In some countries it is not legal to demand details of an employee's previous remuneration as that is regarded as an invasion of privacy. In the United Kingdom, however, it is regarded as a reasonable enquiry; an employer needs to know the calibre of person whom he is hiring. Moreover, the UK income tax deduction system works on a cumulative basis and the employee's previous employer must by law provide his new employer with details of his pay and tax to date in the current tax year.

Regardless of what information you have received about a candidate, it is therefore always prudent when interviewing one for employment to ask sufficient technical questions to ensure that he is genuinely capable of doing what he claims he has done. In general, interviewers do not ask many technical questions (particularly the wide-open kind, such as "How would you decide whether to make these parts in house or to contract them out?") and this is a mistake. You are committing to an indefinite stream of cash payments; you must therefore be sure that the services for which you are paying will be provided, and to an adequate standard. Ask tough questions, trick questions, open questions.

## 5.2e – Employee theft – abuse of facilities and services

Every business has a level of internal theft. Staff use the company stationery, photocopier, telephone and other facilities for their own purposes, and businesses take greatly differing views on this:

- draconian businesses expressly forbid their staff to make even a single personal photocopy or phone call, and have a pay-phone installed, only to be used during designated break periods (this attitude is in keeping with the law and with employees' contracts of employment, but is hardly likely to foster high staff loyalty or performance)
- some businesses are so disorganised and/ or careless that the employees' use of facilities and abstraction of goods from the premises is almost invited (this can go either way: in some businesses staff take extensive advantage of this laxity, whilst in others staff respond by regarding this as trust and not abusing it – however, this is not a chance a business can safely take)
- most businesses accept that occasional use of the facilities and a modest quantity of business goods by staff who are otherwise conscientious and occasionally work extra unpaid hours are acceptable perks (perquisites) of the job, provided that they remain at modest levels

The third attitude above is in keeping with good staff management; staff will work beyond the terms of their contracts for the business, which will likewise allow commensurate non-contractual benefits. But when an employee who habitually leaves on the stroke of closing time regardless of the level of unfinished work wants to photocopy a hundred party invitations, his manager is right to forbid him, or to charge him for it.

Such an attitude must be controlled, however, and maintained as a privilege, not as a right. Use of company vehicles, workshops and materials can rapidly get out of hand if not controlled. Ultimately, loss of control will encourage less conscientious employees and knowledgeable outsiders to use services and to remove goods not for personal use, but for sale for cash. The revenue authorities may also treat such benefits as remuneration and require the company to deduct and remit income tax thereon.

Access to services must be strictly controlled, and under the direct responsibility of specific reliable individuals. For example, only those employees requiring long-distance or international phone calls should have access to such lines, and should be directly responsible for them. Monthly print-outs of the calls should be monitored and the employees should be randomly queried on numbers they have dialled, to make the point that the expenditure is reviewed. The advent of Skype is, however, lessening this problem.

A common example of theft of services is that of an employee running another activity during his working hours. Even if he is not consuming business goods or services in the process, this is effectively fraud as he is obtaining his salary under false pretences by not working the contracted hours. Moreover, such activities almost always involve also the misappropriation of business facilities.

This can only be prevented by close monitoring of employees by managers and this tends to run against a healthy culture of trust. As with all aspects of management, it is a question of balance; employees need to be encouraged to take their own initiatives, but a small percentage may abuse their freedom. When suspicions of unacceptable extra-curricular activities are aroused, pay additional but unobtrusive attention immediately. An oblique warning to an employee at an early stage may be enough to deter him from developing unwanted activities.

## 5.2f – Employee fraud – manipulation of pay

Pay systems should be self-policing; especially those portions of pay which are based on employee performance, in the measure of results or attendance. The majority of performance measurement is carried out by an independent person and is relatively safe, but there are exceptions. For example, the age-old practice of one employee getting another to register his clock-card was once a favourite in factories so large that the discrepancy might not be spotted. It is more difficult in modern, highly automated factories.

If sales or credit control personnel are given bonuses for cash collection targets, an employee who is not going to make his target for cash collection can hold back a large cheque he has collected and bank it in the following month to achieve a particularly high collection and high cash bonus. Not only would the company be losing out on bank interest, but it would be paying for the privilege. The solution, of course, is to use the performance pay scheme described in 3.2e for sales managers, based on the days of debt outstanding at the end of the month; the employee cannot "fudge" that calculation to his advantage.

The general answer is to make all remuneration schemes self-policing. In linear processes, this means remunerating them on what happens downstream from them. If the pay of someone setting up machinery for the following production shift is based on the output of that following shift, then:

- if he takes a long time to do the setting up, the output of the following shift will be reduced and he will lose bonus
- if he hurries the job and the set-up is not quite correct, some of the output of the next shift will have to be reworked and again he will lose bonus

He will get it right – not only because it earns him more money, but because the workers on the downstream shift will have strong words with him if they lose pay because of the inaccurate set-up.

*Real life – a German manufacturer operated a system wherein whenever an employee found a defect in the part-product he received to process, the operator immediately upstream from him lost bonus, even if that employee had not actually created the fault. This turned every single operative into a quality control manager – simple, brilliant, self-policing.*

## 5.2g – Employee theft – removal of goods

With all goods, be they office or workshop consumables, materials, work-in-progress, finished products or equipment, make an assessment of three factors:

- their value to employees or third parties
- their ease of removal
- their ease of resale

and do not underestimate the ingenuity of employees or outsiders in dealing with all three of these issues; if the resale value is high they will go to great lengths to find willing buyers and circumvent difficulties in removal (see 4.1b).

In general, if items are valuable, easy to remove and easy to re-sell, they present a security problem. Even normally honest employees may encounter personal difficulties and be tempted by easy pickings; others have no scruples at any time. The approach is therefore:

- identify the items which meet the above parameters to the greatest extent
- store the items under an appropriate level of physical security
- keep your stocks of the items as low as possible (you should be doing this anyway – see 3.2d – but it may be worth making additional arrangements for high-value easily disposable items)

- appoint specific persons to be responsible for these items – they will then be more closely guarded than if they are stored amongst general items under departmental responsibility
- physically count the items frequently and at irregular, unpredictable intervals
- if someone is caught misappropriating the items, dismiss him immediately and ensure that all other employees know why he has been dismissed

In considering the value and ease of sale of items, take account of their scrap value. For example, you may be making bespoke engineering parts that are of no use to anyone except the manufacturer who has ordered them, but if the parts are made of an easily-reprocessable material such as aluminium, they will present an attractive proposition to those of a criminal bent. Where there is aluminium, there is theft.

## 5.2h – Collusion

There are two areas of collusion:
- between two employees or directors
- between an employee or director and an outside party

Fraud by collusion is not nearly as common as fraud by a single person, since it requires one person to take the risk of suggesting a criminal act to another. Nevertheless, it is common enough to be a genuine concern. In the past it was generally accepted that collusion is so difficult to prevent or detect that financial management was not normally culpable where collusion had occurred. However, the attitude to collusion has hardened, and it is necessary for every financial manager to give careful thought to the possibility whenever a system is introduced or modified, or there is a change in personnel.

There is also passive collusion. *Real life – a new group financial director unearthed a number of frauds perpetrated by a tyrannical managing director whose other directors and senior employees were too terrified to disobey his instructions in setting up spurious transactions which materially overstated the performance of the business (for the purpose of raising finance for expansion). The other directors were effectively colluding by failing to report the transactions. The financial director reported the situation to the chairman and a new managing director was brought in (the finance had already been raised against the falsified results).*

## 5.2i – Segregation of duties

The prime objective of segregation of duties within the financial systems is the detection and correction of processing errors, which are much more likely to occur than collusion towards fraud. However, the prevention of fraud is an important secondary function of the segregation arrangements; if employees are aware that effective segregation and internal check is in force, they are much less likely to embark on any fraudulent activities.

The principal steps in an accounting system are:
- establishing permanent files (customer, product, supplier, material, employee etc data)
- authorisation or initiation of a transaction (sale, return, purchase, return, salary, payment, write-off)
- recording of a transaction (sales ledger, purchase ledger, inventory system, payroll system, bank ledger, journal, general ledger, fixed asset register etc)
- reconciliation of final records
- preparation of financial statements
- review of financial statements

As far as practicable, the above duties in each system should be segregated (vertical segregation). If the above segregations are achieved effectively, not only is each financial system largely self-checking, but an employee will need to collude with another if he is to manipulate the system.
The following examples illustrate some of the possible outcomes when duties are not segregated:

### Purchases system

| *If a person can perform both of these functions:* | *He may be able to:* |
|---|---|
| Create or amend supplier data AND process invoices | Process fictitious invoices, resulting in payments |
| Process invoices AND make payments | Make payments against fictitious invoices |

### Sales system

| *If a person can perform both of these functions:* | *He may be able to:* |
|---|---|
| Despatch products AND write off damaged stock | Despatch products to himself or a colleague and write off the items as scrapped |

| Receive cash from customers AND issue credit notes | Divert cash and square the account with a credit note which is not sent to the customer |

**Payroll system**

| *If a person can perform both of these functions:* | *He may be able to:* |
| Enter new employees on the payroll AND make wages or salary payments | Enter a fictitious employee and pay himself (the author has seen this in practice) |
| Approve time records AND enter them on the payroll | Over-pay colleagues and share the proceeds |

In the former Eastern Bloc of Europe it was common for large factories to be sited by small towns, so that the majority of the town's business came from the factory and the many suppliers in the locality. The result was that almost every supplier or tradesperson from outside the factory was a relative or in-law or drinking friend of one or more persons inside the factory and a high degree of vigilance was necessary. This situation still exists to some extent, and not only in Eastern Europe. Medium-sized businesses in small towns usually need a higher degree of alertness at management level.

A useful tactic is the occasional **rotation of staff duties**, whereupon an employee taking over a hitherto fraudulent activity stands a good chance of noticing the discrepancies. Rotation (within personal capabilities, of course) is good practice anyway, as it broadens employees' skills and provides better cover for holidays and other absences, and for periods between leavers and new staff coming onstream.

## 5.2j – Third party theft and fraud

Where collusion (see 5.2h) is not involved, third-party misdemeanours are generally one of the following:
- outright theft
- obtaining cash for goods or services which are not provided
- overcharging for goods or services which have been provided

The safeguards against third party theft from the business premises are the same as they are for theft by employees: secure storage and control of access. Company property outside the premises should be subject to transit insurance and secure parking of vehicles.

Thorough routine measures such as checking of goods and services received and documenting any deficiencies, together with related checking of supplier invoices (see payables, 4.4) should prevent all but the most ingenious supplier frauds.


## 5.2k – Fraud at high level

*The queen of diamonds let you down; she was just an empty fable*
*The queen of hearts you say you never met*
*Your twisted fate has found you out; now it's finally turned the table*
*Stole your dreams and paid you with regret*

*From "Desperado" by Don Henley and Glenn Frey of the Eagles*
*© Kicking Bear/ Benchmark Music, ASCAP*

Corporate fraud, perpetrated by the directors of a business, is usually for the purpose of falsifying the financial results of the business – see also the real-life example in "Collusion" (5.2h)

If the results are made artificially low, it is usually for one of the following purposes:
- avoidance or postponement of taxation, or transfer of the taxation burden to a country with a lower tax rate
- improving the performance of a related business (eg transferring profits to a fellow-subsidiary)
- "storing up" profits for a later period, perhaps to earn a performance-related bonus or, in the case of a new executive, to demonstrate improvement under his management

If the results are made artificially high, it is usually for one of the following purposes:
- earning a performance-related bonus in the current period
- improving the business's share price or sale value, either for personal gain or, in times of difficulty, to protect one's employment
- avoidance of taxation (normally if the result is below a taxable level, or possibly if a tax advantage will not be available in the following year)
- transfer of profit inward from a country with a higher tax rate

Falsification of figures can be highly subjective. A new financial director will almost always make the most prudent provisions possible on his first financial year-end, so that he does not suffer in the next year (his first full year) from horrors which have occurred in prior years but can no longer be blamed upon his predecessor. Where he crosses the line between justifiably prudent accounting into the area of fraud is highly arguable, particularly where provisions are made for unquantifiable events which may or may not occur.

**The Sarbanes-Oxley Act section 404**, an allegedly preventive measure which followed the Enron and other collapses in the early 21$^{st}$ century, was something of a misconception, aimed as it was against corporate fraud. Documenting accounting systems in excruciating detail does not prevent a CEO and/ or CFO from capitalising expenditure on an unsuccessful oilfield development as an asset; such a transaction will go through the records with all the correct documents and signatures, correctly authorised at the highest level.

What some managing directors fail to understand, or at least conveniently forget, is that **you cannot make money by accounting. You can only shunt profits**:
- **to another period** (usually by bringing them forward from the future, typically by leaving until next year a provision which should be made in this year and covering up the circumstances), or
- **to another place** (usually transferring them to a fellow-subsidiary or a related company)

What they pull into the current year to massage the profits will hit the company in the following year. How easily that is forgotten in the tension of the moment.

There is also the problem of the **double-whammy**. If the directors inflate this year's profit by **$1 million** and forecast future profits on the basis of that figure, then next year will fall short by **$2 million**, because:
- the profits on which next year's projection was based are overstated by $1 million, and
- you will also have to write off the $1 million which should have been written off in the current year

A more mundane example of this occurs when the directors, realising that they are not going to make their monthly target, instruct the finance department not to close off the month until after the first or second working day of the next month. On an average working month of 22 days, the workforce will have to equal 24 days' production in only 20 available days in the following month. DO NOT ACCEDE to such an instruction.

In summary, the main corporate distortions of a practical (one should really say impractical) nature are:
- bringing profits forward from a future period

- bringing profits across from another business
- underproviding for likely liabilities
- underproviding for loss of value of assets
- overvaluing assets
- inconsistent capitalising (eg development projects, intellectual property, dies and moulds)

If you as a controller accede to such instructions, you become a party to them. At the very least, you should record your objections in writing, with a copy to your solicitor.

Dominant chief executives are always a problem, but the best way to deal with them is to give as good as you get. Bullies are weaklings, so take courage and stand your ground.

## 5.2l – Blowing the whistle

As we have considered in 5.2k, you cannot make money by accounting; you can only move profits from one period to another or one business to another. However, some directors fail to understand that fact, or at best refuse to accept it, and may try to achieve a result by fraudulent accounting.

May this never happen to you . . . but if you reach a stage where you have to blow the whistle on a corporate fraud:
- consult your professional institute's legal advisor
- consult your own legal advisor
- compile a full file of documentary evidence (preferably with original documents, not photocopies)
- ensure that the file contains your own written objections to the proposals (see below)
- copy the file to your legal advisor and store your own copy off-site
- then pause to reflect . . . are you REALLY doing the right thing?

At one extreme you may come to the conclusion that the directors are only doing what is best for the company by stretching a point to protect its position. Most companies have at times evened out trading results from period to period. Excess provisions are tucked away in the good times and released in the bad times, and rules on capitalisation of expenditure tend to be relaxed when things are tough. If the effect is mild, you may conclude that the offence is a minor one and register an appropriately mild concern.

At the other extreme you may conclude that:
- what they are doing is defrauding people who are providing funds to the company (probably including suppliers providing credit)

- the house of cards will collapse in the foreseeable future, or at least there is no predictable prospect of the transactions being reversed
- by putting off the inevitable they are delaying corrective action which if taken promptly could remedy the situation, or at least minimise the damage
- you yourself will be associated with the collapse and possibly even be made the scapegoat

If you decide after the most careful reflection that the directors must be prevented from continuing their actions, advise them in writing that you consider their actions to be illegal.

That may have the effect of causing them to back down from what they are about to do. But only allow them a short time in which to do that, otherwise they will return with counter-proposals, moralising arguments and other subterfuges, in the meantime plotting your swift demise, or at least some counter-attack based on your alleged emotional unreliability or some such fabrication, putting you under extreme pressure.

If they do not step back from the brink, give them a 10-minute warning (stretch it to a couple of hours at the most), then pull the plug:

- if the non-executive directors are not complicit in the fraud, then they (especially the chairman) are the people to whom you should report the fraud or intended fraud
- if the non-execs are complicit, the probable best course of action is to instruct your solicitor to contact the auditors – it will then be their responsibility to act

To repeat: may you never have to do that . . . but if you must do it, do not flinch; the consequences are not as bad as you might fear.

*Real life – the new group financial director referred to in section 5.2h never had cause to regret his actions. Years later, he confirmed that he was still satisfied that he had acted in the best interests of the company and all its related parties, and in accordance with the law.*

## 5.3a – Objectives

No matter what are the terms under which the business trades, the financial controller will be involved in the negotiation and agreement of contracts for a variety of issues. If this involves the drafting of a contract for a specific requirement, the controller must be aware of what should be included in the contract to protect the interests of the business (it is normally what is omitted from the contract that will cause you problems). However, even if the contract is a standard pre-printed document (such as a telephone leasing company would provide) the controller needs to check that the contract contains all the necessary conditions, and only those conditions. In such a case, any additions or alterations can be dealt with in a covering letter.

The objectives of this subsection are therefore:
- to consider the terms which exist or should exist in most contracts (these terms are not exhaustive)
- to consider the terms which exist or should exist in specific contracts with which the financial controller is especially likely to be involved
- to give guidance on the drafting of contracts

## 5.3b – Contract structure

Remember that the financial controller is providing administrative, commercial and practical expertise in compiling or reviewing the content of a contract. Legal expertise should be provided by a legal agent appropriately qualified in the law(s) governing the contract.

All countries have their own laws of contract, and some countries such as the USA and the UK have different laws within different parts of the country. Moreover, each business and each contractual situation within the business has its own circumstances which should be dealt with specifically.

However, there are certain conditions (don't use the phrase "terms and conditions"; a term is a condition) and information which should be included in most trading contracts, regardless of their subject. These are, roughly in the order of appearance:

Parties
- the parties to the contract, their representatives and associated parties, and their addresses

Definitions
- the obligations to be implemented under the contract
- the timescale of the obligations (when they are to be met, and when they cease to apply)
- the locations and other factors which define the scope of the actions and obligations
- any exclusions from the scope of the contract
- the legal or professional standards to which the obligations must be carried out
- quantification of the actions (amounts of goods to be delivered, prices to be paid etc)
- any associated objectives of the contract
- any other parameters which must be defined to avoid confusion or disagreement

Reports
- the timing, content and delivery of periodic reports (including invoices and financial statements) to be submitted during the contract
- the timing, content and delivery of the final report

Conduct
- the manner in which the obligations are to be performed
- the parameters which are to be achieved by performing the obligations (this may involve certification by independent parties)
- any other factors which govern the performance of the obligations

Restrictions
- any sensitivities which must be observed (the most common being confidentiality)
- intellectual property
- covenants and other binding limitations
- any other factor which may govern or restrict the performance of the obligations

Administration and conduct
- transport, travel and accommodation related to the contract (what facilities should be used, who is responsible for it, who pays for it)
- insurance against any circumstances arising from the contract (the level of cover and who pays for it)
- communication amongst the parties during the contract
- provision of specific facilities to enable each party to perform its obligations
- security, health and safety

Disputes
- disclosures of difficulties already known to exist (so that neither party can claim that they were unaware of the circumstances)
- warranties and indemnities
- procedure under which any disputes are to be resolved
- country under whose law the contract will be interpreted and under which any disputes can be resolved (conventionally, this should be the country in which most of the obligations are performed, but in practice it tends to be the country of the most powerful party to the contract)

Fees and credit
- definition of the points of completion of obligation (eg deliveries of goods or stages in construction) upon which payments must be made by one party to another
- the amounts (or calculations), currencies, methods, recipients (agents, banks etc) and timing of such payments (remember that the date of payment may not be the date of completion, and that contracts require credit control)
- the reimbursement of outlays properly incurred in performing the obligations
- the payment of any performance bonuses for achieving clearly defined targets
- the payment or deduction of any penalties for failing to achieve clearly defined targets
- any other financial matters relating to the contract

Determination
- homologation, depending on local law (it may be that if a party performs actions stated in the contract, he is deemed to have accepted the contract whether or not he has formally signed it; some countries, including Scotland, legally accept an oral contract if it can be proven)

- definitions of completion of the contract (completions of certain specific obligations, reaching of a certain date, occurrence of an external event etc; there may be more than one possible termination circumstance)
- the rights of the parties on normal completion of the contract
- determination of the contract by default of one of the parties
- the rights of the parties on determination of a contract by default

That is a long list, and there may well be other conditions which should be specified in the contract. However, the above conditions should cover most general trading eventualities, excluding the specific detail of the obligations to be performed (see below).

## 5.3c – Other rules affecting a contract

Contracts are often drafted in an environment in which there are already many rules governing how the parties to the contract must operate (eg tax regulations, health and safety rules). In such cases, DO NOT repeat these regulations in the contract.

If you do, you risk a situation where the regulations are amended and therefore contradict what you have written in the contract, possibly even nullifying the contract. Instead, make reference in the contract to the regulations concerned and if appropriate attach a copy of the regulations to the contract, to be initialled by all parties as understood and as forming part of the contract.

*Real life ~ a team of divers was performing a programme of structural inspection of a number of wellhead platforms in an offshore oilfield. While divers were working below one of the client's platforms, some of the client's personnel threw overboard some heavy containers, narrowly missing the divers. The diving superintendent immediately radioed the client's safety officer to ask him to investigate and prevent a recurrence.*

*Several days later the superintendent received a furious call from the client's chief engineer, pointing out that the contract stated that all accidents and incidents were to be reported immediately to the chief engineer. The superintendent replied that the contract also stated that all diving in the client's oilfield had to be carried out in accordance with the client's diving manual, which was the absolute authority on local diving procedures and which stated that all accidents and incidents must be reported immediately and solely to the client's safety officer, as the superintendent had done.*

*The message bounced around from ego to ego within the client's management structure until, two weeks later, the superintendent radioed the client again to advise that he had still not received any assurance that the incident had been reviewed and steps taken to prevent a repetition. Silence followed, and the contract was completed without the matter ever being resolved, the diving team having instigated its own additional procedures to prevent a recurrence.*

The lesson from this example is clear. Having mentioned that diving was to be performed in accordance with the client's diving manual, the contract should not have contained any diving procedural instructions. The poor drafting was not the fault of the chief engineer or the safety officer, but of the contracts department, and neither the superintendent nor the diving management noticed the contradiction on receiving the contract from the client in the first place.

Therefore when you are drafting a contract in which certain activities are subject to established regulations, do not quote passages from these regulations. Instead:

- if you are certain what these regulations are, refer to them by name (eg "in accordance with the Transfer of Inflammable Materials Act 2005")
- if you are not certain what regulations apply, or if your contract may run long enough to encounter new regulations which are not yet in force, use all-embracing general terminology (eg "in accordance with all national safety regulations and any additional regulations in force on the client's premises")

The second option should always be used where there is any doubt. Note that in the second example there could be conflict between the client regulations and national regulations, so the wording gives precedence to the national regulations.

Regulations which you are likely to encounter include:

- import/ export
- safety during storage, production, transport, usage and other environments
- safety of specific substances, processes or equipment
- national regulations (which may of course differ between two trading countries)
- taxation (where there is possible doubt over tax responsibility, specify who bears any tax payable)
- public or personnel issues

We now consider a few of the main specific contracts that the financial controller will encounter.

## 5.3d – Conditions of sale

Part 5.3b above discusses the requirements of a specific contract for goods, services or facilities. However, the great majority of sales are made under a general contract, not a specific one.

If the contract is not agreed beforehand in writing (as when a retailer sells an item) then there is an implicit contract, and any underlying legislation (but in which country?) together with the actions of the parties will determine how any dispute is settled. Since this is a very unsatisfactory process, all sales should be governed by conditions of sale agreed in writing before the sale is made.

The conditions will vary according to the goods and services being sold, but the following conditions should be present for most goods being sold:
- definitions of the terminology used in the contract
- status of quotations made by the business (ie non-binding)
- the point at which risk in the goods passes to the buyer
- the point at which title to the goods passes to the buyer (note that retention of title is a complex issue and varies from one country to another, and from one product to another; for example, what works in England sometimes does not apply in Scotland, and what may work for building implements may not work for building materials)
- the setting and amendment of prices
- payment methods and credit periods
- warranties
- product liability
- design and other rights
- cancellation or termination of the sales agreement or relationship
- force majeure (the non-acceptance of liabilities resulting from major non-controllable events such as natural disasters, vandalism or civil, political or military upheavals)
- the governing law covering the sale
- any other aspects which could be disputed to the disadvantage of the business

Your legal advisors should be able to compile an appropriate set of conditions for your business. Obtaining the customer's agreement to the conditions, however, is another matter. Ideally, when you accept a new customer you should issue them with two copies of your sales conditions and they should return one copy to you, signed by them as accepted.

In practice, you may find that they send sales orders with their conditions of purchase printed on the back, and if you accept the orders you may be deemed to be accepting their conditions, since their order is the more recent relevant document, and it will favour them rather than you. You may therefore wish to send them a written acknowledgment with your conditions stated on the back, and so on right through the sales documentation. You may consider that the costs of printing your conditions on the back of every sales document exceeds any loss you are likely to incur through disputes, in which case your acknowledgement could simply state "we acknowledge receipt of your order [number and date] in accordance with our conditions of sale as signed by you" or words to that effect.

If this is a problematic area, take legal advice. Consider also whether a customer who presents a lot of problems in this area is worth having.

Remember also that your suppliers will be presenting you with conditions of sale, and you should ensure that you are not buying on disadvantageous conditions.

## 5.3e – Contracts with distributors or agents

For avoidance of doubt (people sometimes use the terms differently):
- a distributor buys your products, and usually some spares and accessories, and sells them on to his customers; he therefore takes ownership of what he buys from you and is your direct customer (below, however, the term "customer" means the end user)
- an agent does not take ownership of your products, although he may hold some on your behalf; he negotiates sales of your products to your customers and takes an agreed commission thereon (he may even commit to collecting your customer debts for you)

Apart from the matters of product ownership, the contractual relationship with a distributor is broadly similar to that with an agent. In addition to the general contract matters (see 5.3b) your contract with the distributor or agent ("D/A") should address the following matters:

Area of operation
- the geographical territory over which the contract is granted
- the degree of exclusivity which the D/A is granted

Products
- the products covered by the agreement (it may not be your whole range)
- the performance (the D/A will wish to ensure that they perform as promised)
- how the products are to be used (incorrect use may result in losses and claims)
- if, when and how upgrades will be developed and introduced to the market, and if so, how older products will be supported
- local variations (eg different power supply, safety regulations, import restrictions)
- instructions and other supporting literature, in the appropriate languages, and adapted to match any variations in your product for local use
- certification (eg fitness for use, freedom from danger, politically acceptable sourcing)
- packaging
- transport
- guarantees (the degree of validity in the D/A's territory must be explicit)
- product liability
- pricing to end customers (this is not a local decision, since you will wish to ensure that your product is sensibly priced in relation to the competition and your own margin requirements – collaboration with the D/A on pricing is usually essential)
- the transfer price to the distributor or commission to the agent (the agent bears less risk, and his commission will therefore normally be less than a distributor's margin)

Service
- the allocation between you and the D/A of responsibility for service to customers
- lead times in delivering products from you to the D/A
- lead times in delivering products from the D/A to the customers
- stockholding (display inventory may be required locally to generate sales; with an agent it will be your inventory, but with a distributor it could be yours or his, so there should be enough to promote sales, but not to cause the distributor a working capital problem, or you will suffer along with him)
- responsibility for repairs (usually arranged locally, but for high-specification products it may be necessary to return them to you, and therefore to provide relief stock to cover the customer during the repair time, especially during the guarantee period)

- maintenance (you have to ensure that the D/A or each customer maintains your products correctly, or you will suffer from repair requirements which should not be your responsibility)
- spares (the D/A will have to hold an adequate supply for immediate availability to local customers, but overstocking will cause you unnecessary outlay in the case of an agent)
- accessories (if profitable, these should be promoted as vigorously as the main products)
- returns (products should not be returned unless absolutely necessary; the greater the distance between you and the D/A, the stricter you must be on controlling returns)

Training
- the D/A, or a local specialist acceptable to both you and the D/A, must be trained to support your products in the field
- the training may involve qualification of local repair and maintenance personnel to a specific standard recognised in your country and the D/A's
- customers themselves may require training to operate your product; whether this is done under your control or the D/A's depends on what resources are available in each area
- in all matters relating to training, all necessary certification needs to be obtained by the people you train, and they will need supporting literature

Intellectual property
- you must retain ownership of your intellectual property (patents, trademarks etc) in all countries in which you operate, and possibly beyond
- you must retain control over sales literature produced by the D/A, or he may over-commit you in terms of support etc or misrepresent you (if possible, provide your own literature with a space for the D/A's logo etc)
- you must retain the right to edit the content of the D/A's website and advertising, to ensure that your products and your business are not misrepresented or over-committed, and that similar goods and services are not passed off by the D/A under your name

As your business and products and the D/A's business develops, it may be necessary to review and amend the contract frequently, so that it continues to reflect and control the relationship between you. This may entail having your own professional advisor(s) in the D/A's territory.

## 5.3f – Importing and exporting documents

Documentation and procedures for importing and exporting goods are a specialist area, best handled by reputable freight handling and forwarding agents unless you have a large enough operation to merit your own impex (import/ export) department. It will then still be a specialist area, requiring specifically experienced and capable personnel, the difference being that they are YOUR personnel.

## 5.3g – Contracts of employment

In most modern countries, contracts of employment are required by law. As with all contracts, the requirements will vary from country to country, but you as a responsible employer will want to have a standard contract which clearly protects the employer and the employee from any untoward behaviour. Every contract should therefore include at least the following details:

Parties
- names, former names, and addresses of the parties to the contract
- job title and description
- duties
- direct superior of employee
- other direct responsibilities (eg a customer services representative may report directly to the sales manager, but may have a strong responsibility to the financial controller for the issuing of sales invoices; nobody should have more than one direct superior, so the controller should be regarded as the representative's "internal customer")

Parameters
- date of starting employment
- duration of employment (or the fact that it is not of a fixed period)
- probation period
- place of work (this may be the general address, or the specific department, as appropriate)
- hours of work, including overtime calculation (if these are governed by detailed regulations elsewhere, do not repeat them in the contract but merely refer to them and attach a copy signed by the employee)

Conduct
- grievance reporting (normally to the direct superior in the first instance, and if satisfaction is not obtained, to a designated senior person or to a personnel manager)
- health and safety (refer to the business's regulations, but do not repeat them – see 5.3c)
- standard of work
- compliance with work regulations
- general behaviour (for example, standard of dress and attitude to customers)
- confidentiality
- intellectual property
- restrictive covenants
- other requirements or restrictions

Benefits
- holidays, with especial reference to when they may and may not be taken, or carried over unused into another year
- compassionate and other non-standard leave
- transport, where provided, and parking facilities
- other facilities specifically provided within the company (fitness room, day-care etc)

Remuneration
- basic pay and calculation
- date and method of payment
- deductions (income tax, social security, savings, subscriptions etc)
- continuity of employment and seniority when an employee moves from one part of the business to another
- pay review process

Termination
- conditions of termination (period of notice, gross misconduct etc)
- misconduct procedure
- requirement for the employee to notify the business immediately of all changes in personal circumstances (eg marriage, new children) which may affect the contract or the pay or statutory conditions
- a statement that employee has read, understood and accepted the contract and the associated regulations (specify these)
- a statement that all changes to the contract (eg promotions, job changes, increases in pay) will be notified in writing, signed by both parties and attached to the contract, thus becoming part of the contract

- employee's and employer's representative's signatures and dates accepting the contract

Earlier (5.3c) we mentioned that if there are other regulations governing the substance of a contract, these should not be repeated in the contract. The contract should only make reference to these other regulations, so that there is no possible contradiction. This is particularly relevant to employment contracts, in which reference may have to be made to:

- statutory conditions of employment (for example, if the business's period of notice is X weeks and the legal minimum period is Y weeks, the conditions should state that the period of notice is "the greater of X weeks and the legal minimum period", so that if the legal minimum changes, there is no need to change all the employee contracts)
- national income tax and social security rates
- business health and safety rules
- special rules relating to the type of work the employee is carrying out
- the business's employee manual

**Do not include termination rights** in a contract of employment, nor in any written form. If you do, the rights become part of the employee's remuneration and are taxable. You must ensure that you make no formal reference to any expectation of termination payments, so that they cannot be considered as remuneration. Termination payments in many countries are considered to be compensation for loss of employment and therefore not subject to tax; you can therefore give a terminated employee a greater benefit for less cost to the business.


## 5.3h – Termination of employment contract

The conditions of termination of an employee are determined by the contract of employment. Over and above meeting the contractual conditions, there are a number of financial actions which either the personnel manager or the financial controller should take immediately. It is very easy to forget these actions, particularly in the case of a sudden departure, so ensure that you have a standing action plan to cover these points and any others which may apply, in accordance with the law under which you are operating:

Consultation
- ensure full legal process has been followed
- ensure full contractual process has been followed
- do not give any expectation of specific termination payments

Resignation .
- obtain a written resignation from the employee, or prepare a notice of termination and obtain the employee's signature thereon
- obtain a written resignation of a directorship if relevant, or a minute of the director's removal from the board
- advise the bank and other external parties for whom the employee was a signatory that the signature is invalid with immediate effect (you may need to ensure that outstanding cheques and transfers are honoured)
- obtain immediate legal advice if the termination is in disciplinary circumstances

Termination payments
- calculate pay to termination date
- calculate outstanding overtime, holiday pay and other dues
- calculate outstanding bonuses
- calculate redundancy payment
- calculate pay in lieu of notice
- obtain from the employee a statement of all outstanding recoverable expenses
- obtain a note of any cash advances made to the employee
- obtain a note of all other outstanding financial matters relating to the employee
- calculate the termination payment(s) from the above
- obtain a signature from the employee for each payment and the supporting calculation

Non-financial facilities
- advise the pension fund of the termination and instruct them to advise the employee accordingly (this may involve a refund from the fund to the employee)
- recover from the employee all membership cards, including any medical cards
- cancel any specific insurance arrangements
- cancel any customer-related documents (eg gate passes to customer premises)
- cancel any related legal documents (eg work permit)
- cancel any memberships (eg local club)

Effects
- recover all keys (factory, office, safe, etc)
- change confidential entry and alarm codes
- recover all files (hard copy and electronic)
- redirect email to an appropriate person

- recover all credit cards, fuel cards etc
- recover corporate frequent flyer cards and other corporate travel cards
- recover the company vehicle and documents and check the vehicle for damage
- recover the employee's laptop computer, mobile phone and other equipment
- recover all manuals and sensitive literature, especially customer and product data
- vacate employee accommodation

If the employee is terminated instantly, swift measures must be taken to complete all of the above actions and any others required. However, in the event of a planned termination, the measures may need to be actioned over an agreed period, often several months. This may be more difficult to control, since it becomes easy to forget some of the actions, so the check-list must be maintained and actioned on the due dates by a responsible person.

## 5.3i – Contracts dictated by other parties

Many of the contracts which a financial controller must review and decide upon are standard contracts produced by external organisations. Examples include:
- insurance policies
- leasing contracts for equipment
- leasing contracts for land and buildings

In these cases there is usually little scope for manoeuvre; it is largely a question of "take it or leave it", the only area of negotiation being the price. Nevertheless, the controller should still review the contracts carefully, using the general contract clauses above (see 5.3b) as an aide-memoire. Where there are conditions that are particularly unacceptable, it may be possible to obtain confirmation in writing from the other party that the condition is modified in your case.

## 5.3j – Drafting contracts

Circumstances may arise in which you have to draft a commercial contract from scratch, such as with a new trading relationship or a contract to carry out a particular service. The way to do this is as follows:

- write down in short notes all that you want to happen and who is to do it
- arrange the notes in the order shown in the sub-headings of "General contracts" above (5.3b)
- review the recommended headings in "General contracts" and add any essentials you have missed

Having prepared a structured set of notes, draft the contract, using a simple bullet-point format.

For example, DO NOT write:
"In the event that the product becomes damaged after sale, and the damage is the fault of the customer, the customer will be required to pay for the repair and any associated costs, but in the event that the repair is required through a defect in the product the distributor will be liable to complete the repair and recover the cost thereof from the manufacturer, except insofar as the repair involves skills beyond the agreed training standard of the distributor's staff, in which case the distributor will return the product to the manufacturer for repair at the manufacturer's expense."

Instead, DO write:
"In the event of damage to the product after sale:
- if it is the customer's fault, the distributor will repair it at the customer's expense, but
- if it results from a product defect, the distributor will repair it at the manufacturer's expense, and
- in either case, if the repair involves skills beyond the distributor's training level, the manufacturer will repair it."

The bullet-point format is much easier to write and to understand, and is just as valid legally, provided that you make it clear whether the points are additive or alternative. Another tabular format which saves much unwanted verbiage is the tick box, which is useful when allocating responsibilities or other features in a sequence of events or requirements. An example is this extract from a service contract under which company X provides payroll processing ("X pay") and accounting ("X a/cs") services to a client:

| Payment of net remuneration to employees | Client | Bank | X pay | X a/cs |
|---|---|---|---|---|
| | | | | |
| Check and sign 2 copies of payroll detail | ✓ | | | |
| Send 2nd copy of payroll detail to X payroll department | ✓ | | | |
| Check and sign 2 copies of bank transfer list | ✓ | | | |
| Send 2nd copy of bank transfer list to X payroll department | ✓ | | | |
| Send list to bank by 27th of month | | | ✓ | |
| Transfer money to employee accounts per transfer list | | ✓ | | |
| Compile payroll journal entry | | | ✓ | |
| Check payroll journal entry and enter in general ledger | | | | ✓ |
| Ensure that net payroll control account squares to zero | | | | ✓ |

Using the above technique you can compress twenty pages of conventional narrative into a four-page contract which is easy to read, easy to understand and more likely to be followed in practice without disputes. Not only that, but if you are working in more than one language it is much easier to translate this format without error or misunderstanding than it is to translate conventional narrative. And it is just as viable in legal terms in most countries. You can also expand the technique by having additional columns for dates or other specifications, and by entering specific information (eg designations of responsible officials) in the boxes instead of ticks.

When you have finished drafting the procedural details of your contract, present your draft to your legal advisors, and have the necessary legal conditions attached. Insist that your legal advisor uses the same simple language (most commercial lawyers are happy to do this).

This approach will work in any modern country if you are working with capable legal advisors, as you are providing the operational framework, leaving the legal embroidery to be stitched around it by the experts.

Stay legal at all times.

## 5.4a – Objectives

The objective of insurance is to protect your business from all non-commercial risks to which it is reasonably expected to be exposed.

What is "reasonably expected" is difficult to define. A business could theoretically be at risk from earthquake, flood, civil unrest, terrorism or war, but the management team may justifiably consider that the likelihood is small enough that the cost of insuring against the risks is not justifiable. There is no perfect definition or quantification of risk.

If the security of a business, as discussed throughout this section, is well-managed, the cost of insurance is likely to be reduced, but one should always view the costs of implementing and maintaining security measures against the savings in premiums. As it is a highly specialised area, you should seek the services of a reputable insurance agent, who will seek the most effective cover at the most economical rates on your behalf. Their commission for doing this will normally be covered by their negotiation of cost-effective premiums on your behalf.

If anything, there is a tendency for managers to over-insure their businesses, to avoid being held responsible for losses which others might argue should have been insured against.

## 5.4b – Types of cover

The physical assets to be considered for insurance are:
- land and buildings including any tenant's improvements
- production equipment (special processes and equipment, such as boilers and lifting gear, may require specific cover)
- road vehicles
- vessels (ships and aircraft)
- goods on site
- goods in transit or on other sites
- office and other non-production equipment
- accounting records and other essential documents

- computer systems
- specialist equipment or substances requiring special care
- cash, on site or in transit
- other aspects of fidelity guarantee
- debts due to the business

Note that it may be incumbent on the business to insure assets that are on loan or lease, even if the title may effectively be held by the lenders or lessors; check the terms of your loan and lease agreements. And where assets are likely to be moved physically, ensure that the terms of the insurance cover all locations at which the assets may be sited (including transit).

Note also that the cost of replacing an asset may considerably exceed the financial value at which that asset is held in the business's books. It may include the following:
- increase in price of the asset (normally dealt with by index-linking, periodic valuation or replacement-cost clauses)
- removing the damaged asset from site, and repairing damage caused by this process
- installing the replacement asset
- testing the replacement asset, and if it is not exactly the same as the damaged asset, training operators and bringing the asset to full operating efficiency
- reconfiguring associated assets which were connected to the damaged asset (all too often the replacement asset is of a newer design, with different connexions and parameters, and the associated assets will not automatically connect with it; this is particularly common in the technology sphere)
- claims from customers arising from production delays

This brings us to the second category of insurance:
- (consequential) loss of profits
- claims from customers or other third parties arising from production delays or other circumstances caused by loss of the asset

Finally, there are legally-oriented issues for which insurance may be needed:
- employer's liability – covering death, injury or distress suffered by employees as a result of their employment
- public liability – covering death, injury, distress or loss to members of the public as a result of the business's activities
- product liability – covering death, injury, distress or loss caused by the business's products

- directors and officers – covering claims made by outsiders against individual members of the management, instead of claiming against the business as an entity
- key personnel – covering the lives or incapacity of persons without whom the business could not operate successfully (remember that few people are quite as indispensable as they may appear)
- professional indemnity – covering alleged professional negligence, where the business is a profession
- fidelity guarantee – covering theft by employees, agents or others closely related to the business in a position of trust over the business's assets
- employee travel – conventional travel cover for employees who travel frequently, possibly covering medical or casualty evacuation from other countries

As with all contracts, force majeure (natural disasters, civil unrest, police or military action) may be excluded from your insurance cover.


## 5.4c – Business continuity and disaster recovery

Multi-site businesses manufacturing similar products have an advantage in disaster planning in that activities can often be transferred from one site to another on a temporary basis in the event of a crisis. But most businesses are capable of being incapacitated by an unforeseen event to the point where the business is unable to function. In such situations, if the business does not return to full operation within a short time it is more likely than not to cease trading completely. Disasters include:

- fire, explosion, flood, earthquake, building collapse or any other major physical occurrence
- cessation of supply from a major supplier (essential supplies should in general be dual-sourced)
- cessation of the major distribution resource
- medium/ long-term breakdown of the information systems

*Real life – having relocated a small aerospace software company near Los Angeles under very hostile circumstances, the author noted that the company's back-up procedure merely involved the head software engineer taking home a back-up of the developing software every night to his surfer pad in Oceanside, some distance down the coast. The author decided to formalise the arrangement and arranged for the newly-appointed auditor to keep the back-up in a fire-proof safe in his office a few hundred metres away in a mall across the freeway, a location which appeared to the author to be much more secure.*

*When the new president returned from his holiday in Hawaii (golfing, not surfing) and learned of this, he tore several strips off the author. The reason? The software engineer's pad on the coast was on the other side of the San Andreas Fault, whereas the accountant's office was only a few hundred metres away, and if an earthquake destroyed the software office, it would also destroy the auditor's office. We live and learn.*

A business should at the very least have:
- an appraisal team who identify the disasters which have some chance of befalling the business
- a response team who will deal with a disaster should it occur
- co-ordination between the two teams to develop AND TEST plans for the main eventualities

The detailed risk evaluation and response planning is beyond the scope of this book, but the rôle of the financial controller merits consideration here.

Of the above events, the one which is most likely fall into the financial controller's domain is the breakdown of the information systems, which could be a disaster in its own right, or the result of one of the other disasters. In such a situation the financial controller and the IT manager would be in charge of the following processes:
- obtaining a back-up set of hardware
- setting up a work site (typically a camp of portable cabin units to house the relevant personnel)
- re-installing the computer system(s) from the back-ups on to the temporary hardware
- setting up the users in the work site and re-establishing contact with customers and suppliers

The immediate reconstruction of the business activities could take place at one or more of:
- the existing premises, under impaired working conditions
- nearby premises rented for the purpose
- the premises of another company in the same group
- by not replicating the activities, but sub-contracting the activities or sourcing the products from another producer (probably unprofitably, but it would retain the customer base, and the loss of profits should be recoverable from the insurers)

The only way of knowing whether the above plan would work would be to rehearse it physically. For the financial controller, this would mean making arrangements with local providers of facilities and then, without warning to them, run a dress-rehearsal to set up:

- a work-site fully connected via a replacement system to all the relevant parties
- orders continuing to flow in from customers, and acknowledgements to go out
- orders continuing to flow out to suppliers
- queries from customers and suppliers to be answered
- all necessary information to and from the rest of the business to be communicated

Continuation of sales invoicing is normally the most important and urgent activity to reconstitute.

The level of detail required for such an operation, and therefore for a successful test, is considerable. Every connexion, every plug, every piece of equipment has to be in place for it to work.

The re-establishment of the other facilities outwith the financial controller's responsibility is beyond the scope of this book. It is a massive simulation exercise (you would not be likely to move into another factory for a few days just to test the disaster plan, but you would be simulating enough of the activities to know that it could work). But the information systems, under the joint care of IT and finance, would be the framework which would hold the plan together.

Business continuity insurance may alleviate part of your losses in the event of a calamity, but you will still be left with the problem of re-creating your business, assuming that there is enough left of it to re-create.

*Real life – in September 2001 Morgan Stanley, one of the world's major financial services businesses, had nearly 2,700 people over 15 floors of the World Trade Center (the "twin towers") in New York. Following a previous attempt to bomb the towers (an unsuccessful bomb in the basement some years earlier) Morgan Stanley had devised an evacuation drill which was practised on several occasions.*

*When the towers were attacked on 11 September, all but 9 of the Morgan Stanley staff were successfully evacuated as a result of their drill. Within hours of the event, Morgan Stanley's clients around the world received an email advising them of the situation and confirming that their investments were unaffected and that all the other Morgan Stanley offices would be open for business as usual the next morning. The email also contained the direct telephone numbers of the senior officials who would field enquiries regarding the various financial services on all continents. The author still holds a copy of that email, a chilling testament to the effectiveness of the disaster plan and the professionalism of the people responsible for implementing it.*

So there is more to do than just the routine inspection of the fire extinguishers and the sprinkler system. You cannot cope for every eventuality, but you should at least identify the major risks facing you (does the nearby river flood from time to time?) and plan and rehearse accordingly. Underpin your success by installing and testing risk management and disaster recovery plans and structures, and ensure that these are absorbed into the fabric and culture of your organisation. It is a well-known statistic that **over 80% of organisations which suffer a sudden deep crisis fail to survive in their original form**.

To obtain reliable advice on business continuity planning, visit the website www.mtjconsulting.co.uk

## 5.4d – Personnel

*Real life – An experienced financial director told the author of a long-past incident in which all the directors of a company were travelling in the same car and were all killed in a crash. When the author asked what happened to the company, he replied cheerfully "It went from strength to strength".*

Whether the reported outcome was true or just his habitual black humour is not known, but in your business you cannot afford to risk emulating Manchester United. Enforce a strict travel policy which ensures that you do not risk an unnecessarily high proportion of key personnel in one car or aircraft. And in some countries you have to give consideration to the safety of rail transport. The policy should of course be tempered with reasonable economy; it is not economically practicable to send everybody separately on every journey.

You may be disappointed to reflect that senior finance people in a mainstream business are probably the most easily replaceable executives in a business, because the discipline of finance is much more similar from one business to another than any other discipline.

# APPENDICES

# APPENDICES

|  |  | pages |  |  |
|---|---|---|---|---|
| General | A1 | 1 | Organisation | *linked* |
|  | A2 | 1 | Product comparison sheet | *linked* |
|  | A3 | 1 | Product lifespan |  |
|  | A4 | 1 | Annual calendar | *linked* |
|  | A5 | 1 | Forex cover plan |  |
|  | A6 | 1 | Capex evaluation using DCF |  |
|  | A7 | 2 | Appraisal format |  |
|  | A8 | 1 | Signing authorities |  |
| Daily, weekly | B1 | 1 | Daily cash position | *linked* |
|  | B2 | 1 | Weekly performance review | *linked* |
| Monthly | C1 | 1 | Monthly accounting timetable |  |
|  | C2 | 1 | Budget template |  |
|  | C3 | 1 | Capex plan | *linked* |
|  | C4 | 1-10 | Budget | *linked* |
|  | C5 | 1 | Monthly report data structure |  |
|  | C6 | 1 | Monthly profit statement | *linked* |
|  | C7 | 1 | Variance report | *linked* |
|  | C8 | 1 | Capital employed statement | *linked* |
|  | C9 | 1 | Cash flow monthly (S&A) | *linked* |
|  | C10 | 1 | Month-end accrual sheet |  |
|  | C11 | 1 | Project report |  |
|  | C12 | 1 | Closure report |  |
| Other | D | 1 | Recommended reading |  |

*Appendices designated "linked" contain figures relating to each other*
*They cover budgetary procedures and subsequent reporting in comparison therewith*
*These appendices are in an imaginary currency, PQ$, for an imaginary year, 20XX-XY*
*The imaginary company is referred to as DEMO COMPANY*

*Comments written in italics on the appendices are purely instructive*
*They would not normally appear on the documents portrayed*

*The main financial statements should be supported by extensive analysis*
*The bulk of this analysis should support the TOP end of the profit statement*
*The mistake most companies make is to analyse their overheads to death,*
*    while ignoring the parts of the business which generate the net variable margin*

| STRATEGIC | MANAGERIAL | OPERATIONAL | PROFIT RESPONSIBILITY | No |
|---|---|---|---|---|

**Marketing Manager** 0
MB Dealmaker

**Sales representatives**
KK Flashman 1
BG Bonus-Chaser 1
GT Mondeo 1

**Sales assistants**
JJ Pattermonger 1
IN Thepost 1

NET SALES
MARKETING MARGIN 12

**Finished Goods Manager** 1
MT Racking

**Goods handlers**
2 per shift 6

**Production manager** 1
JP Handel-Turner

**Total quality manager** 1
QA Perfect

**Production planners**
NE Oldiron 1
ON Schedule 1

**Materials controller** 1
EX Quartermaster

**Inventory assistants**
WE Countem 1
AN Stackem 1

**Shift managers**
MA Morningside 1
SP Siesta 1
FE Nightingale 1

**Shift workers**
Shift A 21
Shift B 21
Shift C 21

MATERIAL COST
DIRECT LABOUR COST
GROSS MARGIN 73

**Marketing Manager** 1
MB Dealmaker

**Marketing staff**
VG Schpieler 1
OK Powerpoint 1

**R&D technical**
XY Boffin 1
SH Spanner 1

**Technical assistants**
To be recruited

MARKETING MARGIN 5

**Financial Controller** 1
VB Tightwad

**Management Accountant** 1
PP Variance

**Finance assistants**
XL Wizard 1
PV Checker 1

**Systems Manager** 1
WZ Kidd

**Reception Personnel** 1
MS Moneypenny

**Admin assistants**
PN Pusher 1
PG Teamaker 1

overheads
borrowing costs
forex costs
taxation
NET PROFIT AFTER TAX 9

**Non-Exec Directors**
JJ Rosencranz
LL Guildenstern

**Chairman**
GN Tonic 1

**Managing Director**
ZZ Top-Mann 1

| 1 | 3 | 18 | 77 | HEADCOUNT 99 |

In larger companies,
departments can be shown in detail on separate sheets and totals thereof shown on this sheet
Where a person holds two posts, the "1" is entered for the main post

The inclusion of headcount numbers indicates which areas may be over- or under-manned

DEMO CO   ORGANISATION   10 Jun 20XX

D:\Ard\Bus\Org\DemOrg

APPENDIX A1

# DEMO COMPANY - PRODUCT COMPARISON

| ATTRIBUTES | DEMO COMPANY | KK LEUNG | MOLYNEUX | UNITED DMA | VAN RENSBURG |
|---|---|---|---|---|---|
| Product | Lancelot | Leopard | MX4 | no comparable offering | Transcope 2 |
| Applications | medical, military | scientific, military | all | | mainly military |
| Capacity | 12,000 | 9,500 | 10,600 | | 14,000 - 14,800 |
| Weight Kg | 24 | 21 | 18 | | 26 |
| Retail price | PQ$384 | PQ$404 | PQ$325 | | PQ$366 |
| Good & bad points | rugged / modules replaceable / heavy over long time | very portable / short re-charge interval / less robust | best display available / very easy to use / delicate outdoors | | good all-round / not best at anything / not worst at anything |
| Date introduced | 20XT | 20X9 | 20XT | | 20XU |
| Reputation | hard-wearing, reliable | accurate, easy to use | industry standard | | favourite with military |
| Successor? | Ranger, 20Y2 | not known, but probable | expected 20XY-Z | not interested at this level | believed to be in 20XZ |

| ATTRIBUTES | DEMO COMPANY | KK LEUNG | MOLYNEUX | UNITED DMA | VAN RENSBURG |
|---|---|---|---|---|---|
| Product | Hannibal | believed to be developing | no comparable offering | TKX 14 | Uniscope 88 |
| Applications | scientific indoors | | | universal, esp educational | mainly science & education |
| Capacity | 7600 (9,200 with G-pack) | | | 8,500 | 8,500 |
| Weight Kg | 26 | | | 19 | 25 |
| Retail price | PQ$372 | | | PQ$348 | PQ$409 |
| Good & bad points | highest accuracy available / high-vol data mapping / long set-up time | | | easy to operate / links to CADOR systems / difficult at high temperatures | competent / no major benefits / no major drawbacks |
| Date introduced | 20XW | | | 20Y1 | 20X0 |
| Reputation | impeccable | | | solid | dependable if slightly clunky |
| Successor? | at concept stage | | | believed to be upgrading | successor expected 20XY |

| ATTRIBUTES | DEMO COMPANY | KK LEUNG | MOLYNEUX | UNITED DMA | VAN RENSBURG |
|---|---|---|---|---|---|
| Product | Geronimo | Ocelot | MQ 21 | no specific product | no comparable offering |
| Applications | all outdoor | all outdoor, esp scientific | mainly vehicle-mounted | TKX 14 regarded as capable | |
| Capacity | 8,800 | 9,100 | 9,400 | | |
| Weight Kg | 29 | 21 | 25 | | |
| Retail price | PQ$391 | PQ$440 | PQ$395 | | |
| Good & bad points | brand universally known / takes heavy punishment / outperformed for accuracy | does everything well / easy to use / no known disadvantages | wide range of applications / any atmospheric conditions / less easily transportable | | |
| Date introduced | planned for Sep 20XX | 20XU | 20XT | | |
| Reputation | clunky | highly regarded worldwide | generally well regarded | | |
| Successor? | imminent (targeting Ocelot) | not known to be developing | new marque expected soon | believed not to be interested | believed under consideration |

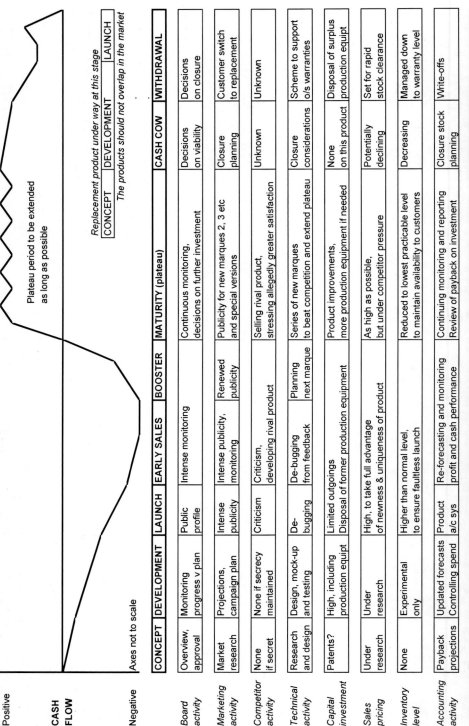

**CASH FLOW** — Positive / Negative

Axes not to scale

Plateau period to be extended as long as possible

Replacement product under way at this stage

| CONCEPT | DEVELOPMENT | LAUNCH |

The products should not overlap in the market

| | CONCEPT | DEVELOPMENT | LAUNCH | EARLY SALES | BOOSTER | MATURITY (plateau) | CASH COW | WITHDRAWAL |
|---|---|---|---|---|---|---|---|---|
| *Board activity* | Overview, approval | Monitoring progress v plan | Public profile | Intense monitoring | | Continuous monitoring, decisions on further investment | Decisions on viability | Decisions on closure |
| *Marketing activity* | Market research | Projections, campaign plan | Intense publicity | Intense publicity, monitoring | Renewed publicity | Publicity for new marques 2, 3 etc and special versions | Closure planning | Customer switch to replacement |
| *Competitor activity* | None if secret | None if secrecy maintained | Criticism | Criticism, developing rival product | | Selling rival product, stressing allegedly greater satisfaction | Unknown | Unknown |
| *Technical activity* | Research and design | Design, mock-up and testing | De-bugging | De-bugging from feedback | Planning next marque | Series of new marques to beat competition and extend plateau | Closure considerations | Scheme to support o/s warranties |
| *Capital investment* | Patents? | High, including production equipt | Limited outgoings | Disposal of former production equipment | | Product improvements, more production equipment if needed | None on this product | Disposal of surplus production equipt |
| *Sales pricing* | Under research | Under research | High, to take full advantage of newness & uniqueness of product | | | As high as possible, but under competitor pressure | Potentially declining | Set for rapid stock clearance |
| *Inventory level* | None | Experimental only | Higher than normal level, to ensure faultless launch | | | Reduced to lowest practicable level to maintain availability to customers | Decreasing | Managed down to warranty level |
| *Accounting activity* | Payback projections | Updated forecasts Controlling spend | Product a/c sys | Re-forecasting and monitoring profit and cash performance | | Continuing monitoring and reporting Review of payback on investment | Closure stock planning | Write-offs |

**PRODUCT LIFESPAN showing the stages which apply to anything from a chocolate bar to a jet airliner**   APPENDIX A3

# DEMO COMPANY – REPORTING CALENDAR 20XX–XY

| Day | APR 20XX | MAY | JUN | JUL | AUG | SEP | OCT | NOV | DEC | JAN 20XY | FEB | MAR |
|---|---|---|---|---|---|---|---|---|---|---|---|---|
| M | 30 |  | 1 | 29 | 3 | 31 | 28 | 2 | 30 | 28 HD | 1 | 1 |
| T | 31 |  | 2 | 30 | 4 | 1 | 29 | 3 | 1 | 29 HD | 2 | 2 |
| W | 1 MA |  | 3 MA | 1 MA | 5 MA | 2 MA | 30 MA | 4 MA | 2 MA | 30 HD | 3 MA | 3 MA |
| T | 2 BM |  | 4 BM | 2 BM | 6 BM | 3 BM | 1 BM | 5 BM | 3 BM | 31 HD | 4 BM | 4 BM |
| F | 3 | 1 | 5 | 3 | 7 | 4 | 2 | 6 | 4 | 1 HD | 5 | 5 |
| M | 6 | 4 | 8 | 6 | 10 | 7 | 5 | 9 | 7 | 4 HD | 8 | 8 |
| T | 7 | 5 | 9 | 7 | 11 | 8 | 6 | 10 | 8 | 5 | 9 | 9 |
| W | 8 | 6 MA | 10 | 8 | 12 | 9 | 7 | 11 | 9 | 6 MA | 10 BF | 10 |
| T | 9 | 7 BM | 11 | 9 | 13 | 10 | 8 | 12 | 10 | 7 BM | 11 | 11 |
| F | 10 DS | 8 | 12 CC | 10 CC | 14 CC | 11 CC | 9 CC | 13 CC | 11 CC | 8 CC | 12 CC | 12 CC |
| M | 13 HD | 11 | 15 FS SC | 13 | 17 | 14 HD | 12 | 16 | 14 | 11 | 15 IA | 15 |
| T | 14 CC | 12 | 16 FS | 14 | 18 | 15 | 13 | 17 | 15 | 12 | 16 IA | 16 |
| W | 15 FA | 13 | 17 FS | 15 | 19 | 16 | 14 | 18 | 16 | 13 | 17 IA | 17 |
| T | 16 FA | 14 | 18 FS | 16 | 20 | 17 | 15 | 19 | 17 | 14 | 18 IA | 18 FM |
| F | 17 FA | 15 CC | 19 FS | 17 | 21 | 18 | 16 | 20 | 18 SU | 15 B1 | 19 IA | 19 HD |
| M | 20 FA | 18 HD | 22 FS FM | 20 | 24 FM | 21 FM | 19 | 23 FM | 21 FM | 18 | 22 IA FM | 22 HD |
| T | 21 FA | 19 | 23 FS | 21 | 25 | 22 | 20 | 24 | 22 | 19 | 23 IA | 23 FS SC |
| W | 22 FA | 20 | 24 FS | 22 | 26 | 23 | 21 | 25 | 23 | 20 | 24 IA | 24 FS |
| T | 23 FA | 21 | 25 FS | 23 | 27 | 24 | 22 | 26 | 24 HD | 21 | 25 IA | 25 FS |
| F | 24 FA | 22 | 26 FS | 24 | 28 | 25 | 23 | 27 | 25 HD | 22 | 26 IA | 26 FS |
| M | 27 FM | 25 FM | 29 | 27 FM | 31 | 28 | 26 FM | 30 | 28 | 25 FM |  | 29 |
| T | 28 | 26 | 30 | 28 |  | 29 | 27 |  | 29 | 26 |  | 30 |
| W | 29 | 27 |  | 29 |  | 30 | 28 |  | 30 | 27 |  | 31 |
| T | 30 FS | 28 |  | 30 |  |  | 29 |  | 31 | 28 |  |  |
| F |  | 29 |  | 31 |  |  | 30 |  |  | 29 B2 |  |  |

**Legend**

- BM – board meeting
- CC – credit control mtg
- MA – monthly accounts
- CC – credit control mtg
- FM – finance dept mtg
- SU – strat plan update (interim year)
- B1 – budget draft 1
- B2 – budget draft 2
- BF – budget final
- IA – interim audit
- FA – final audit
- SC – stock count
- DS – draft stat accounts
- FS – final stat accounts
- HD – holiday
- FS – factory shutdown

[note that the file name and print date/ time should appear on every spreadsheet]

# FOREX COVER PLAN

## CURRENT COMMITMENTS
[currency positions of a PQ$-based business]

### KK$000

| | | NOV | Mth 1 DEC | Mth 2 JAN | Mth 3 FEB | later |
|---|---|---|---|---|---|---|
| Month-end exchange rate | | 1.257 | | | | |
| Accounts receivable | PQ$000 | 1,011 | | | | |
| | currency | 1,271 | | | | |
| Forecast receipts | currency | 1,271 | 520 | 370 | 310 | 71 |
| Accounts (payable) | PQ$000 | (385) | | | | |
| | currency | (484) | | | | |
| Forecast payments | currency | (484) | (201) | (136) | (95) | (52) |
| Currency held/(borrowed) | PQ$000 | 81 | | | | |
| To be absorbed | currency | 102 | 102 | | | |
| | PQ$000 | 707 | | | | |
| Net requirement for cover | currency | 889 | 421 | 234 | 215 | 19 |
| Coverage required | | | 85% | 80% | 80% | |
| | currency | | 358 | 187 | 172 | |
| Already (sold)/ bought | currency | (354) | (209) | (95) | (50) | |
| HEDGE REQUIRED | currency | | (149) | (92) | (122) | |
| | PQ$000 | | (119) | (73) | (97) | |
| | action | | sell | sell | sell | |
| Status | | | sold | ordered | action | |

### GG$000

| | | NOV | Mth 1 DEC | Mth 2 JAN | Mth 3 FEB | later |
|---|---|---|---|---|---|---|
| Month-end exchange rate | | 4.549 | | | | |
| Accounts receivable | PQ$000 | 586 | | | | |
| | currency | 2,666 | | | | |
| Forecast receipts | currency | 2,666 | 1,190 | 880 | 510 | 86 |
| Accounts (payable) | PQ$000 | (1,490) | | | | |
| | currency | (6,778) | | | | |
| Forecast payments | currency | (6,778) | (4,070) | (1,590) | (960) | (158) |
| Currency held/(borrowed) | PQ$000 | 114 | | | | |
| To be absorbed | currency | 519 | 519 | | | |
| | PQ$000 | (790) | | | | |
| Net requirement for cover | currency | (3,594) | (2,361) | (710) | (450) | (72) |
| Coverage required | | | 90% | 85% | 85% | |
| | currency | | (2,125) | (604) | (383) | |
| Already (sold)/ bought | currency | 709 | (209) | (95) | (50) | |
| HEDGE REQUIRED | currency | | 2,334 | 699 | 433 | |
| | PQ$000 | | 1,857 | 556 | 344 | |
| | action | | buy | buy | buy | |
| Status | | | bought | bought | ordered | |

*Note that forex exposure can be considerably more complex, especially when fixed assets, funds and shares in foreign currencies are involved*

*The above is a simplistic view, matching hedging against expected future flows in two different currencies*

*Some companies, in accordance with their particular experiences, do not hedge 100%, particularly on the cash inflow side*

*Note that the above figures only include currently forecast cash flows - transactions in December will cause further flows in January and February*

EXAMPLE    **APPENDIX A5**

# PROJECT: WIDGET-MAKING PLANT

PQ$000 except where in italics

| | 20XX-XY | Aug | Sep | Oct | Nov | Dec | Jan | Feb | Mar | Apr | May |
|---|---|---|---|---|---|---|---|---|---|---|---|
| | 0 | 1 | 2 | 3 | 4 | 5 | 6 | 7 | 8 | 9 | 10 |
| *Unit sales volume 000* | | *951* | *1,847* | *1,932* | *2,041* | *1,939* | *1,842* | *1,750* | *1,575* | *1,417* | *1,276* |
| *Average price PQ$* | | *1.43* | *1.38* | *1.38* | *1.34* | *1.32* | *1.30* | *1.28* | *1.26* | *1.24* | *1.22* |
| **Net sales value** | **0** | **1,360** | **2,549** | **2,666** | **2,735** | **2,559** | **2,395** | **2,240** | **1,984** | **1,758** | **1,556** |
| Direct material | | (495) | (776) | (811) | (857) | (814) | (774) | (735) | (661) | (595) | (536) |
| Direct labour | | (371) | (628) | (657) | (694) | (659) | (626) | (595) | (535) | (482) | (434) |
| Indirect manufacturing costs | | (27) | (34) | (37) | (34) | (31) | (28) | (25) | (22) | (19) | (16) |
| Indirect labour | | (13) | (20) | (22) | (24) | (26) | (28) | (30) | (32) | (34) | (36) |
| Amortisation | | (276) | (276) | (276) | (323) | (323) | (323) | (323) | (323) | (323) | (323) |
| Distribution | | (24) | (24) | (23) | (22) | (21) | (20) | (19) | (18) | (17) | (16) |
| **Direct cost of sales** | **0** | **(1,205)** | **(1,758)** | **(1,826)** | **(1,954)** | **(1,875)** | **(1,799)** | **(1,727)** | **(1,592)** | **(1,470)** | **(1,361)** |
| Marketing & selling | (128) | (98) | (48) | (45) | (42) | (39) | (36) | (33) | (30) | (27) | (24) |
| Projects & other related costs | (23) | (12) | (10) | (10) | (10) | (10) | (10) | (10) | (10) | (10) | (10) |
| Implementation costs | (57) | (106) | - | - | (38) | - | - | - | - | - | - |
| **Total operating cost** | **(208)** | **(216)** | **(58)** | **(55)** | **(90)** | **(49)** | **(46)** | **(43)** | **(40)** | **(37)** | **(34)** |
| **Operating earnings** | **(208)** | **(61)** | **733** | **785** | **691** | **636** | **550** | **470** | **352** | **250** | **162** |
| Taxes    27.0% | 56 | 17 | (198) | (212) | (187) | (172) | (148) | (127) | (95) | (68) | (44) |
| **FORECAST PROFIT AFTER TAX** | **(152)** | **(45)** | **535** | **573** | **504** | **464** | **401** | **343** | **257** | **183** | **118** |
| Inventory | 51 | 35 | 55 | 58 | 61 | 58 | 55 | 52 | 47 | 42 | 38 |
| Accounts receivable | - | 168 | 314 | 329 | 337 | 316 | 295 | 276 | 245 | 217 | 192 |
| Accounts payable | (22) | (47) | (74) | (78) | (82) | (78) | (74) | (70) | (63) | (57) | (51) |
| **Working capital** | **29** | **155** | **295** | **309** | **316** | **295** | **276** | **258** | **228** | **202** | **179** |
| Opening balance | 23 | 2,665 | 2,503 | 2,227 | 1,951 | 2,100 | 1,777 | 1,454 | 1,131 | 808 | 485 |
| Capital spend | 2,642 | 114 | - | - | 472 | - | - | - | - | - | - |
| Amortisation | - | (276) | (276) | (276) | (323) | (323) | (323) | (323) | (323) | (323) | (323) |
| **Fixed capital** | **2,665** | **2,503** | **2,227** | **1,951** | **2,100** | **1,777** | **1,454** | **1,131** | **808** | **485** | **162** |
| **NET CAPITAL EMPLOYED** | **2,694** | **2,658** | **2,522** | **2,260** | **2,416** | **2,072** | **1,730** | **1,389** | **1,036** | **687** | **341** |
| Profit after taxation | (152) | (45) | 535 | 573 | 504 | 464 | 401 | 343 | 257 | 183 | 118 |
| Amortisation | - | 276 | 276 | 276 | 323 | 323 | 323 | 323 | 323 | 323 | 323 |
| Change in working capital | (29) | (126) | (140) | (14) | (7) | 21 | 19 | 18 | 30 | 26 | 23 |
| Capital expenditure | (2,642) | (114) | - | - | (472) | - | - | - | - | - | - |
| Terminal value | - | - | - | - | - | - | - | - | - | - | - |
| **PROJECT CASH FLOW** | **(2,823)** | **(9)** | **672** | **835** | **348** | **808** | **744** | **684** | **610** | **532** | **464** |
| Cost of capital    3.5% | 1.0000 | 0.9662 | 0.9335 | 0.9019 | 0.8714 | 0.8420 | 0.8135 | 0.7860 | 0.7594 | 0.7337 | 0.7089 |
| Discounted cash flow | (2,823) | (9) | 627 | 753 | 303 | 680 | 605 | 538 | 463 | 390 | 329 |
| **CUMULATIVE DISCOUNTED CASH FLOW** | **(2,823)** | **(2,832)** | **(2,205)** | **(1,452)** | **(1,148)** | **(468)** | **137** | **674** | **1,138** | **1,528** | **1,857** |

**Employee** _____    **Period** _____

Interviewer _____    Date _____

Summary _(to cover points from this page and the following page)_ _____

_This page is to assess and record the employee's performance as a team player_
_The following page assesses his performance against objectives set at the previous appraisal_
_Both pages are needed to ensure a balanced performance by the employee, because:_
_- some employees get on well with everyone but achieve little_
_- some employees achieve a lot, but offend a considerable number of people in doing so_

I accept this appraisal of my performance in the period stated above and have agreed the
objectives given to me on the attached sheet for the period stated on that sheet.

Employee _____    Date _____

**How well did the person interviewed work with the following people?**

**Superiors** _____
_____
_____
_____

**Colleagues** _____
_____
_____
_____

**Subordinates** _____
_____
_____
_____

**Other group companies** _____
_____
_____
_____

**Customers** _____
_____
_____
_____

**Suppliers** _____
_____
_____
_____

**Other 3rd parties** _____
_____
_____
_____

Employee _____      Period _____

| No | Objective [EXAMPLES SHOWN] | by Date | With-drawn | Fully Ach'd | Partly Ach'd | Not Ach'd |
|----|---------------------------|---------|------------|-------------|--------------|-----------|
| | **PERSONAL** | | | | | |
| 1 | Develop better working relationships with [suppliers, customers, colleagues, subor-dinates, colleagues, investors etc] | 31 Dec | | | | |
| 2 | Improve skills at [report-writing, XL usage, analysis, performance appraisal etc] | 31 Mar | | | | |
| 3 | Take firmer control of [group, department, procedures, authorisations etc] | 31 Oct | | | | |
| | **PERFORMANCE** | | | | | |
| 4 | Bring rate of [errors, responses, credits, complaints etc] down to X% | 30 Nov | | | | |
| 5 | Ensure that [reports, procedures etc] are completed by X daily, weekly, monthly | immediate | | | | |
| 6 | Ensure that all [procedures] are carried out in accordance with [terms, rules etc] | 31 Oct | | | | |
| | **PROJECTS** | | | | | |
| 7 | Agree objectives for all members of your team for next 5½ months | 22 Oct | | | | |
| 8 | Investigate and determine cause of [fault, losses etc] and recommend solution | 14 Nov | | | | |
| 9 | Set up system for dealing with [problems, information, movements etc] | 30 Nov | | | | |
| 10 | Complete [relocation, reorganisation, tidying, closure etc] of X | 31 Jan | | | | |
| 11 | Devise, agree and implement report high-lighting [problem, opportunity etc] | 16 Jan | | | | |
| 12 | Complete detailed analysis for 20XX-XY [budget, marketing plan etc] | 20 Feb | | | | |

**Training & development needs**

_____
_____
_____
_____

*There are many activities which involve committing a business financially*
*These must be identified and authorities specified for each type of commitment*
*Below are some of the commoner commitments found in everyday businesses*
*Ensure that the authorities are clearly and practically defined, communicated and understood*

*In some cases, monetary limits must be set, above which a higher authority is needed*
*The most common example of this is that of payments from bank accounts (or any outgoing of funds)*

**Planning**
- strategic plan
- budget
- new product development
- new product launch
- marketing campaign
- acquisition of business

**Information systems**
- new user - email
- new user - intranet
- new user - production system
- new user - accounting system
- new user - systems
- web site

**Marketing**
- product development
- major campaign
- consultancy
- external communication

**Sales**
- terms of sale - new
- terms of sale - change
- contract - sales
- contract - services outwards
- sales price
- sales order acceptance
- delivery commitment
- sales commission
- credit note
- letter of credit or similar commitment

**Production**
- capacity plan
- production allocation
- labour hire

**Purchasing**
- new supplier agreement
- purchase order
- contract - materials
- contract - services inwards
- rental or lease
- cash payments

**Capital expenditure**
- budgeted
- unbudgeted
- health, safety & environment
- write-offs
- intellectual property
- disposals
- acquisitions of business
- partnership agreement

**Employment**
- safety
- recruitment - temporary
- recruitment - permanent
- remuneration increase
- other terms of employment
- bonus
- promotion
- severance
- relocation
- training
- absences - contractual
- absences - other

**Finance**
- new bank account
- new financial instrument
- cheque, bank draft etc
- employee expenses
- petty cash payment
- guarantee - bank
- guarantee - other

**Accounting**
- finance manual update
- each individual ledger/ area
- journal entry - routine
- journal entry - non-routine
- monthly operating results
- monthly working papers
- journal entries
- individual ledgers

*Remember that electronic approvals*
*carry the same responsibility as manual signatures*

**JUL 20XX**      **DAY 10**

| | PQ$000 | | | KK$000 | | GG$000 | | PQ$000 | |
|---|---|---|---|---|---|---|---|---|---|
| | Main | Payroll | No 3 | Main | Rate | Main | Rate | Total | Change |
| **Opening balance - budget** | | | | | | | | **(1,213)** | |
| **Actual** | (1,020) | 35 | 56 | (284) | 1.188 | 101 | 4.404 | **(1,145)** | |
| 1 | (1,248) | 35 | 56 | (284) | 1.234 | (127) | 4.567 | **(1,415)** | **(270)** |
| 2 | (1,307) | 35 | 47 | (284) | 1.240 | (151) | 4.601 | **(1,487)** | **(72)** |
| 3 | (1,289) | 0 | 61 | (202) | 1.240 | (121) | 4.598 | **(1,417)** | **70** |
| 4 | (1,054) | 0 | 27 | (174) | 1.251 | (121) | 4.583 | **(1,192)** | **225** |
| 5 | (1,035) | 0 | 27 | (174) | 1.249 | (121) | 4.584 | **(1,174)** | **18** |
| 6 | | | | | | | | | |
| 7 | | | | | | | | | |
| 8 | (1,209) | 0 | 27 | (186) | 1.234 | (138) | 4.567 | **(1,363)** | **(189)** |
| 9 | (1,313) | 64 | 41 | (201) | 1.240 | (109) | 4.601 | **(1,394)** | **(31)** |
| 10 | (1,077) | 28 | 41 | (201) | 1.243 | (101) | 4.589 | **(1,192)** | **202** |
| 11 | | | | | | | | | |
| 12 | | | | | | | | | |
| 13 | | | | | | | | | |
| 14 | | | | | | | | | |
| 15 | | | | | | | | | |
| 16 | | | | | | | | | |
| 17 | | | | | | | | | |
| 18 | | | | | | | | | |
| 19 | | | | | | | | | |
| 20 | | | | | | | | | |
| 21 | | | | | | | | | |
| 22 | | | | | | | | | |
| 23 | | | | | | | | | |
| 24 | | | | | | | | | |
| 25 | | | | | | | | | |
| 26 | | | | | | | | | |
| 27 | | | | | | | | | |
| 28 | | | | | | | | | |
| 29 | | | | | | | | | |
| 30 | | | | | | | | | |
| 31 | | | | | | | | | |

| | | |
|---|---|---|
| *The covering email for this report* | **Budgeted closing balance** | **724**    **724** |
| *should contain comments* | Latest balance | (1,192) |
| *on the main movements of cash* | Forecast closing balance | 756 |
| *for the month* | **Surplus/ (Shortfall)** | **(1,916)**    **32** |

# DEMO CO - weekly performance review

*This report is to maintain constant pressure on the business*

End of week 2, JUL 20XX

| MONDAY MEETING 10.00 12-Jul-20XX | Estimate 05-Jul | Estimate 12-Jul | Forecast 19-Jul | Target 26-Jul | Target 02-Aug | TOTAL FOR MONTH Forecast | Budget | Variance |
|---|---|---|---|---|---|---|---|---|
| Opening orders | 257 | 221 | 264 | 284 | 294 | 257 at sales value | | |
| Orders received | 53 | 129 | 104 | 100 | 100 | 486 at sales value | | |
| Orders despatched | (89) | (86) | (84) | (90) | (90) | (439) at sales value | | |
| **Closing orders** | 221 | 264 | 284 | 294 | 304 | 304 at sales value | | |
| | | | | | | | | |
| **Sales** | **89** | **86** | **84** | **90** | **90** | **439** | 432 | (7) |
| Est value added | 77% | 81% | 80% | 78% | 78% | 79% | 79% | 0% |
| Margin on materials | 69 | 70 | 67 | 70 | 70 | 346 | 342 | 4 |
| Payroll | (49) | (49) | (49) | (49) | (49) | (245) | (243) | (2) |
| Other overheads | (22) | (22) | (22) | (22) | (22) | (110) | (114) | 4 |
| Non-recurring | 0 | 0 | 0 | (9) | 0 | (9) | 0 | (9) |
| **RESULT PRE-TAX** | **(2)** | **(1)** | **(4)** | **(10)** | **(1)** | **(18)** | **(15)** | **(3)** |
| | | | | | | | | |
| Inventory 361 | 338 | 325 | 318 | 315 | 335 | 335 | 304 | (31) |
| | | | | | | | | |
| Opening receivables | 754 | 746 | 740 | 754 | 773 | 754 | 782 | (28) |
| Sales | 89 | 86 | 84 | 90 | 90 | 439 | 432 | 7 |
| VAT on sales | 9 | 9 | 10 | 9 | 10 | 47 | 45 | 2 |
| Cash receipts | (106) | (101) | (80) | (80) | (70) | (437) | (472) | (35) |
| **Closing receivables** | 746 | 740 | 754 | 773 | 803 | 803 | 788 | 15 |
| | | | | | | | | |
| Opening payables | (220) | (143) | (119) | (121) | (141) | (220) | (202) | (18) |
| Direct materials | (20) | (16) | (17) | (20) | (20) | (93) | (92) | |
| Inventory | 23 | 13 | 7 | 3 | (20) | 26 | 37 | |
| Overheads | (22) | (22) | (22) | (22) | (22) | (110) | (123) | |
| Capex & other | 0 | (21) | 0 | 0 | 0 | (21) | (23) | |
| VAT | (2) | (4) | (3) | (4) | (6) | (18) | (18) | |
| Payments | 98 | 74 | 33 | 22 | 12 | 239 | 223 | |
| **Closing payables** | (143) | (119) | (121) | (141) | (197) | (197) | (200) | 3 |
| | | | | | | | | |
| Opening cash | (1,145) | (1,174) | (1,133) | (1,092) | (1,209) | (1,145) | (1,318) | 173 |
| Receipts - customers | 106 | 101 | 80 | 80 | 70 | 437 | | |
| Receipts - other | 0 | 19 | 0 | 21 | 0 | 40 | | |
| Payments - suppliers | (98) | (74) | (33) | (22) | (12) | (239) | | |
| Payments - payroll | (27) | 0 | (2) | (194) | (34) | (257) | | |
| Payments - other | (10) | (5) | (4) | (2) | (11) | (32) | | |
| **CLOSING CASH** | **(1,174)** | **(1,133)** | **(1,092)** | **(1,209)** | **(1,196)** | **(1,196)** | **(3,821)** | **2,625** |

| Risk debts | Total | Current | 30 days | 60 days | 90 days | Comments |
|---|---|---|---|---|---|---|
| HK profiles | 128 | 86 | 0 | 10 | 32 | received 10 Jul 20XX |
| Lima Pacific | 91 | 0 | 10 | 54 | 27 | awaiting Kappa fix |
| Lorenz | 79 | 3 | 19 | 21 | 36 | continuing to decrease |
| Vincenti | 51 | 0 | 0 | 6 | 45 | awaiting translation of manual |
| Other receivables | 391 | 167 | 148 | 37 | 39 | |
| **Total receivables** | 740 | 256 | 177 | 128 | 179 | estimate at 13 Jul 20XX |

| Major projects | | Start | Finish | Stage | Budget | Estimate | Comments |
|---|---|---|---|---|---|---|---|
| Hannibal | NT mk 4 | Jan-XX | Nov-XX | 95% | 21 | 18 | post-launch mods in progress |
| Kappa | KBA | Sep-XW | Jan-XY | 70% | 43 | 55 | retro-fit in final stages |
| | junctions | Mar-XX | ? | 60% | 13 | 13 | subject to graphics quality |
| Military | deflector | Mar-XX | Sep-XX | 90% | 16 | 22 | awaiting call - chase |

| | Prodn | Control | Mkt/Sell | Tech | Other | Staff | Temps | TOTAL |
|---|---|---|---|---|---|---|---|---|
| **Personnel number** | 73 | 6 | 10 | 4 | 12 | **105** | **4** | **109** |

| Day | Cash | Sales | Purchases | Stock | Payroll | Fixed assets | Other | Reports |
|---|---|---|---|---|---|---|---|---|
| | JB, AH | MA, AC | MA, TK | TK, GS | AH, JB | TK, AC | AC, FC | FC, AC |
| MO 23 | Finance dept meeting / Instructions to staff / Chase managers | Finance dept meeting / Instructions to staff / Chase late invoicing / Chase late credits | Finance dept meeting / Instructions to staff / Investigate late items / Send accruals form | Finance dept meeting / Instructions to staff | Finance dept meeting / Instructions to staff | Finance dept meeting / Instructions to staff | Finance dept meeting / Instructions to staff | Finance dept meeting / Finalise timetable / Instructions to staff / Set up report pack / Bring forward papers |
| TU 24 | Post expense claims | Confirm interco bals | Confirm interco bals | | | | | Set timetable / Issue timetable |
| WE 25 | Bank payments | Bad debts / Prepayments | Enter main accruals / Supplier payments / Issue manager accruals | | Payroll run / Payroll payments / Payroll JEs / Print payroll summary | FA register / Disposals / Gains on disposal / Amortisation calc / Summary | Group balance check | Open monthly papers / Open report pack |
| TH 26 | Bank reconciliations / Post to general ledger / Petty cash summary / Post petty cash > GL / Chase o/s points | Sales Cr notes / Sales Cr provision / Chase o/s points | Chase o/s points | Chase o/s points | Payroll thru bank / Chase o/s points | Chase o/s points | Monthly JEs / Chase o/s points / Monthly JEs | Chase o/s points |
| FR 27 | Closing FX rates | Final goods despatch / Final invoices | GRNI list | Final goods despatch | | | | |
| MO 30 | MONTH END / Adjust for late cash / Finalise cash received / Forex differences | MONTH END / Sales ledger control / Reconfirm interco bals | MONTH END / Purchase lgr control / Reconfirm interco bals / Check GRNI / Enter GRNI / Manager accruals | MONTH END / Stock reconciliation / Enter GRNI | MONTH END | MONTH END | MONTH END / Review mtg minutes / Minutes on file / Forex differences / Clear queries | MONTH END |
| TU 1 | | Print aged receivables / Review aged rec'bles / Brief credit control / Bad debts provision | Print aged payables / Manager accruals / Transport accruals / Accruals journal | Close last month / Open new month / Stock provision | Close last month / Open new month | Close last month / Open new month | Clear final queries / Final JEs | Run trial balance / Review trial balance / Final adjustments / Print draft pack / Review draft pack |
| WE 2 | Close last month / Open new month | Close last month / Open new month | Close last month / Open new month | | | | | Finalise draft pack / Issue draft pack / Update audit pack / Finish working papers / Open new GL month |
| TH 3 | Review forex needs | Credit control meeting | | | | | Finish monthly papers / Management meeting / VAT return | Update forecast |

| D:\DBY\Drafts\Maint2 | Comments | TOTAL | Apr 20XX | May 20XX | JUN 20XX | Jul 20XY | Aug 20XY | SEP 20XY | Oct 20XY | Nov 20XY | DEC 20XY | Jan 20XY | Feb 20XY | MAR 20XY |
|---|---|---|---|---|---|---|---|---|---|---|---|---|---|---|
| *At the head of the budget sheet, the estimated sales volume or value per month should be shown, to give an indicator of the activity level, which may influence the costs* | | | | | | | | | | | | | | |
| Current year actual to date | | 62.1 | 5.2 | 15.0 | 5.2 | 14.8 | 3.9 | 4.7 | 3.8 | 5.1 | 4.4 | - | 8.8 | - |
| Forecast for remainder | | 19.9 | - | - | - | - | - | - | - | - | - | 5.0 | - | 6.1 |
| Non-routine items in above | relocating boiler | (19.4) | - | (9.6) | - | (4.3) | - | - | - | - | - | - | (5.5) | - |
| **Current year - routine items** | | **62.6** | **5.2** | **5.4** | **5.2** | **10.5** | **3.9** | **4.7** | **3.8** | **5.1** | **4.4** | **5.0** | **3.3** | **6.1** |
| Safety equipment | | 3.6 | 0.3 | 0.3 | 0.3 | 0.3 | 0.3 | 0.3 | 0.3 | 0.3 | 0.3 | 0.3 | 0.3 | 0.3 |
| Production machinery | | 40.7 | 2.4 | 2.4 | 2.4 | 9.9 | 2.4 | 2.4 | 2.4 | 2.4 | 2.4 | 2.4 | 2.4 | 6.8 |
| Electrical | | 2.4 | 0.2 | 0.2 | 0.2 | 0.2 | 0.2 | 0.2 | 0.2 | 0.2 | 0.2 | 0.2 | 0.2 | 0.2 |
| Water & drainage | | 2.4 | 0.2 | 0.2 | 0.2 | 0.2 | 0.2 | 0.2 | 0.2 | 0.2 | 0.2 | 0.2 | 0.2 | 0.2 |
| Buildings | mainly block B | 8.4 | 0.7 | 0.7 | 0.7 | 0.7 | 0.7 | 0.7 | 0.7 | 0.7 | 0.7 | 0.7 | 0.7 | 0.7 |
| Fittings | | 3.6 | 0.3 | 0.3 | 0.3 | 0.3 | 0.3 | 0.3 | 0.3 | 0.3 | 0.3 | 0.3 | 0.3 | 0.3 |
| Grounds & road surfaces | | 2.4 | 0.2 | 0.2 | 0.2 | 0.2 | 0.2 | 0.2 | 0.2 | 0.2 | 0.2 | 0.2 | 0.2 | 0.2 |
| Other | | 6.0 | 0.5 | 0.5 | 0.5 | 0.5 | 0.5 | 0.5 | 0.5 | 0.5 | 0.5 | 0.5 | 0.5 | 0.5 |
| Other | | 0.0 | - | - | - | - | - | - | - | - | - | - | - | - |
| Other | | 0.0 | - | - | - | - | - | - | - | - | - | - | - | - |
| Other | | 0.0 | - | - | - | - | - | - | - | - | - | - | - | - |
| Other | | 0.0 | - | - | - | - | - | - | - | - | - | - | - | - |
| Contingency | | 6.0 | 0.5 | 0.5 | 0.5 | 0.5 | 0.5 | 0.5 | 0.5 | 0.5 | 0.5 | 0.5 | 0.5 | 0.5 |
| **Budget year - routine items** | | **75.5** | **5.3** | **5.3** | **5.3** | **12.8** | **5.3** | **5.3** | **5.3** | **5.3** | **5.3** | **5.3** | **5.3** | **9.7** |
| (Increase)/ decrease on current year | | (12.9) | (0.1) | 0.1 | (0.1) | (2.3) | (1.4) | (0.6) | (1.5) | (0.2) | (0.9) | (0.3) | (2.0) | (3.6) |
| New layout for hardening area | | 17.1 | - | - | 14.1 | 3.0 | - | - | - | - | - | - | - | - |
| Replacement of electrics on line 3 | | 6.4 | - | - | - | - | - | - | 6.4 | - | - | - | - | - |
| Contingency | | 8.0 | - | 2.0 | - | 2.0 | 2.0 | - | - | 2.0 | - | - | 2.0 | - |
| **Budget year - non-routine items** | | **31.5** | **-** | **2.0** | **14.1** | **3.0** | **2.0** | **-** | **6.4** | **2.0** | **-** | **-** | **2.0** | **-** |
| **TOTAL BUDGET** | | **107.0** | **5.3** | **7.3** | **19.4** | **15.8** | **7.3** | **5.3** | **11.7** | **7.3** | **5.3** | **5.3** | **7.3** | **9.7** |

*The precise layout of a budget template should vary according to the type of expenditure, but the above principles should be followed in general*

*It should be clear why the budgeted expenditure is greater or less (or neither) than that of the current year if the difference is large*

*It may be appropriate to indicate on the schedule the percentage inflation which has been assumed, and the exchange rates assumed if foreign currencies are involved*

*Any other non-regular circumstances should also be highlit*

F:\TWC\FinClose3

| | | Status | TOTAL | Apr 20XX | May 20XX | JUN 20XX | Jul 20XX | Aug 20XX | SEP 20XX | Oct 20XX | Nov 20XX | DEC 20XX | Jan 20XY | Feb 20XY | MAR 20XY |
|---|---|---|---|---|---|---|---|---|---|---|---|---|---|---|---|
| Cooling system for area 4 | N E | in process | 75 | 27 | 34 | 14 | - | - | - | - | - | - | - | - | - |
| New gatehouse | N B | in process | 27 | - | 27 | - | - | - | - | - | - | - | - | - | - |
| Storage racking for fillers | N E | authorised | 13 | - | 13 | - | - | - | - | - | - | - | - | - | - |
| **Forward from previous year** | | | **115** | **27** | **74** | **14** | **0** | **0** | **0** | **0** | **0** | **0** | **0** | **0** | **0** |
| 4-tonne loader | N E | authorised | 23 | 23 | - | - | - | - | - | - | - | - | - | - | - |
| Shikoku R5 robot | N E | authorised | 27 | 22 | 5 | - | - | - | - | - | - | - | - | - | - |
| Gantry for line 7 | N E | authorised | 63 | 15 | - | 27 | 21 | - | - | - | - | - | - | - | - |
| Angled rollers for UV box | N E | authorised | 18 | - | 18 | - | - | - | - | - | - | - | - | - | - |
| 3-way cutters (set of 4) | N E | authorised | 19 | - | - | 19 | - | - | - | - | - | - | - | - | - |
| Hardware for production control | N S | authorised | 35 | - | - | - | - | - | 35 | - | - | - | - | - | - |
| Widening of loading bay | S B | requested | 37 | - | - | - | - | - | 20 | 17 | - | - | - | - | - |
| Dust extractor for area 4 | 2 E | requested | 32 | - | - | - | - | - | 32 | - | - | - | - | - | - |
| Pool car & staff bus | N V | requested | 63 | - | 12 | - | - | - | - | - | 51 | - | - | - | - |
| Infra-red control unit | N E | TBA | 98 | - | - | - | - | - | - | - | - | 98 | - | - | - |
| Powder paint line | 2 E | TBA | 55 | - | - | - | - | - | - | - | - | - | - | 17 | 38 |
| Hardening chamber & racks | S E | TBA | 21 | - | - | - | - | - | - | - | - | - | - | - | 21 |
| Contingency | C | | 24 | 2 | 2 | 2 | 2 | 2 | 2 | 2 | 2 | 2 | 2 | 2 | 2 |
| **TOTAL FOR BUDGET YEAR** | | | **515** | **62** | **37** | **48** | **23** | **2** | **89** | **19** | **53** | **100** | **2** | **19** | **61** |
| **Total to end of current year** | | | **630** | **89** | **111** | **62** | **23** | **2** | **89** | **19** | **53** | **100** | **2** | **19** | **61** |
| Powder paint line | 2 | | 84 | 42 | 42 | - | - | - | - | - | - | - | - | - | - |
| Hardening chamber & racks | S | | 285 | 224 | - | 61 | - | - | - | - | - | - | - | - | - |
| **To be continued into following year** | | | **369** | **266** | **42** | **61** | **0** | **0** | **0** | **0** | **0** | **0** | **0** | **0** | **0** |
| N new | V | vehicles | 63 | - | 12 | - | - | - | - | - | 51 | - | - | - | - |
| 2 second-hand | E | equipment | 356 | 60 | 23 | 46 | 21 | - | 32 | - | - | 98 | - | 17 | 59 |
| S self-build | S | IT systems | 35 | - | - | - | - | - | 35 | - | - | - | - | - | - |
| | B | buildings | 37 | - | - | - | - | - | 20 | 17 | - | - | - | - | - |
| See Appendix A6 | C | contingency | 24 | 2 | 2 | 2 | 2 | 2 | 2 | 2 | 2 | 2 | 2 | 2 | 2 |
| *for capital project appraisal* | | **BUDGET YEAR** | **515** | **62** | **37** | **48** | **23** | **2** | **89** | **19** | **53** | **100** | **2** | **19** | **61** |

**DEMO CO    BUDGET 20XX-XY – CAPEX  PG$000    Printed  16.03  03-FEB-20XX    APPENDIX C3**

# DEMO COMPANY BUDGET SUMMARY — PQ$000

| | 20XX forecast | 20XY BUDGET | diff | 1 Apr | 2 May | 3 JUN | 4 Jul | 5 Aug | 6 SEP | 7 Oct | 8 Nov | 9 DEC | 10 Jan | 11 Feb | 12 MAR |
|---|---|---|---|---|---|---|---|---|---|---|---|---|---|---|---|
| Production workers (heads) | 69 | 74 | 7% | 67 | 67 | 70 | 73 | 73 | 76 | 76 | 76 | 76 | 76 | 76 | 76 |
| Sales volume (No) | 14,444 | 15,070 | 4% | 1,179 | 1,125 | 1,174 | 1,157 | 1,288 | 1,367 | 1,298 | 1,340 | 1,164 | 1,315 | 1,355 | 1,308 |
| Average sales price (PQ$) | 355 | $378.85 | 7% | $373.60 | $373.60 | $373.60 | $373.60 | $373.60 | $382.25 | $382.25 | $382.25 | $382.25 | $382.25 | $382.25 | $382.25 |
| **SALES VALUE** | 5,131 | 5,709 | 11% | 441 | 420 | 439 | 432 | 481 | 523 | 496 | 512 | 445 | 503 | 518 | 500 |
| Direct materials | (1,137) | (1,216) | -7% | (93) | (88) | (92) | (92) | (103) | (109) | (106) | (109) | (95) | (109) | (112) | (108) |
| Value added | 3,994 | 4,493 | 13% | 348 | 332 | 346 | 340 | 379 | 414 | 390 | 403 | 350 | 394 | 406 | 392 |
| | 77.8% | 78.7% | | 79.0% | 79.0% | 79.0% | 78.7% | 78.7% | 79.2% | 78.7% | 78.7% | 78.7% | 78.4% | 78.4% | 78.4% |
| Direct labour | (1,989) | (2,089) | -5% | (166) | (159) | (166) | (168) | (187) | (198) | (179) | (183) | (156) | (174) | (180) | (173) |
| Marketing & selling | (642) | (678) | -6% | (56) | (52) | (53) | (59) | (71) | (55) | (57) | (56) | (51) | (52) | (55) | (61) |
| **GROSS MARGIN** | 1,363 | 1,726 | 27% | 126 | 121 | 128 | 113 | 120 | 161 | 154 | 164 | 142 | 168 | 171 | 158 |
| | 26.6% | 30.2% | | 28.6% | 28.8% | 29.1% | 26.1% | 25.0% | 30.8% | 31.1% | 32.1% | 32.0% | 33.4% | 33.0% | 31.5% |
| Indirect overhead | (1,232) | (1,352) | -10% | (106) | (105) | (119) | (121) | (108) | (107) | (117) | (112) | (110) | (116) | (113) | (120) |
| Operating profit | 131 | 374 | 185% | 20 | 16 | 9 | (8) | 13 | 54 | 38 | 52 | 32 | 52 | 58 | 38 |
| Non-operating items | 29 | 12 | -58% | 1 | 20 | (7) | 1 | 1 | 1 | 1 | 1 | 1 | 1 | 1 | (3) |
| Interest | (52) | (51) | 2% | (4) | (5) | (4) | (4) | (4) | (4) | (4) | (5) | (5) | (4) | (4) | (4) |
| **PROFIT BEFORE TAX** | 108 | 335 | 210% | 17 | 31 | (1) | (10) | 10 | 51 | 35 | 49 | 20 | 49 | 54 | 31 |
| | 2.1% | 5.9% | | 3.9% | 7.4% | -0.3% | -2.4% | 2.0% | 9.8% | 7.0% | 9.5% | 4.4% | 9.7% | 10.5% | 6.2% |
| Adjustments | | 308 | | 2 | 6 | 34 | 26 | 27 | 28 | 28 | 28 | 36 | 30 | 30 | 33 |
| Adjusted profit | | 643 | | 20 | 37 | 32 | 15 | 37 | 79 | 63 | 77 | 56 | 79 | 84 | 64 |
| Working capital | | (173) | | (122) | 32 | (20) | 35 | (31) | (10) | (103) | 10 | 107 | (90) | (35) | 56 |
| Operating cash flow | | 470 | | (103) | 69 | 13 | 50 | 6 | 69 | (41) | 87 | 163 | (11) | 49 | 120 |
| Capex | | (515) | | (62) | (37) | (48) | (23) | (2) | (89) | (19) | (53) | (100) | (2) | (19) | (61) |
| Other cash flow | | (67) | | (17) | 280 | (17) | (132) | (17) | 18 | (57) | (18) | (15) | (57) | (18) | (18) |
| **NET CASH FLOW** | | (112) | | (182) | 312 | (52) | (105) | (13) | (2) | (116) | 16 | 48 | (70) | 12 | 41 |
| Opening bank balance | | (1,291) | | (1,291) | (1,473) | (1,161) | (1,213) | (1,318) | (1,331) | (1,333) | (1,450) | (1,434) | (1,386) | (1,456) | (1,444) |
| **CLOSING BANK BALANCE** | | (1,403) | | (1,473) | (1,161) | (1,213) | (1,318) | (1,331) | (1,333) | (1,450) | (1,434) | (1,386) | (1,456) | (1,444) | (1,403) |
| Inventory | 270 | 271 | 0% | 309 | 302 | 304 | 267 | 253 | 217 | 304 | 296 | 255 | 313 | 320 | 271 |
| Receivables | 810 | 918 | 13% | 794 | 763 | 788 | 787 | 840 | 910 | 913 | 923 | 854 | 883 | 919 | 918 |
| Payables | (301) | (237) | 21% | (201) | (195) | (202) | (200) | (207) | (231) | (217) | (229) | (226) | (223) | (231) | (237) |
| Working capital | 779 | 952 | 22% | 901 | 870 | 889 | 855 | 886 | 896 | 1,000 | 990 | 883 | 973 | 1,008 | 952 |
| Provisions | (39) | (18) | 53% | (16) | (16) | (16) | (16) | (17) | (18) | (19) | (19) | (17) | (18) | (19) | (18) |
| Fixed assets | 1,871 | 1,983 | 6% | 1,904 | 1,903 | 1,914 | 1,907 | 1,879 | 1,937 | 1,925 | 1,946 | 2,001 | 1,970 | 1,956 | 1,983 |
| **NET OPERATING ASSETS** | 2,611 | 2,917 | 12% | 2,789 | 2,757 | 2,787 | 2,746 | 2,748 | 2,815 | 2,906 | 2,917 | 2,866 | 2,924 | 2,945 | 2,917 |
| Bank overdraft | 1,291 | 1,403 | 9% | 1,473 | 1,161 | 1,213 | 1,318 | 1,331 | 1,333 | 1,450 | 1,434 | 1,386 | 1,456 | 1,444 | 1,403 |
| Other finance | 563 | 271 | -52% | 549 | 539 | 521 | 386 | 371 | 400 | 351 | 344 | 330 | 284 | 278 | 271 |
| Debt | 1,854 | 1,674 | -10% | 2,022 | 1,700 | 1,734 | 1,705 | 1,702 | 1,734 | 1,801 | 1,778 | 1,716 | 1,740 | 1,722 | 1,674 |
| Equity | 757 | 1,243 | 64% | 767 | 1,057 | 1,053 | 1,041 | 1,045 | 1,081 | 1,105 | 1,138 | 1,150 | 1,184 | 1,223 | 1,243 |
| **CAPITAL EMPLOYED** | 2,611 | 2,917 | 12% | 2,789 | 2,757 | 2,787 | 2,746 | 2,748 | 2,815 | 2,906 | 2,917 | 2,866 | 2,924 | 2,945 | 2,917 |

| DEMO COMPANY BUDGET RESULTS | PQ$000 | 20XX forecast | 20XY BUDGET | inc | 1 Apr | 2 May | 3 JUN | 4 Jul | 5 Aug | 6 SEP | 7 Oct | 8 Nov | 9 DEC | 10 Jan | 11 Feb | 12 MAR |
|---|---|---|---|---|---|---|---|---|---|---|---|---|---|---|---|---|
| SALES | C4.5 | 5,131 | 5,709 | 11% | 440.5 | 420.3 | 438.6 | 432.3 | 481.2 | 522.5 | 496.2 | 512.2 | 444.9 | 502.7 | 517.9 | 500.0 |
| Direct material | C4.6 | (1,137) | (1,216) | -7% | (92.6) | (88.4) | (92.2) | (92.2) | (102.6) | (108.9) | (105.8) | (109.2) | (94.9) | (108.8) | (112.1) | (108.2) |
| | to sales | -22.2% | -21.3% | | -21.0% | -21.0% | -21.0% | -21.3% | -21.3% | -20.8% | -21.3% | -21.3% | -21.3% | -21.6% | -21.6% | -21.6% |
| VALUE ADDED | C4.5 | 3,994 | 4,493 | 13% | 347.9 | 331.9 | 346.4 | 340.1 | 378.6 | 413.6 | 390.4 | 403.0 | 350.0 | 393.9 | 405.8 | 391.8 |
| | to sales | 77.8% | 78.7% | | 79.0% | 79.0% | 79.0% | 78.7% | 78.7% | 79.2% | 78.7% | 78.7% | 78.7% | 78.4% | 78.4% | 78.4% |
| Direct labour | C4.5 | (1,989) | (2,089) | -5% | (166.3) | (158.7) | (165.6) | (167.7) | (186.7) | (198.2) | (179.3) | (182.7) | (156.5) | (174.4) | (179.7) | (173.4) |
| | to sales | -38.8% | -36.6% | | -37.7% | -37.7% | -37.7% | -38.8% | -38.8% | -37.9% | -36.1% | -35.7% | -35.2% | -34.7% | -34.7% | -34.7% |
| Marketing & selling | C4.6 | (642) | (678) | -6% | (55.7) | (52.2) | (53.1) | (59.4) | (71.4) | (54.6) | (56.6) | (56.1) | (51.2) | (51.9) | (55.3) | (60.8) |
| | to sales | -12.5% | -11.9% | | -12.6% | -12.4% | -12.1% | -13.8% | -14.8% | -10.5% | -11.4% | -11.0% | -11.5% | -10.3% | -10.7% | -12.2% |
| GROSS MARGIN | | 1,363 | 1,726 | 27% | 125.9 | 121.1 | 127.7 | 112.9 | 120.5 | 160.8 | 154.4 | 164.2 | 142.3 | 167.7 | 170.9 | 157.6 |
| | to sales | 26.6% | 30.2% | | 28.6% | 28.8% | 29.1% | 26.1% | 25.0% | 30.8% | 31.1% | 32.1% | 32.0% | 33.4% | 33.0% | 31.5% |
| Factory overhead | C4.6 | (300) | (371) | -24% | (27.9) | (26.6) | (38.9) | (38.4) | (27.1) | (25.2) | (35.4) | (30.2) | (27.4) | (31.4) | (30.3) | (32.0) |
| | to sales | -5.8% | -6.5% | | -6.3% | -6.3% | -8.9% | -8.9% | -5.6% | -4.8% | -7.1% | -5.9% | -6.2% | -6.2% | -5.9% | -6.4% |
| FACTORY MARGIN | | 1,063 | 1,355 | 27% | 98.0 | 94.5 | 88.8 | 74.5 | 93.4 | 135.6 | 119.0 | 134.0 | 114.9 | 136.3 | 140.6 | 125.6 |
| | to sales | 20.7% | 23.7% | | 22.3% | 22.5% | 20.3% | 17.2% | 19.4% | 26.0% | 24.0% | 26.2% | 25.8% | 27.1% | 27.1% | 25.1% |
| Administration | C4.7 | (420) | (427) | -2% | (34.7) | (34.7) | (34.7) | (34.9) | (36.4) | (36.4) | (35.8) | (35.8) | (35.8) | (35.8) | (35.8) | (35.8) |
| Establishment | C4.7 | (170) | (181) | -6% | (14.2) | (14.2) | (15.6) | (17.5) | (14.2) | (14.2) | (14.2) | (14.2) | (14.2) | (15.9) | (14.2) | (18.4) |
| Asset amortisation | C4.9 | (342) | (374) | -9% | (29.0) | (29.3) | (29.7) | (29.8) | (29.9) | (31.0) | (31.1) | (32.1) | (32.8) | (32.8) | (33.0) | (33.5) |
| OPERATING PROFIT | | 131 | 374 | 185% | 20.1 | 16.3 | 8.8 | (7.7) | 12.9 | 54.0 | 37.9 | 51.9 | 32.1 | 51.8 | 57.6 | 37.9 |
| | to sales | 2.6% | 6.5% | | 4.6% | 3.9% | 2.0% | -1.8% | 2.7% | 10.3% | 7.6% | 10.1% | 7.2% | 10.3% | 11.1% | 7.6% |
| Non-operating items | C4.7 | 29 | 12 | -58% | 1.2 | 19.7 | (6.5) | 1.2 | 1.2 | 1.2 | 1.2 | 1.2 | (7.9) | 1.2 | 1.2 | (2.8) |
| Finance | C4.7 | (52) | (51) | 2% | (4.2) | (4.7) | (3.7) | (3.9) | (4.2) | (4.1) | (4.2) | (4.5) | (4.5) | (4.2) | (4.3) | (4.3) |
| PROFIT PRE TAX | C4.10 | 108 | 335 | 210% | 17.1 | 31.3 | (1.4) | (10.4) | 9.9 | 51.1 | 34.9 | 48.6 | 19.7 | 48.8 | 54.5 | 30.8 |
| | to sales | 2.1% | 5.9% | | 3.9% | 7.4% | -0.3% | -2.4% | 2.0% | 9.8% | 7.0% | 9.5% | 4.4% | 9.7% | 10.5% | 6.2% |
| Taxation | C4.10 | (154) | (77) | | (3.9) | (7.2) | 0.3 | 2.4 | (2.3) | (11.8) | (8.0) | (11.2) | (4.5) | (11.2) | (12.5) | (7.1) |
| PROFIT AFTER TAX | | (46) | 258 | | 13.2 | 24.1 | (1.0) | (8.0) | 7.6 | 39.3 | 26.9 | 37.4 | 15.1 | 37.6 | 41.9 | 23.7 |
| Dividends | C4.10 | (38) | (42) | | (3.5) | (3.5) | (3.5) | (3.5) | (3.5) | (3.5) | (3.5) | (3.5) | (3.5) | (3.5) | (3.5) | (3.5) |
| RETAINED PROFIT | C4.3 | (84) | 216 | | 9.7 | 20.6 | (4.5) | (11.5) | 4.1 | 35.8 | 23.4 | 33.9 | 11.6 | 34.1 | 38.4 | 20.2 |

| CAP EMPLOYED | PQ$000 | 20XX forecast | 20XY BUDGET | inc | 1 Apr | 2 May | 3 JUN | 4 Jul | 5 Aug | 6 SEP | 7 Oct | 8 Nov | 9 DEC | 10 Jan | 11 Feb | 12 MAR |
|---|---|---|---|---|---|---|---|---|---|---|---|---|---|---|---|---|
| Inventory | C4.8 | 270 | 271 | 0% | 309 | 302 | 304 | 267 | 253 | 217 | 304 | 296 | 255 | 313 | 320 | 271 |
| Trade acs receivable | C4.8 | 802 | 912 | 14% | 788 | 757 | 782 | 781 | 834 | 904 | 907 | 917 | 848 | 877 | 913 | 912 |
| Prepayments etc | C4.8 | 8 | 6 | -28% | 6 | 6 | 6 | 6 | 6 | 6 | 6 | 6 | 6 | 6 | 6 | 6 |
| Accrued income | C4.8 | - | 0 | na | - | - | - | - | - | - | - | - | - | - | - | - |
| Current assets | C4.8 | 1,080 | 1,189 | 10% | 1,103 | 1,064 | 1,092 | 1,054 | 1,093 | 1,127 | 1,217 | 1,219 | 1,109 | 1,196 | 1,239 | 1,189 |
| Trade acs payable | C4.8 | (181) | (122) | -32% | (108) | (99) | (105) | (100) | (106) | (128) | (112) | (122) | (117) | (112) | (118) | (122) |
| Payroll deductions | C4.8 | (4) | (3) | -20% | (3) | (3) | (3) | (3) | (3) | (3) | (3) | (3) | (3) | (3) | (3) | (3) |
| Sales tax | C4.8 | (93) | (100) | 8% | (78) | (80) | (82) | (84) | (86) | (88) | (90) | (92) | (94) | (96) | (98) | (100) |
| Accruals etc | C4.8 | (23) | (12) | -48% | (12) | (12) | (12) | (12) | (12) | (12) | (12) | (12) | (12) | (12) | (12) | (12) |
| Deferred income | C4.8 | - | 0 | na | - | - | - | - | - | - | - | - | - | - | - | - |
| Current liabilities | C4.8 | (301) | (237) | -21% | (201) | (195) | (202) | (200) | (207) | (231) | (217) | (229) | (226) | (223) | (231) | (237) |
| WORKING CAPITAL | | 779 | 952 | 22% | 901 | 870 | 889 | 855 | 886 | 896 | 1,000 | 990 | 883 | 973 | 1,008 | 952 |
| Inventory | C4.9 | (11) | (2) | -85% | (2) | (2) | (2) | (2) | (2) | (1) | (2) | (2) | (2) | (2) | (2) | (2) |
| Receivables | C4.9 | (28) | (17) | -40% | (15) | (14) | (14) | (14) | (16) | (17) | (17) | (17) | (16) | (16) | (17) | (17) |
| PROVISIONS | | (39) | (18) | -53% | (16) | (16) | (16) | (16) | (17) | (18) | (19) | (19) | (17) | (18) | (19) | (18) |
| Tangibles | C4.9 | 1,434 | 1,597 | 11% | 1,471 | 1,474 | 1,489 | 1,487 | 1,463 | 1,525 | 1,517 | 1,542 | 1,601 | 1,575 | 1,565 | 1,597 |
| Intangibles | C4.9 | 437 | 387 | -12% | 433 | 429 | 425 | 420 | 416 | 412 | 408 | 404 | 399 | 395 | 391 | 387 |
| FIXED ASSETS | | 1,871 | 1,983 | 6% | 1,904 | 1,903 | 1,914 | 1,907 | 1,879 | 1,937 | 1,925 | 1,946 | 2,001 | 1,970 | 1,956 | 1,983 |
| NET ASSETS | | 2,611 | 2,917 | 12% | 2,789 | 2,757 | 2,787 | 2,746 | 2,748 | 2,815 | 2,906 | 2,917 | 2,866 | 2,924 | 2,945 | 2,917 |
| Overdrafts | C4.4 | 1,291 | 1,403 | | 1,473 | 1,161 | 1,213 | 1,318 | 1,331 | 1,333 | 1,450 | 1,434 | 1,386 | 1,456 | 1,444 | 1,403 |
| HP & finance leases | C4.10 | 47 | 28 | | 43 | 39 | 35 | 31 | 27 | 58 | 53 | 48 | 43 | 38 | 33 | 28 |
| Loans | C4.10 | 280 | 124 | | 267 | 254 | 241 | 228 | 215 | 202 | 189 | 176 | 163 | 150 | 137 | 124 |
| Capital grants | C4.10 | 44 | 0 | | 40 | 36 | 32 | 28 | 24 | 20 | 16 | 12 | 8 | 4 | - | - |
| Taxation payable | C4.10 | 154 | 77 | | 158 | 165 | 165 | 85 | 88 | 99 | 69 | 80 | 85 | 57 | 70 | 77 |
| Dividends payable | C4.10 | 38 | 42 | | 42 | 45 | 49 | 14 | 18 | 21 | 25 | 28 | 32 | 35 | 39 | 42 |
| DEBT | | 1,854 | 1,674 | -10% | 2,022 | 1,700 | 1,734 | 1,705 | 1,702 | 1,734 | 1,801 | 1,778 | 1,716 | 1,740 | 1,722 | 1,674 |
| Share capital - ord | C4.10 | 100 | 400 | | 100 | 400 | 400 | 400 | 400 | 400 | 400 | 400 | 400 | 400 | 400 | 400 |
| Share capital - pref | C4.10 | 30 | 0 | | 30 | - | - | - | - | - | - | - | - | - | - | - |
| Profit | C4.2 | 627 | 843 | | 637 | 657 | 653 | 641 | 645 | 681 | 705 | 738 | 750 | 784 | 823 | 843 |
| EQUITY | | 757 | 1,243 | 64% | 767 | 1,057 | 1,053 | 1,041 | 1,045 | 1,081 | 1,105 | 1,138 | 1,150 | 1,184 | 1,223 | 1,243 |
| CAPITAL EMPLOYED | | 2,611 | 2,917 | 12% | 2,789 | 2,757 | 2,787 | 2,746 | 2,748 | 2,815 | 2,906 | 2,917 | 2,866 | 2,924 | 2,945 | 2,917 |

DEMO BUDGET 20XX-XY    CAPITAL EMPLOYED    D:\20XYBUD\BudDraft4    Printed 19.23  23-MMM-20XY    APPENDIX C4.3

| | C-ref | 20XY BUDGET | 1 Apr | 2 May | 3 JUN | 4 Jul | 5 Aug | 6 SEP | 7 Oct | 8 Nov | 9 DEC | 10 Jan | 11 Feb | 12 MAR |
|---|---|---|---|---|---|---|---|---|---|---|---|---|---|---|
| **PROFIT BEFORE TAXATION** | C4.2 | **335** | 17.1 | 31.3 | (1.4) | (10.4) | 9.9 | 51.1 | 34.9 | 48.6 | 19.7 | 48.8 | 54.5 | 30.8 |
| Fixed asset disposals | C4.7 | (2) | | | 7.7 | | | | | | 9.1 | | | |
| Provisions - inventory | C4.8 | (9) | (9.1) | (18.5) | | (0.2) | (0.1) | (0.2) | 0.5 | | (0.3) | 0.4 | | (0.3) |
| Provisions - receivables | C4.8 | (11) | (13.5) | (0.5) | 0.4 | | 1.1 | 1.2 | 0.1 | 0.1 | (1.2) | 0.6 | 0.6 | (0.1) |
| Amortisation of fixed assets | C4.9 | 374 | 29.0 | 29.3 | 29.7 | 29.8 | 29.9 | 31.0 | 31.1 | 32.1 | 32.8 | 32.8 | 33.0 | 33.5 |
| Amortisation of grants | C4.7 | (44) | (4.0) | (4.0) | (4.0) | (4.0) | (4.0) | (4.0) | (4.0) | (4.0) | (4.0) | (4.0) | (4.0) | |
| **Adjusted profit** | | **643** | 19.5 | 37.5 | 32.4 | 15.2 | 36.8 | 79.1 | 62.6 | 76.8 | 56.1 | 78.6 | 84.1 | 63.9 |
| Inventory | C4.8 | (1) | (38.6) | 7.0 | (2.4) | 36.5 | 14.3 | 35.7 | (86.9) | 8.9 | 40.3 | (57.6) | (7.3) | 48.8 |
| Trade accounts receivable | C4.8 | (108) | 16.1 | 31.4 | (24.9) | 0.6 | (52.9) | (70.0) | (2.7) | (10.5) | 68.9 | (29.0) | (35.6) | 0.8 |
| Trade accounts payable | C4.8 | (64) | (99.9) | (6.5) | 7.6 | (2.6) | 7.7 | 24.0 | (13.9) | 11.5 | (2.5) | (3.3) | 8.2 | 6.2 |
| **Working capital movement** | | **(173)** | (122.4) | 31.8 | (19.8) | 34.5 | (30.8) | (10.3) | (103.5) | 9.8 | 106.6 | (89.9) | (34.7) | 55.7 |
| **OPERATING CASH FLOW** | | **470** | (102.9) | 69.3 | 12.7 | 49.7 | 5.9 | 68.8 | (40.8) | 86.6 | 162.7 | (11.3) | 49.3 | 119.6 |
| Assets acquired  tangible | C4.9 | (515) | (62.0) | (37.0) | (48.0) | (23.0) | (2.0) | (89.0) | (19.0) | (53.0) | (100.0) | (2.0) | (19.0) | (61.0) |
| intangible | C4.9 | - | | | | | | | | | | | | |
| Assets sold  both | C4.7 | 30 | | 27.0 | | | | | | | | | | |
| Capital grants | C4.10 | 0 | | | | | | | | | 3.4 | | | |
| HP & finance leases | C4.10 | (19) | (4.0) | (4.0) | (4.0) | (4.0) | (4.0) | 31.0 | (5.0) | (5.0) | (5.0) | (5.0) | (5.0) | (5.0) |
| Loans | C4.10 | (156) | (13.0) | (13.0) | (13.0) | (13.0) | (13.0) | (13.0) | (13.0) | (13.0) | (13.0) | (13.0) | (13.0) | (13.0) |
| Shares issued/(redeemed) | C4.10 | 270 | | 270.0 | | | | | | | | | | |
| Taxation | C4.10 | (154) | | | | (77.0) | | | (38.5) | | | (38.5) | | |
| Dividends | C4.10 | (38) | | | | (38.0) | | | | | | | | |
| **OTHER CASH FLOW** | | **(582)** | (79.0) | 243.0 | (65.0) | (155.0) | (19.0) | (71.0) | (75.5) | (71.0) | (114.6) | (58.5) | (37.0) | (79.0) |
| **NET CASH FLOW** | | **(112)** | (181.9) | 312.3 | (52.3) | (105.3) | (13.1) | (2.2) | (116.3) | 15.6 | 48.1 | (69.8) | 12.3 | 40.6 |
| Opening bank balance | C4.3 | (1,291) | (1,291) | (1,473) | (1,161) | (1,213) | (1,318) | (1,331) | (1,333) | (1,450) | (1,434) | (1,386) | (1,456) | (1,444) |
| **CLOSING BANK BALANCE** | C4.3 | **(1,403)** | (1,473) | (1,161) | (1,213) | (1,318) | (1,331) | (1,333) | (1,450) | (1,434) | (1,386) | (1,456) | (1,444) | (1,403) |

*The above layout is a practical presentation of the reality of the business's operations*
*The balance sheet shows a similar reality ~ the top half shows the substance of the business and the bottom half shows how it is financed between debt and equity*

*Statutory financial statements are much more geared towards quoted groups of companies; hence the emphasis on "investing and divesting activities" etc rather than on operating performance*
*Chief executives are now known more for their acquisitions and disposals rather than for running profitable and cash-generative businesses year-on-year*
*However, the ability to run businesses profitably and cash-positively is far more important than the ability to buy or sell them*

# DEMO COMPANY BUDGET
## OUTPUT

| OUTPUT | PQ$000 | 20XX forecast | 20XY BUDGET | inc | 1 Apr | 2 May | 3 JUN | 4 Jul | 5 Aug | 6 SEP | 7 Oct | 8 Nov | 9 DEC | 10 Jan | 11 Feb | 12 MAR |
|---|---|---|---|---|---|---|---|---|---|---|---|---|---|---|---|---|
| Sales - Lancelot | units | 6,794 | 6,955 | 2% | 482 | 504 | 526 | 548 | 570 | 592 | 614 | 636 | 581 | 642 | 624 | 636 |
| Sales - Hannibal | units | 7,650 | 7,673 | 0% | 697 | 621 | 648 | 609 | 718 | 693 | 635 | 630 | 531 | 606 | 674 | 611 |
| Sales - Geronimo | units | - | 442 | na | - | - | - | - | - | 82 | 49 | 74 | 52 | 67 | 57 | 61 |
| Sales volume | units | 14,444 | 15,070 | 4% | 1,179 | 1,125 | 1,174 | 1,157 | 1,288 | 1,367 | 1,298 | 1,340 | 1,164 | 1,315 | 1,355 | 1,308 |
| Selling price | per unit | $355.23 | $378.85 | 7% | $373.60 | $373.60 | $373.60 | $373.60 | $373.60 | $382.25 | $382.25 | $382.25 | $382.25 | $382.25 | $382.25 | $382.25 |
| SALES VALUE | C4.2 | 5,131 | 5,709 | 11% | 440.5 | 420.3 | 438.6 | 432.3 | 481.2 | 522.5 | 496.2 | 512.2 | 444.9 | 502.7 | 517.9 | 500.0 |
| Accounting period | weekdays | 260 | 260 | | 25 | 20 | 20 | 25 | 20 | 20 | 25 | 20 | 20 | 25 | 20 | 20 |
| Factory shutdown | days | (25) | (25) | | (1) | (1) | - | (10) | - | (1) | - | - | (5) | (2) | - | (5) |
| Production period | days | 235 | 235 | | 24 | 19 | 20 | 15 | 20 | 19 | 25 | 20 | 15 | 23 | 20 | 15 |
| Shift time | hours | 96 | 96 | | 8 | 8 | 8 | 8 | 8 | 8 | 8 | 8 | 8 | 8 | 8 | 8 |
| Shifts | number | 22 | 24 | | 2 | 2 | 2 | 2 | 2 | 2 | 2 | 2 | 2 | 2 | 2 | 2 |
| Available per man | hours | 3,760 | 3,760 | 0% | 384 | 304 | 320 | 240 | 320 | 304 | 400 | 320 | 240 | 368 | 320 | 240 |
| Efficiency | %age | 56.4% | 61.1% | 8% | 62% | 62% | 62% | 62% | 60% | 62% | 62% | 62% | 55% | 60% | 62% | 62% |
| Output time per man | hours | 2,119 | 2,299 | 8% | 238 | 188 | 198 | 149 | 192 | 188 | 248 | 198 | 132 | 221 | 198 | 149 |
| Manpower | heads | 68.8 | 73.5 | 7% | 67 | 67 | 70 | 73 | 73 | 76 | 76 | 76 | 76 | 76 | 76 | 76 |
| Available total | hours | 145,787 | 168,679 | 16% | 15,946 | 12,596 | 13,860 | 10,877 | 14,016 | 14,288 | 18,848 | 15,048 | 10,032 | 16,796 | 15,048 | 11,324 |
| Time per product | hours | 11.48 | 11.25 | -2% | 11.70 | 11.70 | 11.70 | 11.70 | 11.70 | 11.70 | 11.15 | 11.00 | 10.85 | 10.70 | 10.70 | 10.70 |
| Production | units | 12,699 | 14,991 | 18% | 1,363 | 1,077 | 1,185 | 930 | 1,198 | 1,221 | 1,690 | 1,368 | 925 | 1,570 | 1,406 | 1,058 |
| FG stock - opening | units | 1,220 | 791 | -35% | 791 | 975 | 927 | 938 | 711 | 621 | 475 | 867 | 895 | 656 | 911 | 962 |
| FG stock - prodn | units | 14,015 | 14,991 | 7% | 1,363 | 1,077 | 1,185 | 930 | 1,198 | 1,221 | 1,690 | 1,368 | 925 | 1,570 | 1,406 | 1,058 |
| FG stock - sales | units | (14,444) | (15,070) | 4% | (1,179) | (1,125) | (1,174) | (1,157) | (1,288) | (1,367) | (1,298) | (1,340) | (1,164) | (1,315) | (1,355) | (1,308) |
| FG stock - closing | units | 791 | 712 | -10% | 975 | 927 | 938 | 711 | 621 | 475 | 867 | 895 | 656 | 911 | 962 | 712 |
| Pay increase | %age | | | | 0.0% | 0.0% | 0.0% | 2.8% | 0.0% | 0.0% | 0.0% | 0.0% | 0.0% | 0.0% | 0.0% | 0.0% |
| Hourly wage | PQ$ | | | | $9.80 | $9.80 | $9.80 | $10.07 | $10.07 | $10.07 | $10.07 | $10.07 | $10.07 | $10.07 | $10.07 | $10.07 |
| Total wage | | 1,544 | 1,688 | 9% | 156.3 | 123.4 | 135.8 | 109.6 | 141.2 | 143.9 | 189.9 | 151.6 | 101.1 | 169.2 | 151.6 | 114.1 |
| Employment costs | %age | 24.4% | 23.0% | -6% | 23% | 23% | 23% | 23% | 23% | 23% | 23% | 23% | 23% | 23% | 23% | 23% |
| Labour paid | C4.2 | 1,921 | 2,076 | 8% | 192.2 | 151.8 | 167.0 | 134.8 | 173.7 | 177.0 | 233.6 | 186.5 | 124.4 | 208.1 | 186.5 | 140.3 |
| Labour cost per unit | PQ$ | $137.70 | $138.63 | | $141.03 | $141.03 | $141.03 | $144.98 | $144.98 | $144.98 | $138.17 | $136.31 | $134.45 | $132.59 | $132.59 | $132.59 |
| Sales volume | units | 14,444 | 15,070 | | 1,179 | 1,125 | 1,174 | 1,157 | 1,288 | 1,367 | 1,298 | 1,340 | 1,164 | 1,315 | 1,355 | 1,308 |
| Direct labour cost | C4.6 | 1,989 | 2,089 | | 166.3 | 158.7 | 165.6 | 167.7 | 186.7 | 198.2 | 179.3 | 182.7 | 156.5 | 174.4 | 179.7 | 173.4 |

*For the sake of simplicity an average selling price, production time and cost has been used for each product ~ in practice, each product stream would be calculated separately*
*In practice, the incidence of overtime should be forecast to the nearest 1% if there is a premium paid for overtime work~ in this case the workforce is assumed to be of adequate numbers*
*"Labour paid" is the actual amount expected in respect of the volume produced*
*"Direct labour" is the cost relating to the volume sold, the balance between sales and production volume being reflected in the movement of stock value*

# DEMO COMPANY BUDGET — DIRECT COSTS

PQ$000

| DIRECT COSTS | | 20XX forecast | 20XY BUDGET | inc | 1 Apr | 2 May | 3 JUN | 4 Jul | 5 Aug | 6 SEP | 7 Oct | 8 Nov | 9 DEC | 10 Jan | 11 Feb | 12 MAR |
|---|---|---|---|---|---|---|---|---|---|---|---|---|---|---|---|---|
| Direct materials | unit cost | $74.12 | | | $73.93 | $73.93 | $73.93 | $75.04 | $75.04 | $75.04 | $76.86 | $76.86 | $76.86 | $78.09 | $78.09 | $78.09 |
| Consumables | unit cost | $1.01 | | | $0.96 | $0.96 | $0.96 | $0.96 | $0.96 | $0.96 | $0.96 | $0.96 | $0.96 | $0.96 | $0.96 | $0.96 |
| Carriage outward | unit cost | $3.59 | | | $3.67 | $3.67 | $3.67 | $3.67 | $3.67 | $3.67 | $3.67 | $3.67 | $3.67 | $3.67 | $3.67 | $3.67 |
| Direct materials | unit cost | $78.72 | $80.68 | 2% | $78.56 | $78.56 | $78.56 | $79.67 | $79.67 | $79.67 | $81.49 | $81.49 | $81.49 | $82.72 | $82.72 | $82.72 |
| DIRECT MATERIAL C4.2 | | 1,137 | 1,216 | 7% | 92.6 | 88.4 | 92.2 | 92.2 | 102.6 | 108.9 | 105.8 | 109.2 | 94.9 | 108.8 | 112.1 | 108.2 |
| Value added C4.2 | | 3,994 | 4,493 | 13% | 347.9 | 331.9 | 346.4 | 340.1 | 378.6 | 413.6 | 390.4 | 403.0 | 350.0 | 393.9 | 405.8 | 391.8 |
| DIRECT LABOUR C4.2 | | 1,989 | 2,089 | 13% | 166.3 | 158.7 | 165.6 | 167.7 | 186.7 | 198.2 | 179.3 | 182.7 | 156.5 | 174.4 | 179.7 | 173.4 |
| Marketing payroll | | 123 | 106 | -14% | 8.8 | 8.8 | 8.8 | 8.8 | 8.8 | 8.8 | 8.8 | 8.8 | 8.8 | 8.8 | 8.8 | 8.8 |
| Technical payroll | | 86 | 91 | 6% | 7.6 | 7.6 | 7.6 | 7.6 | 7.6 | 7.6 | 7.6 | 7.6 | 7.6 | 7.6 | 7.6 | 7.6 |
| Sales payroll | | 189 | 213 | 12% | 16.7 | 16.3 | 16.7 | 16.5 | 17.5 | 18.4 | 18.4 | 18.7 | 17.4 | 18.6 | 18.9 | 18.5 |
| Commission | | 25 | 29 | 14% | 2.2 | 2.1 | 2.2 | 2.2 | 2.4 | 2.6 | 2.5 | 2.6 | 2.2 | 2.5 | 2.6 | 2.5 |
| Product launches | | - | 22 | na | 2.3 | 2.8 | 2.8 | 4.7 | 7.3 | 1.4 | 0.9 | | | | | |
| Exhibitions | | 24 | 21 | -12% | 4.7 | 3.2 | | | 5.8 | | | | | | | 7.4 |
| Industry seminars | | 7 | 9 | 24% | | | | | | | 2.8 | 2.7 | | | 3.2 | |
| Advertising | | 23 | 44 | 93% | 0.4 | 0.7 | 4.2 | 5.8 | 6.9 | 4.4 | 4.4 | 4.4 | 4.4 | 3.1 | 2.8 | 2.8 |
| Communications | | 18 | 19 | 7% | 1.6 | 1.6 | 1.6 | 1.6 | 1.6 | 1.6 | 1.6 | 1.6 | 1.6 | 1.6 | 1.6 | 1.6 |
| Marketing travel | | 47 | 74 | 57% | 7.4 | 5.2 | 5.2 | 8.3 | 9.2 | 5.2 | 5.2 | 5.2 | 5.2 | 5.2 | 5.2 | 7.1 |
| Bad debts w/off 0.75% | | 93 | 43 | -54% | 3.3 | 3.2 | 3.3 | 3.2 | 3.6 | 3.9 | 3.7 | 3.8 | 3.3 | 3.8 | 3.9 | 3.8 |
| Materials & other | | 7 | 8 | 20% | 0.7 | 0.7 | 0.7 | 0.7 | 0.7 | 0.7 | 0.7 | 0.7 | 0.7 | 0.7 | 0.7 | 0.7 |
| MARKETING C4.2 | | 642 | 678 | 6% | 55.7 | 52.2 | 53.1 | 59.4 | 71.4 | 54.6 | 56.6 | 56.1 | 51.2 | 51.9 | 55.3 | 60.8 |
| Supervisory payroll | | 131 | 165 | 26% | 12.4 | 12.4 | 12.4 | 12.7 | 12.7 | 12.7 | 12.7 | 15.3 | 15.3 | 15.3 | 15.3 | 15.3 |
| Power  prod'n | | 27 | 30 | 11% | 2.7 | 2.2 | 2.4 | 1.9 | 2.4 | 2.4 | 3.4 | 2.7 | 1.9 | 3.1 | 2.8 | 2.1 |
| heating | | 19 | 21 | 10% | 1.7 | 1.7 | 1.7 | 1.7 | 1.7 | 1.7 | 1.7 | 1.8 | 1.8 | 1.8 | 1.8 | 1.8 |
| Gas | | 5 | 5 | -4% | 0.4 | 0.4 | 0.4 | 0.4 | 0.4 | 0.4 | 0.4 | 0.4 | 0.4 | 0.4 | 0.4 | 0.4 |
| Water | | 13 | 14 | 5% | 3.0 | 0.2 | 0.2 | 3.0 | 0.2 | 0.2 | 3.0 | 0.2 | 0.2 | 3.0 | 0.2 | 0.2 |
| Waste disposal | | 2 | 4 | 80% | 0.3 | 0.3 | 0.3 | 0.3 | 0.3 | 0.3 | 0.3 | 0.3 | 0.3 | 0.3 | 0.3 | 0.3 |
| Indirect materials | | 3 | 7 | 123% | 0.5 | 0.5 | 0.5 | 0.5 | 0.5 | 0.6 | 0.6 | 0.6 | 0.6 | 0.6 | 0.6 | 0.6 |
| Maintenance | | 82 | 107 | 30% | 5.3 | 7.3 | 19.4 | 15.8 | 7.3 | 5.3 | 11.7 | 7.3 | 5.3 | 5.3 | 7.3 | 9.7 |
| Security | | 7 | 8 | 20% | 0.7 | 0.7 | 0.7 | 0.7 | 0.7 | 0.7 | 0.7 | 0.7 | 0.7 | 0.7 | 0.7 | 0.7 |
| Cleaning | | 5 | 5 | 6% | 0.4 | 0.4 | 0.4 | 0.9 | 0.4 | 0.4 | 0.4 | 0.4 | 0.4 | 0.4 | 0.4 | 0.4 |
| Other | | 6 | 6 | 0% | 0.5 | 0.5 | 0.5 | 0.5 | 0.5 | 0.5 | 0.5 | 0.5 | 0.5 | 0.5 | 0.5 | 0.5 |
| FACTORY O'HEAD C4.2 | | 300 | 371 | 24% | 27.9 | 26.6 | 38.9 | 38.4 | 27.1 | 25.2 | 35.4 | 30.2 | 27.4 | 31.4 | 30.3 | 32.0 |

Marketing costs in Demo Company are variable costs which drive sales, and as such should be shown in the upper (variable) part of the profit statement
Factory overheads, on the other hand, although related to them making of the products, is a relatively fixed cost and should be shown lower in the profit statement along with the indirect overheads
The inclusion of factory overheads in the inventory valuation, while common practice, is NOT advisable ~ it encourages managers to increase stock levels to reduce reported overhead

| INDIRECT COSTS | | 20XX forecast | 20XY BUDGET | inc | 1 Apr | 2 May | 3 JUN | 4 Jul | 5 Aug | 6 SEP | 7 Oct | 8 Nov | 9 DEC | 10 Jan | 11 Feb | 12 MAR |
|---|---|---|---|---|---|---|---|---|---|---|---|---|---|---|---|---|
| Admin payroll | | 77 | 73 | -5% | 6.1 | 6.1 | 6.1 | 6.1 | 6.1 | 6.1 | 6.1 | 6.1 | 6.1 | 6.1 | 6.1 | 6.1 |
| Finance & costing payroll | | 109 | 116 | 6% | 9.2 | 9.2 | 9.2 | 9.2 | 9.2 | 9.2 | 10.1 | 10.1 | 10.1 | 10.1 | 10.1 | 10.1 |
| Other staff costs | | 25 | 28 | 10% | 2.3 | 2.3 | 2.3 | 2.3 | 2.3 | 2.3 | 2.3 | 2.3 | 2.3 | 2.3 | 2.3 | 2.3 |
| Office supplies | | 10 | 8 | -16% | 0.7 | 0.7 | 0.7 | 0.7 | 0.7 | 0.7 | 0.7 | 0.7 | 0.7 | 0.7 | 0.7 | 0.7 |
| Management travel | | 24 | 28 | 15% | 2.3 | 2.3 | 2.3 | 2.3 | 2.3 | 2.3 | 2.3 | 2.3 | 2.3 | 2.3 | 2.3 | 2.3 |
| Telecoms | | 31 | 36 | 16% | 2.6 | 2.6 | 2.6 | 2.8 | 2.8 | 2.8 | 2.8 | 2.8 | 2.8 | 2.8 | 2.8 | 2.8 |
| Fees - audit, tax etc | | 28 | 34 | 20% | 2.8 | 2.8 | 2.8 | 2.8 | 2.8 | 2.8 | 2.8 | 2.8 | 2.8 | 2.8 | 2.8 | 2.8 |
| Fees - legal etc | | 27 | 16 | -42% | 1.3 | 1.3 | 1.3 | 1.3 | 1.3 | 1.3 | 1.3 | 1.3 | 1.3 | 1.3 | 1.3 | 1.3 |
| Licences etc | | 18 | 23 | 27% | 1.9 | 1.9 | 1.9 | 1.9 | 1.9 | 1.9 | 1.9 | 1.9 | 1.9 | 1.9 | 1.9 | 1.9 |
| Insurance | | 30 | 34 | 12% | 2.8 | 2.8 | 2.8 | 2.8 | 2.8 | 2.8 | 2.8 | 2.8 | 2.8 | 2.8 | 2.8 | 2.8 |
| Miscellaneous | | 41 | 32 | -21% | 2.7 | 2.7 | 2.7 | 2.7 | 2.7 | 2.7 | 2.7 | 2.7 | 2.7 | 2.7 | 2.7 | 2.7 |
| **ADMINISTRATION** | C4.2 | 420 | 427 | 2% | 34.7 | 34.7 | 34.7 | 34.9 | 36.4 | 36.4 | 35.8 | 35.8 | 35.8 | 35.8 | 35.8 | 35.8 |
| Council taxes | | 108 | 113 | 4% | 9.4 | 9.4 | 9.4 | 9.4 | 9.4 | 9.4 | 9.4 | 9.4 | 9.4 | 9.4 | 9.4 | 9.4 |
| Building utilities | | 23 | 19 | -17% | 1.6 | 1.6 | 1.6 | 1.6 | 1.6 | 1.6 | 1.6 | 1.6 | 1.6 | 1.6 | 1.6 | 1.6 |
| Property insurance | | 31 | 38 | 22% | 2.8 | 2.8 | 2.8 | 2.8 | 2.8 | 2.8 | 2.8 | 2.8 | 2.8 | 2.8 | 2.8 | 7.0 |
| Other | | 8 | 11 | 40% | 0.4 | 0.4 | 1.8 | 3.7 | 0.4 | 0.4 | 0.4 | 0.4 | 0.4 | 2.1 | 0.4 | 0.4 |
| **ESTABLISHMENT** | C4.2 | 170 | 181 | 6% | 14.2 | 14.2 | 15.6 | 17.5 | 14.2 | 14.2 | 14.2 | 14.2 | 14.2 | 15.9 | 14.2 | 18.4 |
| Disposals NBV | C4.3 | (29) | | | 0.0 | (8.5) | (7.7) | 0.0 | 0.0 | 0.0 | 0.0 | 0.0 | (12.5) | 0.0 | 0.0 | 0.0 |
| Proceeds | | 30 | | | - | 27.0 | | | | | | | 3.4 | | | |
| Net gain/ (loss) | C4.3 | 4 | 2 | | 0.0 | 18.5 | (7.7) | 0.0 | 0.0 | 0.0 | 0.0 | 0.0 | (9.1) | 0.0 | 0.0 | 0.0 |
| Grants amortised | | 48 | 44 | | 4.0 | 4.0 | 4.0 | 4.0 | 4.0 | 4.0 | 4.0 | 4.0 | 4.0 | 4.0 | 4.0 | - |
| Other | C4.3 | (23) | (34) | | (2.8) | (2.8) | (2.8) | (2.8) | (2.8) | (2.8) | (2.8) | (2.8) | (2.8) | (2.8) | (2.8) | (2.8) |
| **NON-OPERATING** | C4.2 | 29 | 12 | -58% | 1.2 | 19.7 | (6.5) | 1.2 | 1.2 | 1.2 | 1.2 | 1.2 | (7.9) | 1.2 | 1.2 | (2.8) |
| Interest   overdraft | 3.25% | 42 | 44 | 5% | 3.5 | 4.0 | 3.1 | 3.3 | 3.6 | 3.6 | 3.6 | 3.9 | 3.9 | 3.8 | 3.9 | 3.9 |
| HP/ lease | 3.75% | 3 | 2 | -50% | 0.1 | 0.1 | 0.1 | 0.1 | 0.1 | 0.1 | 0.2 | 0.2 | 0.2 | 0.1 | 0.1 | 0.1 |
| loans | 2.50% | 7 | 5 | -26% | 0.6 | 0.6 | 0.5 | 0.5 | 0.5 | 0.4 | 0.4 | 0.4 | 0.4 | 0.3 | 0.3 | 0.3 |
| **FINANCE** | C4.2 | 52 | 51 | -2% | 4.2 | 4.7 | 3.7 | 3.9 | 4.2 | 4.1 | 4.2 | 4.5 | 4.5 | 4.2 | 4.3 | 4.3 |
| Direct labour | C4.6 | | 2,089.1 | | 166.3 | 158.7 | 165.6 | 167.7 | 186.7 | 198.2 | 179.3 | 182.7 | 156.5 | 174.4 | 179.7 | 173.4 |
| Marketing | C4.6 | | 105.6 | | 8.8 | 8.8 | 8.8 | 8.8 | 8.8 | 8.8 | 8.8 | 8.8 | 8.8 | 8.8 | 8.8 | 8.8 |
| Technical | C4.6 | | 91.2 | | 7.6 | 7.6 | 7.6 | 7.6 | 7.6 | 7.6 | 7.6 | 7.6 | 7.6 | 7.6 | 7.6 | 7.6 |
| Sales | C4.6 | | 212.6 | | 16.7 | 16.3 | 16.7 | 16.5 | 17.5 | 18.4 | 18.4 | 18.7 | 17.4 | 18.6 | 18.9 | 18.5 |
| Supervisory | C4.6 | | 164.5 | | 12.4 | 12.4 | 12.4 | 12.7 | 12.7 | 12.7 | 12.7 | 15.3 | 15.3 | 15.3 | 15.3 | 15.3 |
| Administration | C4.7 | | 73.2 | | 6.1 | 6.1 | 6.1 | 6.1 | 6.1 | 6.1 | 6.1 | 6.1 | 6.1 | 6.1 | 6.1 | 6.1 |
| Finance & costing | C4.7 | | 115.8 | | 9.2 | 9.2 | 9.2 | 9.2 | 9.2 | 9.2 | 10.1 | 10.1 | 10.1 | 10.1 | 10.1 | 10.1 |
| **Total payroll cost** | Memo | | 2,852.0 | | 227.1 | 219.1 | 226.4 | 228.6 | 248.6 | 261.0 | 243.0 | 249.3 | 221.8 | 240.9 | 246.5 | 239.8 |

# DEMO COMPANY BUDGET
## WORKING CAPITAL PQ$000

| | 20XX forecast | 20XY BUDGET | inc | 1 Apr | 2 May | 3 JUN | 4 Jul | 5 Aug | 6 SEP | 7 Oct | 8 Nov | 9 DEC | 10 Jan | 11 Feb | 12 MAR |
|---|---|---|---|---|---|---|---|---|---|---|---|---|---|---|---|
| Raw materials | 55 | 76 | 38% | 58.9 | 61.5 | 61.5 | 68.4 | 72.6 | 70.5 | 72.8 | 63.3 | 72.5 | 74.7 | 72.1 | 75.7 |
| Work in progress | 32 | 30 | -5% | 23.6 | 24.6 | 24.6 | 27.4 | 29.0 | 28.2 | 29.1 | 25.3 | 29.0 | 29.9 | 28.9 | 30.3 |
| Finished goods | 171 | 153 | -10% | 214.1 | 203.6 | 206.0 | 159.7 | 139.5 | 106.7 | 190.4 | 194.9 | 141.7 | 196.1 | 207.1 | 153.3 |
| Packaging | 12 | 12 | 0% | 12.0 | 12.0 | 12.0 | 12.0 | 12.0 | 12.0 | 12.0 | 12.0 | 12.0 | 12.0 | 12.0 | 12.0 |
| Inventory - at cost | 270 | 271 | 0% | 308.6 | 301.6 | 304.0 | 267.5 | 253.1 | 217.5 | 304.4 | 295.5 | 255.2 | 312.8 | 320.1 | 271.3 |
| Provision - damage  0.6% | (11) | (2) | -85% | (1.9) | (1.8) | (1.8) | (1.6) | (1.5) | (1.3) | (1.8) | (1.8) | (1.5) | (1.9) | (1.9) | (1.6) |
| INVENTORY  C4.3 | 259 | 270 | 4% | 306.7 | 299.8 | 302.2 | 265.9 | 251.6 | 216.2 | 302.6 | 293.7 | 253.7 | 310.9 | 318.2 | 269.7 |
| Receivables mth 1  30 | 444 | 500 | | 440.5 | 420.3 | 438.6 | 432.3 | 481.2 | 522.5 | 496.2 | 512.2 | 444.9 | 502.7 | 517.9 | 500.0 |
| Receivables mth 2  15 | 232 | 259 | | 220.4 | 220.3 | 210.2 | 219.3 | 216.2 | 240.6 | 261.3 | 248.1 | 256.1 | 222.5 | 251.4 | 259.0 |
| Receivables mth 3  5 | 65 | 84 | | 67.2 | 58.6 | 73.4 | 70.1 | 73.1 | 72.1 | 80.2 | 87.1 | 82.7 | 85.4 | 74.2 | 83.8 |
| Receivables  total | 741 | 843 | 14% | 728.1 | 699.2 | 722.2 | 721.7 | 770.5 | 835.2 | 837.7 | 847.4 | 783.7 | 810.5 | 843.4 | 842.7 |
| Sales tax  8.25% | 61 | 70 | 14% | 60.1 | 57.7 | 59.6 | 59.5 | 63.6 | 68.9 | 69.1 | 69.9 | 64.7 | 66.9 | 69.6 | 69.5 |
| Group trade balances | | 0 | na | | | | | | | | | | | | |
| Prepayments etc | 8 | 6 | -28% | 5.8 | 5.8 | 5.8 | 5.8 | 5.8 | 5.8 | 5.8 | 5.8 | 5.8 | 5.8 | 5.8 | 5.8 |
| Accrued income | | 0 | na | | | | | | | | | | | | |
| Receivables - book | 810 | 918 | 13% | 794.0 | 762.7 | 787.6 | 787.0 | 839.9 | 909.9 | 912.6 | 923.1 | 854.2 | 883.2 | 918.8 | 918.0 |
| Provision - returns  0.5% | (18) | (4) | -77% | (3.6) | (3.5) | (3.6) | (3.6) | (3.9) | (4.2) | (4.2) | (4.2) | (3.9) | (4.1) | (4.2) | (4.2) |
| Provision - bad debts  1.5% | (10) | (13) | 26% | (10.9) | (10.5) | (10.8) | (10.8) | (11.6) | (12.5) | (12.6) | (12.7) | (11.8) | (12.2) | (12.7) | (12.6) |
| RECEIVABLES  C4.3 | 782 | 901 | 15% | 779.5 | 748.7 | 773.2 | 772.6 | 824.4 | 893.2 | 895.8 | 906.2 | 838.5 | 866.9 | 901.9 | 901.2 |
| Direct materials | | | | 92.6 | 88.4 | 92.2 | 92.2 | 102.6 | 108.9 | 105.8 | 109.2 | 94.9 | 108.8 | 112.1 | 108.2 |
| Days purchases outstanding | | | | 25 | 25 | 25 | 25 | 25 | 25 | 25 | 25 | 25 | 25 | 25 | 25 |
| Payable for direct materials | 90 | | na | 77.2 | 73.7 | 76.8 | 76.8 | 85.5 | 90.8 | 88.2 | 91.0 | 79.1 | 90.7 | 93.4 | 90.2 |
| Overhead creditors | 10 | | na | 9.5 | 9.5 | 9.5 | 9.5 | 9.5 | 9.5 | 9.5 | 9.5 | 9.5 | 9.5 | 9.5 | 9.5 |
| Capex creditors  5 days | 10 | | na | 10.3 | 6.2 | 8.0 | 3.8 | 0.3 | 14.8 | 3.2 | 8.8 | 16.7 | 0.3 | 3.2 | 10.2 |
| Total purchases | 110 | | na | 97.0 | 89.3 | 94.3 | 90.2 | 95.3 | 115.1 | 100.8 | 109.3 | 105.3 | 100.5 | 106.1 | 109.8 |
| Sales tax  11.25% | 12 | | na | 10.9 | 10.1 | 10.6 | 10.1 | 10.7 | 12.9 | 11.3 | 12.3 | 11.8 | 11.3 | 11.9 | 12.4 |
| External trade payables | 181 | 122 | -32% | 107.9 | 99.4 | 104.9 | 100.3 | 106.1 | 128.0 | 112.2 | 121.6 | 117.1 | 111.8 | 118.0 | 122.2 |
| Group trade balances | 0 | 0 | na | | | | | | | | | | | | |
| Payroll deductions | 4 | 3 | -20% | 3.2 | 3.2 | 3.2 | 3.2 | 3.2 | 3.2 | 3.2 | 3.2 | 3.2 | 3.2 | 3.2 | 3.2 |
| Value added sales tax | 93 | 100 | 8% | 78.0 | 80.0 | 82.0 | 84.0 | 86.0 | 88.0 | 90.0 | 92.0 | 94.0 | 96.0 | 98.0 | 100.0 |
| Accruals | 23 | 12 | -48% | 12.0 | 12.0 | 12.0 | 12.0 | 12.0 | 12.0 | 12.0 | 12.0 | 12.0 | 12.0 | 12.0 | 12.0 |
| Deferred income | 0 | 0 | na | | | | | | | | | | | | |
| PAYABLES  C4.3 | 301 | 237 | | 201.1 | 194.6 | 202.1 | 199.5 | 207.3 | 231.2 | 217.4 | 228.8 | 226.3 | 223.0 | 231.2 | 237.4 |

| FIXED ASSETS | 20XX forecast | 20XY BUDGET | inc | 1 Apr | 2 May | 3 JUN | 4 Jul | 5 Aug | 6 SEP | 7 Oct | 8 Nov | 9 DEC | 10 Jan | 11 Feb | 12 MAR |
|---|---|---|---|---|---|---|---|---|---|---|---|---|---|---|---|
| **Vehicles** Additions CC3 | | | | | | | | | | | | | | | |
| Disposals neg | | | | | | | | | | | | | | | |
| pos | | 63.0 | | | 12.0 | | | | | | 51.0 | | | | |
| Cost | 227.3 | 279.9 | 23% | 227.3 | 228.9 | 228.9 | 228.9 | 228.9 | 228.9 | 228.9 | 279.9 | 279.9 | 279.9 | 279.9 | 279.9 |
| Disposals neg | | (10.4) | | | (10.4) | | | | | | | | | | | |
| pos | | 1.9 | | | 1.9 | | | | | | | | | | | |
| Charge | | (62.5) | 25.0% | (4.7) | (4.8) | (4.8) | (4.8) | (4.8) | (4.8) | (4.8) | (5.8) | (5.8) | (5.8) | (5.8) | (5.8) |
| Amortn | (104.8) | (165.4) | 58% | (109.5) | (112.4) | (117.2) | (122.0) | (126.8) | (131.6) | (136.4) | (142.2) | (148.0) | (153.8) | (159.6) | (165.4) |
| NBV | 122.5 | 114.5 | -7% | 117.8 | 116.5 | 111.7 | 106.9 | 102.1 | 97.3 | 92.5 | 137.7 | 131.9 | 126.1 | 120.3 | 114.5 |
| **Equip't** Additions CC3 | | 380.0 | | 62.0 | 25.0 | 48.0 | 23.0 | 2.0 | 34.0 | 2.0 | 2.0 | 100.0 | 2.0 | 19.0 | 61.0 |
| Disposals neg | | (28.3) | | (6.0) | | (8.1) | | | | | | (14.2) | | | |
| pos | | | | | | | | | | | | | | | |
| Cost | 606.0 | 957.7 | 58% | 662.0 | 687.0 | 726.9 | 749.9 | 751.9 | 785.9 | 787.9 | 789.9 | 875.7 | 877.7 | 896.7 | 957.7 |
| Disposals neg | | | | | | | | | | | | | | | | |
| pos | | 8.1 | | 6.0 | | 0.4 | | | | | | 1.7 | | | |
| Charge | | (79.6) | 10.0% | (5.5) | (5.7) | (6.1) | (6.2) | (6.3) | (6.5) | (6.6) | (6.6) | (7.3) | (7.3) | (7.5) | (8.0) |
| Amortn | (168.9) | (240.4) | 42% | (168.4) | (174.1) | (179.8) | (186.0) | (192.3) | (198.8) | (205.4) | (212.0) | (217.6) | (224.9) | (232.4) | (240.4) |
| NBV | 437.1 | 717.3 | 64% | 493.6 | 512.9 | 547.1 | 563.9 | 559.6 | 587.1 | 582.5 | 577.9 | 658.1 | 652.8 | 664.3 | 717.3 |
| **IT sys** Additions CC3 | | 35.0 | | | | | | | 35.0 | | | | | | |
| Disposals neg | | 0.0 | | | | | | | | | | | | | |
| pos | | | | | | | | | | | | | | | |
| Cost | 606.0 | 641.0 | 6% | 606.0 | 606.0 | 606.0 | 606.0 | 606.0 | 641.0 | 641.0 | 641.0 | 641.0 | 641.0 | 641.0 | 641.0 |
| Disposals neg | | | | | | | | | | | | | | | | |
| pos | | 0.0 | | | | | | | | | | | | | |
| Charge | | (156.8) | 25.0% | (12.6) | (12.6) | (12.6) | (12.6) | (12.6) | (13.4) | (13.4) | (13.4) | (13.4) | (13.4) | (13.4) | (13.4) |
| Amortn | (168.9) | (325.7) | 93% | (181.5) | (194.1) | (206.7) | (219.3) | (231.9) | (245.3) | (258.7) | (272.1) | (285.5) | (298.9) | (312.3) | (325.7) |
| NBV | 437.1 | 315.3 | -28% | 424.5 | 411.9 | 399.3 | 386.7 | 374.1 | 395.7 | 382.3 | 368.9 | 355.5 | 342.1 | 328.7 | 315.3 |
| **Property** Additions | | 37.0 | | | | | | | 20.0 | 17.0 | | | | | |
| Disposals neg | | 0.0 | | | | | | | | | | | | | |
| pos | | | | | | | | | | | | | | | |
| Cost | 606.0 | 643.0 | 6% | 606.0 | 606.0 | 606.0 | 606.0 | 606.0 | 626.0 | 643.0 | 643.0 | 643.0 | 643.0 | 643.0 | 643.0 |
| Disposals neg | | | | | | | | | | | | | | | | |
| pos | | 0.0 | | | | | | | | | | | | | |
| Charge | | (24.7) | 4.0% | (2.0) | (2.0) | (2.0) | (2.0) | (2.0) | (2.1) | (2.1) | (2.1) | (2.1) | (2.1) | (2.1) | (2.1) |
| Amortn | (168.9) | (193.6) | 15% | (170.9) | (172.9) | (174.9) | (176.9) | (178.9) | (181.0) | (183.1) | (185.2) | (187.3) | (189.4) | (191.5) | (193.6) |
| NBV | 437.1 | 449.4 | 3% | 435.1 | 433.1 | 431.1 | 429.1 | 427.1 | 445.0 | 459.9 | 457.8 | 455.7 | 453.6 | 451.5 | 449.4 |
| **Intangbl** Additions | | 0.0 | | | | | | | | | | | | | |
| Disposals neg | | 0.0 | | | | | | | | | | | | | |
| pos | | | | | | | | | | | | | | | |
| Cost | 606.0 | 606.0 | 0% | 606.0 | 606.0 | 606.0 | 606.0 | 606.0 | 606.0 | 606.0 | 606.0 | 606.0 | 606.0 | 606.0 | 606.0 |
| Disposals neg | | | | | | | | | | | | | | | | |
| pos | | 0.0 | | | | | | | | | | | | | |
| Charge | | (50.4) | 8.33% | (4.2) | (4.2) | (4.2) | (4.2) | (4.2) | (4.2) | (4.2) | (4.2) | (4.2) | (4.2) | (4.2) | (4.2) |
| Amortn | (168.9) | (219.3) | 30% | (173.1) | (177.3) | (181.5) | (185.7) | (189.9) | (194.1) | (198.3) | (202.5) | (206.7) | (210.9) | (215.1) | (219.3) |
| NBV | 437.1 | 386.7 | -12% | 432.9 | 428.7 | 424.5 | 420.3 | 416.1 | 411.9 | 407.7 | 403.5 | 399.3 | 395.1 | 390.9 | 386.7 |
| **TOTAL** Cost | 2,651.3 | 3,127.6 | 6% | 2,707.3 | 2,733.9 | 2,773.8 | 2,796.8 | 2,798.8 | 2,887.8 | 2,906.8 | 2,959.8 | 3,045.6 | 3,047.6 | 3,066.6 | 3,127.6 |
| Amortn | (780.4) | (1,144.4) | | (803.4) | (830.8) | (860.1) | (889.9) | (919.8) | (950.8) | (981.9) | (1,014.0) | (1,045.1) | (1,077.9) | (1,110.9) | (1,144.4) |
| NET BOOK VALUE  C4.3 | 1,870.9 | 1,983.2 | 6% | 1,903.9 | 1,903.1 | 1,913.7 | 1,906.9 | 1,879.0 | 1,937.0 | 1,924.9 | 1,945.8 | 2,000.5 | 1,969.7 | 1,955.7 | 1,983.2 |
| AMORTN CHARGE  C4.2 | 342.0 | 374.0 | 9% | 29.0 | 29.3 | 29.7 | 29.8 | 29.9 | 31.0 | 31.1 | 32.1 | 32.8 | 32.8 | 33.0 | 33.5 |

| DEMO COMPANY BUDGET FINANCE PQ$000 | | 20XX forecast | 20XY BUDGET | inc | 1 Apr | 2 May | 3 JUN | 4 Jul | 5 Aug | 6 SEP | 7 Oct | 8 Nov | 9 DEC | 10 Jan | 11 Feb | 12 MAR |
|---|---|---|---|---|---|---|---|---|---|---|---|---|---|---|---|---|
| Facility | | 1,500 | 1,500 | 0% | 1,500 | 1,500 | 1,500 | 1,500 | 1,500 | 1,500 | 1,500 | 1,500 | 1,500 | 1,500 | 1,500 | 1,500 |
| Headroom | | (209) | (97) | -54% | (27) | (339) | (287) | (182) | (169) | (167) | (50) | (66) | (114) | (44) | (56) | (97) |
| **OVERDRAFTS** | **C4.3** | **1,291** | **1,403** | **9%** | **1,472.9** | **1,160.6** | **1,212.9** | **1,318.2** | **1,331.2** | **1,333.5** | **1,449.8** | **1,434.2** | **1,386.1** | **1,455.9** | **1,443.5** | **1,402.9** |
| Hire purchase | | 47 | 28 | -40% | 43 | 39 | 35 | 31 | 27 | 58 | 53 | 48 | 43 | 38 | 33 | 28 |
| Finance leases | | - | 0 | na | - | - | - | - | - | - | - | - | - | - | - | - |
| **HP & FIN LEASES** | **C4.3** | **47** | **28** | **-40%** | **43.0** | **39.0** | **35.0** | **31.0** | **27.0** | **58.0** | **53.0** | **48.0** | **43.0** | **38.0** | **33.0** | **28.0** |
| Bank loans | | 0 | 0 | na | - | - | - | - | - | - | - | - | - | - | - | - |
| Trade authority loans | | 280 | 124 | -56% | 267.0 | 254.0 | 241.0 | 228.0 | 215.0 | 202.0 | 189.0 | 176.0 | 163.0 | 150.0 | 137.0 | 124.0 |
| **LOANS** | **C4.3** | **280** | **124** | **-56%** | **267.0** | **254.0** | **241.0** | **228.0** | **215.0** | **202.0** | **189.0** | **176.0** | **163.0** | **150.0** | **137.0** | **124.0** |
| Grants received | | 124 | 124 | 0% | 124.0 | 124.0 | 124.0 | 124.0 | 124.0 | 124.0 | 124.0 | 124.0 | 124.0 | 124.0 | 124.0 | 124.0 |
| Amortisation | | (80) | (124) | 55% | (84.0) | (88.0) | (92.0) | (96.0) | (100.0) | (104.0) | (108.0) | (112.0) | (116.0) | (120.0) | (124.0) | (124.0) |
| **CAPITAL GRANTS** | **C4.3** | **44** | **0** | **-100%** | **40.0** | **36.0** | **32.0** | **28.0** | **24.0** | **20.0** | **16.0** | **12.0** | **8.0** | **4.0** | **0.0** | **0.0** |
| Opening balance | | 143 | 154 | 8% | 154.0 | 157.9 | 165.1 | 164.8 | 85.4 | 87.7 | 99.5 | 69.0 | 80.2 | 84.7 | 57.4 | 69.9 |
| Tax on result | 23.0% | 154 | 77 | -50% | 3.9 | 7.2 | (0.3) | (2.4) | 2.3 | 11.8 | 8.0 | 11.2 | 4.5 | 11.2 | 12.5 | 7.1 |
| Tax (paid)/ refunded | | (143) | (154) | 8% | - | - | - | (77.0) | - | - | (38.5) | - | - | (38.5) | - | - |
| **TAX PAYABLE** | **C4.3** | **154** | **77** | **-50%** | **157.9** | **165.1** | **164.8** | **85.4** | **87.7** | **99.5** | **69.0** | **80.2** | **84.7** | **57.4** | **69.9** | **77.0** |
| Opening balance | | 27 | 38 | 41% | 38.0 | 41.5 | 45.0 | 48.5 | 14.0 | 17.5 | 21.0 | 24.5 | 28.0 | 31.5 | 35.0 | 38.5 |
| Dividends declared | | 38 | 42 | 11% | 3.5 | 3.5 | 3.5 | 3.5 | 3.5 | 3.5 | 3.5 | 3.5 | 3.5 | 3.5 | 3.5 | 3.5 |
| Dividends paid | | (27) | (38) | 41% | - | - | - | (38.0) | - | - | - | - | - | - | - | - |
| **DIVS PAYABLE** | **C4.3** | **38** | **42** | **11%** | **41.5** | **45.0** | **48.5** | **14.0** | **17.5** | **21.0** | **24.5** | **28.0** | **31.5** | **35.0** | **38.5** | **42.0** |
| Ordinary shares | | 100 | 400 | 300% | 100.0 | 400.0 | 400.0 | 400.0 | 400.0 | 400.0 | 400.0 | 400.0 | 400.0 | 400.0 | 400.0 | 400.0 |
| Preference shares (redeemed) | | 30 | 0 | -100% | 30.0 | - | - | - | - | - | - | - | - | - | - | - |
| **SHARE CAPITAL** | **C4.3** | **130** | **400** | **208%** | **130.0** | **400.0** | **400.0** | **400.0** | **400.0** | **400.0** | **400.0** | **400.0** | **400.0** | **400.0** | **400.0** | **400.0** |
| Ordinary shares | | 400 | 400 | 0% | 400.0 | 400.0 | 400.0 | 400.0 | 400.0 | 400.0 | 400.0 | 400.0 | 400.0 | 400.0 | 400.0 | 400.0 |
| Preferences shares | | 0 | 0 | na | - | - | - | - | - | - | - | - | - | - | - | - |
| **SHARE PREMIUM** | **C4.3** | **400** | **400** | **0%** | **400.0** | **400.0** | **400.0** | **400.0** | **400.0** | **400.0** | **400.0** | **400.0** | **400.0** | **400.0** | **400.0** | **400.0** |
| PRIOR YR PROFIT | C4.3 | 627 | | | | | | | | | | | | | | |

**MONTHLY REPORT STRUCTURE - a schematic view of how to build a powerful suite of monthly financial reports using an MS Excel spreadsheet**

| Accounting period | 3 |
| --- | --- |

| General ledger accounts | | Analysis |
| --- | --- | --- |
| Codes | Headings | codes |
| 001001 | | IRMC |
| 001002 | | IRMP |
| 002006 | | |
| 002007 | | |
| etc | | |

| Lookup values for current period - units 1,000 | | | |
| --- | --- | --- | --- |
| Opening | Prior Period | This Period | Cumulative |
| General ledger balances for specific periods using period number and lookup formula  Recommend round to 000 or 000.0 | | | |
| Totals to equal 0 | | | |
| Non-financial figures for specific periods using lookup formula as above | | | |
| Summaries collected in required format using 4-letter codes and SUMIF formula (examples shown on left) | | | |
| Figures used for management reports as required on subsequent sheets | | | |

| General ledger cumulative balances - units 1.00 | | | | |
| --- | --- | --- | --- | --- |
| Opening | Periods | | Pre-audit | Final |
| 0 | 1 2 3 4 5 6 7 8 9 10 11 12 | | 13 | 14 |
| | General ledger cumulative balances for each period  Use system facility to download into spreadsheet  Download first on to separate sheet in same file  Check alignment with accounts codes  Then copy cumulative values into column for this period | | For adjustments  Same process | |
| | Totals to equal 0 | | | |
| | Non-financial figures entered manually (eg sales volumes, exchange rates, personnel numbers) | | | |
| | Summaries collected in required format for trend analysis | | | |

| | |
| --- | --- |
| Raw material cost | IRMC |
| Raw material provisions | IRMP |
| Work in progress cost | IWPC |
| Work in progress provisions | IWPP |
| Finished goods cost | IFGC |
| Finished goods provisions | IFGP |

*The above layout is highly flexible, allowing insertion of rows to accommodate new general ledger codes*
*Even if the general layout is highly unsuitable, the information can be summarised in a format which feeds the management reports directly*
*Where a high volume of analysis is required, additional columns of analysis codes can be used (eg to differentiate market sectors or production lines)*
*The reports can be designed to draw from the period and cumulative columns for current period figures*
*The reports can also provide trend analysis by linking with the period columns*
*Non-financial measures are easily obtained by linking the reports with the statistical information entered directly below the ledger download*
*That gives powerful information such as average prices, output per person etc and enables useful automatic variance analysis*
*The budget should be entered as a separate sheet in similar format, derived from your budget model*

## OPERATING RESULT

| | | June 20XX Period | | | June 20XX Cum've | | |
|---|---|---|---|---|---|---|---|
| | | Budget | ACTUAL | Variance | Budget | ACTUAL | Variance |
| Sales volume - units | | u 1,174 | u 1,161 | u (13) | u 3,478 | u 3,553 | u 75 |
| | | | | | | | |
| SALES VALUE | | 438.6 | 421.7 | (16.9) | 1,299.4 | 1,323.6 | 24.2 |
| Average sale price per unit | | $374 | $363 | $(10) | $374 | $373 | $(1) |
| | | | | | | | |
| Direct materials | | (92.2) | (93.7) | (1.5) | (273.2) | (276.4) | (3.2) |
| Average material price per unit | | $(79) | $(81) | $(2) | $(79) | $(78) | $1 |
| Value added | | 346.4 | 328.0 | (18.4) | 1,026.2 | 1,047.2 | 21.0 |
| Average value added per unit | | $295 | $283 | $(13) | $295 | $295 | $(0) |
| | % | 79.0% | 77.8% | -1.2% | 79.0% | 79.1% | 0.1% |
| Direct labour | | (165.6) | (168.4) | (2.8) | (490.5) | (499.6) | (9.1) |
| Marketing and selling | | (53.1) | (55.5) | (2.4) | (160.9) | (167.8) | (6.9) |
| GROSS MARGIN | | 127.7 | 104.1 | (23.6) | 374.7 | 379.8 | 5.1 |
| Average gross margin per unit | | $109 | $90 | $(19) | $108 | $107 | $(1) |
| | % | 29.1% | 24.7% | -4.4% | 28.8% | 28.7% | -0.1% |
| Factory overhead | | (38.9) | (36.5) | 2.4 | (93.4) | (118.2) | (24.8) |
| Factory margin | | 88.8 | 67.6 | (21.2) | 281.3 | 261.6 | (19.7) |
| Average net contribution per unit | | $76 | $58 | $(17) | $81 | $74 | $(7) |
| | % | 20.3% | 16.0% | -4.2% | 21.7% | 19.8% | -1.9% |
| Administration | | (34.7) | (33.5) | 1.2 | (104.1) | (102.4) | 1.7 |
| Establishment | | (15.6) | (15.4) | 0.2 | (44.0) | (44.9) | (0.9) |
| Asset amortisation | | (29.7) | (29.8) | (0.1) | (88.0) | (89.7) | (1.7) |
| OPERATING PROFIT | | 8.8 | (11.1) | (19.9) | 45.2 | 24.6 | (20.6) |
| | % | 2.0% | -2.6% | -4.6% | 3.5% | 1.9% | -1.6% |
| Non-operating items | | (6.5) | (7.7) | (1.2) | 14.4 | 16.2 | 1.8 |
| Finance | | (3.7) | (3.7) | - | (12.6) | (11.7) | 0.9 |
| PROFIT BEFORE TAX | | (1.4) | (22.5) | (21.1) | 47.0 | 29.1 | (17.9) |
| | % | -0.3% | -5.3% | -5.0% | 3.6% | 2.2% | -1.4% |
| Taxation | | 0.3 | 6.6 | 6.3 | (10.8) | (5.2) | 5.6 |
| Profit after tax | | (1.0) | (15.9) | (14.9) | 36.2 | 23.9 | (12.3) |
| Provision for dividend | | (3.5) | (3.6) | (0.0) | (10.5) | (10.6) | (0.1) |
| Retained profit | | (4.5) | (19.5) | (14.9) | 25.7 | 13.4 | (12.4) |
| | | | | | | | |
| Fixed asset disposals | | (7.7) | - | 7.7 | 10.8 | 14.2 | 3.4 |
| Grants amortised | | 4.0 | (5.0) | (9.0) | 12.0 | 3.0 | (9.0) |
| Forex gains/ (losses) | | - | (5.0) | (5.0) | - | (7.3) | (7.3) |
| Exceptional Items | | - | - | - | - | - | - |
| General provision | | (2.8) | - | 2.8 | (8.4) | 4.0 | 12.4 |
| Non-operating items | | (6.5) | (10.0) | (3.5) | 14.4 | 13.9 | (0.5) |

*The figures in light print (unit values and percentages against sales) are as important as the monetary figures*
*They give an immediate indication of the reasons for the variances - see Appendix C7 for further analysis*

*Note that gross margin and profit before tax are given greater emphasis than sales*
*This is because they are far more important in considering the business's performance - see 3.1c*

*If there are large provision movements, consider highlighting them separately as non-operating items*

*It is also informative to present the actual results in a landscape 12-month columnar format*
*This highlights the trends - for example, the June result differs greatly from the overall performance . . . why?*

## June 20XX

| | | Result Budget | Actual | VARIANCE | VARIANCES Volume | Price | Other |
|---|---|---|---|---|---|---|---|
| Sales volume | units | u 1,174 | u 1,161 | u (13) | -1.1% | | |
| Sales value | PQ$000 | 438.6 | 421.7 | (16.9) | (4.9) | (12.0) | |
| Price per unit | PQ$ | $373.59 | $363.22 | $(10.37) | -1.1% | -2.7% | |
| Materials | PQ$000 | (92.2) | (93.7) | (1.5) | 1.0 | (2.5) | |
| Cost per unit | PQ$ | $(78.53) | $(80.71) | $(2.17) | -1.1% | 2.7% | |
| Val added per unit | PQ$ | $295.06 | $282.52 | $(12.54) | | -4.3% | |
| | | 79.0% | 77.8% | -1.2% | | | |
| Direct labour | PQ$000 | (165.6) | (168.4) | (2.8) | 1.8 | (4.7) | |
| Marketing & selling | PQ$000 | (53.1) | (55.5) | (2.4) | | | (2.4) |
| Gross margin | PQ$000 | 127.7 | 104.1 | (23.6) | (2.0) | (19.2) | (2.4) |
| Margin per unit | PQ$ | $108.81 | $89.66 | $(19.14) | | | |
| | | 29.1% | 24.7% | -4.4% | | | |
| Other overhead | PQ$000 | (118.9) | (115.2) | 3.7 | | | 3.7 |
| Operating profit | PQ$000 | 8.8 | (11.1) | (19.9) | (2.0) | (19.2) | 1.3 |

### SALES VOLUME VARIANCE  -1.1%  (4.9)
1. Cut-back on order levels from Krakowiecz (4.8)
2. Delayed shipment to Dynaflex (3.7)
3. Unbudgeted new customer - Lauwerier BV 4.8
Other variances [this is the balancing figure on each section] (1.2)

### SALES PRICE VARIANCE  -2.7%  (12.0)
1. Refund to Fliegertech for damage in transit (7.2)
2. Discount on Norfolk militray contract (first consignment only) (2.6)
3.
Other variances (2.2)

### MATERIALS VOLUME VARIANCE  -1.1%  1.0
1. Use of automatic beveller on lines 2, 3 & 4 - scrap reduction 2.3
2. Re-work on Hannibal Mk 2 (0.9)
Other variances (0.4)

### MATERIALS PRICE VARIANCE  2.7%  (2.5)
1. Change of nickel supplier to Fresno Industries 3.1
2. Movement in exchange rates on CHF & SGD (1.4)
3. Increase in polymer prices worldwide (3.0)
Other variances (1.2)

### DIRECT LABOUR VARIANCE  1.8  (4.7)
1. Fewer temporary workers used 1.4
2. Overtime to make-up breakdown time on line 1 (3.6)
3.
Other variances 0.4 (1.1)

### OVERHEAD VARIANCE  3.7
1. Reduced maintenance resulting from installation of rev counters 1.6
2. Reduced management travel 2.2
3. Unbudgeted repair to no 2 store (0.9)
Other variances 0.8

*If you do not have a standard costing system, you should create a simple, effective variance analysis*
*You MUST have a meaningful volume measurement, even if it is only hours charged, miles travelled etc*

| CAPITAL EMPLOYED PQ$000 | Opening Actual | Prior Per Actual | CURRENT PERIOD Budget | CURRENT PERIOD ACTUAL | CURRENT PERIOD Variance | CASH FLOW ACTUAL Period | CASH FLOW ACTUAL Cum've | P | COMMENTS |
|---|---|---|---|---|---|---|---|---|---|
| Inventory | 270 | 282 | 304 | 361 | (57) | (79) | (91) | | Cash flow is normally reported in the format of Appendix C9 |
| Trade acs receivable | 802 | 707 | 782 | 754 | 28 | (47) | 48 | | However, this layout is easier for non-financial managers |
| Prepayments etc | 8 | 9 | 6 | 7 | (1) | 2 | 1 | | It does cut a few corners, but not materially |
| Current assets | 1,080 | 998 | 1,092 | 1,122 | (30) | (124) | (42) | | Current assets are shown gross (provisions deducted below) |
| Trade acs payable | (181) | (121) | (105) | (141) | 36 | 20 | (40) | | Always adjust your budgeted opening balance sheet |
| Payroll deductions | (4) | (5) | (3) | (7) | 4 | 2 | 3 | | to the actual opening balance sheet |
| Sales tax | (93) | (77) | (82) | (95) | 13 | 18 | 2 | | to enable automatic cash flow comparison with budget |
| Accruals etc | (23) | (17) | (12) | (16) | 4 | (1) | (7) | | This has been assumed here |
| Current liabilities | (301) | (220) | (202) | (259) | 57 | 39 | (42) | | |
| WORKING CAPITAL | 779 | 778 | 889 | 863 | 26 | (85) | (84) | | Gross working capital change, indicating cash movement |
| Inventory | (11) | (5) | (2) | (4) | 2 | | | P | Movement in provisions included in profit movement |
| Receivables | (28) | (19) | (14) | (18) | 4 | | | P | Movement in provisions included in profit movement |
| PROVISIONS | (39) | (24) | (16) | (23) | 6 | (2) | (17) | | |
| Cost | 2,651 | 2,741 | 2,774 | 2,789 | (15) | (49) | (138) | P | Movement in amortisation included in profit movement |
| Amortisation | (780) | (833) | (860) | (881) | 21 | | | | |
| FIXED ASSETS | 1,871 | 1,908 | 1,914 | 1,908 | 6 | | | | |
| NET OP'ING ASSETS | 2,611 | 2,661 | 2,787 | 2,749 | 38 | | | | Net operating assets are the substance of the business |
| Overdrafts | 1,291 | 1,086 | 1,213 | 1,145 | 68 | 35 | 27 | | |
| HP & finance leases | 47 | 39 | 35 | 74 | (39) | (13) | (39) | | |
| Loans | 280 | 254 | 241 | 241 | - | | | | |
| Capital grants | 44 | 36 | 32 | 32 | - | | | P | |
| Taxation payable | 154 | 161 | 165 | 171 | (6) | 10 | 17 | | |
| Dividends payable | 38 | 45 | 49 | 49 | - | 4 | 11 | | |
| DEBT | 1,854 | 1,621 | 1,734 | 1,712 | 23 | 36 | 16 | | |
| Share capital - ord | 100 | 400 | 400 | 400 | - | - | 300 | | |
| Share capital - pref | 30 | - | - | - | - | - | (30) | | |
| Profit | 627 | 640 | 653 | 637 | 16 | 39 | 82 | P | Total adjusted for provision movements and amortisation |
| EQUITY | 757 | 1,040 | 1,053 | 1,037 | 16 | 39 | 352 | | This format does not identify disposal gains or losses |
| | | | | | | | | | Capital employed finances the net operating assets |
| CAPITAL EMPLOYED | 2,611 | 2,661 | 2,787 | 2,749 | 38 | (59) | 146 | | This equals the movements in the "Overdrafts" row |

CASH FLOW

# DEMO COMPANY BUDGET
## CASH FLOW — PQ$000

| | PERIOD | | | CUMULATIVE | | |
|---|---|---|---|---|---|---|
| | Budget | Actual | Variance | Budget | Actual | Variance |
| **PROFIT BEFORE TAXATION** | (1.4) | (22.5) | (21.1) | 47 | 29 | (18) |
| Fixed asset disposals | 7.7 | 28.7 | 21.0 | (11) | (4) | 7 |
| Provisions - inventory | - | (0.7) | (0.7) | (9) | (7) | 2 |
| Provisions - receivables | 0.4 | (1.1) | (1.5) | (14) | (10) | 4 |
| Amortisation of fixed assets | 29.7 | 52.0 | 22.3 | 88 | 113 | 25 |
| Amortisation of grants | (4.0) | (4.0) | - | (12) | (12) | - |
| **Adjusted profit** | 32.4 | 52.4 | 20.0 | 89 | 110 | 20 |
| Inventory | (2.4) | (79.0) | (76.6) | (34) | (91) | (57) |
| Trade accounts receivable | (24.9) | (45.0) | (20.1) | 23 | 49 | 27 |
| Trade accounts payable | 7.6 | 39.0 | 31.4 | (99) | (42) | 57 |
| **Working capital movement** | (19.8) | (85.0) | (65.2) | (110) | (84) | 26 |
| **OPERATING CASH FLOW** | 12.7 | (32.6) | (45.3) | (21) | 26 | 47 |
| Assets acquired    tangible | (48.0) | (56.1) | (8.1) | (147) | (148) | (1) |
| intangible | | | | | | |
| Assets sold    both | - | 7.6 | 7.6 | 27 | 11 | (17) |
| Capital grants | | | | | | |
| HP & finance leases | (4.0) | 35.0 | 39.0 | (12) | 27 | 39 |
| Loans | (13.0) | (13.0) | - | (39) | (39) | - |
| Shares issued/ (redeemed) | - | - | - | 270 | 270 | - |
| Taxation | - | - | - | - | - | - |
| Dividends | - | - | - | - | - | - |
| **OTHER CASH FLOW** | (65.0) | (26.5) | 38.5 | 99 | 120 | 21 |
| **NET CASH FLOW** | (52.3) | (59.1) | (6.8) | 78 | 146 | 68 |
| Opening bank balance | (1,160.6) | (1,086.1) | 74.5 | (1,291) | (1,291) | - |
| **CLOSING BANK BALANCE** | (1,212.9) | (1,145.2) | 67.8 | (1,213) | (1,145) | 68 |

Printed  16:44  03-Jul-20XX

## COMMENTS

*Reporting in landscape format offers several advantages:*
1. *It enables commentary directly alongside the figures*
2. *It greatly reduces narrative report compilation time*
3. *It enables easy replication of prior period comments*
4. *It does not require a high level of reporting skill*

*The actual cash flow, profit and capital employed should also be presented in a month-by-month layout (identical to the budget layout in C4.2, C4.3 and C4.4) so that trends are clearly highlit*

*How detailed should the figures be?*
*A good rule of thumb is that they should be to 3 digits, (except for the overall totals, which could run to 4 digits)*

*3 digits are sufficient to give meaningful comparison, and yet still be easily assimilated mentally*

# MANAGERS' COMMITMENTS                    APPENDIX C10

**Manager** _____    **Department** _____

The information below is required by the finance department by: | **[date]** |

If you have committed the company to costs during this month, and these costs have not yet been invoiced to us, we need to accrue an estimate of these costs, so that our monthly financial result is realistic.

Please would you therefore note any commitments you have made this month which have not yet been invoiced, and submit this to the financial controller by the date shown above. A reasonably accurate round-sum estimate will suffice if you do not know the exact cost. Ignore items costing less than £500, unless they are part of a larger cost item. If you have no costs accrued, please enter "NIL" in the cost column.

DEVELOPMENT PROJECTS                                          Cost UK£

_____    _____
_____    _____
_____    _____
_____    _____
_____    _____

EXTERNAL SERVICES (professional, technical etc)              Cost UK£

_____    _____
_____    _____
_____    _____
_____    _____
_____    _____
_____    _____

ABNORMAL PURCHASES (capital expenditure and other one-off items)   Cost UK£

_____    _____
_____    _____
_____    _____
_____    _____
_____    _____

OTHER EXTERNAL COSTS (eg travel, accommodation)             Cost UK£

_____    _____
_____    _____
_____    _____
_____    _____
_____    _____

OTHER INTERNAL COSTS (eg staff overtime etc)                Cost UK£

_____    _____
_____    _____

**BUDGET**

| | Prior Year | Q1 | | | Q2 | | | Q3 | | | Q4 | | | TOTAL YEAR 1 | % | TOTAL YEAR 2 |
|---|---|---|---|---|---|---|---|---|---|---|---|---|---|---|---|---|
| | Mar-XX | Apr-XX | May-XX | Jun-XX | Jul-XX | Aug-XX | Sep-XX | Oct-XX | Nov-XX | Dec-XX | Jan-XY | Feb-XY | Mar-XY | | | |
| Net sales | - | - | - | - | 16.9 | 20.3 | 25.3 | 15.2 | 8.4 | 33.4 | 50.2 | 66.7 | 83.4 | 319.8 | 193% | 937.7 |
| Direct materials | - | - | - | - | (6.3) | (7.6) | (9.5) | (5.7) | (3.1) | (12.6) | (18.8) | (25.0) | (31.3) | (119.8) | -194% | (352.1) |
| Gross margin | - | - | - | - | 10.6 | 12.7 | 15.8 | 9.5 | 5.3 | 20.8 | 31.4 | 41.7 | 52.1 | 199.9 | 193% | 585.6 |
| | - | - | - | - | 62.7% | 62.6% | 62.5% | 62.5% | 63.1% | 62.3% | 62.5% | 62.5% | 62.5% | 62.5% | | 62.5% |
| Other direct costs | - | - | (0.7) | - | (1.8) | (5.2) | (5.9) | (4.7) | (0.9) | (3.7) | (5.5) | (7.2) | (9.1) | (44.7) | -162% | (117.1) |
| Logistics | - | - | - | - | (1.0) | (1.2) | (1.5) | (0.9) | (0.5) | (2.0) | (3.0) | (4.0) | (5.0) | (19.1) | -196% | (56.6) |
| Other operating costs | - | - | - | - | (11.0) | (11.0) | (11.0) | (11.6) | (11.6) | (11.6) | (11.6) | (11.6) | (11.6) | (102.7) | -66% | (170.0) |
| Non-operating items | - | - | (1.7) | (11.0) | (3.5) | - | - | - | - | - | - | - | - | (16.2) | 7% | (15.0) |
| Interest | - | - | - | - | (0.1) | (0.1) | (0.2) | (0.2) | (0.2) | (0.3) | (0.3) | (0.3) | (0.2) | (1.9) | 47% | (1.0) |
| **BUDGETED RESULT** | 0.0 | 0.0 | (2.4) | (11.0) | (6.8) | (4.8) | (2.8) | (7.9) | (7.9) | 3.2 | 11.0 | 18.6 | 26.2 | 16.3 | 1372% | 226.9 |
| Inventory | - | - | - | 12.6 | 15.2 | 19.0 | 17.1 | 12.4 | 25.2 | 37.6 | 50.0 | 62.6 | 70.0 | 70.0 | | 70.0 |
| Receivables | - | - | - | - | - | - | - | - | - | - | - | - | - | | | |
| Payables | - | - | - | (11.4) | (10.6) | (12.4) | (11.9) | (6.1) | (10.1) | (20.9) | (28.2) | (35.5) | (40.3) | (40.3) | (1.6) | (38.7) |
| Working capital | - | - | - | 1.2 | 4.6 | 6.6 | 5.2 | 6.3 | 15.1 | 16.7 | 21.8 | 27.1 | 29.7 | 29.7 | (1.6) | 31.3 |
| Fixed assets | - | - | - | - | - | - | - | - | - | - | - | - | - | | | |
| **BUDGETED NET ASSETS** | 0.0 | 0.0 | - | 1.2 | 4.6 | 6.6 | 5.2 | 6.3 | 15.1 | 16.7 | 21.8 | 27.1 | 29.7 | 29.7 | | 31.3 |
| Borrowings | - | - | - | 14.6 | 24.8 | 31.6 | 33.0 | 42.0 | 58.8 | 57.2 | 51.3 | 38.0 | 14.4 | 14.4 | 224.3 | (209.9) |
| Equity | - | - | - | (13.4) | (20.2) | (25.0) | (27.8) | (35.7) | (43.7) | (40.5) | (29.5) | (10.9) | 15.3 | 15.3 | (225.9) | 241.2 |
| **BUDGETED PROJECT CAPITAL** | 0.0 | 0.0 | - | 1.2 | 4.6 | 6.6 | 5.2 | 6.3 | 15.1 | 16.7 | 21.8 | 27.1 | 29.7 | 29.7 | | 31.3 |

**ACTUAL**

| | Prior Year | Q1 | | | Q2 | | | Q3 | | | Q4 | | | TOTAL YEAR 1 | % | TOTAL YEAR 2 |
|---|---|---|---|---|---|---|---|---|---|---|---|---|---|---|---|---|
| | Mar-XX | Apr-XX | May-XX | Jun-XX | Jul-XX | Aug-XX | Sep-XX | Oct-XX | Nov-XX | Dec-XX | Jan-XY | Feb-XY | Mar-XY | | | |
| Net sales | - | - | - | - | 14.8 | 25.2 | 29.8 | 0.0 | 0.0 | 0.0 | 0.0 | 0.0 | 0.0 | 69.8 | | 0.0 |
| Direct materials | - | - | - | - | (5.4) | (8.8) | (10.2) | - | - | - | - | - | - | (24.4) | | 0.0 |
| Gross margin | - | - | - | - | 9.4 | 16.4 | 19.6 | 0.0 | 0.0 | 0.0 | 0.0 | 0.0 | 0.0 | 45.4 | | 0.0 |
| | - | - | - | - | 63.5% | 65.1% | 65.8% | - | - | - | - | - | - | 65.0% | | |
| Other direct costs | - | - | - | - | (5.0) | (6.9) | (6.9) | - | - | - | - | - | - | (18.8) | | 0.0 |
| Logistics | - | - | - | - | (0.2) | (0.9) | (1.1) | - | - | - | - | - | - | (2.2) | | 0.0 |
| Other operating costs | - | - | - | - | (5.3) | (5.2) | - | - | - | - | - | - | - | (10.5) | | 0.0 |
| Non-operating items | - | - | - | - | - | (0.3) | (9.3) | - | - | - | - | - | - | (9.6) | | 0.0 |
| Interest | - | - | - | - | - | - | - | - | - | - | - | - | - | | | |
| **PROJECT RESULT** | 0.0 | 0.0 | 0.0 | 0.0 | (1.1) | 3.1 | 2.3 | 0.0 | 0.0 | 0.0 | 0.0 | 0.0 | 0.0 | 4.3 | | 0.0 |
| Inventory | - | - | - | - | 20.8 | 18.2 | 24.8 | - | - | - | - | - | - | 0.0 | | 0.0 |
| Receivables | - | - | - | - | 2.0 | 0.3 | 0.2 | - | - | - | - | - | - | | | |
| Payables | - | - | - | - | (17.2) | (15.8) | (16.5) | - | - | - | - | - | - | | | |
| Working capital | - | - | - | - | 5.6 | 2.7 | 8.5 | - | - | - | - | - | - | | | |
| Fixed assets | - | - | - | - | - | - | - | - | - | - | - | - | - | | | |
| **NET PROJECT ASSETS** | 0.0 | 0.0 | 0.0 | 0.0 | 5.6 | 2.7 | 8.5 | 0.0 | 0.0 | 0.0 | 0.0 | 0.0 | 0.0 | 0.0 | | 0.0 |
| Borrowings | - | - | - | - | 10.2 | 4.2 | 4.2 | - | - | - | - | - | - | | | |
| Equity | - | - | - | - | (4.6) | (1.5) | 4.3 | - | - | - | - | - | - | | | |
| **NET PROJECT CAPITAL** | 0.0 | 0.0 | 0.0 | 0.0 | 5.6 | 2.7 | 8.5 | 0.0 | 0.0 | 0.0 | 0.0 | 0.0 | 0.0 | 0.0 | | 0.0 |

*This format enables top management to see at a glance the progress of a project against its plan – the best reports are single-page reports, and this is a good example*

**DEMO PROJECT**  **RESULTS - YEAR ENDED 30 JUNE 20XX**  **UK£000**  **APPENDIX C11**

CLOSURE ESTIMATE    MONTH-END ESTIMATES OF REMAINING BALANCES

| | North Branch | South Branch | SEP 20XX | OCT 20XX | NOV 20XX | DEC 20XX | JAN 20XY | FEB 20XY | MAR 20XY | APR 20XY | MAY 20XY | JUN 20XY | JUL 20XY | AUG 20XY | SEP 20XY |
|---|---|---|---|---|---|---|---|---|---|---|---|---|---|---|---|
| Inventory | 5,555 | - | 5,555 | 5,335 | 4,310 | 1,868 | - | | | | | | | | |
| Due from customers - external | 1,236 | - | 1,236 | 1,566 | 2,310 | 1,915 | 930 | | | | | | | | |
| Other debtors | 432 | - | 432 | - | - | - | 38 | | | | | | | | |
| Sales tax recoverable | 345 | 22 | 367 | 262 | 62 | 65 | (15) | | | | | | | | |
| Prepayments & accrued income | 22 | - | 22 | 29 | 26 | 17 | 13 | | | | | | | | |
| Loan to Demo Hong Kong | - | 31 | 31 | 31 | - | - | - | | | | | | | | |
| Equipment & vehicles | 77 | - | 77 | 69 | 66 | 60 | 57 | | | | | | | | |
| Corporate tax | 111 | - | 111 | 100 | 100 | 100 | 100 | | | | | | | | |
| Deferred tax | 99 | - | 99 | - | - | - | - | | | | | | | | |
| Cash | 2 | 11 | 13 | 9 | 10 | 7 | 4 | | | | | | | | |
| **Assets** | **7,879** | **64** | **7,943** | **7,401** | **6,884** | **4,032** | **1,127** | 0 | 0 | 0 | 0 | 0 | 0 | 0 | 0 |
| Due to suppliers | (999) | (44) | (1,043) | (1,129) | (687) | (200) | (142) | | | | | | | | |
| Other creditors | (111) | - | (111) | (86) | (33) | - | - | | | | | | | | |
| Tax creditors | (33) | - | (33) | (33) | (55) | - | - | | | | | | | | |
| Accrued expenses | (44) | (33) | (77) | (75) | (55) | (32) | (32) | | | | | | | | |
| Due from/ (to) other Demo cos | (200) | 200 | 0 | - | - | - | - | | | | | | | | |
| Employee terminations | - | - | 0 | (84) | (40) | (40) | - | | | | | | | | |
| Property evacuations | - | - | 0 | (16) | (3) | (3) | (3) | | | | | | | | |
| Closure expenses | - | - | 0 | - | - | - | - | | | | | | | | |
| Contingency | - | - | 0 | | | | | | | | | | | | |
| **Liabilities** | **(1,387)** | **123** | **(1,264)** | **(1,423)** | **(818)** | **(275)** | **(177)** | 0 | 0 | 0 | 0 | 0 | 0 | 0 | 0 |
| **Net recoverable** | **6,492** | **187** | **6,679** | **5,978** | **6,066** | **3,757** | **950** | 0 | 0 | 0 | 0 | 0 | 0 | 0 | 0 |
| Finance from Demo Group | (2,222) | - | (2,222) | (731) | (731) | (689) | 53 | | | | | | | | |
| Bank deposits/ (overdrafts) | (2,727) | 6 | (2,721) | (3,766) | (3,950) | (1,800) | 229 | | | | | | | | |
| Other bank funds | - | - | 0 | - | - | - | - | | | | | | | | |
| **NET VALUE** | **1,543** | **193** | **1,736** | **1,481** | **1,385** | **1,268** | **1,232** | 0 | 0 | 0 | 0 | 0 | 0 | 0 | 0 |

Annotations:

- Inventory decreases as it is disposed of
- Customer cash can become difficult to collect in a closure situation
- Miscellaneous item appearing as an item is sold
- Sales tax will not follow normal patterns, but will move with disposals
- Prepaid rentals etc may not be recoverable
- Internal debts may give scope for maneouvre
- Fixed assets tend to lose much of their value (especially office items)
- Recoverable against prior period profits?
- Deferred tax will not be recoverable
- Liquid cash will often be needed for removals, decommissioning etc
- Ensure that supplies are available for you to complete items for sale
- Additional creditors may arise from the closure process
- Can this be set back against any losses from prior periods?
- Accrued items should steadily be eliminated
- Can the group be used cost-effectively as a banker?
- Liabilities will almost certainly arise in respect of employees
- Property may require to be restored to its original condition
- Legal costs, property dilapidations etc
- Contingency may or may not be needed
- Can the group be used cost-effectively as a banker?
- The intention is normally for this to be the single remaining balance
- It may be appropriate to place funds on interest-earning deposit

**The Goal**
**Eliyahu Goldratt and Jeff Cox**
**Available in several editions from Amazon**
Written as a novel, this book begins slowly, strangely and simply. But over the first few chapters it gathers pace and involves the reader in a number of familiar industrial problems as the protagonist is given three months in which to turn a factory into profitability, or else it will be closed. This book was compulsory reading for management in various companies in which the author has worked. Later editions have a few theoretical chapters after the main story.

**Continuous Improvement**
**Wayne Scott Ross**
**Management Books 2000 Ltd - ISBN 1-85252-427-8**
**ISBN 1-85252-427-8**
A succinct and handy guide for the financial controller who needs to understand the factors which affect the performance of his production line. It is based on manufacture, but the principles thereof apply to a variety of linear and parallel business processes. If you wonder what the terms Kan-Ban and Kaizen mean, this is an easy read where you will quickly find the answer clearly presented.

*The author re-emphasises that the principles of efficient production apply to many processes, not just to manufacturing. For example, the author has streamlined the preparation and production of monthly management accounts in a number of businesses using simple prinicples of production. Whether you are manufacturing machine parts, mixing chemicals, building houses or washing up after a dinner for ten people, the principles of efficient process flow are the same. You may even have cause to advise your suppliers and customers to improve their efficiency, to the benefit of your own business.*

**Marketing Plans**
**How to prepare them; how to use them**
**Malcolm McDonald**
**Butterworth Heinemann**
**ISBN-13: 978-0750683869 available from Amazon**
In a class of its own, this book is almost an encyclopaedia. Authoritatively written in a style which is easy to assimilate, it has clear graphics and tabulations which are expanded and linked clearly by the narrative. There are exercises for the reader and a host of other features, all presented with simple, impeccable clarity. An essential guide to the front end of the business.

**The Report Report**
**Alasdair Drysdale**
**Management Books 2000 Ltd - ISBN 1-85252-452-9**
Financial controllers have to write reports: small one-page briefings, larger narratives to support grant applications, major reports to support a proposed acquisition, etc. The Report Report, as its name suggests, is written as a report, and covers all aspects of report writing and preparation, including content, layout, language style, politics, choice of words, use of numbers and a host of other considerations, right through to packaging and final presentation. Indispensable.

**Croner manuals**
**Google "Croner" and review list of publications**
Croner manuals deal comprehensively with UK employment law, and there are separate manuals for various branches of that law. Subscribers receive frequent updates covering changes in the law, and other facilities are provided. This range is mainly for personnel managers, but there are a number of issues, especially in relation to termination of employment, which are of direct relevance to financial controllers and directors.

## A

| | |
|---|---|
| Acccounts payable ledger | 4.4p |
| Accountant | 1.1c |
| Accountant - duties | 1.2c |
| Accountants, professional | 1.4j |
| Accounting calendar, month-end | App C1 |
| Accounting records - archiving | 2.4f |
| Accounting records - filing | 2.4f |
| Accounting records - numbering | 2.4f |
| Accounting records - storage | 2.4f |
| Accounts payable duties | 1.2c |
| Accounts payable system | 4.4 |
| Accounts receivable duties | 1.2c |
| Accounts receivable ledger | 4.3x |
| Accruals | 2.3c |
| Accruals sheet | App C10 |
| Additions to fixed assets | 4.6d |
| Administration - general | 3.3l |
| Administration department | 1.3b |
| Agents | 5.3e |
| Annual calendar | App A4 |
| Annual financial statements | 2.5c |
| Annual financial statements - audit | 2.5h |
| Annual financial statements - liquidity | 2.5g |
| Annual information | 4.5p |
| Appraisal form (2 parts) | App A7.1-2 |
| Appraisals | 1.2e |
| Archiving of accounting records | 2.4f |
| Attitudes - to external organisations | 1.4a |
| Auditors | 1.4j |
| Authorities for signing | App A8 |

## B

| | |
|---|---|
| Back-end loading | 3.2c |
| Bad & doubtful debts | 4.3u |
| Balance sheets | 2.2j |
| Bank & cash | 4.7 |
| Bank & cash - cash disbursements | 4.7e |
| Bank & cash - cash receipts | 4.7d |
| Bank & cash - cheque payments | 4.7e |
| Bank & cash - closing accounts | 4.7c |
| Bank & cash - credit cards | 4.7j |
| Bank & cash - deposits | 4.7h |
| Bank & cash - foreign currency | 4.7f |
| Bank & cash - general ledger | 4.7l |
| Bank & cash - loans, HP & leases | 4.7i |
| Bank & cash - objectives | 4.7b |
| Bank & cash - opening & closing a/cs | 4.7c |
| Bank & cash - petty cash | 4.7k |
| Bank & cash - reconciliations | 4.7g |
| Bank & cash - signing authorities | 4.7e |

| | |
|---|---|
| Bank & cash - systems | 4.7 |
| Bank & cash - transfers | 4.7e |
| Bank & cash - travel expenses | 4.7j |
| Bank interest - actual against budget | 3.2c |
| Bank loans | 3.2i |
| Banks, bankers | 1.4g |
| Barriers to rapid month-end reports | 2.3d |
| Bespoke products | 4.3e |
| Bill of materials | 4.1e |
| Billing - at frequent intervals | 3.2d |
| Blowing the whistle | 5.2l |
| Board of directors | 1.1d |
| BOM | 4.1e |
| Borrowing costs | 3.1j |
| Breakeven health-check | 3.1k |
| Breakeven level | 3.1k |
| Breakeven: actual ratio | 3.1k |
| Budget - capex | 3.2g, App A6, C3 |
| Budget model | App C4.1-10 |
| Budget template | App C2 |
| Budgeting - documentation | 3.5d |
| Budgeting - final version | 3.5g |
| Budgeting - financial model | 3.5e |
| Budgeting - interim updates | 3.5h |
| Budgeting - objectives | 3.5a |
| Budgeting - overall process | 3.5b |
| Budgeting - review & approval | 3.5f |
| Budgeting - timescale | 3.5c |
| Business continuity | 5.4c |
| Business objectives | 1.1a |
| Business planning | 3.3, 3.4 |
| Business planning - considerations | 3.4e |
| Business planning - controller's rôle | 3.4l |
| Business planning - elements of plan | 3.4h |
| Business planning - incremental | 3.4i |
| Business planning - objectives | 3.4a |
| Business planning - other approaches | 3.4i |
| Business planning - overall process | 3.4b |
| Business planning - planning team | 3.4d |
| Business planning - production | 3.4j |
| Business planning - review | 3.4m |
| Business planning - scale & detail | 3.4c |
| Business planning - side-activities | 3.4k |
| Business planning - SWOT analysis | 3.4f |
| Business planning - targeted | 3.4i |
| Business planning - typical format | 3.4n |
| Business planning - zero-based | 3.4i |
| Buying of materials | 3.2d |

## C

| | |
|---|---|
| Calculation of remuneration | 4.5h |

| | |
|---|---|
| Calendar - monthly | 2.4b |
| Calendar - yearly | App A4 |
| Calendar, annual | App A4 |
| Capex budget | 3.2g, App A6, C3 |
| Capex DCF | App A6 |
| Capex evaluation | App A6 |
| Capital employed - specimen layout | App C8 |
| Capital employed reports | 2.2j |
| Capital expenditure budget | 3.2g |
| Capital expenditure reports | 2.1j |
| Capital gearing | 3.2c |
| Capital leases | 3.2i |
| Cash | 3.2 |
| Cash disbursements | 4.7e |
| Cash flow monthly - specimen layout | App C9 |
| Cash flow reports | 2.2k |
| Cash flow, daily | App B1 |
| Cash flow, weekly | App B2 |
| Cash receipts | 4.7d |
| Cash reports (daily) | 2.1k |
| Cash supervisor duties | 1.2c |
| Casual or part-time labour | 4.5l |
| CEO | 1.1d |
| CFO | 1.1c |
| Chairman | 1.1d |
| Cheque payments | 4.7e |
| Cheque signing authorities | 4.7e |
| Chief accountant | 1.1c |
| Chief executive officer | 1.1d |
| Chief financial officer | 1.1c |
| Closure reports | 2.2m |
| Clsoure progress statement | App C12 |
| Collusion | 5.2h |
| Commitments sheet | App C10 |
| Company cars | 1.3d |
| Company credit cards | 4.7j |
| Components - off-the-shelf | 3.2d |
| Computer hardware | 4.6l |
| Computer software | 4.6l |
| Conditions of sale | 5.3d |
| Consignment stocks - receipt of | 4.4l |
| Consignment stocks - to customers | 4.3s |
| Consolidated reports | 2.2q |
| Constraint management | 3.2d |
| Contractors | 1.4f |
| Contracts | 3.3h, 5.3 |
| Contracts - conditions of sale | 5.3d |
| Contracts - distributors or agents | 5.3e |
| Contracts - drafting | 5.3j |
| Contracts - employment | 5.3g |

| | |
|---|---|
| Contracts - import or export | 5.3f |
| Contracts - other parties | 5.3i |
| Contracts - other rules | 5.3c |
| Contracts - purchasing | 4.4d |
| Contracts - structure | 5.3b |
| Contracts - termination of employment | 5.3h |
| Contracts (production) department | 1.3m |
| Contracts manager | 1.1e |
| Contracts of employment | 4.5d |
| Controller's master file | 1.1g |
| Corporate fraud | 5.2k, 5.2l |
| Costing supervisor duties | 1.2c |
| Credit cards | 4.7j |
| Credit control | 3.2e |
| Credit control - X-Co | 3.2e |
| Credit control department | 1.3i |
| Credit control review | 3.2e |
| Credit management in dept | 3.2e |
| Credit notes - sales of goods | 4.3q |
| Credit notes - sales of services | 4.3r |
| Credit notes, purchases from suppliers | 4.4n |
| Culture - finance department | 1.2b |
| Culture - general | 1.1f |
| Currency hedging | 4.7f |
| Currency hedging | App A5 |
| Customer debit notes | 4.3p |
| Customer files | 4.3c |
| Customer service targets | 3.3f |
| Customer statements | 4.3t |
| Customers - can't pay/ won't pay | 3.2e |
| Customers - contract | 1.4c, 1.4d |
| Customers - general | 1.4b, 1.4d |
| Customers - visits to their premises | 1.4b |
| Customers, new (credit rating etc) | 4.3b |
| **D** | |
| Daily cash flow | App B1 |
| Days of inventory | 3.2d |
| Days of production | 2.1c, 3.2c |
| Days of purchases | 3.2c |
| Days of sales | 3.2c |
| Debit notes - customers | 4.3p |
| Debtors - can't pay/ won't pay | 3.2e |
| Deductions from pay | 4.5k |
| Delivery drivers | 3.2e |
| Departmental management | 1.2g |
| Departmental reports | 2.2i |
| Departments - administration | 1.3b |
| Departments - finance | 1.2 |
| Departments - information technology | 1.3e |
| Departments - inventory control | 1.3n |

| | |
|---|---|
| Departments - land and buildings | 1.3f |
| Departments - maintenance | 1.3o |
| Departments - marketing | 1.3g |
| Departments - other | 1.3 |
| Departments - personnel | 1.3c |
| Departments - production (contracts) | 1.3m |
| Departments - production (manufr) | 1.3k |
| Departments - production (services) | 1.3l |
| Departments - research & development | 1.3j |
| Departments - sales | 1.3g |
| Departments - transport (distribution) | 1.3h |
| Deposits | 4.7h |
| Despatch of finished goods | 4.1m, 4.3i |
| Development costs | 4.6l |
| Direct (variable) costs | 3.1e |
| Direct labour | 3.1e |
| Direct materials - cost | 3.1e |
| Direct materials - delivery | 3.1e |
| Direct materials - usage | 3.1e |
| Director - team playear | 1.1d |
| Director, divisional | 1.1d |
| Director, executive | 1.1d |
| Director, financial | 1.1d |
| Director, functional | 1.1d |
| Director, managing | 1.1d |
| Director, non-executive | 1.1d |
| Director, regional | 1.1d |
| Directors, board of | 1.1d |
| Disaster recovery | 5.4c |
| Disclosure items | 2.5f |
| Discontinuation of product | 3.2d |
| Discretionary costs | 3.1h |
| Distribution (transport) department | 1.3h |
| Distributors | 5.3e |
| Divisional directors | 1.1d |
| Divisional head office | 1.4q |
| Double whammy | 5.2k |
| Doubtful debts | 4.3u |
| Dowturns | 3.1m |
| Drafting contracts | 5.3j |
| Duties - accountant | 1.2c |
| Duties - accounts payable | 1.2c |
| Duties - accounts receivable | 1.2c |
| Duties - cash supervisor | 1.2c |
| Duties - costing supervisor | 1.2c |
| Duties - fixed assets supervisor | 1.2c |
| Duties - payroll supervisor | 1.2c |
| Duties, rotation of | 5.2i |
| Duties, segregation of | 5.2i |

**E**

| | |
|---|---|
| Elements of profit performance | 3.1b |
| Employee fraud | 5.2d |
| Employee theft | 5.2d |
| Employee theft - removal of goods | 5.2g |
| Employment contracts | 4.5d, 5.3g |
| Employment, termination | 4.5f |
| Engineering department | 3.3j |
| Engineering manager | 1.1e |
| Equipment set-up | 3.2d |
| Executive director | 1.1d |
| Expenses | 4.7j |
| Export documents | 5.3f |
| External organisations | 1.4 |

**F**

| | |
|---|---|
| Facilities, granting & receipt of | 4.4h |
| Fellow subsidiaries | 1.4r |
| Filing - sales & receivables | 4.3v |
| Filing - sales contracts | 4.3w |
| Finance department - culture | 1.2b |
| Finance leases | 3.2i, 4.7i |
| Finance staff development | 1.2d |
| Finance staff duties | 1.2c |
| Financial controller - definition | 1.1c |
| Financial controller - objectives | 1.1a |
| Financial director | 1.1c |
| Financial reporting conventions | 2.2f |
| Financial reporting priorities | 2.2e |
| Financial statements | 2.5c |
| Financial statements - disclosure items | 2.5f |
| Finished goods control | 4.1l |
| Finished goods despatch | 4.1m |
| Finished goods inventory | 3.2c |
| Fixed assets | 4.6 |
| Fixed assets - additions & transfers in | 4.6d |
| Fixed assets - amortisation | 4.6g |
| Fixed assets - capital expend budget | 4.6b |
| Fixed assets - cash control | 3.2g |
| Fixed assets - computer hardware | 4.6l |
| Fixed assets - computer software | 4.6l |
| Fixed assets - definitions | 4.6c |
| Fixed assets - development costs | 4.6l |
| Fixed assets - funding | 3.2g |
| Fixed assets - general ledger | 4.6i |
| Fixed assets - goodwill | 4.6l |
| Fixed assets - insurance | 4.6k |
| Fixed assets - intangible | 4.6l |
| Fixed assets - physical verification | 4.6j |
| Fixed assets - register | 4.6h |
| Fixed assets - revalue, reclassification | 4.6f |

| | | | |
|---|---|---|---|
| Fixed assets - system | 4.6 | Incentives | 3.3 |
| Fixed assets - tooling | 4.6c | Incremental planning | 3.4i |
| Fixed assets supervisor duties | 1.2c | Indirect costs | 3.1f |
| Fixed assets, amortisation (depn) | 4.6g | Information technology | 1.3e |
| Fixed costs | 3.1f | In-house manufacture | 3.1g |
| Following year - preparation | 2.5i | Insurance | 5.4 |
| Foreign currency transactions | 4.7f | Insurance - business continuity | 5.4c |
| Foreign exchange | 3.2i | Insurance - disaster recovery | 5.4c |
| Foreign exchange reports | 2.2n | Insurance - types of cover | 5.4b |
| Forex hedging | App A5 | Insurance, fixed assets | 4.6k |
| Fraud & Theft | 5.2 | Insurers | 1.4l, 5.4 |
| Fraud & Theft - collusion | 5.2h | Intangible fixed assets | 4.6l |
| Fraud & Theft - corporate | 5.2k | Internal check, purchases & payables | 4.4s |
| Fraud & Theft - double whammy | 5.2k | Inventory - bill of materials (BOM) | 4.1e |
| Fraud & Theft - employee fraud | 5.2d | Inventory - contracting businesses | 4.1c |
| Fraud & Theft - employee theft | 5.2d | Inventory - finished goods control | 4.1l |
| Fraud & Theft - high level | 5.2k | Inventory - finished goods despatch | 4.1m |
| Fraud & Theft - limitations | 5.2c | Inventory - general ledger | 4.1o |
| Fraud & Theft - manipulation of pay | 5.2f | Inventory - material master file | 4.1d |
| Fraud & Theft - moving profits | 5.2k | Inventory - physical security | 4.1b |
| Fraud & Theft - removal of goods | 5.2g | Inventory - product routing file | 4.1h |
| Fraud & Theft - rotation of duties | 5.2i | Inventory - raw materials control | 4.1j |
| Fraud & Theft - Sarbanes-Oxley act | 5.2k | Inventory - service businesses | 4.1c |
| Fraud & Theft - segregation of duties | 5.2i | Inventory - standard costs file (labour) | 4.1g |
| Fraud & Theft - third party | 5.2j | Inventory - standard costs file (material) | 4.1f |
| Fraud & Theft - whistle-blowing | 5.2l | Inventory - standard costs file (o'head) | 4.1g |
| Functional director | 1.1d | Inventory - work in progress control | 4.1k |
| **G** | | Inventory control - finished goods | 3.3i |
| Gearing | 3.2c | Inventory control - raw material | 3.3i |
| General ledger purchases & payables | 4.4r | Inventory control - work in progress | 3.3i |
| General ledger sales & Receivables - | 4.3z | Inventory control department | 1.3n |
| General ledger, bank & cash | 4.7l | Inventory count - allocation of duties | 4.2e |
| General ledger, fixed assets | 4.6i | Inventory count - consumables | 4.2p |
| General ledger, payroll | 4.5n | Inventory count - contract work in prog | 4.2s |
| General manager | 1.1e | Inventory count - counting methods | 4.2l |
| Goods on consignment - receipt of | 4.4l | Inventory count - cyclical counting | 4.2q |
| Goods, theft of | 5.2g | Inventory count - entry into system | 4.2o |
| Goodwill | 4.6l | Inventory count - goods in transit | 4.2i |
| Grant-awarding bodies | 1.4i | Inventory count - goods inwards | 4.2g |
| Granting credit - new customer | 3.2e | Inventory count - goods outwards | 4.2h |
| Grants & grant applications | 3.2i | Inventory count - instructions | 4.2c |
| Group companies | 1.4r | Inventory count - intra-group inventory | 4.2j |
| Group head office | 1.4q | Inventory count - issues arising | 4.2n |
| **H** | | Inventory count - items at other sites | 4.2r |
| Hedging | 4.7f, 4.7h | Inventory count - obsolete/ damaged | 4.2k |
| High level fraud | 5.2k | Inventory count - pre-count actions | 4.2d |
| Hire purchase | 3.2i, 4.7l | Inventory count - recording the count | 4.2m |
| **I** | | Inventory count - responsibility | 4.2b |
| Impact | 1.1h | Inventory count - site plan | 4.2f |
| Import documents | 5.3f | Inventory count - valuation | 4.2p |

| | | | |
|---|---|---|---|
| Inventory ledger | 4.1n | Manipulation of pay | 5.2f |
| Inventory reports | 2.1c | Manufacturing (production) dept | 1.3k |
| Inventory system | 4.1 | Manufacturing manager | 1.1e |
| Invoice processing - purchases | 4.4i | Margins & mark-ups | 3.1d |
| IT department | 1.3e | Market downturns | 3.1m |
| **J** | | Market upturns | 3.1n |
| Journal | 2.4d | Marketing against gross margin | 3.1i |
| **K** | | Marketing and sales department | 1.3g |
| Kaizen | App D | Marketing manager | 1.1e |
| Kan-Ban | App D | Mark-ups & margins | 3.1d |
| **L** | | Master file - controller | 1.1g, 1.3g, 1.3j |
| Land and buildings department | 1.3f | Material master file | 4.1d |
| Leases (finance) | 4.7i | Material price files | 4.4c |
| Leasing companies | 1.4h | Materials - buying | 3.2d |
| Legal advisors | 1.4n | Maximising profit | 3.1 |
| Leverage | 3.2c | Meetings | 3.3n |
| Liquidity | 2.5g | Miscellaneous payables | 4.4q |
| Loans | 4.7i | Month-end accounting calendar | App C1 |
| Local debt finance | 3.2i | Month-end papers | 2.4 |
| Losing money | 5.1 | Month-end reports | 2.2b |
| Losing money - cash management | 5.1 | Month-end reports - barriers | 2.3d |
| Losing money - fixed assets | 5.1 | Month-end timetable | 2.3e |
| Losing money - inventory & production | 5.1 | Monthly calendar | 2.4b |
| Losing money - payroll & expenses | 5.1 | Monthly management reports | 2.3, App C5-12 |
| Losing money - purchases & payables | 5.1 | Monthly reporting amendments | 2.2d |
| Losing money - sales & receivables | 5.1 | Monthly reporting model | 2.2c, 2.2d |
| Lowering selling prices | 3.1c | Monthly reviews, payroll | 4.5o |
| **M** | | Monthly working papers | 2.4c |
| Maintenance department | 1.3o | Montnly financial report - structure | App C5 |
| Make-or-buy decision | 3.1g | **N** | |
| Makrketing costs | 3.1i | Narrative reports | 2.2o |
| Management - constraints | 3.2d | New customer | 3.2e |
| Management accounts - timetable | 2.3e | New customer - granting credit | 3.2e |
| Management accounts - to final a/cs | 2.5e | New financial year - preparation | 2.5i |
| Management cycle | 3.3b | Non-executive director | 1.1d |
| Management objectives | 1.1a | Notes & coin | 4.7k |
| Management team | 1.1e | Numbering of accounting records | 2.4f |
| Manager, contracts | 1.1e | **O** | |
| Manager, engineering | 1.1e | Objectives - business | 1.1a |
| Manager, general | 1.1e | Objectives - financial controller | 1.1a |
| Manager, manufacturing | 1.1e | Objectives - management | 1.1a |
| Manager, marketing | 1.1e | Off-the-shelf components | 3.2d |
| Manager, operations | 1.1e | Operating statement - specimen | App C6 |
| Manager, production | 1.1e | Operations manager | 1.1e |
| Manager, research & development | 1.1e | Optimising cash | 3.2 |
| Manager, sales | 1.1e | Optimising profit | 3.1 |
| Manager, technical | 1.1e | Order processing - purchases | 4.4e |
| Managers' commitments sheet | App C10 | Organisation chart | App A1 |
| Managing a department | 1.2g | Organisations, external | 1.4 |
| Managing director | 1.1d | Other departments | 1.3 |

| | |
|---|---|
| Other group companies | 1.4r |
| Overdrafts | 3.2i |
| Overheads reports | 2.1g |
| Overseas debt | 3.2i |
| Overseas travel | 4.7j |
| **P** | |
| Pain - passing it on | 3.3c |
| Papers, month-end | 2.4 |
| Part-time labour | 4.5l |
| Passing on pain | 3.3c |
| Payables - control (see Purchases) | 3.2f |
| Payables ledger | 4.4p |
| Payables reports | 2.1h |
| Payables system | 4.4 |
| Payments, payroll | 4.5m |
| Payroll | 4.5 |
| Payroll - annual information | 4.5p |
| Payroll - calculation of remuneration | 4.5h |
| Payroll - casual or part-time labour | 4.5l |
| Payroll - contracts of employment | 4.5d |
| Payroll - general ledger | 4.5n |
| Payroll - monthly reviews | 4.5o |
| Payroll - net pay, deductions etc | 4.5k |
| Payroll - payments | 4.5m |
| Payroll - period | 4.5j |
| Payroll - personnel budget | 4.5b |
| Payroll - personnel file | 4.5e |
| Payroll - recruitment | 4.5c |
| Payroll - system | 4.5g |
| Payroll - termination of employment | 4.5f |
| Payroll - verification of remuneration | 4.5i |
| Payroll manipulation | 5.2f |
| Payroll supervisor duties | 1.2c |
| Pension trustees | 1.4o |
| Performance pay | 3.3d |
| Period payroll | 4.5j |
| Personnel appraisal form (2 parts) | App A7.1-2 |
| Personnel budget | 4.5b |
| Personnel department | 1.3c |
| Personnel file | 4.5e |
| Petty cash | 4.7k |
| Physical verification of fixed assets | 4.6j |
| Planning | 3.3 |
| Planning - incremental | 3.4i |
| Planning - targeted | 3.4i |
| Planning - zero-based | 3.4i |
| Preparation for year-end | 2.5d |
| Price & volume | 3.1c |
| Prices - effect of raising or lowering | 3.1c |
| Price-volume table | 3.1c |
| Prior year figures | 2.2b |
| Process flow | 3.2d |
| Product comparison | App A2 |
| Product design | 3.2d |
| Product development reports | 2.1i |
| Product discontinuation | 3.2d |
| Product lifespan | App A3 |
| Product price files | 4.3d |
| Product routing file | 4.1h |
| Production (contracts) department | 1.3m |
| Production (manufacturing) dept | 1.3k |
| Production (services) department | 1.3l |
| Production inefficiency | 3.1e |
| Production manager | 1.1e |
| Production output & incentives | 3.3g |
| Production reports | 2.1d |
| Production set-up time | 3.1e |
| Profit | 3.1 |
| Profit performance - elements | 3.1b |
| Profit reports | 2.2g |
| Profit statement - specimen layout | App C6 |
| Project management | 3.2d |
| Project progress statement | App C11 |
| Project reports | 2.2l |
| Property lessors | 1.4m |
| Public sector bodies | 1.4i |
| Purchase invoices, dispensing with | 4.4i |
| Purchase invoices, non-inventory | 4.4j |
| Purchase invoices, services & facilities | 4.4k |
| Purchase requisitions | 4.4e |
| Purchases & Payables | 4.4 |
| Purchases - consignment goods | 4.4l |
| Purchases - credit notes | 4.4n |
| Purchases - general ledger | 4.4r |
| Purchases - internal check | 4.4s |
| Purchases - invoices | 4.4i |
| Purchases - ledger | 4.4p |
| Purchases - material price files | 4.4c |
| Purchases - miscellaneous | 4.4q |
| Purchases - non-inventory | 4.4g |
| Purchases - order processing | 4.4e |
| Purchases - receipt of facilities | 4.4h |
| Purchases - receipt of goods | 4.4f |
| Purchases - receipt of services | 4.4h |
| Purchases - returns to suppliers | 4.4m |
| Purchases - supplier files | 4.4b |
| Purchases - supplier statements | 4.4o |
| Purchases contracts | 4.4d |
| Purchasing department | 3.3k |
| Purchasing tactics | 3.3k |

**Q**

| | |
|---|---|
| QUADCOMBS (Eli Goldratt) | 3.2d |

**R**

| | |
|---|---|
| R&D manager | 1.1e |
| Raising selling prices | 3.1c |
| Raw material levels | 3.2c |
| Raw materials control | 4.1j |
| Receipt of goods - inventory | 4.4f |
| Receipt of goods - non-inventory | 4.4g |
| Receipt of goods - purchasing | 4.4f |
| Receivables - can't pay/ won't pay | 3.2e |
| Receivables - miscellaneous | 4.3y |
| Receivables - reports | 2.1f |
| Receivables - see Sales | 4.3 |
| Receivables ledger | 4.3x |
| Reclassifications of fixed assets | 4.6f |
| Reconciliation, bank accounts | 4.7g |
| Recruitment | 1.2f, 4.5c |
| Regional directors | 1.1d |
| Register of fixed assets | 4.6h |
| Reminders to customers | 4.3t |
| Remuneration, calculation | 4.5h |
| Remuneration, verification | 4.5i |
| Reporting calendar | App A4 |
| Reporting conventions | 2.2f |
| Reporting priorities | 2.2e |
| Reports - areas of reporting | 2.3 |
| Reports - assets & liabilities | 2.2j |
| Reports - capital employed | 2.2j |
| Reports - capital expenditure | 2.1j |
| Reports - cash (daily) | 2.1k |
| Reports - cash flow | 2.2k |
| Reports - closures | 2.2m |
| Reports - completion & collation | 2.2r |
| Reports - consolidated | 2.2q |
| Reports - departments or sectors | 2.2i |
| Reports - foreign exchange | 2.2n |
| Reports - inventory | 2.1c |
| Reports - monthly management | 2.3, App C5-12 |
| Reports - narrative | 2.2o |
| Reports - other | 2.2p |
| Reports - overheads | 2.1g |
| Reports - payables | 2.1h |
| Reports - product development | 2.1i |
| Reports - production | 2.1d |
| Reports - profit | 2.2g |
| Reports - projects | 2.2l |
| Reports - receivables | 2.1f |
| Reports - sales | 2.1e |
| Reports - variances | 2.2h |

| | |
|---|---|
| Reports, month-end | 2.2b |
| Research & development | 3.3j |
| Research & development - cash control | 3.2h |
| Research & development - customer-facing | 3.2h |
| Research & development department | 1.3j |
| Research & development manager | 1.1e |
| Returns from customers | 4.3o |
| Returns to suppliers | 4.4m |
| Revaluations of fixed assets | 4.6f |
| Reviews and appraisals | 1.2e |
| Rotation of staff duties | 5.2i |

**S**

| | |
|---|---|
| Sales & Receivables | 4.3 |
| Sales - bad debts | 4.3u |
| Sales - bespoke products | 4.3e |
| Sales - consignment goods | 4.3s |
| Sales - contract filing | 4.3w |
| Sales - credit notes (goods) | 4.3q |
| Sales - credit notes (services) | 4.3r |
| Sales - customer debit notes | 4.3p |
| Sales - customer files | 4.3c |
| Sales - deductions | 4.3n |
| Sales - despatch of goods | 4.3i |
| Sales - enquiries | 4.3f |
| Sales - filing | 4.3v |
| Sales - general ledger | 4.3z |
| Sales - invoices (goods) | 4.3k |
| Sales - invoices (services) | 4.3m |
| Sales - ledger | 4.3x |
| Sales - new customers | 4.3b |
| Sales - order processing | 4.3h |
| Sales - product price files | 4.3d |
| Sales - provision of services | 4.3j |
| Sales - returns | 4.3o |
| Sales - sales contracts | 4.3g |
| Sales - sales price files | 4.3l |
| Sales - statements, reminders | 4.3t |
| Sales commissions | 4.3n |
| Sales contracts | 4.3g |
| Sales credit notes | 3.3o |
| Sales discounts | 4.3n |
| Sales enquiries | 4.3f |
| Sales force targets & incentives | 3.3e |
| Sales invoice processing (goods) | 4.3k |
| Sales invoice processing (services) | 4.3m |
| Sales ledger | 4.3x |
| Sales manager | 1.1e |
| Sales of services | 4.3j |
| Sales order processing | 4.3h |
| Sales price files | 4.3l |

| | |
|---|---|
| Sales rebates | 4.3n |
| Sales reports | 2.1e |
| Sales support targets | 3.3f |
| Sarbanes-Oxley act | 5.2k |
| Sector reports | 2.2i |
| Segregation of duties | 5.2i |
| Selling costs | 3.1i |
| Service industries - work in progress | 3.2d |
| Services department | 1.3l |
| Services, receipt of | 4.4h |
| Set-up time | 3.1e, 3.2d |
| Shared service centres | 1.2h |
| Shareholders | 1.4p |
| Short-term deposits | 4.7h |
| Side-activities | 3.4k |
| Signatories | 4.7e |
| Signing authorities | App A8 |
| Source & application - specimen layout | App C9 |
| Speculative costs | 3.1h |
| Staff development - finance | 1.2d |
| Staff recruitment | 1.2f |
| Staff reviews & appraisals | 1.2e |
| Standard costs file (labour) | 4.1g |
| Standard costs file (materials) | 4.1f |
| Standard costs file (overheads) | 4.1g |
| Statements from suppliers | 4.4o |
| Statutory financial statements ("stats") | 2.5c |
| Stock - see Inventory | 4.1 |
| Storage of accounting records | 2.4f |
| Storekeeping | 3.2d |
| Strategic plan - typical format | 3.4n |
| Strategic planning | 3.4 |
| Supplier files | 4.4b |
| Supplier returns | 4.4m |
| Supplier statements | 4.4o |
| Suppliers - contractors & sub-contractors | 1.4f |
| Suppliers - general | 1.4e |
| Supply terms | 3.2f |
| SWOT analysis - preparation | 3.4f |
| SWOT analysis - use for planning | 3.4g |
| Systems, payroll | 4.5g |
| **T** | |
| Targeted planning | 3.4i |
| Team player | 1.1d |
| Technical manager | 1.1e |
| Technical support | 1.3j, 3.3j |
| Termination of employment | 4.5f, 5.3h |
| Terms of supply | 3.2f |
| Theft | 5.2 |
| Theft of goods | 5.2g |

| | |
|---|---|
| Third party fraud or theft | 5.2j |
| Timetable - month-end reporting | 2.3e |
| Tooling | 4.6c |
| Transfer pricing | 3.2i |
| Transfers of fixed assets | 4.6d, 4.6e |
| Transport (distribution) department | 1.3h |
| Travel expenses | 4.7j |
| Travel, overseas | 4.7j |
| Treasury | 3.2i |
| **U** | |
| Upturns | 3.1n |
| **V** | |
| Value added | 3.1l |
| Value added per hour | 3.1l |
| Variable (direct) costs | 3.1e |
| Variance analysis - specimen layout | App C7 |
| Variance reports | 2.2h |
| Vendor files | 4.4b |
| **W** | |
| Weekly cash flow | App B2 |
| Whistle-blowing | 5.2l |
| Work in progress - service industries | 3.2d |
| Work in progress control | 4.1k |
| Working capital - product design | 3.2d |
| Working capital against annual sales | 3.2c |
| Working capital control - inventory | 3.2d |
| Working papers - balance sheet | 2.4d |
| Working papers - monthly | 2.4c |
| Working papers - profit statement | 2.4e |
| **X** | |
| X-C0 (credit management in depth) | 3.2e |
| **Y** | |
| Year-end preparation | 2.5d |
| Year-end processes | 2.5b |
| **Z** | |
| Zero-based planning | 3.4i |